DOCUMENTARY EXPLORATIONS

15 interviews with Film-makers

G. Roy Levin has made a number of short films which don't satisfy him, but he is working on others which he hopes will. He lives in Vermont, where he taught film at Goddard College before starting this book. Earlier, he'd taught French, theater and film at the Solebury School.

Much of Levin's time has been spent in theater work. While at the Yale Drama School, he cofounded a cabaret theater and coproduced and directed an English revue at the Village Gate in New York City. Later, he was drama director at the Jewish Community Center in Rochester. His play *Humphrey, Armand and the Artichoke* has been produced in London, Brussels and Baltimore. His one-act play *Henry-Henrietta* was done at the Caffe Cino in New York.

Roy Levin was born in 1931 in Philadelphia. He went to Oberlin, got an M.A. in French literature from Columbia, spent a year at the Sorbonne in Paris and has an M.F.A. from the Yale Drama School.

In 1969 Levin received a grant from the National Endowment for the Humanities to do a study of the documentary film. It was this study that led to the present book.

DOCUMENTARY EXPLORATIONS

15 INTERVIEWS WITH FILM-MAKERS

G. ROY LEVIN

GARDEN CITY, NEW YORK
DOUBLEDAY & COMPANY, INC.
1971

Documentary Explorations: 15 Interviews with Film-makers was published simultaneously in a hardcover edition by Doubleday & Company, Inc.

THIS BOOK IS DEDICATED TO

JORDAN, BRYNA AND MAURIE, 11, 9, AND 7,

AND TO ALL THOSE OF THEIR GENERATION.

CONTENTS

ACKNOWLEDGMENTS

To all the film-makers for the interviews and their time and trouble for the photos, biographies, filmographies and clarification of small but essential details; to Edith Bloom, a most excellent, helpful typist; to Ben Gruberg and Sandra Robinson for various and sundry aids at crucial moments; to Bossie, the Potoks, and the Lee St. commune for their hospitality when I needed a place to work on the book; to Ludi Kowalewicz for undertaking so many difficult transcriptions; to Lena, my mother; to Jacques Ledoux of the Cinémathèque Royale de Belgique, to Regina Cornwell and Willard Van Dyke of the Museum of Modern Art and to the British Film Institute for making it possible for me to see so many documentaries; to the National Endowment for the Humanities for the grant that made much of the work for the book possible; to all those kind people and friends who helped in small but important ways, from reading a bit of the manuscript to making a call to arrange for a meeting; and finally, to Judy, who was of help in more intangible ways,

many thanks.

G.R.L.

Notes in the Guise of an Introduction

I would like to speak of two things here. One, the making of the book, and two, some of my own thoughts about documentary film.

I. Books often appear as though they materialized out of thin air. From reading articles about authors, and biographies and autobiographies, I am not unaware of the problems that authors have, yet still I have a feeling of mystification about books. Generally, if someone wants an explication of a text, he buys a book dealing specifically with that. But I think it worthwhile to speak of this here because the making of this book has certain similarities to the making of a cinéma-vérité film—one of the main subjects that interested me in doing these interviews.

How to begin? Perhaps with this very question, which is one Ed Pincus raises: how does a film-maker start a cinéma-vérité film when he has so much background information that the viewer doesn't have? And how can the interview tell you, the reader, everything that is not included, such as the influence of the personalities of the people involved, the mood of the moment and the environment in which the interview took place?

I could say that the book is about documentary films, truth, fiction, objectivity, subjectivity, reality, etc.; and, further, that my attitudes toward these subjects are the very things that influenced the making of the book: choice of film-makers, how I did the interviews and edited them and how I gathered and wrote all the other material in the book—including these words. It is also presumably clear that my prejudices affected the questions I asked, the tone of the interview, how I related to the film-maker and he to me and, most importantly, the effect all this had on what the film-maker said.

As I write this, I still do not know what the order of the interviews will be. Chronological, by nationality, for contrast? All three would ignore the order in which I did the interviews and edited them, and the fact that the earlier interviews influenced the later ones and that the earlier editing work influenced the succeeding editing work. Does this matter?

I did not do these interviews primarily as a film critic or historian of the documentary film—I'm neither, and have no wish to be either. It's not that I wasn't interested in historical, technical or critical points, but that my main purpose was to learn something. I wanted to know about—and I suspect reveal—these film-makers as people, because it's the person who makes the films. If the interviews are successful, it is at least in part due to my being as personal and intimate with the film-makers as the situation permitted; and when this was not possible, by being impersonal, suggestive, tactful, and perhaps even slightly dishonest at times by not fully saying what I thought, by shading my opinions. In brief, even if the interviews appear to be objective, they are not.

Have I then manipulated reality and distorted the truth? I think not. I did not want confrontations. I wanted the film-makers to speak as revealingly as possible about themselves and their work. And if I am not guilty of deceit or a betrayal of trust—and again, I think I am not—I think these interviews are then fair and honest. But objective?

Yes, to a degree, in spite of my subjectivity. At least in letting the men speak for themselves. I worked very hard at ordering the rambling of taped conversations so that neither the ideas expressed nor the manner of expression got distorted; and, more important, I think mostly successfully. By what criteria, you ask? or whose? Clearly mine. What are they? They're self-evident in the interviews, and based on a substantial comprehensive understanding of the subject.

I also note that I left in a few shots of the camera and tape recorder, not to be chic, but to remind the viewer that the words he reads exist only as an interviewer-created reality. Also, ellipses [. . .] have been put in to avoid inventing questions where there is a break in the logic and as a reminder that deletions have been made where I considered material redundant or irrelevant—and not, I believe, to avoid statements which might conflict with my preconceived ideas.

There are now questions I wish I had asked but did not, questions I let slip by only half-answered, clues I missed for exploring certain points; but I was often preoccupied with listening, responding, juggling the order of the questions in my mind, trying to keep a logical order to the interview without dampening spontaneity—and, at times, with mundane matters like being tired or hungry or a plane I had to catch or an appointment I wanted to keep. But it is six of one and half a dozen of the other, vices are an integral part of virtues, and if I succeeded in obtaining worthwhile interviews, it is not only in spite of my failings as an interviewer, but perhaps also because of these failings.

II. Undocumented opinions.

As implied above, this book is not meant to be a critical study, and for this reason I refrain from expressing my opinions about the work of the film-makers interviewed. To do that here without detailing the reasons for my likes and dislikes would be unfair and not particularly illuminating. Besides, many of my opinions are expressed in the interviews where the context makes them more meaningful.

What, then, are the aims of the book? To offer a broad picture of the history and nature of the documentary film as a genre, insights into the work of each man interviewed, a sense of the film-maker as a person, and to raise basic questions about the form, effect and resultant social implications of documentary and its various uses. The interviewees selected do not represent a comprehensive worldwide survey of the documentary film, but they do represent those traditions and aspects that are essential and relevant to the documentary as it is known in the United States and the West today. It is on the basis of these criteria that the men in this book have been chosen. I regret that Alberto Cavalcanti, Joris Ivens, Pare Lorentz, Chris Marker, Alain Resnais, Paul Rotha, Roberto Rossellini, Peter Watkins, several Canadian film-makers and Newsreel are not included, but circumstances and space limitations have made this impossible.

A definition of documentary? Fifteen interviews with documentary film-makers and still it would be difficult to find a satisfactory one. The classic definition is John Grierson's: "The creative treatment of actuality," but though rich in implication it is hardly sufficient. Defining the word today is further complicated by the introduction of documentary techniques into fiction films so that at times it is difficult to say whether a film is completely fictional or documentary. This is true not only of a number of underground films of recent years but also of comparatively big-budget productions like Haskell Wexler's *Medium Cool* and Agnès Varda's *Lions Love*.

Grierson, for example, the "father" of English documentary, felt that documentaries should be used for purposes of propaganda. Paul Rotha, a very respected documentary film-maker himself and the author of the standard text on the subject, feels that documentary films should have an ameliorative social purpose and that they should be produced by groups rather than by individuals with egocentered sensibilities. Many of the French see little difference between documentary and fiction; rather, they see each as a personal, artistic expression. Some Americans tend to see it as an impersonal and objective gathering of data. Many would see social purpose as a necessary ingredient. To a good part of the public it implies something "educational" and boring.

At best, a definition of documentary is like any definition of an ongoing form of art: useful in indicating its concerns and raising provocative questions, but limiting and therefore falsifying.

If one wishes to discuss the subject, the point is not to tie it up with string and lock it up in a box, but to be stimulated and perhaps to learn something. Suffice it here to say that the main attributes of documentary as generally understood are: it treats reality, past or present (or future?), either by direct recording or by some indirect means as compilation or reconstruction; very often it is concerned with social problems, which means, almost by definition, such subjects as the poor and the alienated; recently it has often come to include hand-held cameras (i.e., shakiness, grain, bad focus as acceptable) and direct interviews.

Though the above takes into account the principal ostensible features of documentary, it ignores what I see as the underlying problem of documentary: objectivity vs. subjectivity, or, the question of interpretation and its validity. The point is raised here not because it is the kind of problem that has *a* solution—it doesn't—or to reiterate the obvious—that finally everything we do or say is in some sense subjective. Rather, my purpose is to clarify and insist on that which is undoubtedly clear to many but which is often ignored or obfuscated and which should be clear to everyone: 1. that footage of actual events can be made to lie or distort the facts; 2. that documentaries and documentary-like material (newsreels, etc.) are a mixture of the objective and the subjective (of fact and fiction, if you like); 3. that those films that pretend to pure objectivity are highly suspect; and 4. that every film is the result of many subjective choices, as: what to shoot and what to omit, how to shoot (framing, angle, lighting, etc.) and the fact of editing (omitting certain shots, juxtaposing shots or sounds unconnected in reality, etc.).

These observations are hardly new; they take on their proper significance, however, when considering the fact that a large proportion of the population of this country receives a large percentage of its information from television, which presents documentaries and documentary-type material with the a priori assumption that *because* it is documentary—even simply because it is *film*—that it is presenting "reality" and therefore the unquestionable objective truth about a subject.

Furthermore, not only do documentaries give us information that shapes our attitudes on many crucial issues, the *manner* in which the information is presented influences our attitudes toward the various problems and, by extension, the way we as a society deal with these problems of vital local, national, international and even global concern—like the nuclear arms race, pollution, overpopulation, racism, Vietnam, demonstrations and protests and cultural trends such as the youth movement. To take only one example, note television's changing attitude toward the Vietnam War over the past ten years, from general approval of U.S. actions to at least a questioning stance, if not outright disapproval. This came about not so much through the differences in the actual footage shown—much of it in fact would be interchangeable—but through the editorial comment that accompanied the footage and from allowing dissenting opinions to be heard. The *facts*—or the footage—have not radically changed over the years, simply the *opinion* about the facts.

Or, let there be no mistake that television is a free and open medium, for documentaries or anything else. The three networks will almost never air films not produced under their own auspices and completely supervised by their own staffs. Furthermore, since commercial television is completely dependent for its existence on advertising revenue, it is apt to refrain from making strong statements about anything for fear of offending advertisers or viewers and thereby adversely affecting revenues. And because commercial television represents large investments of capital and great influence in government circles (this is finally the only way to get—and keep—a television license), it is inevitable that the networks and stations are controlled by members of the establishment. This includes the very wealthy, the influential in national economic and political affairs—and, by extension, in an indirect but real way, the government. Therefore, almost by definition, those in control of television are in favor of keeping the status quo, for obvious reasons as well as for more subtle ones like self-censorship. This clearly makes it difficult for minority or dissident voices to be heard on this medium and makes television's objectivity highly suspect.

Educational television does provide a certain alternative to commercial TV, but it has remained rather limited because even its funds come in good part from the government and from large foundations that finally have the same desire for the status quo as do the commercial networks.

The importance of documentary film, then, should not be underestimated. In addition to the effects discussed above, it has also influenced our perception of the world, our awareness of other peoples and cultures and our knowledge of social injustice. It continues to remind us of certain essential facts of life which contemporary society would in many ways have us deny: the concrete reality of the physical world and the existence of people as individual, human, living beings.

Marshfield, Vt., Jan. 17, 1971.

A Brief Outline of the History of Documentary Film[1]

This is not meant to be a comprehensive survey of the documentary film but to present a broader picture of the genre so that the interviews can be read within a more meaningful context. If important films or film-makers have been omitted, these omissions are due to a lack of space—or are oversights—and I hereby extend my apologies.

PRIMITIVE ORIGINS: LUMIÈRE (as vs. Méliès)

From its very inception the cinema can be seen as divided into two main categories which remain essentially the same even today: the realistic (or documentary) film as represented by Lumière, and the fiction film as represented by Méliès.

Lumière's films, called *actualités* or *documentaires*, like other films of this kind from other countries, lasted less than a minute and consisted of footage of everyday events shot from a fixed camera position. In 1895 contemporary audiences found them new and exciting: it was the shock of seeing moving reality reproduced upon a screen for the first time. Typical titles include: *Workers Leaving the Lumière Factory, Baby at the Breakfast Table, Demolition of a Wall, Arrival of a Train at Ciotat Station, A Boat Leaving the Harbor.*

The beginnings of the fiction-film tradition can be seen in the work of Méliès, a magician turned film-maker who made fantasy films in his own studio in Paris and who discovered many of the techniques basic to film. In spite of their age, many of them remain fascinating and humorous today. Some of the best-known titles are: *The Conjurer*, 1899, *A Trip to the Moon*, 1902, and *The Palace of the Arabian Nights*, 1905.

Films similar to those of Lumière were being produced in other countries at the same time. In the United States they were made principally by Edison; typical titles are: *Chinese Laundry*, 1894, *Execution of Mary Queen of Scots*, 1895, *The Irwin-Rice Kiss*, 1896, *New York Steam Elevated Railway*, 1897, and *President McKinley's*

[1] Most of the material for this outline was taken from *The Liveliest Art* by Arthur Knight, *Documentary Film* by Paul Rotha (with Sinclair Road and Richard Griffith), *The Film Till Now* by Paul Rotha and Richard Griffith and "The Museum of Modern Art Department of Film Circulating Programs" (hereafter "MOMA Programs").

Inauguration, 1898. Some of these, such as *The Irwin-Rice Kiss*, were staged in Edison's studio in West Orange, New Jersey.

Brief moments of recorded reality, these Lumière and Edison films can be seen in the tradition of the newsreel, or news-documentary, one of the basic forms of the genre. However, from the very beginning, as the titles of these men's films perhaps indicate, the American tradition tended more toward the theatrical than did the French tradition.

MODERN ORIGINS: VERTOV AND THE KINO-EYE

The first major step toward evolution of documentary as the genre we know today came out of Russia during and immediately after the Bolshevik Revolution of 1917, principally in the work of Dziga Vertov, who edited actuality footage into newsreels; one of these series was called "Kino-Pravda."[2] Other newsreels or *actualités* simply recorded moments of reality; Vertov's differed essentially in having a social purpose—to help in the task of indoctrinating and informing the people about the Revolution. Also relevant is the theory of film-making Vertov developed called "Kino-Eye," and which Rotha describes as

> a scientific, experimental study of the visible world. It seeks to collect and to catalogue for our pleasure and edification the actualities of contemporary life. It sorts out the pertinent from the irrelevant and places it on the cinema-screen.[3]

Thus, in theory and practice, even at this formative primary source, the main characteristics of documentary are seen to be the interpretative editing of film that directly recorded reality for a social purpose.

THE FIRST DOCUMENTARIES: FLAHERTY

About the same time as Vertov was working in Russia, the first documentaries as we know them today were being made by the American Robert Flaherty. His *Nanook of the North*, 1922, a study of Eskimo life in northern Canada made to advertise a fur company, Revillon Frères, is one of the key films in the history of the genre. Previous travel films were merely photographed records;

[2] Literally "Camera-(or Film-)Truth" and also the meaning of the French phrase "cinéma-vérité," which was taken from Vertov.
[3] Rotha and Griffith, op. cit., p. 244.

Nanook was an interpretation of the life that the film-maker himself observed; it

> built up a dramatic picture of the struggle for life in a hostile environment by careful observation and sensitive recording of hunting, fishing, the construction of shelter, and the relationship between the individual and the family and [the] community.[4]

Flaherty went on to make other important films in this same tradition, like *Moana*, 1926, about Samoan life and culture, and *Man of Aran*, 1934, about the Aran Islanders and their struggle against the sea.

Flaherty's films are often seen as romantic because of the basic theme of man against nature and the idealistic view of man so often found in his work. Because of this they are often criticized for being unrealistic and for not exploring social themes implicit in the subject matter. Though there is some truth to this criticism, Flaherty remains one of the seminal and most important figures in all of documentary history because of the interpretative, evocative and human quality of his work and for the example and standards he set for succeeding film-makers.

CITY REALISM

A completely different and antiromantic tradition of documentary film began with Alberto Cavalcanti's *Rien que les heures*, 1926, a non-literal, impressionistic study of Paris, and Walter Ruttman's *Berlin, The Symphony of a Great City*, 1927, a day in the life of that city. Though many of Cavalcanti's techniques stemmed from the avant-garde films and surrealist movement of the time, the film was nevertheless documentary in its use of real locations and in contrasting rich and poor to make a social comment. "Ruttman emphasized visual rhythms in his cutting . . . and strove to give his films a symphonic organization. The result was widely influential in suggesting to film-makers how the motifs of everyday life could be patterned thematically."[5] Because of this and their exploration of the harsh realities of city life, such films are referred to as "city symphonies."

Joris Ivens, from Holland, also started out in this tradition. *The*

4 "MOMA Programs," p. 34.
5 Ibid., p. 28.

Bridge, 1928, is a study of the movements of a railroad bridge; *Rain*, 1929, the study of a rain shower in Amsterdam; and *Philips-Radio (Industrial Symphony)*, 1931, a study of the Philips-Radio factory in Holland—another "symphony" film and one of the earlier documentaries sponsored by industry.

HISTORIC (PROPAGANDIST) RECONSTRUCTIONS

The reconstructed historic, propagandist films that came out of the Russian Revolution are another essential step in the evolution of the documentary form. Their purpose, as Vertov's, was to instruct the Russian people about the Revolution and to win them over to the Communist cause. They started with almost no film tradition behind them and a shortage of film stock and film equipment, and were thus forced to find new ways to use film to express their ideas, essentially in the area of editing. Lev Kuleshov came to the conclusion that it was not the shot in itself which was important but the juxtaposition of two images that gives each individual shot its importance and emotional force. V. I. Pudovkin was concerned with the use of close-ups not for pointing up details but as an organic way to say something. And Sergei Eisenstein evolved a theory that he paralleled with Japanese hieroglyphics: the juxtaposition of two dissimilar images that took on a new meaning by their contrast with one another.[6]

These theories were put to use in the creation of some of the most important and memorable works in the history of film—what Rotha calls the "propagandist" tradition of documentary film. They were mainly reconstructions of real events using the actual locations in which these revolutionary events took place, and they often had an extraordinary feel of reality about them. More specifically, it is worth quoting Rotha on *Ten Days That Shook the World (October)*, 1928, by Sergei M. Eisenstein and Grigori Alexandrov:

> [It] undertook the selection and presentation of actual events and persons, not for accurate historical description but for the expression of a definite viewpoint which conformed with a definite political regard for the affairs of 1917. . . . This, you may say, is merely the result of propagandist aim. It is. But it is also something more. It is creating a form of documentary approach which gives new meaning to familiar things; not

[6] For an excellent discussion of this subject, v. *The Technique of Film Editing* by Karel Reisz and Gavin Millar, pp. 26–40.

> representing persons and things as they are, but relating them in such a manner to their surroundings that they temporarily are transformed by the powers of the film into material which can be shaped to take on different significances according to the director's aim; in this case to serve a political end by means of a dialectical treatment.[7]

(This lesson, that film material could be shaped to take on different meanings, was one to be remembered time and time again by documentarians, especially in the propaganda films of World War II.)

Potemkin, 1925, Eisenstein's reconstruction of a mutiny in the time of the Czar, is one of the most famous of all films in the history of the cinema. "It introduced a new film technique, providing a newly conscious conception of the manipulation of film material to communicate physical sensation."[8] Here, and in other Eisenstein films, the masses are the hero. In Pudovkin's films the hero is an individual who is idealized and presented as a personification of the masses; among his most important films are: *Mother*, 1926, based on Gorky's novel of the same name and actual incidents; *The End of St. Petersburg*, 1927, based "on the orthodox Communist view of the war and revolution, rather than on a strictly historical account"[9]; and *Storm over Asia*, 1928, about "the early years of the U.S.S.R. and of foreign intervention and which has been widely praised for complex cutting and careful editorial construction, the naturalism of the acting, and the freely experimental nature of the film."[10]

COMING TO MATURITY: GRIERSON AND THE BRITISH

These are the predecessors and influences from which the documentary movement grew. It came into existence as a continuing movement only with the creation of the English Empire Marketing Board Film Unit in 1929, under the supervision of John Grierson. This movement is of signal importance

> because of its continuity, its consistent purpose of public information and public service, and its volume. Its leader, John Grierson . . . saw in film a means of bridging the enormous gaps of comprehension and sympathy in the complex society

[7] Rotha, op. cit., pp. 93–94.
[8] "MOMA Programs," p. 23.
[9] Ibid., p. 24.
[10] Ibid., p. 24.

> of our times. He and the group gathered around him . . . sought to "bring alive" to the citizen the services of government and industry by dramatizing them in terms of human values, and he daringly sought financial support from government and industry themselves.[11]

When the E.M.B. was about to be abolished in 1933, the Film Unit came under the direction of the General Post Office, renamed the Crown Film Unit in 1940. But the basic premises held throughout these changes. It could be added that the "E.M.B. also represented the first attempt to portray the working-class of Britain as a human, vital factor in present-day existence."[12]

These films too were propagandistic, but in a less pointed manner than the word usually implies; the films were meant to spread information and a rather benign message of democratic idealism and a belief in the workingman. The method, in Grierson's phrase, was "the creative treatment of actuality"[13]; "You photograph the natural life, but also, by your juxtaposition of detail, create an interpretation of it."[14] Also, the Film Unit is one of the very rare examples of a group of film-makers working together as a group with an essentially single purpose for a sustained period of time. And indeed, every important English documentary film-maker of these years worked either directly or indirectly with this group.

The movement had its simple beginnings with *Drifters*, 1929, the only film personally directed by Grierson, about North Sea herring fishermen. Then followed films that recorded the work of miners and glass blowers. Later, production became more sophisticated to meet the requirements of explicating more complicated subjects; there were dramatic reconstructions, direct interviews and other innovations in technique.

Among important films produced by these Film Units are: *Granton Trawler*, 1934, directed by Edgar Anstey, about dragnet fishing; *Song of Ceylon*, 1934, directed by Basil Wright, regarded as one of the classics of the documentary film:

> Wright's use of a seventeenth-century commentary over pictures of Singhalese life today was the first consistent attempt to use sound in counterpoint rather than in complement to the visuals and results in mounting contrast between what is heard and

[11] Ibid., p. 37.
[12] Rotha, op. cit., p. 97.
[13] *Cinema Quarterly*, vol. 2, no. 1, p. 8.
[14] *Grierson on Documentary*, Forsythe Hardy, ed., pp. 81–82.

what is seen, between the old Singhalese culture and the impact on it of industrial civilization.[15]

Housing Problems, 1935, directed by Arthur Elton and Anstey, was influenced by *The March of Time*'s journalistic style and used direct interviews with people from the slums; *Night Mail*, 1936, directed by Harry Watt and Wright, poetically records the night mail train from London to Glasgow:

> By intimate observation of the postal workers at their jobs, it pictures the dignity of ordinary labor, while the poetic ending celebrates the meaning of mail to the man in the street. The complex mixing of natural sound, music, and the commentary in verse by W. H. Auden make this film a technical aesthetic landmark in documentary, and, indeed, in the history of the sound film itself.[16]

North Sea, 1938, produced by Cavalcanti and directed by Watt, uses dramatic reconstruction and actors to tell of the ship-to-shore radio service.

Among other countries that have produced important documentary films, Belgium should be mentioned for the large body of work produced there by Henri Storck: *Misère au Borinage*, 1933, made with Joris Ivens, and *Les Maisons de la misère*, 1938, two of the earliest films of social protest; and his films on art, notably *Le Monde de Paul Delvaux*, 1947, and *Rubens*, 1949.

THE UNITED STATES: TOWARD MATURITY

There was a strong touch of documentary in a number of Hollywood films of the thirties in their direct or implied social criticism of the American system that had brought on the suffering of the Depression. Gangster films, while frequently exploiting the material, nevertheless often attacked official corruption. A film like *I Am a Fugitive from a Chain Gang*, 1932, based on factual material, was a powerful indictment of the inhuman chain gang system in the South, and King Vidor's *Our Daily Bread*, 1934, "showed a heterogeneous band of unemployed people finding their salvation working together on a farm cooperative."[17]

[15] "MOMA Programs," p. 37.
[16] Ibid., p. 38.
[17] Knight, op. cit., p. 240.

But documentary production was sporadic here until the mid-thirties. In 1935 *The March of Time* came to the American screen from Time-Life, Inc., and Louis de Rochemont, complete with the impersonal, stridently authoritative voice of the narrator, Westbrook Van Voorhis. Blending actuality footage with staged interviews and at times with staged events, in dramatic rather than descriptive fashion, the films have been criticized for their very conservative bias and manipulation of events. From a historical point of view they "exerted profound and world-wide influence on screen journalism and the documentary,"[18] and

> in their thirteen issues a year the editors managed to keep their material timely, lively and even, on occasion, controversial. Indeed, so successful was "The March of Time" during the late thirties, that RKO-Radio Pictures was inspired to launch a rival reel, "This is America." For most Americans, these spelled documentary. They knew nothing else.[19]

It was in 1936, however, that the American documentary movement as such came into its own with Pare Lorentz' *The Plow That Broke the Plains.* Commissioned by the Roosevelt New Deal Resettlement Administration,

> it was a dramatic account of the tragic misuse of our Great Plains that led to the disastrous Dust Bowl of the mid-thirties. Like President Roosevelt's famous "fireside chats," this was a report to the nation on its government's efforts to meet the emergency.[20]

In 1937 Lorentz went on to make *The River,*

> A panoramic view . . . of the Mississippi River basin, of the vast industrial and agricultural expansion that led to its exploitation and ruin, and of the later efforts to control its flood by reforestation and the Tennessee Valley Authority. . . . [It] has come to be considered a masterpiece of the American screen.[21]

[18] "MOMA Programs," p. 32.
[19] Knight, op. cit., p. 249.
[20] Ibid., p. 250.
[21] "MOMA Programs," p. 40.

Other key films of this era are:

The City, 1939, by Willard Van Dyke and Ralph Steiner. Made for exhibition at the 1939 New York World's Fair, and sponsored by the American Institute of Planners, it was a plea for city planning done with technical expertise, even humor, and, as with Lorentz' work, a concern for social problems.

Power and the Land, 1940, Joris Ivens' first American film, centered "on the coming of electricity to rural districts and the human advantages it brings to farmers . . . it is chiefly an emotional impression of American farm life. . . . It features an actual farm family of the Middle West."[22]

The Land, 1942, by Robert Flaherty, with the collaboration of his wife, Frances Flaherty, and edited by Helen Van Dongen. This is a personal film about American agriculture during the Depression narrated by Flaherty himself. Because of the social implications of the film, the Agriculture Department, which had sponsored it, refused to release it for theatrical distribution. (And the U. S. Film Service was disbanded shortly thereafter by Congress.)

Louisiana Story, 1948, also by Flaherty, was concerned with the discovery of oil and the building of an oil rig in the Louisiana swamps as seen through the eyes of a Cajun boy.

The American documentary film thus "grew originally out of a world in depression,"[23] and, like the British, had a concern for social problems, but with a probably more direct emotional appeal.

WORLD WAR II: DOCUMENTARY-PROPAGANDA

With the coming of World War II documentary flourished as it never had before and as it never has since. As a tool for propaganda there was no better instrument than film, and all combatants mobilized their film industries for this purpose. Generally, the aim of these films was threefold: 1. to produce training and morale-building films for the armed forces; 2. to strengthen the morale of the public and keep it informed of the progress of the war; and 3. to inform other nations of one's own efforts in the war to gain support for one's goals. The documentary-propaganda film was an integral part of this international struggle for survival, and some of these films that came out of the war are among the best ever made in this genre, though today we would view their content, in spite of their technical innovations and excellence, from a different point of view.

22 Ibid., p. 40.
23 Rotha, op. cit., p. 213.

WORLD WAR II: GERMANY

The war propaganda film could be said to have had its start with the creation of the German Ministry of Propaganda in 1933 under the direction of Goebbels.

> The Soviet *Potemkin* was at first the model he held up to German film-makers, but he soon abandoned all fictional forms in favor of a type of documentary film in which the factual content of the photographic material used disguised the editorial manipulation of that material toward predetermined ends. Psychologically adept, technically brilliant, these films were highly effective.[24]

The best of the German film-makers was Leni Riefenstahl, previously an actress in romantic features. Her *Triumph of the Will*, 1934–36, documents the first Nazi Party conference in Nuremberg in 1934. Actually the conference was staged for the purpose of being filmed, "For ultimately, both Goebbels and Hitler realized, the enthusiasm of the Party members at Nuremberg was less important than the transmission of that enthusiasm to the millions of ordinary Germans everywhere who would see the film in their theatres."[25] Apotheosizing Hitler and the Nazi mystique of nationalism and the *Übermensch*, the film remains, in spite of its message and because of its art, one of the most brilliant documentary films ever made.

Olympia, 1936–38, also by Riefenstahl, and again at least partially staged for the camera, recorded the 1936 Olympics and was again brilliantly photographed and edited. Even here the Nazi mystique of joy and victory through physical strength permeated the film.

Baptism of Fire (*Feldzug in Polen*), 1940, was about the conquest of Poland, and was shown to countries about to be attacked to convince them that resistance was pointless. *Victory in the West* (*Sieg im Westen*), 1941, about the fall of France, was similarly used in that country.

Though the claim was and is still sometimes made that pictures do not lie, it is clear that they can be made to lie, and to lie extremely well by various means, especially in the way they are

24 "MOMA Programs," p. 41.
25 Knight, op. cit., p. 198.

edited—the juxtaposition of shots, the use of narration, etc. Though German propaganda films perhaps distorted the facts more grossly than others, it was a principle used by all countries in their effort to make footage take on the meaning they wanted it to have; this is one of the marvelous possibilities of documentary for the person in control—and one of the great dangers for the people to whom such films are shown.

WORLD WAR II: ENGLAND

In Britain, with a comparatively long tradition of documentary film-making, the many well-trained and experienced documentary film-makers joined forces with fiction film-makers to produce a large number of effective wartime films "to train men, to hearten the homefront, and to tell the world that Britain stood resolute, if alone, against the Nazi holocaust."[26]

Among the important films to come out of this era are: *Listen to Britain*, 1942, directed by Humphrey Jennings, one of the most important directors of the time; a kaleidoscopic impression of the country at war, it explores "the uses of sound in the motion picture, whether directly recorded natural speech, music, poetic commentary or the sounds of daily life."[27] *Target for Tonight*, 1941, directed by Harry Watt, about the intricate planning for a bombing mission over Germany, gave the airmen in the film "the chance of being themselves. To Watt went the credit of being the first to depict the human undercurrents of war on a scale which documentary had not previously attempted."[28] *World of Plenty*, 1943, produced and directed by Paul Rotha, was a compilation film important to the history of the genre in revealing

> almost for the first time how much form and sense could be given footage shot at many different times and places, for different purposes. Its most important and most original element was its attempt to give the audience a voice in the film itself; the voices of men in the street interrupt the narration of the old "voice of God" commentator to argue with his platitudes and to give a common-sense view on the topic of nutrition and on the world-wide paradox of plentiful food production existing side by side with starvation.[29]

[26] "MOMA Programs," p. 42.
[27] Ibid., p. 42.
[28] Rotha, op. cit., p. 251.
[29] "MOMA Programs," p. 43.

Desert Victory, 1943, directed by David MacDonald and the RAF Film Production Unit, documents the British victory over Rommel's Afrika Korps in North Africa. And *Diary for Timothy*, 1945, also directed by Jennings, tells of the last few months of the war in the form of a diary to a newborn child and, in this writer's opinion, remains touching even today for its humanity and personally felt need not to make the same mistakes, to create a new world.

Some British fiction films of the time also had documentary qualities in recording various aspects of the war in fictionalized form, as *One of Our Aircraft Is Missing*, 1942, directed by Michael Powell.

WORLD WAR II: UNITED STATES

In the United States, following the example of the Germans and British, Hollywood directors (Capra, Ford, Huston, Wyler, etc.) joined American documentary film-makers to help the war effort. For the men in the service there were indoctrination films and films to keep them abreast of the events of the war. There were also propaganda and incentive films made for the general public and wartime factory workers; others were made for distribution overseas to present the "American way of life" and to counteract fascist propaganda.

The best-known of the indoctrination films are the *Why We Fight* series produced by Col. Frank Capra for the War Department. They were designed to inform the American serviceman about the origins and progress of the war through explication and dramatization of the events that led up to the conflict. All of the films in the series were compilations that used existing footage, including earlier documentaries, newsreels, combat footage and even material from Axis films.

> The prolonged, repeated study and examination of existing documentary films . . . gave this production group a familiarity with documentary techniques and led them to break completely with the techniques of fictional dramatisation. . . . This was what made their pictures more convincing than comparable films made for the Air Force or the Navy groups which had not been so indoctrinated and who therefore tended to use . . . a fictional style instead of the documentary one.[30]

There is no doubt about the power of manipulated pieces of film as seen in this series, including the excellent and even in-

[30] Rotha, op. cit., p. 310, note 1.

novative use of editing, sound and visual; but *The March of Time*-like narrator and the blatant chauvinism of most of these films give them little appeal as to their content when seen today—at least by this viewer. But seen in their historical context they are extremely impressive indeed.

Among important films of this series are: *Prelude to War*, 1943, produced and directed by Capra; *The Nazis Strike*, 1943, produced and directed by Capra and Major Anatole Litvak; and *The Battle of Russia*, 1944, directed by Lt. Col. Anatole Litvak, which, in this writer's estimation, is one of the best of the series in being less blatantly chauvinistic and shrill.

The Army-Navy Screen Magazine, produced by Col. Leonard Spiegelgass and Brig. Gen. E. L. Munson, was issued bimonthly with the purpose of keeping the serviceman abreast of the events of war at home and on the front. Other films were also produced primarily for the serviceman, but in the form of reportage rather than compilation. The best of these, in the opinion of this writer, and of others, is *The Battle of San Pietro*, 1944, directed by Major John Huston. Using combat footage, the film tells the story of the difficult and costly taking of the small mountaintop village of San Pietro, but contrary to most other wartime documentaries, this one is quietly realistic, understated and deeply sympathetic to the men dying for a piece of earth without the pretense that death is somehow denied in patriotism; and Huston's own dry, cracked voice for the narration, instead of a loud, strident one, adds to the dignity of its statement. (It was also, expectedly, a film that had censorship problems.)[31]

Other films in this last category are: *Memphis Belle*, 1944, directed by Lt. Col. William Wyler, and *The Fighting Lady*, 1945, produced by Louis de Rochemont with photography under the supervision of Edward Steichen. This latter film is one of the more famous documentaries to come out of the war, and its reputation is one of excellence; for this viewer, however, its tone, set by the honey-voiced narration of Robert Taylor, debases the men in the film and their effort to fight the war.

Civilian propaganda films were produced by the Office of War Information and were shown throughout the country. Some titles are: *Fellow American*, 1942, directed by Garson Kanin; *War Town*, 1943; *Report from the Aleutians*, 1943, directed by Huston; *Know*

[31] For further discussion of this film, and a banned Huston wartime documentary, *Let There Be Light*, v. interview with Huston in *Film: Book 2, Films of Peace and War*, edited by Robert Hughes, Grove Press, Inc., New York, 1962. On *Let There Be Light*, also v. Van Dyke interview, p. 183, note 6.

Your Ally, Britain, 1944, directed by Capt. Anthony Veiller; and one of the most celebrated films in this category, *The True Glory,* 1945, an Anglo-American production edited jointly by Carol Reed and Garson Kanin, which tells the story of the war from D-Day to V-E Day and is known for the complex message it communicates, often in human terms, and its effective use of varied kinds of narration.

Films for overseas propaganda, produced by the Overseas Branch, OWI, to present the American way of life, were made with simple story lines and a reliance on a balance between the visuals and the words since the films had to be released in many languages. Where Hollywood film-makers dominated the Armed Service film units, here American documentary film-makers were in the majority; among them were Alexander Hammid, Irving Jacoby, Boris Kaufman, Irving Lerner, Lawrence Madison, Sidney Meyers and Willard Van Dyke. Some of the titles are: *The Autobiography of a Jeep,* 1943, produced and written by Joseph Krumgold; *Valley of the Tennessee,* 1944, directed by Alexander Hammid; *San Francisco,* 1945, about the beginnings of the U.N., produced and directed by Willard Van Dyke; and *Toscanini: Hymn of the Nations,* 1945, produced by Irving Lerner and directed by Hammid.

WORLD WAR II: RUSSIA

Compilation films were not among the best work that came out of Russia during the war, but rather their features,

> [which] stood out as achievements of remarkable skill and power. . . . The passionate and almost indescribable violence and horrors of the fighting on the Russian front were also of a character that could not be escaped. Films like *Defeat of the Germans near Moscow* (1942), *Siege of Leningrad* (1942), *The Battle for the Ukraine* (1943) and *The Battle of Orel* (1943) brought out the cruel anonymity of total war. . . . In the hands of Dovjenko especially, the material from the battlefronts became a vast piece of orchestration on the one single, relentless theme. It was not personalised in the manner of the Western films, but still full of humanity.[32]

The machinations of the politicians undoubtedly contributed to the problems of the film-makers, as it was often difficult to know

[32] Rotha, op. cit., pp. 289–90.

what was the accepted version of a particular battle, especially in the first years of the war when the fight was going badly.

POST-WORLD WAR II: ITALY AND NEO-REALISM

In brief, World War II saw the flowering of the documentary film in the innovation of techniques and exploration of themes. However, since the war, documentary film production has waned; without continuing sponsorship only one important documentary movement has sustained itself—the Canadian. But with the rise of television this is perhaps understandable given that medium's potential production funds and enormous audience. This is not to say that worthwhile documentary films have not been produced since the war, and among the most significant, at least historically, are those from the Italian neo-realistic school.

Very little if anything of consequence came from the Italian film industry in the years before or during the war, either in documentary or fiction feature films—Mussolini's dictatorship was apparently not conducive to creativity. However, after the war there arose one of the most important movements not only for the documentary but also for the fiction film—the neo-realist movement. It had its roots in Luchino Visconti's *Ossessione,* made in 1942 in the midst of the war and in spite of censorship problems. Based on James M. Cain's novel (uncredited) *The Postman Always Rings Twice,* the film had

> the deep attachment to the vitality of the working-class life, the uncompromising photography of Italian streets . . . and the determination to show how poverty, overcrowding and sordid living-conditions affect the humanity of men, women and children alike.[33]

Roberto Rossellini's *Open City,* 1945, was the first and key film of the movement as such. It "sought to re-create, as accurately as possible, the tensions, the trials and the heroic resistance of the common people of Rome during the years of the Nazi occupation."[34] Very few of the actors were professionals, it was photographed when and where possible, often with hidden cameras, and with poor film stock and little money.

> Its roughness, its lack of finish became a virtue. And the cumulative power of Rossellini's feeling for his subject was translated

[33] Roger Manvell, *New Cinema in Europe,* p. 18.
[34] Knight, op. cit., p. 223.

into a visual intensity that made the picture sometimes almost unbearable to watch. Here was true realism—the raw life of a tragic era. "This is the way things are," said Rossellini in presenting his film. It became the credo of the entire neo-realistic movement.[35]

Other significant neo-realist films followed. *Paisan*, 1946, Rossellini's second film and generally considered his best, records the life of the Italians and the Americans in their relationship of conquered to conqueror, again drawing its material from the raw life of the people. Vittorio de Sica's *Shoeshine*, also 1946, with a screenplay by his frequent collaborator, Cesare Zavattini, is a passionate realistic study of destitute children after the war, and his *Bicycle Thieves*, 1948, is about the misery and degradation of unemployment. Also in this group are Luigi Zampa's *To Live in Peace*, 1946, and *Angelina*, 1947; Alberto Lattuada's *Without Pity*, 1947; and *The Earth Trembles*, 1948, by Visconti. Later films in the genre, such as *Bitter Rice*, 1949, *Rome, 11 O'Clock*, 1952, and *Three Forbidden Stories*, 1953, exploited the neo-realistic method rather than explored its subject matter and technique.

As the Italian film industry got back on its feet, it generally went the way of most commercial cinema, though some films in this realistic-documentary tradition continued to be made, as *Umberto D*, 1952, by De Sica, and some of the earlier films of Fellini.

The neo-realist Italian movement, with its serious exploration of social themes, the use of non-actors to re-create stories based on the reality of the lives of the people in the actual settings where they originally took place was re-created documentary in its best sense. Furthermore, it helped intellectuals, especially in the United States, to begin to take film seriously, and made young film-makers aware that films could be made cheaply and without the oversophisticated, prohibitively expensive machinery of the Hollywood studios.

POST-WORLD WAR II: OTHER COUNTRIES

Documentary was put to use after the war by Britain to prepare its people for the postwar world—problems of housing, a new economy, etc.—and to to help the returning veteran. But the flowering of the British documentary movement had passed—the Crown Film Unit was abolished in 1952—and production remains sporadic and uneven.

[35] Ibid., p. 224.

In the United States a number of films were also made to help the veteran readjust to peacetime life and the nation to a peacetime economy, but the government film agencies were soon reduced in scope or abandoned and very little of the dynamic of wartime production remained.

Indeed, as mentioned above, only one sustained documentary movement has appeared since the war, the National Film Board of Canada, a government-sponsored organization founded in 1939 under the direction of John Grierson, and which has steadily continued to produce worthwhile films. Among them are: *Corral*, 1954, and *City of Gold*, 1956, by Colin Low and Wolf Koenig; the *World in Action* series, "which analyzed post-war problems and dramatized the concept of the United Nations as a working partnership dedicated to the co-operative solution of such problems"[36]; the *Canada Carries On* series, whose purpose was "to give the Canadian public 'the living sense of what is going on in Canada and in the rest of the world in relation to Canada,'"[37] and which achieved wide distribution; *Lonely Boy*, 1962, by Wolf Koenig and Roman Kroitor, an early cinéma-vérité film about the pop singer Paul Anka; and *Pour la suite du monde* (*Moontrap*) by Michel Brault and Pierre Perrault, 1963, about an isolated island community, again in cinéma-vérité style.

Among other significant or noteworthy films to have appeared since the war are:

GREAT BRITAIN:

The World Is Rich, 1947, Paul Rotha;
Waters of Time, 1950, Basil Wright; and
World Without End, 1952, Rotha and Wright.

Films which could be listed under the general category of Free Cinema[38] and which generally dealt with working-class people in a broader social context than had been done before in British documentary or fiction films (earlier British documentary put the working classes on the screen almost solely in terms of their work) are:
Thursday's Children, 1955, Lindsay Anderson;
Momma Won't Allow, 1955, Karel Reisz and Tony Richardson;
Every Day Except Christmas, 1957, Lindsay Anderson; and
We Are the Lambeth Boys, 1958, Karel Reisz.

[36] Rotha, op. cit., p. 333.
[37] Ibid., p. 336.
[38] V. Anderson biography and interview, pp. 58–62.

FRANCE:

La Bataille du rail, 1946, René Clément;
Farrébique, 1947, Georges Rouquier;
Guernica, 1950, Alain Resnais;
Hôtel des Invalides, 1952, Georges Franju;
Les Poussières, 1955, Georges Franju;
Nuit et brouillard, 1955, Alain Resnais, a remarkably moving study of the German concentration camps;
Les Maîtres fous, 1958, Jean Rouch;
Description d'un combat, 1960, Chris Marker;
Le Joli Mai, 1963, Chris Marker;
science films, Jean Painlevé.

UNITED STATES:

Muscle Beach, 1948, Irving Lerner and Joseph Strick;
The Quiet One, 1948–49, Sidney Meyers;
On the Bowery, 1956, Lionel Rogosin;
The Savage Eye, 1959, Ben Maddow, Sidney Meyers, Joseph Strick;
Come Back Africa, 1959, Lionel Rogosin;
Football, 1961, Jim Lipscomb;
Primary, 1960, Richard Leacock, D. A. Pennebaker, Al Maysles, Terry Filgate;
Happy Mother's Day, 1963, Richard Leacock;
Scorpio Rising, 1963, Kenneth Anger;
Don't Look Back, 1966, D. A. Pennebaker;
Titicut Follies, 1967, Frederick Wiseman;
Monterey Pop, 1967, D. A. Pennebaker;
High School, 1969, Frederick Wiseman;
Salesman, 1969, the Maysleses, Charlotte Zwerin;
Gimme Shelter, 1970, the Maysleses, Charlotte Zwerin.

CONTEMPORARY TRENDS

The most significant trends in documentary film-making since the war have been cinéma-vérité and documentaries made for television. Some of the wider implications of cinéma-vérité are discussed in the Introduction and in the interviews. Suffice it here to say that its origins lie mainly in World War II: the enormous amount of combat footage shot in 16mm. led to a greater acceptance of 16mm. as a professional medium and to a proliferation of 16mm. cameras and projectors; also, professionals started to use 16mm. for its lightness, cheapness and portability—all much greater in 16mm. than in 35mm. This gave them the means to shoot outside the studio much more easily and to capture reality as it happened—or to create this appearance. In time, tape recorders with acceptable sound were produced—the Nagra, invented by Stefan Kudelski, is considered the best and is the one most commonly used; and finally a portable rig capable of recording synchronized sound was created—one of the first was by Richard Leacock, Al Maysles and D. A. Pennebaker while working for Robert Drew (v. Leacock and Pennebaker interviews for further comments).

At about the same time—the early sixties—the phrase "cinéma-vérité" itself came into use in France in reference to the films of Jean Rouch and Chris Marker. The term generally refers to films that use such techniques as: synch-sound interviews, the hand-held camera, the direct recording of reality (supposedly) without the interference of the film-maker/cameraman, who is purported to be almost an instrument himself without involvement in the particular situation, and non-manipulative editing of the footage. These techniques have enormously influenced not only documentary film-making but also fiction films.

Documentaries made for television are an important trend because: 1. television remains the biggest and, in most countries, the only sponsor with sufficient funds to support continuing production and the means of "distribution"; 2. television has an enormous potential audience—literally the world; and 3. these two facts have important social and political implications. The effect of all this for good is questionable, but certainly never before has there been so much information available to so many people about so many subjects of vital concern to their well-being.

Many television documentaries use cinéma-vérité techniques, but contrary to a basic precept of cinéma-vérité there is often an omniscient narrator who imposes certain attitudes on the material by a seemingly impartial and objective commentary that is patently manipulative. And only rarely do any of these films go beyond their bureaucracies to express any direct personal point of view. Furthermore, because television producers have more influence in conceiving and deciding on the final shape of documentaries than the film-makers themselves, they have been a key factor in the development of the TV documentary. Among those producers and programs which have been most influential are:[39]

[39] For further details about these programs, v. *Documentary in American Television*, by A. William Bleum, Appendix III.

ABC:

John Secondari, *Close-Up!* series, c. 1960–63;
Secondari and Helen Jean Rogers, *The Saga of Western Man* series, c. 1963–64.

CBS:

Edward R. Murrow and Fred W. Friendly, the *See It Now* series, c. 1953–55;
Fred W. Friendly, *CBS Reports* series, c. 1959–63;
Burton Benjamin, *The Twentieth Century* series, c. 1958–63;
Warren Wallace.

NBC

Henry Salomon, *Victory at Sea* series, 1952–53;
Salomon and Donald B. Hyatt, the *Project XX* series, c. 1955–63;
Hyatt, *The World of ——* series, c. 1961–62;
Irving Gitlin, *DuPont Show of the Week*, c. 1962–64, and the *White Paper* series, c. 1960–64;
Reuven Frank and Lou Hazam.

FREE-LANCE:

Robert Drew and David Wolper.

Among TV documentary film-makers (besides those interviewed in this book) who should be mentioned are:
American: Bill Jersey, Jim Lipscomb and Gregory Shuker.
English: Denis Mitchell and Ken Russell.
Canadian: Beryl Fox and Douglas Leiterman.

Though television has cut back on its production of documentaries in recent years, it nevertheless continues to provide an outlet, even if limited and narrow in point of view, for a number of worthwhile documentaries that explore a variety of subjects.

In this same area, the growth of cable television with its many possible channels and the promise of cassette TV hold great potential for documentary, including the use of tape instead of film as a recording medium and the possibility of reaching larger audiences through these alternative means of distribution. Because of this and the recent availability of comparatively cheap portable video systems (as little as $2000), there are a growing number of groups working in this area of "amateur" television. (V. Shamberg-Cort interview for further comments.)

OTHER POSSIBILITIES

At the same time there is another trend in documentary in the United States and elsewhere, that of the protest/propaganda film. Coinciding with the rise of dissent throughout the West in the past ten to fifteen years there has been a small, steady stream of documentary films made mainly by non-professionals on very low budgets in a usually unpolished, rough style and covering principally subjects of social protest from a radical point of view. These films reach their public—mainly college students and the already radicalized—through a kind of "underground" non-commercial network consisting of various political, social and/or cultural groups which have their own film lists and distribution centers. Typical and one of the more important and longer-lasting ones is Newsreel, a politically left-oriented group which distributes, and makes, radical (often propagandistic) films.

Also, besides the comparatively wide distribution of a few well-known and popular documentary films there is now wider distribution of other documentaries through the increasingly important commercial 16mm. circuit—colleges, clubs, political organizations, etc. It is conceivable, though not yet so, that this market will one day be large enough to pay basic costs—even if not large profits—for some low-budget documentaries; and though perhaps more true in the United States, it is also partially true in Europe. Indeed, the growth of this 16mm. market, along with cable TV and video cassette systems, are possibly important trends for financing and distributing documentaries other than through the more traditional and restrictive outlets.

NON-HISTORICAL CONCLUSION

Documentary has never been a popular form, in good part because it does not conform to our standards of entertainment. In recent years, however, cinéma-vérité films of rock stars and concerts have gained popularity—and greater profits. But popularity—pleasing a large number of people—does not necessarily imply value, and the economic profits that might accrue from such films are not necessarily the solution of the essential problem of financing documentary films. First, it is likely that such profits would be used to make other popular and economically profitable documentary—or fiction?—films which, in relying on such subjects as stars of the entertainment or other worlds, deny too large a part of the reality that documentary would record for our possible benefit. Secondly, there would be the temptation to exploit people, events or our gullibility, to hoke up, falsify or even create events—possibly without regard for consequences—to flatter the audience for the sake of greater popularity and financial profit, which would deny the very essence of documentary, treating reality as it exists in actuality; and if this be the only solution for financing and gaining a greater audience for documentaries, then it is perhaps better for documentary to remain as it has in the past, comparatively unpopular, misunderstood and slightly dusty.

But why the insistence on documentary as distinguished from other film forms? Because even though fiction films can perhaps finally give us deeper and more profound perceptions about the world, documentary, if only by directly recording moments of reality, can show and tell us things that fiction films cannot because of fiction's *embellishment* of reality. And finally, because of its inherent obligation to reality, whether in the form of the simplest travel film or description of a work process or in complex portraits of movements, events or people, documentary will surely continue to have its place in the world of film.

BRITAIN

BASIL WRIGHT

Basil Wright was born in 1907. He attended Corpus Christi College in Cambridge, where he took an Honours degree in classics and economics. He was twice film critic for *The Spectator*, and broadcast regularly for a number of years with the BBC Critics program. Wright has also lectured extensively on film in many countries and has served on a number of film festival juries, including Venice, Mannheim, Tours and Krakow.

In 1947 he worked with Julian Huxley and John Grierson at UNESCO in Paris "preparing the first international plans for the use of film in fundamental education and mass communication." (B.W.) In 1962 and 1968 he spent six months lecturing on film at the University of California. In 1967 he visited Uganda for UNESCO and prepared a report on the use of film and TV, and in 1969, again for UNESCO, he and Peter Hopkinson conducted a course in screenwriting at the Film Institute of India in Poona. In 1970 he taught a course on documentary film in the United Arab Republic. Since 1970 he has been writing a book on film, tentatively entitled *The Long View*.

Wright is a Fellow of the British Film Academy, a Governor of Bryanston School and President of the International Association of Documentary Film Makers. In the past he has also been a Governor of the British Film Institute, President of the Scientific Film Association, Chairman of the National Film Archive Committee, a Council Member of the Royal College of Art, a Council Member of the Society of Authors and President of the London Regional Council of the United Nations Association.

Wright is unmarried and lives in a small house on the Chilterns.

FILMOGRAPHY*

E.M.B. FILM UNIT

1930: *Conquest.* A compilation film edited by B.W. under John Grierson's supervision. Dealt with the history of the development of the North American continent and included clips from films like *The Covered Wagon, The Iron Horse,* etc. Silent.

Lumber. Another compilation film about the extraction and transport of timber in Canada. Sound: no narration, but musical score specially composed by Denis Arundell. (Note: this film was subsequently re-edited and put out with a different track under the title *King Log.*[1])

1931: *The Country Comes to Town.* First professional directorial job; also scripted and edited. Camera by James Burger and B.W. Sound.[1]

1932: *O'er Hill and Dale.* Script, direction, editing, photography. Depicted the life of a shepherd on the Cheviot Hills, Scotland, during the spring lambing season. Sound.[1]

Gilbraltar. Script, direction, editing, photography. Educational film about the rock. Silent.

Shot some extra material for Flaherty's *Industrial Britain.*[1]

1933: Expedition (alone) to the West Indies. Directed and photographed some 36,000 feet of 35mm. film. Out of this made a number of educationals (silent). Also *Liner Cruising South,* a film about a luxury cruise (silent); *Cargo from Jamaica,* an impression of the banana industry much noted at the time for pioneer work in montage (silent); *Windmill in Barbados,* a film on old and new methods in the sugar industry, edited silent by B.W., but sound added later by Cavalcanti.

G.P.O. FILM UNIT

1934: *Song of Ceylon.* Script, direction, photography, editing. Assistant was John Taylor. Music by Walter Leigh. Commentary

* Supplied by the film-maker.

1 "These were part of a batch of films sold to a commercial distributor who added commentary and music without our having much control." [B.W.]

spoken by Lionel Wendt. (Awarded a Gold Medal and the prize for the Best Film from Any Source at the Brussels Film Festival.)

Shot some extra material for *Coalface.*

Shot several sequences for the jazz section of *BBC The Voice of Britain.*

1935: Produced some films under Grierson's supervision, including *The Fairy on the Phone* (directed by William Coldstream).

1936: Codirected *Night Mail* with Harry Watt. Photography by H. E. Fowle, Jonah Jones. Editing by R. Q. McNaughten. Verse by W. H. Auden. Music by Benjamin Britten. Sound by Cavalcanti.

Produced or associate-produced various G.P.O. films, including Len Lye's *Rainbow Dance.*

REALIST FILM UNIT

1937: Left G.P.O. Film Unit and founded Realist (with John Taylor and Cavalcanti).

Produced *The League at Work,* film directed by Stuart Legg about the League of Nations.

Children at School. Script, direction, editing. Photography by Adrian Jeakins. Commentary written by Tom Driberg and spoken by H. Wilson Harris. (Made for British Commercial Gas Association.)

1938: *The Face of Scotland.* Script, direction, editing. Photography by Adrian Jeakins. Music by Walter Leigh. Commentary written by B.W. and spoken by G. N. Carstairs. (Made for Films of Scotland Committee.)

FILM CENTRE

1939: Left Realist in charge of John Taylor and joined Film Centre. Associate producer on *The Londoners* (directed by John Taylor). Producer, *Men of Africa* (directed by Alex Shaw).

1940: *Harvest Help.* Direction and editing. Government propaganda short featuring Michael Redgrave, Rachel Kempson and Hay Petrie.

1940–44: Produced, among countless films for the war effort: *The Harvest Shall Come* (directed by Max Anderson); *Canteen on*

Wheels (directed by Jay Lewis); *Subject for Discussion* (directed by Hans Nieter); *Lift Your Head, Comrade* (script by Arthur Koestler; directed by Michael Hankinson); *Neuropsychiatry 1943* (directed by Michael Hankinson).

CROWN FILM UNIT

1945–46: As Producer in Charge produced, among others, *Diary for Timothy* and *A Defeated People* (both directed by Humphrey Jennings) and *Children on Trial* (directed by Jack Lee).

INTERNATIONAL REALIST

1947: After visit to New York to discuss international production possibilities with Grierson and Legg, set up International Realist, with Pat Moyna, as adjunct to Realist Film Unit.

1948: *Bernard Miles on Gun Dogs.* Production, script, direction, editing. Photography by Ron Craigen. Narration written by Antony Steven and spoken by Bernard Miles. Music by Doren Carwithen.

1950: *Waters of Time.* Produced. Scripted, codirected and edited with Bill Launder. Photography by Reg Hughes. Narration written by Paul Dehn and spoken by James McKechnie, John Slater, Paul Dehn, Felix Felton. Music by Alan Rawsthorne. For Port of London Authority.

1953: *World Without End.* Produced. Codirected and edited with Paul Rotha. Photography in Thailand by Adrian Jeakins; in Mexico by Carlos Carbajal. Narration written by Rex Warner and spoken by Michael Gough. Music by Elisabeth Lutyens. Associate producer was John Alderson. For UNESCO.

Produced *The Drawings of Leonardo da Vinci.* Directed by Adrian de Potier. Photography by Adrian Jeakins. Script and narration by Michael Ayrton. Used voices of Laurence Olivier and C. Day Lewis. Color.

1955: *The Stained Glass at Fairford.* Production and direction. Photography by Adrian Jeakins. Script by John Betjeman, spoken by John Betjeman and Robert Donat. Music by Julian Leigh. For Arts Council. Color.

1956: Produced *One Wish Too Many,* feature film directed by John Durst. For Children's Film Foundation.

MARSDEN FILM PRODUCTIONS

1957: Formed Marsden as partnership between my mother, Gladys Wright, and myself. We took a unit to Greece and shot material for two films:

1958: *The Immortal Land.* Produced by Gladys and Basil Wright. Directed and edited by Basil Wright. Assistant editor was Adrian de Potier. Photography by Adrian Jeakins. Adviser on Greek Art was Michael Ayrton. Narration by Rex Warner, spoken by Michael Redgrave, Leo Genn, John Gielgud, Minos Volonakis. Extracts from Greek Drama spoken by Katina Paxinou and Alexis Minotis. Music by James Bernard. Associate producer was John Alderson. Color. (Awarded the Council of Europe Gold Medal and Greek Sculpture First Prize at the Bergamo Film Festival.)

1959: *Greek Sculpture.* Produced by Gladys and Basil Wright. Codirected by Michael Ayrton and B.W. Photography by Adrian Jeakins. Edited by B.W. Assistant editor was Adrian de Potier. Narration written by Michael Ayrton and spoken by Leo Genn. Music by Humphrey Searle. Color.

REALIST FILM UNIT/ANVIL FILMS

1960: *A Place for Gold.* Production, direction, editing. Script and narration by Paul Dehn. With voices of James McKechnie and David Markham. Photography by Adrian Jeakins. Music by James Bernard. Assistant editor was Adrian de Potier. For Worshipful Company of Goldsmiths. Color.

1970: Planning *The Discovery of Nautilus*, a film about a new kind of sculpture developed by Michael Ayrton. In color, with photography by Adrian Jeakins and music by Humphrey Searle.

1971: Possible color film in collaboration with Michael Ayrton and with photography by Adrian Jeakins, on three great equestrian statues—Marcus Aurelius (Rome), Colleoni (Venice) and Gattamelata (Padua).

December 20, 1969, at Basil Wright's home, near Henley-on-Thames, England.

G. Roy Levin: I thought we could start by asking how you started making films.

Basil Wright: Most naturally I find it boring to have to repeat it. It's coming out like a formula now. When I was in Cambridge—I was a student there from 1926 to 1929—I changed my intention from being the world's greatest novelist-playwright-poet to being a film director, for the simple reason that I suddenly realized from the films I saw that here was a new art which very few people had had the opportunity yet to experiment with. The films which influenced me in this particular manner were Alfred Hitchcock's early silent film called *The Lodger*, E. A. Dupont's film *Variety* and *The Student of Prague*. And these films suddenly made me realize that this was a new form of creative expression, a new art form, so why not? you know, go in.

I think, too, I'd been terribly influenced by cinema since I was very young. I saw *Cabiria* when it first came out in 1913, and then there were some American films, one about a railroad called *The Juggernaut*, and another one about red Indians, and heaven knows what; anyhow they were all very moral and all very sad, but to this day I can see these visuals on my mind. They really had a most tremendous effect on me. I was, I suppose, four or five years old at the time I'm talking about. I also saw *The Last Days of Pompeii*, which was an immense Italian super in which everything fell down and crushed people. So I think I had been very much influenced in that way, and also during my public school days—which means, you must realize, in England, private school days. I'd been awfully impressed by Griffith's *Way Down East*, *Orphans of the Storm*, Stroheim, Fritz Lang, all that sort of thing. It had all been building up, but it wasn't until I was at Cambridge and I saw *The Lodger* and *Variety* that I definitely got interested in films, and began secretly to see the banned Russian films like Pudovkin's *Mother*. But the whole thing sort of codified in my mind, and I said, "This is what I must do." So when I left Cambridge I tried to get a job in films somehow—you know, I got introductions and that sort of thing. Then I went to the Film Society performance in London at which they showed *Potemkin* for the first time. It had been banned for years, even for private showing. The supporting program to *Potemkin* was the premiere of John Grierson's *Drifters*, and as soon as I saw *Drifters* I knew this was the sort of film I wanted to make. I tried to find out his address, and while I was looking for it he wrote to me out of the blue because he'd seen an amateur film I'd made, asked would I come see him and offered me a job to edit a film for him. That was in late 1929.

G.R.L. What was the name of your film that he'd seen?

B.W. Oh yes, it was called *Strandfest*; it was a film very much influenced by Dziga Vertov and that sort of thing. I'd been on vacation and I'd shot a lot of things at some swimming pool in Germany and at a fair, you know, roundabouts and carousels and all that, and then I just edited them all together. Apparently Grierson was impressed with the way I edited the film, and so I got my first job. He paid me seven pounds ten to edit the film and it cost me twelve pounds. I've never forgotten that. Then, as you know, we worked very closely together for many years, and I think we are still sort of in telepathic communication.

G.R.L. At the G.P.O. and the Empire Marketing Board, were you all consciously aware of wanting to change social conditions? Was there a group spirit?

B.W. Well, of course there was a group spirit. The awareness of wanting to change social conditions was, I think, there. Grierson used to get very impatient with us, I mean my generation, Arthur Elton, Edgar Anstey and myself and various others around at the time, because we were interested in film art, and he said, "Okay, you're interested in film art. I'll do a bargain with you. You must get interested in social betterment." He never used the word revolution. I'm exaggerating a little here because all of us were left-wing in any case; but what he had to do was get our minds off the glorious new technique of the Russian cinema and onto the fact that first of all we were civil servants and were responsible for spending public money, and secondly, that any new development in film aesthetic must be disciplined by the demands of the subject at hand; therefore the subject that one was dealing with must control the technique, or the experimental technique. We all came from different areas, from different points of view, and we were all interested in the creative possibilities of cinema. Grierson's great genius was to get this group of people to concentrate not just on the idea of social reform or social revolution, but on social reform through capitalism. All the money we ever got for making documentary was from British Conservative governments, or from monopoly capitalism, like oil, or gas, or chemicals, and that sort of thing. So you see, he gave us a double discipline. He made us discipline ourselves to our duties as citizens, and to forcing the monopoly capitalists to make progressive films. We proved to them that by so doing they were doing themselves a lot of good.

G.R.L. Were you all friends? Did you talk to each other about your ideas, about the films you were making? Did you look at each other's films, scripts and rushes?

B.W. To begin with, Grierson regarded rushes as rather a private affair. I think he was right. The rest of the unit were not allowed to see any individual's rushes, and I appreciated that—I think everybody did. You see, he was a very good—and very tough—producer, and he liked to say about your rushes exactly what he thought, even including spitting on the floor. And he felt that it was not good for somebody to undergo this amongst all his contemporaries. It would have been like the Red Guards in China, or something of that sort. Criticism of one's work by one's colleagues and contemporaries usually came when the film was finished. And I still think this is a good idea, and I am not personally in favor of collective bullying or breast-beating, because I don't think it really makes the film any better.

As to whether we discussed things, my goodness, yes. I could take you round a series of pubs in Soho and tell you the point we left one pub because the beer quality went down and went to another one. But in those pubs were Robert Flaherty, and Grierson, and Cavalcanti and anybody who happened to be in London concerned with films, talking like mad. And we little boys, the ones who were learning to make our little films, we were there. If you weren't on location, you were there in the evening, arguing and arguing, talking and talking, and Grierson was marvelous there too, for he would put on a different attitude. Still be quite tough, but then he would talk much more freely and without the sense of discipline which he had to keep and always kept in the more formal matters, you know, seeing rushes, or looking at rough cuts—which is of course even more important. Well, his genius as a producer is to me quite extraordinary. I owe him practically everything I have in life, as a film-maker, because of his ability to understand someone else's potentialities and drag them out of him without imposing his own ideas at all.

G.R.L. Do you mean his perception in seeing, for example, rough cuts and saying what was good and what was bad?

B.W. His perception in seeing rushes and saying, "It's not good enough. Go back and do it again." He'd say, "You know perfectly well you could have shot that better." He didn't say how I should have shot it. He said, "Just look, you only have to look at that sequence—how's it going to cut? It's no good. Go back tomorrow and shoot it again." He'd do that on the telephone when you were five hundred miles away. And he was very tough. He was quite frightening. But it happened, and he was always right.

G.R.L. When you directed a film, for example, how free were you to work as an individual?

B.W. Completely. Absolutely completely, except that somebody else was paying for it. Grierson was my producer, he was responsible to the government or to Shell[1] or whatever it was. Obviously he had his duty there, and he was always telling us, "All right, you're responsible to the people putting up the money for this film to make it a good film." He didn't say to make it what they wanted, because we didn't always do that. We used to persuade them afterwards that the result was what they wanted, and they usually were very pleased. The sponsors were very seldom disappointed, in the end.

G.R.L. In the abstract color film by Len Lye, *Colour Box,* I believe the only message of any kind is at the very end where there is something about postal rates, and—

B.W. Well, that was simply Grierson. Len Lye got an introduction to Grierson and showed him this film and Grierson said, "This man is terribly important, we must get him going." Then he said to Len, "Okay, it's quite easy; put a bit on the end—I'll give you the material—about how the postal charges on parcels have been reduced by so and so and so"—whatever it was, I think it was that. And Len put it on the end, and it became a commercial, an advertising film. And yet quite a few cinemas in London paid rent to show the film, because the public liked it so much.

G.R.L. One thing that Paul Rotha talks about over and over in his book[2] is the idea of making films in groups. He says that one shouldn't make documentary films as an individual but as part of a team.

B.W. But be careful not to misunderstand this point of view. I think Rotha has always said—and I agree with him—that it's dangerous, unless you know you're a genius, to become a lone-force individual film-maker having allegiance to nobody. In fact, I think that great genius Robert Flaherty did suffer from being a lonely man. There were many wasted years in his life in which no films happened, because he was living in a hard, hard world where people were not waiting with money and checkbooks to do anything for him. I know Grierson was always very sad that he couldn't succeed in getting Flaherty somehow into our group so that he could have sold the old boy to some sponsor or other. But Flaherty didn't like that, and this was that love-hate relationship which went on between

1 Shell Marketing and Refining Company.
2 *Documentary Film.*

Grierson and Flaherty all the time, because the moment anybody really attacked Flaherty, Grierson leapt to his defense; and the rest of the time Flaherty and Grierson were bitching it away like mad.

Now, getting back to Rotha. I think what he means is that the success of the British documentary movement, and the reason why it lasted for so long—let us put it at a minimum of twenty-five years—was that it was a unified group of people who agreed on their general policy about the use of the film medium in terms of sociology, economics, education, information, or what you now call mass communication, and that apart from the fact that they used to meet together very regularly and discuss all these things, they eventually got so that if any member found himself in Baghdad or Chile or Chicago or somewhere and was offered some sort of deal for a film, his reactions would be identical with almost any other member in the group in the sense that he would say to himself, "Okay, what strings are attached to this offer? Will the money involve my having insufficient freedom to express the subject offered in terms of creative film-making?" In other words, "I musn't take the job if I am going to be forced to do a falsity, to treat the subject in a way in which I shall be insincere and incorrect."

We were all of us, I think, very much imbued with this idea, which certainly came from the fact that we worked as a group. Let's be quite clear what we mean by a group here: I'm talking about a group of about 150 people, not a group of 10. Of course there were others such as trainee cameramen, editors, young people coming up who subsequently became famous and so on, but who were all still being influenced by this attitude, this atmosphere, this ambience, in which we all lived. It was almost like a reflex action. We reacted terribly quickly to certain stimuli, always in the same way. And always, I would like to say, positively, not negatively, in the sense that we were interested in anything that was said or offered to us which could possibly turn into a positive, valuable piece of film expression. This is what really kept us going from the time when Grierson stopped being a film director, after he made *Drifters*, until television came in, in the late fifties, I suppose.

G.R.L. It sounds like it was a happy time.

B.W. Oh, it was a marvelous time. It's like saying to the impressionists, "It was a happy time then, the great period of impressionism, which will pass into history." I think this period of British documentary has passed into history the same way.

But everything is different now. I believe documentary has passed almost totally into television, which is where it should be, and where it would have been had there been television in 1929. But it fascinates me that all documentary television is done by a new generation. None of the old guard of documentary went into television, except Paul Rotha, and he himself, I think, would agree that it didn't work. He went into BBC as director of television documentary, and it only lasted for about eighteen months. It was nobody's fault; it was simply that television is different. Television is quite different from film. Making a film for television is not the same thing as making a documentary film for the cinema screen.

G.R.L. Would you want to say why?

B.W. Well, simply because of the nature of the medium and the circumstances under which you'll see it. A little while ago we were talking about Richard Cawston's TV program *Born Chinese*. Now there's a perfect example of how to make a film which is in fact designed to catch a television audience. It could also catch other audiences, but it's designed for television. Now in this film he uses brilliantly all the things you had to throw out when you were making a cinema documentary. In this particular film, he uses all the shots in which people are looking at the camera or have suddenly spotted the camera, even though he was using, as television people do, long-focus lenses. And, as you know, in the old documentary days, as soon as someone looked at the camera, you threw that shot out because the illusion of reality had been lost. In this film, he builds this whole element up simply because the whole thesis of the film is that the Chinese rather despise the Europeans and can't recognize one European from another because they're all pink, and that sort of thing. Having built this up, he is then able to get all those shots of the Chinese population of Hong Kong, who happen to be glancing at the camera, to mean something quite important. He uses this to prove the truth of his thesis; and if you haven't seen the film I don't want you to get the wrong idea, because it's a very sincere, honest film about human relationships.

Anyhow, this is one of the differences I see between film and TV. And we've got to have two separate names for them. Because I want to see from now on a generic thing called motion picture, including one thing which means film, and another which means television program.

G.R.L. The technique, if you will, of people looking at the camera is common enough in certain kinds of contemporary films. I'm sure you've seen that.

B.W. Only recently. Only since television. That's the point I'm making. I was interested in Cawston quite early on. Indeed *Born Chinese* is a comparatively old film. He saw this point and deliberately used it. Well, now, of course, in ciné-vérité, it's almost wrong—people shouldn't be looking straight at the camera all the time. But there *is* a point about the intimacy of television. The use of close-up in intimacy, to a degree, which was only thought of previously by Robert Flaherty in *Nanook of the North* and *Moana*, and, oh, by Edgar Anstey and John Taylor when they made films like *Housing Problems* in 1935 where they took the most cumbersome apparatus in the world—a sound camera, a crew of eight—and interviewed people directly in the worst slums of London. This was a freak at the time. It's now become a new technique, if you like.

G.R.L. It was all 35mm.?

B.W. Of course it was all 35mm. No magnetic tape. Nothing.

G.R.L. Do you think that the films made by you and the other people working with Grierson helped to bring about social change? *Cathy Come Home*, for example, I was told, brought about a debate in Parliament and supposedly helped bring about a change in the housing laws. Are there any examples like that? Did you feel you were changing anything?

B.W. I hadn't expected that the films one made were going to cause social change. I think our feeling was that it was a total use of the means of mass communication which would bring about change. And as you know, Grierson developed this very much during the war in Canada, where he became concerned with more than film, with the whole question of mass communication. And as you also know, as documentary developed, we related it more and more to other means. You had the film, and you had a kit which was the film and a filmstrip and teachers' notes, and wall posters—you know, everything. I think we should have been extremely vain if we thought that any *particular* film we made at that time was going to create a tremendous difference in life. What we were trying to do was to make it possible for ordinary citizens to get an idea of the arguments pro and con in certain circumstances, and an idea of why certain things—like smoke pollution or slums—existed, and how they could be put right. We never made political films, but we would show films as a result of which people would argue about a problem from different points of view. We felt documentary was a policy of the use of the media of communication which could, over a period, change the feeling, the atmosphere of thinking, the attitudes of people without bullying them. We always felt there was great danger in trying to change people's points of view by bludgeoning them, mentally, aesthetically, or any other way.

G.R.L. These films were seen by a lot of people?

B.W. Oh yes, by a damn sight more than people think, because in order to get them shown, Grierson realized that he had to have his own circuit, the non-theatrical as opposed to a theatrical circuit, because who was going to book documentaries into public cinemas in those days?

G.R.L. How was this "private circuit" built up?

B.W. Free distribution, encouragement to people to buy 16mm. projectors, traveling vans with 16mm. projectors in them. You had the government, the big cartels, ICI,[3] Shell. They set up libraries. If you set up a library and say that you've got 250 films of various categories, largely educational, you'll find groups that will have projectors who will want them. Then you offer them to non-paying audiences to guarantee that you're not doing it commercially, and as long as they promise they are not charging for entrance, you send them the films, and they only have to pay the cost of mailing it back. They provide the projector, or you can send your mobile projectors out, which I think is a less satisfactory way. As soon as you start this, you create an interest in it, and in the idea of the purchase and use of projectors. On top of this was the whole film society movement, which was terribly important to us in England in the thirties, and which was using mainly 35mm. films at the time and therefore hiring public theaters for private shows. Anyhow, this was all happening outside the ordinary range of cinema, and this became a growing market. When I speak of market, I mean a market for the dissemination of ideas rather than for making profits, and big industry and government found it perfectly worth doing. You must also remember there was no direct political propaganda involved in this at all.

G.R.L. Were there any problems with people who had radical political ideas and wanted to express them?

B.W. Our problem was seldom with people who had right-wing political ideas and wanted to express them. Most of them—whether in home or imperial questions—usually played along with us, and turned themselves into our left-wing level, because they knew on which side their bread was buttered. I'm not talking purely politically now, I'm talking about basic mental attitudes, which included the attitude of the commercial firms that wanted their brand names stuck on every shot of the film. You had to explain to them that it would do them no good because they would make the film unviable. In general, we found the conservative people far more understanding of the possibilities of the use of our media than the left-wingers. In fact, when Labour came in with a tremendous majority after the war, I said to my colleagues in documentary, "Now our troubles are really starting," and I was right, because the left-wing socialists

[3] Imperial Chemical Industries, Ltd.

and all the members of the co-operative movement and the socialist movement hadn't a clue as to how to use film. We used to long to go back to the gorgeous liberal days of ICI and Shell—we really had trouble with the Left.

G.R.L. Why was that?

B.W. Because they were narrow-minded, doctrinaire and almost entirely lacking in imagination. They wanted films of propaganda that were bent into very, very narrow lines. It's almost impossible to tell you what we suffered with the first Socialist government, how they nearly destroyed the whole movement. Of course, there were a number of individuals and groups who were complete exceptions, like S. C. Leslie, who used to be with B.C.G.A. before the war and sponsored all those sociological films, and then after the war was in the *Britain Can Make It*[4] thing, put on by the Council for Industrial Design. He was one of the exceptions, but on the whole one went into the sort of narrow religious thing you get where other people's points of views cannot possibly be reconciled or even entertained. Their whole attitude towards the use of cinema was just plain stupid. Now, I lived through all of this so I don't want to go into more details. You can always see where two negatives come together. During the war documentary people had been working themselves to death practically, were exhausted and wanted to be inspired by a new and vigorous and very positive challenge; and instead they were faced with a lot of bitchy old doctrinaire politicians who simply ran documentary and themselves and everybody into the ground because they created or represented a negative attitude.

G.R.L. *Diary for Timothy* struck me most of all the wartime films I saw here, and what struck me about it was that there was a passion about setting the world right. There was a given, in that everybody knew his function in the world and what had to be done: we had to win the war and then everything would be fine and dandy. And in the last line of the film, if I remember correctly, the narrator asks, "Will you, Timothy, be greedy like your forebears?" Not just in a material way, but greed in a spiritual way, which seemed to me a very radical statement.

B.W. That statement was made by an old and very famous gentleman named E. M. Forster.[5] He wrote the commentary.

G.R.L. I found it touching, because now the world seems to be askew, we don't know what's right. Very little is clear-cut.

B.W. Of course, but at any point in history you're entitled to ask

[4] An exhibition and campaign showing Britain's achievements and know-how; it was followed up by a government film series using the same generic title. [B.W.]

[5] Forster died in 1970.

a question and try and give a directive, and this is what *Diary for Timothy* tried to do. When I showed it to all these Asian students in Poona, where I was teaching last November—remember I told you we showed them over 150 films—I thought, they won't give a hoot what this bloody thing is about. On the contrary, it made a most tremendous effect on them. They were coming up and discussing it with me for days afterwards because of what it said, and its approach. They didn't necessarily know about E. M. Forster just because he wrote *A Passage to India* or anything of that sort. And they hadn't been in London during the war. They were struck by the technique of the film, and the cross-cutting between the performance of *Hamlet* and the air raid—though they had never seen an air raid. But it was the ideology you've just mentioned that struck them, because it would strike anybody. They'd had independence in 1947, and this year they were looking at their country as it was. They had seen the ideas, felt the promises made, then experienced what happened afterwards. The curious thing is that if you make a film like *Diary for Timothy*, it remains valid simply because of the fact of what it talks about; and the hopes it expresses are still valid. The fact that they haven't come true is part of history, or part of the dilemma or predicament of the human race.

G.R.L. I see it also in relationship to what you were talking about a moment ago—how the Labour government, which came in after the war, was more doctrinaire than a liberal government might have been; but perhaps being doctrinaire would have been a problem of any government after the war. It wasn't so clear then what had to be done and how one should go about it.

B.W. Yes, although we of documentary film were very clear about the possibilities and the role of the United Nations, more particularly of specialized agencies like UNESCO and UNICEF. May I remind you of the feature-length documentary which Paul Rotha and I made for UNESCO, in 1953? It was called *World Without End*. Paul filmed in Mexico and I filmed in Thailand and we put our material together to show that the basic human problems and their solutions are the same everywhere and are part of everyone's conscience. Of course, we turned more and more in the direction of the U.N. because there wasn't much finance at home, and because of what we felt was lacking in the public relations or the communications system of the Labour government. This is not a criticism of what the Labour government did otherwise. I'd like to make that clear. And if Stafford Cripps[6] had had his way that

[6] Sir Richard Stafford Cripps, 1889–1952; Member of Parliament, 1931–50; Chancellor of the Exchequer, 1947–50.

would have been different, because he backed the documentary idea 100 per cent and used to have documentary people around regularly once a fortnight to talk to him about it. But he was one person in the Cabinet; the other people seemed not to understand about the use of mass media, the possibilities of film, that sort of thing. Only Cripps did, and he had far too much to do otherwise, to do other than encourage it.

G.R.L. Perhaps we could go on to the question of TV, and documentary and objectivity. One of the problems I see is that documentaries on television are generally presented as being objective when it's clear—at least to me—that they have a definite point of view, a bias; and I think documentaries should make their points of view clear—it's more honest and makes it easier to evaluate the material being shown. We're all prejudiced in one way or another—and the film-maker does choose what he shoots, the questions he asks, and he manipulates the material in the editing.

B.W. Well, are you talking about ciné-vérité?

G.R.L. I'm talking mainly about television—but it's often true even in other kinds of documentaries.

B.W. Look, as far as I'm concerned, if I make a film it's an expression of my personal opinion. For Christ's sake why should I make a film that isn't an expression of what I feel? What I try to do is say what I feel in a fair and reasonably objective manner, and if I have feelings of great passion about something, I don't necessarily put them all into a film; it depends on the subject. I regard the film as an art. I don't pretend that any film I make is going to be a work of art—though I always hope something of that sort will turn up. But the point is, if I am making a film about children starving to death in Biafra, I have a point of view, which is that no children anywhere in the world should starve to death, and therefore something is bloody awful wrong with humanity. That's Biafra. I'm not talking about a film I've made there, but what would happen if I were making a film there. First of all I would have to find out what was the situation between the federal government and the Biafrans, the situation between Harold Wilson and whatever the name of your president is, Nixon, and whoever else is concerned, and then what was the situation, and what was the status of these charitable organizations who are concerned, and that sort of thing. And I should be trying in that way to be objective. Having taken my stand that the bloody thing has got to be stopped somehow, I would then try to make a film—sorry, I would then try to write a script or plan a film based on all the possible information I could get. And I would plan it in the interests of the starving children not try just from a doctrinaire attitude to take the House of Commons' point of view, or the federal point of view, or the American point of view, or whatever it was, but would try and do a balanced statement of the situation. I don't know how balanced it would be in the end, but it would not be plugging one point of view simply for the sake of plugging one point of view. It would be trying to make a film which would have a strong emotional, aesthetic effect on the people who saw it in the direction of saving the poor children and their mothers and fathers from starving to death. You see, you're asking for this terrible objective-truth thing, which you cannot get if you use any form of the mass media because they're not designed for that. As Marshall McLuhan, in his muddle-headed sort of way, has pointed out, they don't know what they're doing.

G.R.L. It just seems to me that it should be made clear for people who are not terribly sophisticated that news and documentary television programs are biased.

B.W. Again, you see, what do you mean by biased?

G.R.L. I mean that at least in America the networks generally reflect a government, a fairly conservative point of view.

B.W. In this country, we know that. When the Prime Minister does a television broadcast and all our networks, all three of them, show him at the same time, we deeply resent this because this is *not* a government edict. The networks are perfectly free not to show it, and yet by some inner agreement they do, which means, you see, when the Prime Minister or the leader of the opposition does what they call a party political broadcast on television, everybody looks up the program in the newspapers, and they switch off. This is the lowest viewing figure you could ever possibly imagine in this country. Which shows bias defeating its own end, if you see what I mean. But I think that the public at large has got a fairly healthy cynicism about this sort of thing.

I notice in America you have a sort of play-by-play description of the Vietnam War going on on television; of course, we in Britain, choosing not to deal with it so much, don't see so much of that in our television news. I don't think we have as much television news as you do in America. This is why I think you can't talk about bias. I'm talking about general documentary programs on television which are dealing with matters of public concern, like health or alcoholism, or name anything, the pill. Yes, you know, poor old Sophocles with *Oedipus Rex* and Euripides with *The Trojan Women*, were they suffering from bias in putting these programs across? Well, okay, so does the author of *Cathy Come Home*, so do people who make films on documentary subjects—they're putting across a point of view. Are you really saying that putting across a point of view is bias?

G.R.L. What I'm concerned about is the pretense of objectivity. For example, in the news, for years in the U.S., we had a blow-by-blow account of the Vietnam War, and as the footage and accompanying commentary were presented, it almost always took the government point of view as if it were an objective point of view—which I think is dangerous.

B.W. My answer to that is, if that happened, what did the public do? Did they believe the whole bloody thing? Or did they spit in his eye?

G.R.L. Well, I guess finally they spit in his eye, but it took a long, long time—a longer time than it should have.

B.W. Well, the point is whether your television service, your mass communication service creates the right sort of climate of opinion. You see, in this country, I think on the whole we're going to spit in the eye rather than agree with something we see on television. And I hate to say it, but I've got a terrible feeling that in your great country there's slightly more tendency—I'm talking about your television audience—to accept rather than spit in the eye first. I don't know, this is only a feeling. We are less exposed to television here, of course, because we don't have so many channels, and we don't spend so much time looking at it as you do, and it isn't on all the time either. God knows how long it will last, but we are still more discriminating. God knows most people in this country seem to have the bloody machine on all the time anyhow; but I don't think we are so indiscriminate in its use as in your country.

G.R.L. Do you know the films of, for example, the Maysles brothers, Pennebaker, Leacock, Wiseman?

B.W. Yes, I know, *Titicut Follies* and so on.

G.R.L. Well, the phrase cinéma-vérité started with the French—

B.W. Oh, you mean ciné-vérité starting with Jean Rouch?

G.R.L. Right, with Rouch and Marker. But there's no question that they then used this technique to state clearly how they felt about a subject. But it seems to me that it's used in its purest or most perverted form—I'm not sure which—in the U.S. by people like those I've mentioned. And some people feel this really is objective because you set the camera up and you roll, and that this really is the only way to make an "objective" documentary.

B.W. As you know, when Grierson was asked about it, he said, "You mean that film called *Nanook of the North* when Flaherty went with a camera and lived with an Eskimo family?" Ciné-vérité. He stuck the camera up and showed what they were doing.

G.R.L. But he staged scenes.

B.W. Well, he cut half an igloo off, otherwise how could you see what's happening inside? What's that got to do with it? If you take a camera crew into somebody's house and live with them, you're cutting one of the walls away in a sense, aren't you? I think that ciné-vérité is something which documentary people have been longing to do for years. I was talking about *Housing Problems* earlier. There they took the bloody apparatus down into the slums and they interviewed these people direct, but it was a very cumbersome process. You couldn't be foot-loose. You couldn't flash about. It all had to be laid on on the spot. I think ciné-vérité is basically a matter of degree. You've got to decide how far you're going to carry the technique. You cannot actually have ciné-vérité because neither the director nor the cameraman or the camera are invisible; therefore ciné-vérté cannot exist; it could only exist if the people concerned didn't know that there was a camera and a cameraman there. What ciné-vérité people are doing is to identify themselves so much with the people that they get used to them being there, and therefore don't notice them as much.

I'm not by any means against this. Last year there was this tremendous colloquium on ethnographical films at UCLA, and all the ethnographers, including Jean Rouch, turned up. And there was this great quarrel about if you go to film a primitive tribe, the mere act of putting a camera there and a tape recorder there is destroying the purity of life of that tribe. Which I think is absolute cock. I believe the first thing an ethnographer has got to do is put the camera and tape recorder obviously and blatantly there before the people know what it is, even. And Rouch is on this side of the fence too. He says the hell with it. He does more. He says he explains to them, "This is a camera, this is a tape recorder. Come on, let's have fun." So this is very much a question of degree, and a question of honesty, and a question of not deceiving yourself.

I think the best ciné-vérité I've ever seen is a Canadian film done by Tanya Ballantyne called *The Things I Cannot Change*. She took her unit into a low-income family in Montreal, a little sort of French-Canadian Irishman and his wife with more children than I can remember. They lived with this family for three weeks, during the course of which the woman had yet another baby, and we saw it born. And this film was edited very deliberately, very carefully, edited more in the direction of truth than falsity than any I've seen—it's difficult to explain without your having seen the film. But what happens in this film, and you kind of *know* this is going to happen, is that the husband becomes a sort of epic character. He's one of the most odious little people you could have ever met. He's a bully, he's a coward, he's stupid, he's affectionate, he's clever, he's uneducated. And they shot everything which happened to him, and they edited the film very brilliantly. Indeed, some of it is absolutely straight shooting, not edited. The husband had a fight in the street—which happened without the crew knowing it was going to happen, because the film crew was always with them, either with him or with the wife and the children; but anyhow, this fight in the street ends up with the man getting in trouble with the police. The police went to take him down to the police station for a report, and he won't go because he feels they'll keep him a night in a cell. The reason he feels this is that it has happened to him once before, and he can't bear to be in prison. The point is that the film-makers combine these two sequences, one absolutely real one where the man is found by the police and he goes and hides, that sort of thing, and afterwards, in order to explain it, they insert an interview with him where he explains *why* he had this reaction to the police; they then cross-cut the real thing happening with the interview which explains it. Which is also a very curious piece of editing, because you are seeing the man in two different moods at two different times, which actually makes it more ciné-vérité than you could possibly believe.

Now, here you've got a point. You musn't despise the ciné-vérité people. What you must stop from doing is thinking that just by sticking up their camera they're doing something. It's by using their camera imaginatively and attempting insofar as it's humanly possible to identify themselves with or to become invisible to the people they're filming, that they've got their strength. Compare the original version of Ricky Leacock's *Happy Mother's Day*, with the buggered-up one they put on the television networks and you will see what I mean.

G.R.L. There are moments in cinéma-vérité films that are passionately moving, that I think one doesn't find in other films. They're rare. I think it depends on the person being filmed. I think a film like *Salesman* is at moments very moving. I think the Maysles are going further in that film because, in part, they do use editing, and I feel that the objective cinéma-vérité treatment of just turning on the camera is not, does not give us the most truthful statement.

B.W. I agree. It's what I just mentioned, and of course the combination of ciné-vérité with compilation—that sort of thing—like the Canadian film on genocide, *Memorandum*, which is one of the greatest films which I have ever seen in this genre, and which I'm always showing to my students—where you deliberately make a setup for ciné-vérité and then you stage some of it and yet somehow you get a lot of the best of ciné-vérité out of it. Like anything else, ciné-vérité is a technique that can be used by itself, or very often can be combined with other techniques to say what you want to say, to express what you want to express.

G.R.L. I think it's clear that the British documentaries of the thirties and the forties, and of the fifties, when people like Anderson and Reisz started to make films, were very valid and worthwhile for their time. But do you think that these and other early documentary films remain valid today?

B.W. I think you've got to rephrase that question to, Do you think *films*, not just documentaries, remain valid? As I told you earlier, I've been going to the cinema since 1913 and one of the most extraordinary things is how some films remain valid and some don't. Films that impressed you terribly twenty, thirty or forty years ago, when you see them again you can't imagine why the hell you thought they had anything at all. Other films that impressed you equally remain equally impressive.

It's terribly difficult for me to understand. It's partly maybe the emotional mood in which you see a film, partly the age period in which you see it—you know, it may have become old-fashioned and out of date, whereas another picture has got something in it that is universal and permanent. I only mention this because I think it applies to all film, as well as certainly applying to documentary. It interests me very much when I go from time to time to places like UCLA to lecture on the history of documentary, and I of course show films regularly. I'll show a film that was made twenty years ago which had a great reputation at the time. When I see it, I realize that it's dying its death in front of my student audience, but worse still, it's dying its death in front of me because it has ceased to exist. After all, most films are very ephemeral. Film is a very ephemeral medium. There are films that fit the particular moment, but only that. There are other films that have a quality of permanence, an element of the universal. And I'm sure this is probably true of books, and plays, and everything. I think documentary is the same.

The thing you must also remember is that the volume of production of documentary increased all the time. When we were making films like *Night Mail,* there were far fewer films made each year. But by the time people were making films in the fifties, the output of documentary, including all the educational films, the technical films and the film kits, was absolutely colossal, so that the number of winners out of the whole field would seem to be smaller, because the volume was greater. If you go back to 1933–34, you've got very few films to choose from, and the whole thing was much more concentrated because we were deeply involved, profoundly involved, in experimenting in the use of the film medium.

G.R.L. Compared to today, Flaherty is perhaps an odd example of documentary because in many cases the films are really fictionalized. In *Moana*, for example, the ceremonial rites shown didn't exist then.

B.W. That's not fair. It is very true of *Man of Aran*, but it's not true of *Moana*.

G.R.L. I thought that when he went to Samoa that the tattooing ritual, for example, was no longer practiced.

B.W. You're thinking of *Man of Aran*. When he went to Aran, the practice of going out to harpoon and catch the basking sharks to get oil for their lamps had long since ceased; he had to teach them how to do it. If you want to argue about *Moana*, well, he said nothing about the bad behavior of the New Zealanders or the Australians as the mandatory powers looking after the island. There again you've got to be fair. You can't expect a man to make a film showing every aspect of everything. No one will want to see it. Flaherty was not only a great personal friend of mine; I still regard him as one of the world's great film-makers. And all right, you want to criticize him, then I can criticize him as easily as you like, you see, because he didn't show anything about colonial exploitation in *Moana*. And he falsified the story in *Man of Aran*, which is the film of his I dislike most, although I think his shooting of the stormy seas is perhaps one of the most terrific bits of cinema in the history of the medium. I still love *Louisiana Story* for all its faults, and I think that *The Land* is absolutely tremendous. This is his big film, the film in which he didn't understand what he was doing—he was too busy trying to express his feelings. He was just in absolute fury and agony at what he'd found out about American agriculture, what was happening to the people involved. And the fact that in the narration of the film he used his own voice is very poignant to me too.

G.R.L. I really wasn't criticizing Flaherty. I was trying to say that he does get to an essential truth even though one might say it's a romantic, partially idealized truth.

B.W. Well, look what happens in *Louisiana Story*. He brings together the simple, the primitive and the modern technological in a romantic landscape; they interrelate, they interweave and then they part again. And yet both sides have retained their integrity throughout the film. It's a very beautiful film. People complain this is oversimplified, but the hell with that. The gorgeous thing about Bob Flaherty is that he was one of the few film-makers that knew you've *got* to oversimplify. Most people overcomplicate things. Or am I wrong?

G.R.L. I think they're damn good films, but I also think they're in some ways romantically falsified.

B.W. Look, I was just answering all the criticism that I am always hearing and making some on my own, because I admire the boy too much not to give him the honor of criticism. I regarded him as a very dear personal friend, a marvelous man.

G.R.L. I very much enjoyed your film *Waters of Time*, particularly the use of sound and the intercutting. There was also the innovative use of sound in *Song of Ceylon*. Were there other examples of such use of sound that you knew about? What gave you the idea to try to use sound that way? It seems to me that even now sound is the one part of film that is rarely used terribly imaginatively.

B.W. Well, I don't know about *Waters of Time*—by that time I was a bit long in the tooth and knew it. But *Song of Ceylon* was an experiment. I've just been back to Ceylon and feel very emotive about it because everything I thought about the country then, the people, the religion, proved to be absolutely true. It's just the same. *Ceylon* was a unique experience in my life. It's the only film I've made that I really loved, and it was in fact a religious experience. I went to Ceylon, as you know, to make four travelogues for the Tea Propaganda Board, and I shot four travelogues; but while I was doing it, I had these extraordinary, inexplicable inner impulses, which made me shoot sequences and things that I couldn't have logically explained. But as soon as I got into the cutting room, they all fell into their places, like the birds flying up, that sort of thing. I had no reason to shoot them; in fact, they were shot at a time when I'd finished shooting for the day and was very tired, but something forced me to shoot a number of shots and the thing built up to a tremendous amount of internal tension, breaking out into expression, coming from one's subconscious very much, I think, and this was all. A sort of magnetic field was created in which we were operating. When I say "we," I mean Walter Leigh, who did the music and the sound, and myself. That month the G.P.O. Film Unit had gotten a sound studio and Cavalcanti had just come there with the express purpose of thinking about how to use sound. And the studio was being used for all sorts of sound experiments all the time. But this film grew like a tree growing out of one's navel. Each morning there would be another branch there; you'd have to sort of cut it off, or prune it, or keep it as it was, and gradually the film emerged. I still cannot understand. I walked into an unconscious process, shot the material and turned it into the film it is, which has the curious validity of being loved and admired and delighted in by the Ceylonese of today, the young people there today, which surprised me last month when I was there. I was terribly pleased at that, you see.

G.R.L. I've seen the film just recently again—it's still very impressive.

B.W. Well, this was a magical film, you see. I can't think of the rules of that. *Waters of Time* was like a reprise, or a repetition. All right, here is a film which certainly did make use of the soundtrack, but was much more elaborately and consciously planned with the use of various voices and visual techniques—including one of the earliest uses of shooting from a helicopter. I like that film quite a lot. It's not an important film because it's only descriptive. It doesn't say anything terribly important about life. It describes the complexity of the great port without going into a number of things which might have been gone into, like labor problems, and this and that, and economic problems.

G.R.L. I think maybe I liked it because it had a very human feeling about it.

B.W. What does that mean?

G.R.L. I guess it had those qualities we respond to as being human and alive.

B.W. Yes, we actually did use real characters, the people who took the boat through the lock, and the man who brought in this huge ship. They were real. I wanted to show them exactly as they were. Remember that awful old man on the telephone who shifted the ships from one dock to the other? I said, "All right. He's real. This is what happens." Now I think that film has a certain elegance about it. I haven't seen it for years, but in fact I could see that one again, I think. But I had much more money for that, much more technical facilities than in *Song of Ceylon.*

G.R.L. Are you working on any film projects now?

B.W. No. I've just signed a contract for a fairly large book on a reassessment of the motion picture, which I have to start writing almost at once. I'm getting quite interested in it, because this might be the point where one starts to query all the attitudes towards the history of cinema that have so far been taken. Like that extraordinary myth about the silent film, which never existed.[7] But I have to put a footnote there, because certain avant-garde directors, including Stan Brakhage in particular, have in some cases actually specified that no sound should be attached to their films. Otherwise silent film is nonsense.

G.R.L. How long have you known Brakhage?

B.W. I knew him for one long, gorgeous day in San Francisco in 1962 when they were having a sort of mini-festival of his films. I was there and James Broughton, who's an old friend of mine, said, "Would you like to meet Stan?" I said, "Yes, I would." We saw his films, then the two of us sat down and had a real wham-bam delightful screaming argument which went on for hours and hours and was only interrupted by the arrival of Pauline Kael. Brakhage has always interested me very much. I wish I could remember the exact film—it was one of the *Dog*[8] films—when he suddenly said, "Now there must be absolutely no sound." To my mind this is deliberately depriving yourself of an element of cinema. Though I'm not arguing against it. I simply said to him, "Do you think your film is strong enough to stand it?" He did, and he still does, and good luck to him.

G.R.L. Do you know *Window Water Moving Baby?*[9]

B.W. Oh, yes. I think it's a very beautiful film.

G.R.L. Is that a documentary?

B.W. I'll ask you a question in return. What is a documentary?

G.R.L. Well, Grierson says it's "the creative treatment of actuality." We all know that definition.

B.W. A clumsy description, and he admitted that it was no good. But let it stand.

[7] Wright is referring to the fact that even in the days of the silent film there was accompanying sound; in large theaters in cities there were orchestras of varying sizes to accompany the film and provide sound effects, and at times there were full orchestras with especially composed scores, as for Griffith's *Birth of a Nation;* and in small-town theaters there was at least a pianist to play mood music.

[8] Brakhage made a series of films in several parts with the title *Dog Star Man.*

[9] By Stan Brakhage.

LINDSAY ANDERSON

Lindsay Anderson was born in 1923, in Bangalore, India, where his father was serving in the British Army. He went to England by the time he was two, attended English public school and then Oxford, where he began to study classics. He served in the Intelligence Corps of the British Army during the war and then returned to Oxford to study English and act in some amateur theater productions.

In 1946, while still at Oxford, Anderson cofounded *Sequence*, an anti-establishment film magazine, and was one of its main editors and contributors until its demise in 1952. That same year he wrote *Making a Film*, about the production of Thorold Dickinson's *Secret People*. In 1955, at the National Film Theatre, he organized a festival of John Ford's films. With Karel Reisz and Tony Richardson, Anderson was instrumental in starting the Free Cinema movement (1956–59), which showed British shorts at the National Film Theatre, including several of Anderson's, and whose program was radical.* On *March to Aldermaston*, 1958, he was one of the directors and supervised the editing. And in 1969 he was appointed a Governor of the British Film Institute.

Since 1948 Anderson has directed not only documentary films, but a number of television films (though never a TV documentary), television commercials and two features. He has done some acting from time to time, written numerous articles on film and worked extensively in the theater as a director, mainly at the Royal Court, where he is now an associate director. Recently he directed the play *Home*, with John Gielgud and Ralph Richardson, in London and New York.

(The above material was taken from *Lindsay Anderson* by Elizabeth Sussex.)

* "1956, the year of Suez and of Hungary, was a crucial point in British culture of the 'fifties. It was the year that . . . Osborne's *Look Back in Anger* [was produced] at the Royal Court Theatre, as well as the year Free Cinema began; in politics it was the beginning of the New Left." (Elizabeth Sussex, *Lindsay Anderson*, p. 31)

FILMOGRAPHY*

FILMS

1948: *Meet the Pioneers.* Richard Sutcliffe Ltd. Directed by Lindsay Anderson. Produced by Desmond and Lois Sutcliffe. Photographed by John Jones and Edward Brendon. Edited by Lindsay Anderson and Edward Brendon. Art adviser: Eric Westbrook. Music arranged by Len Scott. Commentary spoken by Lindsay Anderson. 33 minutes.

1949: *Idlers That Work.* Richard Sutcliffe Ltd. Directed by Lindsay Anderson. Produced by Richard O'Brien. Photographed by George Levy. Music from Ralph Vaughan Williams and Aaron Copland. Continuity: Lois Sutcliffe. Unit assistants: Bill Longley, Geoff Oakes, Ernest Slinger and George Wilby. Commentary spoken by Lindsay Anderson. 17 minutes.

1952: *Three Installations.* Richard Sutcliffe Ltd. Directed by Lindsay Anderson. Produced by Dermod Sutcliffe. Photographed by Walter Lassally. Additional photography by John Jones. Assistant cameraman: Desmond Davis. Edited by Derek York. Orchestral music from Copland, Gillis and Khachaturian; Conveyor Boogie by Alan Clare (piano) and Johnny Flanagan (drums). Sound recording by Charles Green. Production manager: John Exley. Unit assistant: Vincent Young. Commentary spoken by Lindsay Anderson. 28 minutes.

Wakefield Express. The Wakefield Express Series Ltd. Directed by Lindsay Anderson. Produced by Michael Robinson. Photographed by Walter Lassally. Songs by Snapethorpe and Horbury Secondary Modern Schools; Band Music by Horbury Victoria Prize Band. Production assistant: John Fletcher. Commentary spoken by George Potts. 33 minutes.

1953: *Thursday's Children.* World Wide Pictures (A Morse Production). Written and directed by Guy Brenton and Lindsay Anderson. Photographed by Walter Lassally. Music by Geoffrey Wright. Commentary spoken by Richard Burton. With children from the Royal School for the Deaf, Margate. 20 minutes.

O Dreamland. A Sequence Film. Directed by Lindsay Anderson. Camera and assistance: John Fletcher. 12 minutes.

* From *Lindsay Anderson* by Elizabeth Sussex.

1954: *Trunk Conveyor*. Richard Sutcliffe Ltd./National Coal Board. Directed by Lindsay Anderson. Produced by Dermod Sutcliffe. Photographed by John Reid. Camera assistant: Gerry Godfrey. Edited by Bill Megarry. Assistant editor: James Vans Collina. Songs by Bert Lloyd; Concertina, Alf Edwards; Guitar, Fitzroy Coleman. Production manager: Peter Woodward. Commentary spoken by Lindsay Anderson. 38 minutes.

1955: *Green and Pleasant Land.*
Henry.
The Children Upstairs.
A Hundred Thousand Children.
National Society for the Prevention of Cruelty to Children. (Basic Film Productions). Directed and scripted by Lindsay Anderson. Produced by Leon Clore. Photographed by Walter Lassally. *Henry* 5½ minutes; the others each 4 minutes.

£20 a Ton.

Energy First. National Industrial Fuel Efficiency Service. (Basic Film Productions). Directed by Lindsay Anderson. Produced by Leon Clore. Photographed by Larry Pizer. Production manager: John Fletcher. Each about 5 minutes.

Foot and Mouth. Central Office of Information for the Ministry of Agriculture, Fisheries and Food (A Basic Film Production). Written and directed by Lindsay Anderson. Produced by Leon Clore. Photographed by Walter Lassally. Edited by Bill Megarry. Technical adviser: J. C. Davidson, M.R.C.V.S. Production manager: Philip Aizlewood. Commentary spoken by Lindsay Anderson. 20 minutes.

1957: *Every Day Except Christmas*. Ford of Britain (A Graphic Production). Directed by Lindsay Anderson. Produced by Leon Clore and Karel Reisz. Photographed by Walter Lassally. Music by Daniel Paris. Recording and sound editing by John Fletcher. Assistants: Alex Jacobs, Brian Probyn and Maurice Ammar. Commentary spoken by Alun Owen. 40 minutes.

1963: *This Sporting Life*. Independent Artists (A Julian Wintle/Leslie Parkyn Production). Directed by Lindsay Anderson. Produced by Karel Reisz. Screenplay by David Storey, based on his novel *This Sporting Life*. Photographed by Denys Coop. Camera operator: John Harris. Edited by Peter Taylor. Assistant editor: Tom Priestley. Art director: Alan Withy. Set dresser: Peter Lamont. Dress designer: Sophie Devine. Music composed by Roberto Gerhard and conducted by Jacques-Louis Monod. Sound editor: Chris Greenham. Sound recording: John W. Mitchell and Gordon K. McCallum. Casting: Miriam Brickman. In charge of production: Albert Fennell. Assistant director: Ted Sturgis. Production manager: Geoffrey Haine. Continuity: Pamela Mann. Make-up: Bob Lawrence. Hairdresser: Ivy Emmerton. Propertyman: Ernie Quick. 134 minutes.

1966: *The White Bus.* United Artists (A Woodfall Film Presentation). Directed by Lindsay Anderson. Executive producer: Oscar Lewenstein. Associate producer: Michael Deeley. Original story and screenplay by Shelagh Delaney. Photographed by Miroslav Ondricek in black and white and color. Edited by Kevin Brownlow. Art director: David Marshall. Music by Misha Donat. Sound editor: John Fletcher. Sound recording: Peter Handford. Casting director: Miriam Brickman. Assistant director: Kip Gowans. Production manager: Jake Wright. 46 minutes.

1967: *Raz Dwa Trzy—The Singing Lesson.* Contemporary Films (Warsaw Documentary Studios). Directed by Lindsay Anderson. Chief of production: Miroslaw Podolski. Photographed by Zygmunt Samosiuk. Edited by Barbara Kosidowska. Arrangement of songs: Ludwik Sempolinski. Piano accompaniment: Irena Klukowna. Sound editor: Henryk Kuzniak. Sound recording: Malgorzata Jaworska. Assistant director: Joanna Nawrocka. 20 minutes.

1968: *If . . .* Paramount (A Memorial Enterprises Film). Directed by Lindsay Anderson. Produced by Michael Medwin and Lindsay Anderson. Screenplay by David Sherwin, from the original script *Crusaders* by David Sherwin and John Howlett. Director of photography (in color and black and white): Miroslav Ondricek. Cameraman: Chris Menges. Camera operator: Brian Harris. Camera assistant: Michael Seresin. Edited by David Gladwell. Assistant editors: Ian Rakoff and Michael Ellis. Production designed by Jocelyn Herbert. Wardrobe: Shura Cohen. Music composed and conducted by Marc Wilkinson; 'Sanctus' from the *Missa Luba* (Philips recording). Dubbing editor: Alan Bell. Dubbing mixer: Doug Turner. Sound recordist: Christian Wangler. Casting director: Miriam Brickman. Assistant director: John Stoneman. Production manager: Gavrik Losey. Assistant to the producers: Neville Thompson. Assistants to the director: Stephen Frears and Stuart Baird. Continuity: Valerie Booth. Make-up: Betty Blattner. Construction manager: Jack Carter. 112 minutes.

TELEVISION FILMS

Episodes in *The Adventures of Robin Hood* series. Incorporated Television Programme Company (Weinstein Productions for Sapphire Films). Directed by Lindsay Anderson. Executive producer: Hannah Weinstein. Associate producer: Sidney Cole. Script supervisor: Albert G. Ruben. Photographed by Ken Hodges. Supervising editor: Thelma Connell. Art supervisor: William Kellner. Sound: H. C. Pearson. Assistant director: Christopher Noble. Production manager: Harold Buck. Each 25 minutes.

1955: "Secret Mission." Screenplay by Ralph Smart. Music: Edwin Astley.

1956: "The Impostors." Screenplay by Norman Best. Music: Edwin Astley.

"Ambush." Screenplay by Ernest Borneman and Ralph Smart. Music: Albert Elms.

"The Haunted Mill." Screenplay by Paul Symonds. Music: Edwin Astley.

"Isabella." Screenplay by Neil R. Collins. Music: Edwin Astley.

December 3, 1969, London, in a pub in Notting Hill Gate where Lindsay Anderson was preparing to shoot a commercial.

G. Roy Levin: When you first started working in films, why did you make documentaries?

Lindsay Anderson: Well, of course, we'd have to define the word "documentary." I always fall back on Grierson's definition—I think it's his—which defines documentary as "the creative interpretation of actuality."[1] And one of the things that has fouled up the discussion of documentaries, I think, in recent years has been the identification of documentary with information or even instruction. Maybe it's a word that has outlived its usefulness, because I think that it no longer has a very clear significance.

Certainly as far as I am concerned, I started making what we could call industrial documentaries because an opportunity to make such films simply fell into my lap, and to a great extent that is how my career has proceeded. I didn't set out with a burning and effective ambition to make films. I came away from the university with a vague theory that I would like to make films and with an interest in film and theater; and, quite by chance, really through a personal contact, I was given the opportunity of making an industrial advertising film for a factory making mining machinery in the north of England. I was given this opportunity by rather enlightened people who wanted something that was more than a merely hard-sell film, and was offered creative opportunities to convey the spirit of the place. And that's how I started making films. In other words, it really didn't just happen, and of course short films and particularly documentary films are the easiest form to start on as a film-maker, and I think that this quite obviously played a part in it. It was a long time before someone like myself was acceptable in Britain as a feature or dramatic film-maker, because the conservatism in the British film industry in the late forties and through the mid-fifties was such that really new talent was not acceptable. Even when I had established myself as a theater director I wasn't judged competent or trustworthy. For instance, to direct the film version of a play that I had done called *The Long, the Short and the Tall*,[2] such

[1] Grierson's definition is slightly different: "the creative treatment of actuality."
[2] Original play, by Willis Hall, directed by Anderson at the Royal Court Theatre. London, 1959.

was the conservatism of the industry at that time that it was not considered that I could be entrusted to direct the film version. So really at that stage the only alternative *was* documentary.

G.R.L. This has changed, hasn't it?

L.A. Well, except for myself, this changed completely in the late fifties, through the process of history, and maybe a little bit through some of the efforts that myself and my friends made with our movement called Free Cinema. After *Saturday Night and Sunday Morning,* with which Karel Reisz made a directorial debut with an unknown actor, Albert Finney, the dam burst and new directors were not only acceptable, they were actually sought after. Then followed the usual folly, of course, in which the industry proceeded to be as unselective in its choice of directors as before it had been restrictive.

G.R.L. The idea of a social conscience in making films . . . in other words, films that are concerned with contemporary social issues, were these things you were concerned with from the very beginning?

L.A. I think it is just something that is a part of my approach to life, my imaginative impulse. I think that insofar as one is an artist—which is something I would like to be, or claim to be—that one doesn't set out to fulfill a program when one makes a film or creates a work of art. One instinctively chooses the approach that reflects one's nature, and my nature finds the social relationships of human beings as important and as significant as their personal relations. Documentary is certainly a form, I think, that stresses the social relationships, because the nearer you get to the individual study and the psychological study, the more you are forced towards a dramatic effort and an imaginative creation and that takes you away from actuality, which is in fact the basic material of documentary.

G.R.L. Didn't this happen literally with a film like *Cathy Come Home?*[3]

L.A. *Cathy Come Home* is something of a hybrid. I like the film very much and I think it has served its purpose extremely well, but on artistic grounds it probably suffers from its documentary basis. And if you were to consider it as a documentary you might say that it suffered because of the admixture of fictional elements. It doesn't quite create a new creative form of its own, but on the other hand it isn't trying to do that; I think what it set out to do it did very well. To continue on that track, I think a film

[3] A BBC film about housing problems in England. It was directed by Ken Loach and produced by Tony Garnett. See interview with them for details. Also see comments on film in interview with Richard Cawston.

like *Poor Cow*[4] perhaps shows the difficulty of making the transition from a documentary to a dramatic form. Though *Poor Cow* has a lot of very strikingly original and beautifully handled things in it, what is weak about it in the end is its scenario conception, in the areas where it has to transcend the documentary and become a creative invention. It's there that I think it fails.

G.R.L. In *Sequence 3* you wrote, "During the thirties young people who were seriously interested in the cinema tended to go into documentaries, and since documentary-makers believed in the importance of their job and were on the whole given a great deal of freedom, the results were very good. But today things are not the same. Few of us are any longer able to summon up that ardent proselytizing enthusiasm for social-democracy which was the inspiration of the documentary movement."

L.A. That was written in 1949, of course, or even 1948; that's twenty years ago.

G.R.L. I'm not trying to hold you to that.

L.A. No, I think it's true of its time. I think that was a reaction against the Griersonian conception of documentary, which was basically narrow even though Grierson also talked about a broader creative interpretation in documentary. You know, like all intelligent people he contradicted himself, because he also talked about documentary as primarily a social propaganda weapon. I think that there always has been a good deal of the Philistine in Grierson in the sense that he instinctively is a bit scornful of purely creative values and put the stress too much on information. The results of this, of course, were shown when he tried to cope with feature film production in Group Three, the experiment where the government put money into film production and Grierson was put in charge of Beaconsfield studios with John Baxter in the late forties and early fifties. His production program was a total disaster because it was shown that he really knew nothing and understood nothing about what we may simply term "feature film." He was out of his depth.

G.R.L. I recently saw *A Diary for Timothy*[5] and I found it touching and moving. One of the reasons was that it presented a world that was comparatively simple, where everyone seemed to understand what the world was about, where one was going and the function of

[4] Directed by Ken Loach, 1967, and starring Carol White.

[5] Produced by Basil Wright and directed by Humphrey Jennings in 1944–45 for the Crown Film Unit. (The film recapitulates the last months of the war in a style that greatly depends on montage effects, and questions whether the world will be a better place when peace comes.)

one's life in an ordered world. And compared to what I see life to be today, I found that touching.

L.A. I think this absolutely true. But you've got to remember that Jennings was something of a maverick in the British documentary movement and that he was certainly never a typical Griersonian documentary film-maker. He was completely exceptional. Jennings is a complicated case in that he was a poetic film-maker who came from the realm of a cold intellectual background and was warmed into imaginative life by the tremendously emotional atmosphere of wartime. And that he happened to be making those films at that particular time is what made him into an artist in cinema. I don't think he would ever have done it otherwise, and it is significant that after the war he never succeeded in recapturing the emotional fervor of his wartime films. There is no doubt too, I think, that in the conditions of today, with its murky, undecided realities—or something like that—it is much more difficult than it was in Jennings' time to achieve that kind of positive creative statement. (I seem to have said all this before somewhere.) There's also the simple fact that when Jennings made his wartime films there was a Crown Film Unit to pay for them, and now no one has got money for documentaries. If you make them now they won't be shown. And if you make them for television you really are asked to make purely informational films, because for television nobody has the time or the money to spare on really creative work.

G.R.L. Is there a particular reason why you never worked for the BBC?

L.A. Well, I'm not a very institutional kind of person, and the institutions are, on the whole, suspicious of me. One or two attempts have been made to do work for the BBC. I met the editors of a television magazine program called *Tonight*, which was what John Schlesinger started on, and I was strongly resented by them because they thought they did in twenty-four hours what it took me over six months to do—and what they thought I did less well. In other words, they didn't understand the creative effort or the poetic quality of a film like *Every Day Except Christmas*; all they saw was a five-minute TV news item about porters in Covent Garden. There was another attempt for me to do a film for the BBC which fell through because I wasn't on the staff.

And when I was directing a play in Poland I was approached by Granada[6] to make a film for them and I said I would. When I came back I talked to them, but the difficulties and complications were so

[6] An independent London commercial television station as opposed to the BBC, which is government-sponsored and without commercials.

great that I found it was easier for me to go back to Warsaw and make a film for a documentary studio there.[7]

G.R.L. But BBC does produce a great number of documentaries. Do you look on these as strictly informational?

L.A. Most of them. I suppose BBC documentary at its prime is represented by someone like Richard Cawston, who makes such films about the Royal Family,[8] or sort of jumbo films about the BBC,[9] and they are certainly creatively totally uninteresting. They are public-relations jobs. I mean, what documentaries can you tell me about that have creative significance on the BBC?

G.R.L. I thought *Cathy Come Home* was a very exciting film.

L.A. Well, it is a very exciting film, but *Cathy Come Home* we've discussed and anyway some claim it wasn't a documentary, but rather something that falls in between documentary and a feature, and it's inevitable that Ken Loach should go on to make feature films.

G.R.L. Yes, but I think that whole question and that distinction between documentary and feature films becomes more and more difficult to define.

L.A. I don't think that it does. I think that if we have any respect for words we might as well give them a true significance. There is a clear distinction between the creative and poetic use of invented elements, and documentary at its purest and most poetic is a form in which the elements that you use are the *actual* elements. It is the manipulation of the *actual* world into, as far as I am concerned, a poetic form—and that is documentary. If you invent your characters, invent your situation, then you go on from documentary into a different form.

G.R.L. That sounds like a good distinction, but in the kind of films that are made today it's difficult at times to make that distinction—Agnès Varda's *Lions Love,* for example. My point is that it isn't always clear to what degree certain incidents in the film are or are not documentary—that is, actual incidents. And one of the problems is that when documentary techniques, especially cinéma-vérité techniques, are used in what are presumably fiction films, the distinction—

L.A. I'm sorry. If we're going to use words we should be accurate in our use of them. It isn't a question of technique, it is a question of the material. If the material is actual, then it is documentary. If the material is invented, then it is not documentary, and Agnes Varda is not really a documentary film-maker.

[7] *The Singing Lesson,* 1967.
[8] *Royal Family,* 1969.
[9] *This Is the BBC,* 1959.

G.R.L. Well, for the viewer, at times it's difficult to know if the material has been invented or if it is real.

L.A. Well, that doesn't matter. If you get so muddled up in your use of the term, stop using it. Just talk about films. Anyway, very often when we use these terms, they only give us an opportunity to avoid really discussing the film.

G.R.L. Then let's go back to that quote of yours about the "ardent proselytizing enthusiasm for social-democracy" of documentarists of the thirties, and the image of an ordered world with a purpose during World War II, when Jennings made his best films, and contrast that with what many see today as a less ordered, less comprehensible world, where it is not clear how one can cope. If one accepts this very broad definition and is concerned about it, as I think you are, do you think that documentaries can do anything to change the situation, and should that be one's aim? I'm not exactly sure who "one" is.

L.A. I was wondering about that.

G.R.L. Well, let's say anyone concerned with the problem. Or do you feel that a more fundamental kind of change is necessary, let's say a basic psychological human change?

L.A. But you see, you are talking from the outside, like a critic or a university lecturer. An artist cannot think like that, an artist doesn't sit down and think, now should one, in this particular historical context, do such and such. I mean, the way an artist develops or picks on a subject and decides what he is going to do to a large extent depends on his own imaginative development, his development as an artist, and often that will catch him unawares. So an artist is as likely to be surprised by the work he does as other people who see it. I don't sit down and think, now in the present state of society what should one do. I just think, here I am living from day to day, there are certain possibilities, I wonder what would be the best thing to do next. Then you look around and see what offers itself, and somehow you end up doing something. It is for the critic to answer the kind of question you are asking.

G.R.L. Perhaps. But I'm not asking the question as a critic; for me it's a personal question. Let me put it this way: you worked on *March to Aldermaston*[10] and I would guess that part of the reason you worked on it was because you thought the cause was worthwhile.

[10] A film about the first Easter protest march to the nuclear weapons factory in Aldermaston in 1958 which was sponsored by the Campaign for Nuclear Disarmament; five other directors besides Anderson worked on the film: Derrick Knight (also the producer), Stephen Peet, Derek York, Kurt Lewenhack and Karel Reisz.

L.A. Yes, but how do you define the cause in *March to Aldermaston?* You may say that it was about nuclear disarmament, or you might say it was about individuals in an increasingly conformist society choosing a way of testing minority belief. Those are two rather different subjects. In fact, the answer to me is probably both. Both things attracted me, but probably the second thing more.

G.R.L. This is closer to the impetus behind your work in your fiction films, is it not?

L.A. Probably.

G.R.L. Then let me ask the question a different way. From your films, I would take it that you do not see the world as a particularly satisfactory place.

L.A. I would have to be a maniac if I did.

G.R.L. Okay. Given that fact, and concern about it, someone might become a social worker. People like Tony Garnett and Ken Loach feel committed to making films that have direct social comment. Everybody does what he can. So I'm not in any sense making a judgment. What I'm asking is, do you feel that making films like Garnett and Loach make, or other documentaries that have direct social comment, can help change anything—that is, society?

L.A. I think that this is a hypothetical question. It has very little bearing on whether such films, so to speak, should be made. I think that the most important thing is for people to find out what creatively satisfies the most and make that. I think that our ability to change the world is exceedingly limited, although I think it's a good thing to feel that we can or that we should. The idea of changing the world can be interpreted in a very large number of ways. I think that this obviously plays for the completely narrow informational film. Everything depends on the context within which a film is made. I think that equally, on an imaginative level, a film like *This Sporting Life* can change the world. But Tony Garnett wouldn't agree with me. He has a narrower view than I have.

G.R.L. I think that he would agree to a certain extent but add that it was only a part of the kind of change that has to take place—that political, economic changes also have to be made.

L.A. He talks about change from some kind of Marxist position, whereas, in fact, I grow increasingly skeptical of those kinds of solutions. I don't really see change in terms of an effort towards an attainable good end. I think it's just part of the continual structure to which in fact I can see no end. To that degree, in the last twenty years, having been through a period of cautiously optimistic left-wing thinking or aspiration, and having seen that really wither away, I come to the conclusion that in the end the artist is on his own.

Therefore, to that extent, I would consider myself to have an anarchistic rather than a socialist position. I think that a socialist society is as liable to victimize the artist as any other. In fact, we've seen it happen. It's probably more liable to victimize the artist than a capitalist society because a capitalist society is, in certain ways, less efficient.

G.R.L. In the United States, for example, there is, in a real sense, more freedom than in Eastern socialist countries. But in the United States there is an economic control over the arts even though it's unwritten and unspoken. Do you see this kind of indirect control as more pervasive?

L.A. In purely pragmatic terms I think that in Russia Andy Warhol couldn't make his films. I haven't seen them and I don't think I'd like them particularly; but it's quite a good thing that he can make them. I think that in Russia there would not be a film like *Easy Rider*. If I, as an artist, had to make a choice between living in America and Russia, I know which I'd choose. That is based purely on self-interest, which in the end is our first obligation. That's because the first obligation of any human being, and particularly of any artist, is to survive.

G.R.L. At any cost?

L.A. Well, at any cost that falls short of his extinction in terms of being an artist, if you like, or being what we may define as a "human being." I don't rate survival purely in terms of breathing.

G.R.L. Do you hope to make more documentaries? Would you like to?

L.A. Well, I'm very deeply skeptical about the possibility of getting the money to make a documentary with all of it being shown when I've made it. I think documentary as a subject in a poetic medium is still a very beautiful and gratifying form to work in, but I don't really enjoy making films that are not shown.

G.R.L. Is part of the reason why you still like documentaries that it is less of a hassle, less cumbersome and complicated than making feature films? That you have more personal control?

L.A. Yes, I think that is undoubtedly so. I mean it was rather marvelous to make that film in Poland with a unit of about four or five people and with a minimum of fuss. Of course, in Britain—it's more the pity—even in documentary you're exposed to union requirements and regulations. But with documentaries you are sort of, yes, you are nearer to full personal control of your material. Equally, I think it is a more modest form. That's all right, there is nothing wrong with that.

G.R.L. Do you always keep very tight control of the shooting, camera setups and the like, and the editing?

L.A. Absolutely, particularly the editing.

G.R.L. Is it because of union regulations that you have an editor who—

L.A. I'm also somewhat clumsy with my hands and I couldn't edit a sound track, you know. I work with an editor and I'm always delighted to work with someone who can give me ideas, but basically I hold myself responsible for the editing.

G.R.L. Have you seen any cinéma-vérité films, by the Maysles brothers, for example?

L.A. Yes. And Richard Leacock.

G.R.L. What do you think of their films, of this style?

L.A. Again I would judge each film individually. I think on the whole that it has the merits and the demerits of journalism, which include a certain superficiality and a certain emphasis on effect. This is something I don't like very much.

G.R.L. Certain film-makers who work in this style would claim, I think, that cinéma-vérité gives you truth in being objective and—

L.A. Complete nonsense. There is no such thing as objective truth in art. All art is more or less subjective; that's just a rationalization of what they can do best. And we shouldn't try to make out that because we can do a thing it is therefore the best thing.

G.R.L. But many documentaries try to give the impression of being objective, of presenting the truth.

L.A. This is very naïve. There is no such thing. People are often very naïve about cinema. There are still a lot of people just as naïve as the audiences that saw that train that drew into the station.[11] It just depends where you put the camera and what you show. There is a basis of selection to all these things.

G.R.L. Do you like to make commercials?

L.A. I don't mind too much making them. It's a way of making money, and I would always rather make a good commercial than make a bad film. And it's quicker.

G.R.L. You work on the editing with these?

L.A. Oh yes, you must, yes.

G.R.L. You apparently have to start shooting now, but let me finish with one last question. It's rather a personal one, but one that bothers me; and though I don't think there's any final answer, I'd like to know what you would say about it. It's this: Given the fact

[11] Anderson is referring to an early (1895 or '96) *actualité* film by the Lumière brothers, either *Arrival of a Train at Ciotat Station*, or *A Train Entering a Station.*

that the world we live in seems so unsatisfactory in so many ways—overpopulation, pollution, the arms race, Vietnam, dehumanization of life, everything that many people have talked and written about and have unsuccessfully tried to do something about for years—given all this, does one have the right to ignore it in one's work, to just go on and do one's own little thing? Like making personal films?

L.A. You have to, otherwise you'll go mad. You have to try and find the single image that implies everything instead of trying to make the film that contains everything specifically. You have to.

RICHARD CAWSTON

Richard Cawston was born in 1923, in Weybridge, Surrey, and was educated at Westminster School and Oxford. In 1947, after five years as a wartime officer in the Royal Signals Regiment, he joined the BBC Television Service. At first he was a film editor; then from 1950 to 1954 he was producer of the original *Television Newsreel*, being responsible for nearly seven hundred editions (including all the BBC's coronation newsreels). After this he was associated with a number of studio productions, including *Panorama*, but since 1955 he has specialized in producing documentary films. In June 1965 he was appointed to the newly created post of Head of Documentary Programmes, BBC Television.

FILMOGRAPHY*

1954: *We Live By the River.* (For the first Eurovision exchange series.) Produced by Richard Cawston. Directed by Jack Howells. Photographed by Clifford Hornby. Film editor: Richard Cawston.

1955: *V.E. plus Ten.* (One-hour film about the postwar decade.) Produced by Richard Cawston. Commentary written and spoken by Patrick O'Donavan. Film editor: Dennis Edwards. (A Compilation Film)

1956: The *Away From It All* series. I. "Into the Country." Produced by Richard Cawston. Directed by Stephen Hearst. Commentary by Christopher Chataway. Photographed by A. A. Englander F.R.P.S. Film editor: Sheila S. Tomlinson. II. "Into the Backwaters." Produced by Richard Cawston. Directed by Stephen Hearst. Commentary by Christopher Chataway. Photographed by Charles de Jaeger. Film editor: Keith Latham. III. "Into the Mountains." Produced by Richard Cawston. Directed by Stephen Hearst. Com-

* Supplied by the film-maker.

mentary by Christopher Chataway. Photographed by: Terry Hunt. Film editor: Tony Essex. IV. "On an Island." Produced by Richard Cawston. Directed by Stephen Hearst. Commentary by Christopher Chataway. Photographed by Peter Hamilton. Film editor: Alan Martin.

1957: The *Half the World Away* series. (A series of three films on Delhi, Hong Kong and Singapore.) Produced by Richard Cawston. Directed by Stephen Hearst. Commentary by Christopher Chataway. Photographed by Peter Hamilton. Sound by Michael Colomb. Film editor: Harry Hastings.

The Man at Dover. (A study of the refugee in Britain.) Produced by Richard Cawston. Written and directed by Richard Cawston and Pamela Wilcox Bower. Photographed by Charles de Jaeger. Film editor: Harry Hastings.

The Big Gamble. (About the British seaside holiday.) Produced by Richard Cawston. Directed by Richard Cawston and Pamela Wilcox Bower. Cameraman: James Balfour. Film editor: Sheila S. Tomlinson. Commentary spoken by Jack Warner.

Onion Johnnie. (Won First Prize at the Vancouver International Film Festival of 1958.) Produced by Richard Cawston. Directed by Stephen Hearst. Photographed by Ken Higgins. Film editor: Sheila S. Tomlinson. Commentary spoken by Jacques Brunius.

1958: *Never Never*. (About hire purchase.) Written, directed and produced by Richard Cawston. Introduced by Morris West. Photographed by Douglas Wolfe. Film editor: Sheila S. Tomlinson. Script adviser: Campbell Fraser. Production assistant: Barbara Saxon.

Lost City. (A "portrait" of J. B. Priestly.) Written, directed and produced by Richard Cawston. Photographed by Gerry Pullen. Film editor: Sheila S. Tomlinson. Recorded by Robert Saunders and Graham Turner. Production assistant: Barbara Saxon. Narrated by: J. B. Priestly.

A Prime Minister Remembers. (A forty-five-minute "interview" with Lord Attlee.) Directed and produced by Richard Cawston. Film cameraman: Peter Sargent. Film editor: Philip Wrestler. Production assistant: Barbara Saxon.

On Call to a Nation. (A seventy-five-minute study of the doctors' view of the Health Service.) Written, directed and produced by Richard Cawston. Photographed by Eric Deeming. Recorded by Robert Saunders and Frank Dale. Sound editor: Eric Brown. Film editor: Harry Hastings. Production assistant: Barbara Saxon.

1959: *This Is the BBC* (Winner of the British Film Academy Award for the best specialized film of 1959.) Written, directed and produced by Richard Cawston. Photographed by Kenneth Westbury. Sound by Robert Saunders and Michael Colomb. Film editor: Harry Hastings. Production assistant: Barbara Saxon.

1960: *The Lawyers.* (Practicing barristers and solicitors in an eighty-five-minute documentary about themselves.) Written, directed and produced by Richard Cawston. Commentary spoken by Colin Wills. Photographed by Eric Deeming. Recorded by Robert Saunders and Peter Jarvis. Film editor: Joseph Sterling. Production assistant: Barbara Saxon.

1961: *Television and the World.* (Winner of the Screenwriters' Guild Award for the best documentary script, 1961, the Silver Medal of the Television Society, 1961, the Guild of Television Producers and Directors' Award for the best factual production, 1962, and the Italia Prize for Television Documentaries, 1962.) Written, directed and produced by Richard Cawston. Commentary spoken by Michael Flanders. Photographed by Kenneth Westbury. Sound by Michael Colomb and Robert Saunders. Film editor: Harry Hastings. Production assistant: Barbara Saxon.

1962: *The Monarchy.* (A study of the significance of the Throne in Britain, made for the tenth anniversary of the Queen's accession.) Directed and produced by Richard Cawston. Written and narrated by Patrick O'Donovan. Film editor: Kenneth Bilton. Production assistant: Barbara Saxon.

The Schools. (A seventy-five-minute survey which takes the audience through the entire educational system in England and Wales—both state and independent—for students from the ages of five to eighteen, and in which all the comments are made by practicing teachers.) Written, directed and produced by Richard Cawston. Photographed by Hugh Wilson. Sound by Grahame Whatling and Patrick Whitaker. Film editor: Roy Fry. Production assistant: Barbara Saxon.

1963: *The Pilots.* (A seventy-minute study of the profession of the modern airline pilot, which follows in detail a flight by a Boeing 707 from London to Beirut, and in which practicing pilots from Britain's three major airlines take part.) Written, directed and produced by Richard Cawston. Photographed by Dick Bush. Sound by

Robert Saunders, Robin Green, John Hore. Film editor: Roy Fry. Production assistant: Barbara Saxon.

The Exporters. (A fifty-six-minute impression of the world of the British businessman involved in export.) Written, directed and produced by Richard Cawston. Photographed by Peter Sargent. Sound by Robert Saunders and Philip Young. Film editor: Roy Fry. Production assistant: Barbara Saxon.

1964: *Supersonic.* (A seventy-minute story from the earliest beginnings of supersonic passenger aviation, featuring the Anglo/French Concord and its American competitors, and those people who are opposed to the whole idea of supersonic travel.) Written, directed and produced by Richard Cawston. Commentary spoken by Michael Flanders. Photographed by Dick Bush. Sound by Robin Green and Robert Saunders. Film editor: Roy Fry. Production assistant: Barbara Saxon.

Shellarama—A Dimitri de Grunwald Production. (A fifteen-minute film made in Supertechnirama 70 and Technicolor for world-wide Cinerama distribution showing the excitement of getting oil out of the ground and the pleasure it gives to people everywhere in the form of petrol.) Written and directed by Richard Cawston. Photography by Stanley Sayer. Film editor: Fred Burnley. Sound editor: Norman Savage. Sound mixer: Gordon McCallum.

1965: *Born Chinese.* (A fifty-seven-minute film about the character of the Chinese people. This documentary was filmed in Hong Kong and is centered around a single Chinese family, born in China, now living in one of the Hong Kong government vast housing estate flats.) Directed and produced by Richard Cawston. Film editor: Larry Toft. Photographed by Peter Bartlett. Recorded by Peter Richardson. Dubbing mixer: Patrick Whitaker. Production assistant: Barbara Saxon. Narrated by Anthony Lawrence.

1966: *I'm Going to Ask You to Get Up Out of Your Seat.* (A sixty-minute film telling the story of Billy Graham's 1966 Greater London Crusade. It shows the star performers and television, press and business methods that are involved in the elaborate Graham organization.) Written, directed and produced by Richard Cawston. Photographed by Peter Bartlett. Sound by Peter Edwards. Dubbing mixer: Patrick Whitaker. Film editor: Angus Newton. Production assistant: Barbara Saxon.

1967: *The Story of the Queen Mary*. (A sixty-minute film to commemorate the end of the *Queen Mary* as a transatlantic passenger liner. The film includes a brief history of the passenger trade on the Atlantic from its very beginning and tells the whole story of the *Queen Mary* herself.) Directed and produced by Richard Cawston. Commentary written by Anthony Lawrence. Commentary spoken by Kenneth More. Photographed by Peter Bartlett. Sound recorded by Bob Roberts. Dubbing mixer: Stanley Morcom. Film editor: Michael Bradsell. Production assistant: Barbara Saxon.

1969: *Royal Family*. (A 105-minute documentary about the Queen and her family on and off duty. Shot during a whole year in cinéma-vérité style by a BBC team. A BBC-ITV consortium was set up to handle this project.) Directed and produced by Richard Cawston. Commentary spoken by Michael Flanders. Commentary written by Anthony Jay. Photographed by Peter Bartlett. Sound recorded by Peter Edwards. Dubbing mixer: Patrick Whitaker. Research: Roger Cary. Production assistant: Barbara Saxon. Film Editor: Michael Bradsell.

December 19, 1969, at the BBC TV Center, Wood Lane, London.

G. Roy Levin: Would you want to say something about how you got started making films?

Richard Cawston: Well, I was one of those people who was always going to make films ever since I was in school—and I made films in school. But this was interrupted by the war, so I never got started on a career until after the war, and of course now I'm talking about 1947. In '46 I came out of the army. In those days if you were going to be a film-maker, it meant only one thing, feature films, and so I was going to make feature films.

G.R.L. Didn't the G.P.O. and the Empire Marketing Board mean anything to you?

R.C. Yes, there was the Crown Film Unit, a certain amount of documentary work, but there was no television very much, you see, at that time. One was interested entirely by what one saw in the cinema, and the place that documentaries took in those days in the cinema was a very minor role in relation to feature films.

G.R.L. I know something about documentaries at that time because I'm specifically interested, but did people in England know about them at the time? Were they important? For example, did you see them and say, "Those are really nice films?"

R.C. I don't think the general public knew much about documentaries in those days. I mean, as a schoolboy I was a mad cinemagoer, and I went several times a week. I used to go and sit in the gods of the Royal Court Theatre, which is now a theater, but which was in those days a repertoire cinema, and I used to see everything I could see. The people who were with me at school used to do this also, although the amateur films we made together at school were documentaries, of course. We made films about our life in the school and this kind of thing, but the kind of film-making that one set one's sights on in those days was feature film-making; that was the thing to be in as a career. Good documentaries were so rare that one didn't visualize documentary film-making as a career in those days. The news theaters were filled with incessant sunsets and travelogues, and I think there was floating through the cinema in those days—just before the war and just after it—what I call a kind of documentary sewage. These films were fillers; they got the horrible word "shorts," which they still have to live with. The word "short" became synonymous with documentary and it's done documentary a terrible disservice in terms of the cinema distribution world.

In those days, which were the days before television, anybody going to the cinema expected to get their money's worth of screen entertainment. They expected two features, an A picture and a B picture, and they expected two or three shorts in between, and these didn't have to do the job of getting people into the cinema. The box office was geared to the star system and that was what got the people into the cinema. The feature films did the work of popular appeal. The documentary only had to be loud enough to hide the noise of the ice cream papers and the hats and coats being stuffed under the seats. There was a terrible load of junk being turned out in one-reel form, and when the distributors bought them, all they wanted to know was how long these things were, because they were planning programs around them and they became a terrible kind of subsidiary entertainment. Now, of course, there were a few good ones, but they were isolated. I mean, for instance, the work that Grierson did, the work that was done in the war itself. Documentaries played a very important role of keeping up morale, and an educational role. People like Humphrey Jennings,[1] who influenced me a great deal, the Crown Film Unit, which was a wonderful organization in this country, the National Film Board of Canada, which Grierson started over there—all did wonderful work; but there were relatively few of these things. I mean, if you count up the films made by Grierson and by the Crown Film Unit, they would probably be in the hundreds. If you count up the features that were turned out by Hollywood during the same period, they would be in the thousands. And so the film business in those days meant automatically the feature film business, and any young person who was keen thought of feature films.

Directors were regarded as people on a very high plane—I mean, I didn't ever think I would ever be good enough to be a director. I didn't set my sights so high. In those days, 1946, and '47, when I came out of the war at the age of twenty-three and wanted to get on with the business of making films, I thought of a director as Carol Reed or David Lean and a few people of that stature—I'm talking about the British cinema. One didn't think one would ever be that good, and so I set my sights only on being a film editor to start with. I thought, well, if I can become a film editor, then maybe sometime in the future I might be able to direct, or perhaps I might be on the other side and become an associate producer or something like that. Looking back, it's extraordinary how the

[1] Historical Outline, pp. 17–18.

role of film director has become much more something that everyone can set their sights on—everybody thinks he's a film director nowadays. In those days it was almost like wanting to be a Prime Minister or President.

So I came out of the army and I decided to be a film editor, but I couldn't get a job as a film editor because there was a union closed shop. It still exists, but it was very strong at that time. The union policy was to reaccommodate all the people who had been in the forces, give their jobs back to them, and any new people, like me, were just absolutely out of it. I had a very, very difficult year trying to get into the cinema here. I went and stayed with relatives in Beverly Hills on the doorstep of Hollywood and then tried the whole process there, and it was the same. A, they had a union closed shop too, and they couldn't give me work. B, you know how Hollywood is—for every one person who gets in, there are about a thousand hanging about trying to get in. C, I was a foreigner and I didn't have a work permit in the United States and this was the strongest anti-immigrant period ever, because the immigrants were pouring into the United States after a four-year period in which they couldn't pour in.

It was very bleak, so I came to television, which was very much a second choice at that time. Somebody said, "Why don't you try television?" and I wrote to television and got an interview. They said they were just about to form a film unit in BBC television, which was very small in those days—we were ahead of the American equivalent, but we were still very small. I think the whole staff here were only about five hundred in television. The total number of sets was thirty-three thousand, I remember, when I joined. Now it's . . . fifteen million. It really was a very pioneering time. Fortunately I came and I said, "I'll do anything just to get into a visual medium. I've given up films. I can't do it." And they said, "Well, it so happens we are just about to form a small film unit to produce newsreels of our own." And there was a job for an assistant librarian. I applied and I got the job for six pounds five shillings a week.

Then things moved so fast it just wasn't true. It was just one of those strokes of luck because the BBC didn't recognize the cinema union and so there was no restriction, and within three months not only was I assistant librarian, I was also assistant editor, I was choosing the music for the newsreel, I was helping to do the recording sessions, I was assisting the cameramen, I was helping to write the commentaries—and by the end of the year I had done all the film jobs because we all did everything, as often happens when you're in on a pioneering thing. I quite quickly became officially an assistant film editor because there were only two of us then. And then I became an editor and cut hundreds of newsreels, and two years later I became producer of the newsreel. So I moved very quickly, and I stayed on making newsreels altogether for six years—two years as an editor and four years as a producer.

Then the newsreel was disbanded and taken over by the BBC News Division—an internal reorganization. And those of us who had become film-makers by that method . . . my God, we'd made a lot of footage in that time. You have to get flying hours in this business, you have to handle footage. We used to finish at one o'clock in the morning every night. I got TB as a result of the over-hours, but nevertheless, at the end of six years, I had had the equivalent of about twenty-five years' experience in the film industry if you measure by footage. They were not very enlightened films, of course, newsreels, but we thought we were making better newsreels than anybody else. And by then I had been bitten by the documentary bug and so had a number of the rest of us here, and I decided then to concentrate on making long documentaries.

G.R.L. What gave you the idea of making long documentaries? Were there examples that got you enthusiastic?

R.C. I think it was not so much examples as the satisfaction one got out of working with real material as opposed to fictional material. I realized this was a medium in which the newsreel was only scratching the surface of what could be done, that there could be, perhaps, a lot of work done in this factual field of film-making which hadn't really been properly done in the cinema.

Now I think that one must—I'm jumping ahead a bit now—but one must really give BBC the credit it deserves for the enormous shot in the arm it has given documentaries down these years, because its philosophy has been to provide space in peak hours for documentary films. More I think than anyone else in the world. Therefore we were playing to a large public, not just to minorities as specialized films did, not to educational audiences, not to industrial audiences. We were not the "sewage" of the cinema, the hat-and-coat-and-ice-cream category. We were playing to audiences with documentaries as a form of entertainment in their own right, and the most important thing that happened was when commercial television started up in this country in 1956. We then had competition, and this was an enormous shot in the arm, because what the documentary then had to do from that time onward was to compete for the audience against the alternative of pure entertainment on the other channel. It had to compete for its audience in an open market in a way I don't think it ever had to do in its history either here or anywhere else in the world. I mean, as I said earlier, in the cinema it was the feature film that got the audience in. It was the stars that made them pay their money. Here we were competing for an audience which had the option of turning their switch to the other channel. Therefore we had to make documentaries as exciting to watch as entertainment films. And this I think has done the documentary film more good than anything, and it has certainly formed the theory I have been following all through my career—that a documentary should be entertaining. Of course, people want information, but they acquire far more information if it comes to them in the form of entertainment, because it's painless information, painless education. I think this is one of the great mistakes, if I may say so, about the American setup of having a channel labeled "educational." The label, a misnomer anyway, sort of says to the audience, "If you want to be educated, watch this channel. If you want to be entertained, watch one of the others." We don't take that view here. We take the view that education and entertainment and information should always be one and the same thing.

Down the years I have been trying to develop the long documentary and get away from this terrible label of "short." I was one of the first few people to make long documentaries *regularly* in this country, and by that I mean feature-length. There had been a few down the years, of course, but as a regular thing I started about 1958 making documentaries which ran seventy-five minutes. And to hold an audience in a competitive situation with that length of program means it really has got to have some sort of dramatic form to it; it has to have a story line. I've always built a story line into my documentaries so that there are characters that people can identify with and there's a developing plot that makes people want to watch to see what happens, as well as all the factual information which is also there.

That's one of the things I've worked on, the long documentary, and of course it's accepted nowadays. We have a fifty-minute documentary every Tuesday night on BBC 1. We have a forty-five-minute documentary every Saturday night on BBC 2. This is very largely the result of the work I think that was done by just a few of us in television who were concerned with making long documentaries in the late fifties and sixties.

Another thing I've been interested in is the removal of the commentary from the documentary. I made a film called *This Is the BBC* in 1959 which was about the BBC itself. It was a terrible job to be given, but I decided that if the BBC was going to make a self-portrait there was no conceivable way of writing a commentary. What line do you take if you write a commentary? Do you take a hard-sell line telling everybody how wonderful the BBC is? No. Because it then looks like a public-relations film. Do you take a soft-sell line in which you mildly criticize? No. Because why should you damn your own organization with faint praise, and why should you use British understatement ad absurdum, which is what would have happened. So I thought, well, we won't have a commentary. We will make a sound track which is a montage of people talking and of programs being put out, and all of the information will in fact be concealed in the dialogue of the people who are talking. It was a very complicated film to make, and it was certainly influenced by films Humphrey Jennings had made in the Crown Film Unit during the war. In particular he made a film called *Listen to Britain*,[2] a twenty-minute film which impressed me a lot. And I thought if he could do that without a commentary for twenty minutes, I think I can do one for an hour. At the time it was publicized as the longest documentary that had been made without a commentary.

Again, this has now become a fairly commonplace technique, but it was a sort of ambitious and daring thing to do at that time because it could have been a terrible failure. In fact, it was such a risk, we organized a sneak show. We had an invited audience of about thirty people to come and see the film before it was actually finished, and I quizzed them for over two hours afterwards to find out what they got from it. A lot of the long documentaries that are made nowadays are not in my view good enough. They don't hold the audience, and I think it's a very difficult form of film-making; the reason I've stayed on with it rather than follow my original ambition of working with feature films is that I find it so exciting—because it's difficult. When it comes off it's immensely satisfying.

The other thing that I've believed in and which has now also become accepted practice is the abolition of the script before you shoot the film. This has become totally vindicated nowadays by the use of ciné-vérité techniques. But it was my view always that the producer or director, call him what you like, the creator of the film, should also be the writer—and I'm not talking about the commentary, if there is a commentary; that can be written later by somebody else. But the authorship, in the broad sense, should be in the hands of the director. And the reason for that is that if you write a script in advance of making a documentary, then the

[2] 1942.

film can only be as good as the script, no better. If you confine yourself to making a kind of plan of what you're going to do but allow the film to develop during the shooting, allow events to happen which you couldn't have forseen, allow yourself the opportunity of catching the odd-line of dialogue which nobody could have thought of in writing a script . . . you find gems, and you have to pick them up.

G.R.L. I can see that the Billy Graham film[3] was very likely created as you worked.

R.C. Yes, it was.

G.R.L. *The Pilots* also? Or did you have that structure in mind before you started?

R.C. A structure—yes. My script for *The Pilots* was two pieces of paper, and it wasn't a script. I don't mean to say that nothing is written down. I'm saying it's got to be done by the same man who is the director, because there's a certain amount in his head in the form of things he hopes to be able to do if the opportunity arises, and this couldn't possibly be put on script by one man and given to another man to direct. *The Pilots* was two sheets of paper; one sheet said that the film will follow a single Boeing 707 crew from London to Beirut, and then it will show them resting at Beirut. We will show every detail of that flight. We will show the crew arriving at the airport, meeting each other, doing their flight briefing, their preparation for take-off, the landing at intermediate stops such as Frankfurt and Rome, the night flying, and then the landing at Beirut. Then we will see them resting at Beirut, and then getting ready for the next leg to Delhi. So I simply put that down. Then on another sheet of paper I said this story will be intercut by sequences about the pilot's job, and these sequences will deal with pilot training, air traffic control, airport conditions, the pros and cons of British and American aircraft, etc.

Now at that stage it was really a shopping list, not a script. This was material that I needed to shoot in order to go on developing the film in the cutting room, which is the ultimate place where the documentary is really made. This is another reason why you can't have the script in minute detail—because so much creative work can be done in the editing, and the creation which is done in the editing arises from the actual celluloid itself, from what you see when you look at the material on the moviola.[4] Now *The Pilots* is a very good example of something that we couldn't have put in the script. The editor was showing me a certain sequence

[3] *I'm Going to Ask You to Get Up Out of Your Seat,* 1966.
[4] A viewing machine used in editing.

he'd cut of the pre-take-off checks in the cockpit. When we came to the end of the sequence, he had left the soundtrack of the pilots' voices on by mistake. The next shot he had joined was a shot of the aircraft taxiing out, because what we were going to do was to cut from the cockpit with all the chatter going on to the sound of the plane taxiing along. But he hadn't put in the exterior sound, he'd left the chatter running; and as it ran through the moviola he said, "Oh, I haven't done this bit yet," and there was a picture on the screen of a long shot of the plane taxiing but the sound that was coming out of the loudspeaker was the chatter of the voices inside. I said, "That's the way we're going to make this film!" Suddenly, the machine gave me the idea: why don't we look at the outside of the airplane and hear the voices inside? And we carried this technique right through. We even had the night shot, you remember, when he put his landing lights on and we still could hear them inside the cockpit, but we were looking at the shot from a totally different angle—from outside the plane. This was not a new idea in other films, but it was a new idea for an aviation film, to have the inside dialogue and the outside pictures together. And this came totally from one of those inspirations you get from the damn machine itself. So this really illustrates my point. Nobody would have put that in the script.

G.R.L. Probably true—accidents in art are often happy ones.

R.C. Cutting is a very creative place for me, and I think this is why all directors ought to be editors first—because the mere looking at the material constantly gives you ideas. Just running a bit of film backwards and forwards will suddenly give me an idea of some kind of sound track, some kind of music, some kind of cut we can make which I couldn't have visualized, some juxtaposition of ideas, which are suggested to you by looking at the material; and I like to leave that door open. I spend a lot of time in the cutting room with my films.

With ciné-vérité it is imperative not to have a script because you film things as they happen. The Billy Graham film, of course, had an over-all plan, but I didn't know what he was going to say on certain occasions, I didn't know who he would turn to when he arrived on the station platform, how the crowd would react and so on, and therefore with a technique where the dialogue comes from real life and even where the events come from real life, you really couldn't have a detailed script. This was true in *Royal Family* too, where we just had to allow the events as they took place to help shape the film.

Another thing we've found is the advantage of the director himself doing the research. Maybe he goes and meets fifty people when he only wants one—I met fifty pilots before deciding which crew I was going to feature. You meet a particular man and you say to yourself, he's got something; I think if I come back with a camera I can get something out of him. If I ask him certain questions, I think he will give interesting answers. You don't ask the questions during your research, you store them up in your mind because you know it would be better to come back in a month's time with a camera, then ask the questions and get a spontaneous answer. In other words, I think that the "script" which you're creating as director is a kind of contract with yourself to come back and do something yourself. If you went out and wrote to me, "I've interviewed fifty pilots, I think if you go back with your cameras you'll find X interesting," I'd then go back and find that to me X isn't interesting, and I don't get him reacting the same way. Perhaps X doesn't like me as much as he liked you, so he behaves differently in my presence than he would in your presence. Therefore this dichotomy of preparation and directing has created a disadvantage. I believe that solo working is very important.

G.R.L. A few brief questions about *The Pilots*. For example, when they have coffee in the airplane, when they check into the hotel, when they're in the bar, when the captain goes to sleep, when they're sitting on the veranda talking—were those all setups?

R.C. Well, in those days we were working with 35mm. cameras, which were very heavy. We couldn't use ciné-vérité techniques then. They were setups, yes. Everything. In those days, the way we had to work was to observe very carefully what happened in reality, then set it up to re-create reality as accurately as we could. It was the director's job, when he did stage anything, to stage it not with his own ideas, but simply to reproduce what he had seen happening during research. We filmed what we could of the actual flight from London to Beirut, and we had two tape recorders running throughout, which recorded everything that happened. We recorded all the intercom and all the talk between the crews, and we got what pictures we could on board, which were limited, because it is very difficult to film on the flight deck. We then came back and had the flight simulator for a whole night when it wasn't being used, and with the aid of these tape recorders which told us what had happened during the flight, we restaged the events. That little incident about a navigator going sick and the pilot hearing this just as they were approaching Beirut, and having to tell the navigator he was going to have to go on to Delhi, well, that really happened, and we got the lines of dialogue they used, and so on, off the tape recorder, and then we restaged it. So, to some extent with that film, we were obliged to restage. Nowadays, I think, with the light 16mm. cameras, we could probably make the film without any restaging.

G.R.L. What were the shooting ratios in *The Pilots* and the Billy Graham film?

R.C. I think *The Pilots* was about ten to one,[5] eight to one maybe. One used to shoot lower ratios on 35mm., and with staged situations. With ciné-vérité you go on turning until you have what you want. Billy Graham was a high-ratio film deliberately, about twenty to one. I always knew that that would be a high-ratio film.

G.R.L. I believe the phrase cinéma-vérité was first applied to the work of French film-makers like Rouch and Marker. In the United States one uses the phrase in reference to the work of people like the Maysles brothers, Leacock, Pennebaker, Wiseman. Can you say what you think about their films? About this trend towards the use of cinéma-vérité?

R.C. I think there was an era when a great deal of baloney was said about ciné-vérité. I think it became a pseudo art form in its own right. It isn't an art form; it's simply one of the tools of the trade which are available to film-makers, and it should be used where it is the appropriate tool, but where other methods are more appropriate, then they should be used also. I personally, and most of us working in this department here—there are about thirty directors—we use that kind of technique, but as a tool, not as an end in itself.

G.R.L. I would like to take things more slowly, but you have that conference soon, so let me jump to something else. How do you feel about documentary and objective truth, and how TV often presents documentaries as if it were understood that they were objective?

R.C. Well, I think there's room for both kinds. I think there is at one end of the scale the totally objective type of program which is what I have made more myself; at the other end of the scale there is the fully subjective, committed documentary which is made by a man who wants to use it to say something himself. Now the extreme example of that is Peter Watkins' *The War Game*, which he made in this department. Peter Watkins is a film-maker—a brilliant genius of a film-maker—who wanted to say some things about life and he was using film to put over his own views. That is perfectly legitimate, so long as it is clearly labeled, so that the audience when they see it know this is Peter Watkins' view of

5 This means that ten times more footage was shot than was used in the final film.

something. We do a certain number of subjective films like that. The difficulty is that it's a very limited field. You cannot base an entire film-making career saying what you want to say yourself, because people will get bored with you. By the time Peter Watkins has made about five subjective films, they will know roughly what Peter Watkins wants to say, and that, I would have thought, would be the limit of the number of totally subjective films that any one man could make. I think that on the other hand, with objective film-making, you could go on forever because you are presenting other people's views.

G.R.L. Do you feel that *The Pilots* and the Billy Graham film were objective?

R.C. Yes, I do. In the Billy Graham film I have been proved to be objective in the sense that people who hold both points of view about Billy Graham, people who like him and people who don't like him, were both satisfied by that film. It could be read either way. The Billy Graham organization itself liked it very much, and the anti-Billy Graham people also liked it. They both felt it strengthened their attitudes, that the information was there. I think that the research that you do is a very important feature of objectivity. With *The Pilots* I interviewed nearly a hundred pilots and had their remarks all written down, and in that way I found out what kind of views they held. If 70 per cent of the pilots thought one thing, then this is the view that I would consider should be in the film. Let us take the argument of which type of aircraft are better, British or American. I found that the pilots in this country were more or less equally divided on this subject; therefore in my final film I had the same number on both sides of that particular argument. I had two in favor of British aircraft, and I had two against. They reflected what I had found, by my own kind of private Gallup poll, to be the truth. It was not *my* view of whether British aircraft were better or inferior, it was an attempt to put over *their* view by doing enough research.

G.R.L. Is this the view that you take generally in the documentaries that you do and have done for BBC?

R.C. Not always. I did one film in particular which was subjective, and I felt I was entitled to be subjective because the work I did was an original piece of research which had never been done before. This was when I went around the world and studied world television. I studied the impact that television was making on the developing countries. I went to twenty countries to study this as part of my research. I did a ten-week trip for this. Nobody else had done this particular study and I therefore felt entitled to draw my own conclusions. The conclusion, very simply, was that there was a lot of unsuitable junk being dumped into countries where it shouldn't be shown. Westerns for example, being shown to Africans.

G.R.L. What was the title of that film?

R.C. *Television and the World.* It's that big one up there,[6] the film that won the Italia prize. It was also used for the opening night of Channel 13 in New York.

G.R.L. Is that a particular favorite of yours?

R.C. It was a favorite film in the sense that I think it did some real good. It opened the eyes of people all over the world to the fact that television could go wrong if it was used wrongly, and in fact it has been instrumental in restraining certain countries from opening television services before they were ready to do so. Therefore it's had a definite effect, apart from informing people.

[. . .]

G.R.L. What about a film like *Cathy Come home,*[7] for example. I'm not sure one could say it was objective—it had a point of view, a bias if you like, and this was made clear in the film. But did you think it was a fair and honest film, and in this way objective?

R.C. Well, first of all, *Cathy Come Home* was not a documentary. It was a play, a play in which all the information was drawn from life, and so it was a documented play. It's a form of film which I prefer to call the drama-documentary or the dramatized documentary, making use of actors. I think it was slightly unfair in that the author took one couple and made all the terrible things happen to them that he could. Now, in real life, these terrible things had of course happened, but they happened to different people. They hadn't all happened to one; so from that point of view it was a slight caricature. I think that nevertheless it was a terribly valuable and important program. My only reservations about it were that it borrowed documentary techniques so much that the audience were slightly misled into believing it was a documentary, that it wasn't acted, and that these were real people.

G.R.L. There were credits, though.

R.C. There were credits, but I think they didn't quite do enough to label it as a play. But this is not a serious objection to it. It was a wonderful piece of work, but I don't call it a documentary.

G.R.L. When I saw the film on Billy Graham in one of the screening rooms here at BBC, the young man who threaded the

[6] He was referring to a framed prize certificate hanging on the wall.
[7] A BBC film about housing problems in England. It was directed by Ken Loach and produced by Tony Garnett. See interview with them for details. Also see comments on film in interview with Lindsay Anderson.

Steenbeck[8] for me knew the film, and he didn't like it—because he thought it was against Billy Graham. It seemed fairly clear to me—though apparently this is not true for everybody—that it was somewhat biased against certain aspects of the Billy Graham Crusade. Personally I found the bias—perhaps one could say editorializing—to be fair and just. For example, intercutting Billy Graham saying, "Would you please come up to the platform" with shots of people selling pop and hot dogs and literature outside I presume was meant to say that there was an aspect of commercialism in the Crusade. Now this comment wasn't made by use of cinéma-vérité, right? because you arbitrarily cut from one thing to another to make your point. I think that that's fair—but I don't think it's objective.

R.C. I do. I think it's objective if you draw the information which leads you to put the film together in that way from a very large number of people. Hundreds of people told me they felt that this was a commercialized situation; and where I say objective I mean I was reflecting their views in putting the film together in that way—not my own; and that is my definition. Of course, you can say there is no such thing as an objective film, that because it is made by a human being who has got his own weaknesses and who is fallible it must always to some extent be subjective. The definition for me is this: what is the intention? If the intention is to be objective, that's as far as you can go. The film-maker then does his best to be objective. He does his best not to allow his own prejudice to influence the decisions. Supposing I had privately been wildly in favor of Billy Graham, supposing I had been a passionate Billy Graham follower, and I wanted to make an objective film, I still should have allowed the views of these hundreds of thousands of people who thought it was commercial to influence me enough to put the film together in that way. Supposing I had been violently anti-Billy Graham personally, I still should have been sufficiently influenced to do what in fact I did do, which was to allow him to make the best possible sermon he could make—I filmed something like eight sermons during that Crusade and selected the very best bits of all of them to give him the best presentation of his case. I feel that when you're being objective, it's like being a lawyer on both sides of a case. While you're presenting one side of the case, you do the best you can for your client. You then do a kind of two-faced act and present the other side of the case and do the best you can for your other client. Now, that's what I was doing with the Billy Graham film: I was giving both sides the best deal

8 Another, more sophisticated type of viewing machine used in film editing.

I could. If I'd been subjective, I'd have allowed the audience to know my own views about Billy Graham by giving only one side of the case.

G.R.L. The next is perhaps a delicate question: if one worked for the BBC—or for that matter for any network in any country—and felt that the society one lived in had many faults, how much of a chance is there to say something about that and to genuinely try to change that society? I don't think that the Labour government directly tells you or anyone else here what to do or say. I'm talking of something more subtle, of the degree to which the government in power influences over-all policy. Here in England you have a state-owned network, and power works in certain ways. In the United States the networks are private and governmental influences are probably more indirect, more economic.

R.C. Well, one thing, I spend my time when I'm in America telling people that the BBC has nothing to do with the government. This really is the most independent form of organization; it's publicly owned but it's not government-controlled. The government in power really has no effect on it at all. The government is always one of the BBC's enemies in the sense that we constantly tell them we will do things our own way. We're owned by the public and financed directly by the public, and the government really has no effect on us, and this is why we like working here. I'm not doing a BBC public-relations line here—I mean, I'm saying that this is literally why I choose to work here. The BBC operates within itself, it has its own policies. We have to require producers not to do certain things—they are very basic rules—a sort of folklore. "Don't create racial hatred," is one of our philosophies. "Be fair" is another. "Give a proper hearing to all sides of any argument" is another philosophy. They're very simple, morally accurate beliefs, and I think that in other countries, on the other hand, very different systems operate. France and Italy are two examples where the government has an enormous bearing on what is done. When there's an election and the government changes, so the television service changes, and the officials running it change. It is an instrument of government in those places. I think that there isn't any equivalent anywhere of the BBC quite. NHK in Japan is supposed to be a copy of it, and I think to some extent it is. I think that it is very difficult in the United States to have an organization which is totally free of pressures. The pressures there are mainly commercial, of course, and they come through the association with sponsorship and the high costs of programing which have developed. I would not work in an organization which was subject to political pressures because I think this is the most dangerous of all. I think it's much more dangerous than commercial pressure.

G.R.L. I've talked to some film-makers here who have worked for BBC and have been glad of it because they've had a chance to do certain things they couldn't have done elsewhere; but they left after a time because they felt there was a subtle kind of pressure, an unspoken set of rules which they couldn't accept, and that they finally could not make the films they wanted to make—radical films.

R.C. Well, I think you've talked to one or two people who have had arguments with the BBC that I know about, but this has never been an argument with the government. *The War Game* is a very good example, if you like. It was decided not to put that film on television. Now you could take a view—Peter Watkins, who was a very emotional young man, took the view—that this was because the BBC was pandering to a government situation. This was not in fact true because I was involved in this and I can tell you about the decision that was made. I wanted it to go on television. I was in favor of Peter Watkins making it—of course I wanted it to go on; I was backing him. At the same time I think it was an extremely difficult decision that had to be made. I wouldn't have liked to have had the responsibility of making that decision, and I was therefore quite happy to refer it higher up in the BBC to somebody else. And if you refer something higher up, you have to be prepared to accept what they tell you. And the reason for the decision basically was not a political one, and it was certainly a BBC decision; the main reason for not putting it on was the fact that television is an indiscriminate means of distribution. You don't know the circumstances in which your audience are viewing. There is no means of stopping an old, nervous person from watching a very frightening program on television. It is different in the cinema, because an old, nervous person coming into the cinema is immediately surrounded by the company of the audience, and they are protected in a sense by the fact that the audience is there. We knew that if we put *The War Game* on, there would be numbers of such people who would be so frightened by that film that they might even commit suicide, and we didn't feel that we could take the risk of scaring people to that extent.

So we went all out to get it a theatrical release, instead. Now, if it had been a political decision not to show it, it wouldn't have been released at all. This is a case where Peter Watkins, if you interviewed him, might give you the other point of view. He would probably tell you that the BBC is a place where he was not allowed to show that film. But in fairness, no other organization in the world would have had the courage to *make* it in the first place. I think if you work in an organization which is very courageous about what it will make, the price you have to pay is that occasionally something is made which the very creators of the program, namely the BBC, subsequently feel shouldn't be shown.

G.R.L. The story that I heard or read about, because I've never gotten to speak to Peter Watkins, is that not only could it not be shown on television, but that there was a great deal of trouble to get it shown to anybody, and that the BBC did not want it shown outside.

R.C. The BBC did want it shown outside. I think there were some BBC people who didn't but more people who did, and the people who did won.

[. . .]

G.R.L. Do you think that documentaries can help to change society, particularly TV documentaries, since they have such an enormous audience?

R.C. I'm sure they have done already. They've changed society basically in that people are far better informed than they were before. There's no question, if you take a man of twenty-two now and if you could take a man of twenty-two twenty years ago, they would be totally differently informed people. A great deal of that difference is due to the information that they receive through TV. I mean, before we had television and television documentary nobody knew who their politicians were, what sort of people they were, what the rest of the world was like. It's given an enormous amount of information about other countries. It's created therefore much more tolerance in my view than existed in the days of ignorance, because intolerance to some extent comes out of ignorance. I'm sure that society is better informed and that must be a good thing, because people can then draw their conclusions on the basis of information instead of ignorance.

That's the main thing it's done. In addition to that I'm sure it has influenced society in terms of behavior. It's shown people how other people behave and I think it's far better that people should imitate the widest possible cross section of the real world rather than doing what they used to in the thirties, which was to imitate—or rather to envy—Hollywood. You see, Hollywood used to be the main mass influence before the war. Hollywood films used to show people living a life of luxury, and in my view they created a great deal of unhappiness without meaning to do so. They created unhappiness because they made people discontented with their own lives; they gave a false image. Now people realize that really the rest of the world is pretty much like themselves, and they don't feel so discontented, and I think this is a good thing.

G.R.L. Personally, do you feel that documentaries and TV should help try to change, ameliorate social conditions?

R.C. I think that TV should—TV is a link; its job is to reflect society, not to influence it, but in reflecting society accurately, one tries to reflect, as it were, the spearheads of society. One tries to take people who are slightly ahead in their thinking, communicate their thoughts to the masses, which enables those who are a little lagging behind to catch up with the ones up front. And in that way, of course, it must help change society, because if your progressive thinkers have decided, for example, that there should be world population control, that there should be more tolerance, that colonial countries should be independent and should have their own governments—various humanitarian attitudes which are now more or less accepted amongst ordinary thinking people—then those attitudes can be communicated to the masses through documentary, and then the masses will be able in due course to adjust their thinking to the thoughts of the leaders. Of course, where there are two opposing points of view, then it's right that these should be shown equally. I would think that in the days before television, it would have been extremely difficult to get capital punishment abolished, which happened yesterday in this country. And I think television has played a part in bringing the mass of people into this line of thinking so that politicians have now been able to take this step, knowing it won't be unpopular.

TONY GARNETT AND KENNETH LOACH

Tony Garnett was born April 3, 1936, in Birmingham, England, the son of a toolmaker; he attended primary school there and won a scholarship to Birmingham Central Drama School. After acting in provincial repertory for eighteen months he studied experimental psychology at London University while continuing to act in television and repertory plays. He later became a story editor and then a producer at BBC-TV, where he and Loach met and began to work together.

Kenneth Loach was born June 17, 1936, in Nuneaton, England; he studied law at Oxford, where he also acted. He took the director's course at BBC and became a television director there.

The two collaborated at the BBC on the series of "Wednesday Plays" and other plays and video dramas, among them fictionalized social documentaries (a blend of fact and fiction) such as David Mercer's *In Two Minds*, the story of a schizophrenic girl based on real case histories, and *Cathy Come Home*, which dramatized the housing problems in England and which won a number of prizes. *Up the Junction*, another of their TV collaborations, was made into a feature film.

In 1965 Loach won the TV Director of the Year Award from the British TV Guild. He made his first theatrical film as director of *Poor Cow*; his second is *Kes*, which is Garnett's first feature. Garnett and Loach both recently left BBC and subsequently formed their own production company, Kestrel Films, Ltd.

Loach lives with his wife, Lesley, and their three children in London. Garnett, who is single, also lives in London.

FILMOGRAPHY*

FOR BBC-TV:

1966–67: Garnett produced twelve television plays; among them are: *The Lump,* directed by Jack Gold, a story of industrial conflict; *Drums Along the Avon,* written by Charles Wood, about Indian immigrants; and *Voices in the Park,* which dealt with London's popular Speakers' Corner.

"Wednesday Plays"; Garnett was story editor on thirty-four original seventy-five-minute plays; Loach directed a number of them.

Z *Cars* series; Loach directed three episodes.

The Coming Out Party and *The End of Arthur's Marriage,* two TV plays written and directed by Loach.

For the five following films or plays, though the United Artists' press release is not clear, I presume that Loach was the director and Garnett the producer:

In Two Minds; Loach and Garnett's first collaboration; about a schizophrenic girl, based on real case histories.

Up the Junction; about a rich girl who goes to live in London's working-class Battersea area.

Cathy Come Home; script by Jeremy Stanford; v. note p. 99.

The Golden Vision; about soccer.

The Big Flame; script by Jim Allen; about industrial disputes on the docks of Liverpool.

FEATURES:

1968: *Poor Cow.* National General Pictures Release (Technicolor). Produced by Joseph Janni. Screenplay by Nell Dunn, Kenneth Loach, based on the novel by Nell Dunn. Directed by Kenneth Loach. Director of photography: Brian Probyn. Art Director: Bernard Sarron. Production manager: David Anderson. Associate producer: Edward Joseph. Assistant to producer: John Goldstone. Editor: Roy Watts. Music: Donovan. 104 minutes.

1969: *Kes.* A Woodfall Films presentation. A Kestrel Films production. Screenplay by Barry Hines, Ken Loach, Tony Garnett, based

* It was not possible to obtain a complete or accurate filmography for either Loach or Garnett in time for publication except for *Poor Cow* and *Kes;* the information here was taken from press releases by United Artists for *Kes.* Unless by pure chance, the listing is not in chronological order.

on *Kestrel for a Knave* by Barry Hines. Produced by Tony Garnett. Directed by Ken Loach. Photography: Chris Menges. Editor: Roy Watts. Art director: William McCrow. Music composed and conducted by John Cameron. Production supervisor, David Griffiths. Assistant director: Keith Evans.

November 30, 1969, London, at Ken Loach's home.

G. Roy Levin: I had a good talk with Tony while driving over here, but unfortunately I have none of it on tape.

Ken Loach: He's probably got a photographic memory and can get it all down later.

G.R.L. No such luck. But maybe we can go over some of it later. To start with, though, why don't you tell me mundane things like how you got started making films.

K.L. Unemployed actor, repertory director doing murder plays. . . . Then I applied for a job with the BBC when BBC 2[1] was starting. They needed a lot of people and were prepared to take just about everybody, which was fortunate.

This was about 1962–63. We did a three-week course during which one was told how to fill up wardrobe forms, and when to apply to the make-up lady for make-up. Then a series of studio drama productions during the course of which this whole group of us got fed up with working in the studio and asked if our money could be spent on film rather than studio. Making films was sort of a development of that. And that's it, really. Because most of our films were made for the BBC in fact. I've only made three or four films outside the BBC, two features and two television films, one of which hasn't been shown and was a straight documentary—the only straight documentary I've really done.

G.R.L. Which was that?

K.L. A film for the Save the Children Fund which is in a state of some confusion, because they weren't too pleased with what we got. And the others are films for London Weekend Television.[2] We're just finishing one that was made in Liverpool. It's about a working-class funeral. It takes place over three or four days before the funeral and in a way it's a record of those days, the relationships between the family and some assessment of that old chappie who was dying. He was an old militant.

G.R.L. Was this about someone who actually died?

Tony Garnett: Well, it was written by a friend of ours, Neville Smith, who's an actor. It was based on the life of his father, who died last year. So the inspiration for it and the source material are personal, but it's fiction in the sense that none of the characters directly correspond to his real family.

[1] The second channel of the BBC.

[2] A commercial television station, as opposed to BBC, which is government-owned and -operated.

G.R.L. And, as with *Cathy Come Home*,[3] you use actors?

T.G. Yes. Except what do you mean by the word "actors"? You see, we've got the problem in this country of British Actors' Equity in which they say that everyone who takes part in a play must be an existing member of Equity. You just can't ask somebody to be in it and then get them to join, because they've got to be already in Equity. This causes problems for us, because they say that they'll be trained and have experience in repertory and these are very often the people we don't want, although one sympathizes with a trade union in a capitalist society—most of them out of work, and so on. Artistically, though, it makes it very difficult for us.

G.R.L. These are non-professionals, people who haven't acted before? Where did you cast that film?

T.G. Well, most of the people in that film entertain in the workingmen's clubs, so that they are professionals or semiprofessionals in the sense that they get up in front of an audience and play the guitar, or tell funny stories or whatever they do, and they get paid for what they do; but they're not actors in any conventional sense. They were chosen partly because they're the people we wanted, and partly because they happen to be members of the union, because they are entertainers. You know, there are problems, and if you want somebody who is not a professional, in the accepted sense of a member of the union, then you're into a big hassle.

K.L. But in fact these people have got the ability to make a fictional situation believable in front of a camera. We try to get people who can draw on their own lives, on their experience —so they bring it in, so they're not emoting, not a blank sheet of paper on which you and they write the part. You try to find people who have it in their own experience.

[3] A television film made for the BBC that uses actors and a fictional form but is based on actual facts about the housing problem in Britain. The story is built around a young working-class couple whom we see go from comparative material ease to desperate situations after the husband has an accident and cannot find work. They are forced to live in an abandoned bus with their children, the husband and wife are split up when she and the children go to a halfway house where only women and children are permitted when they can't find housing they can afford. In the final moment, after the husband has all but disappeared, the children are taken from the mother to be put in a state home because of her inability to provide and care for them. Though perhaps seemingly stereotypical and obvious in bare outline, the texture of the film has a genuine feel of reality to it and is often comic, touching and moving. (Carol White, later the star of *Poor Cow* and other films, plays the wife.)

G.R.L. Did you go to Liverpool and around the clubs to look for these people? Did you have a casting call?

K.L. Yes.

G.R.L. Which?

[Laughter.]

K.L. We've got quite a lot of contacts up there in the clubs and we cast a lot from amongst those, and then there were some people we knew. It's gotten to be a kind of a family affair now.

G.R.L. Did you do the same for *Cathy Come Home?*

K.L. No, not really, that was done in the London area, and they are all actors.

T.G. They've acted before in other films and plays.

K.L. Of course, there were one or two that we picked up in the provinces, in Birmingham, but they were more accepted actors.

G.R.L. Were any of the people in *Cathy Come Home* actually from these homes, these halfway houses? They certainly had the feel of real people—their faces, for example.

K.L. Quite a lot of them were, in fact. The ones that were in the script as non-speaking parts, we found from the streets nearby. So they are just ordinary families, from a poorer area, and some of those families might well end up in halfway houses. The ones who have any speech are actresses who do professional theater work.

T.G. They've got some contact with reality though, not just their agent.

G.R.L. Let's say you were going to do *Cathy Come Home* now, would you use Carol White and Ray Brooks, the boy who played her husband, again? Would you use those kind of people again?

K.L. Probably not, in fact.

T.G. Unless we were forced to.

K.L. That's Carol as she was, not as she is today. I think she's probably different. . . .

T.G. From Carol now.

K.L. I guess her circumstances have changed considerably.

G.R.L. She was hard up then?

T.G. No, but since then she's become what is called a film star and been to Hollywood and, you know, she's gone on to all that circuit. I mean, it's a different girl in some ways from the girl she was then. Then she had more contact in her daily life with the kind of daily life that most people are in contact with. It wasn't in that enervating atmosphere of show business, which we hate.

K.L. Also, she hadn't done so much work; she'd had a long gap where she hadn't worked at all. When people have done a lot of work their edge tends to be blunted, really. If she hadn't gone on to become a film star, you know, if she had just worked regularly, I think the odds are again that the edge is blunted. You become too pat.

G.R.L. Tony was saying in the car that if he made *Cathy Come Home* again he'd make it much more radical. Perhaps you'd like to say how you feel about that, or perhaps Tony would like to say why again.

T.G. Well, it's a feeling we both share. We've changed since then. I think we wouldn't be so happy with adapting such a liberal position towards that subject. We would be more definite and more political.

K.L. The great weakness of it is that everybody can claim it as their own. You know, every politician can say, "Oh yes . . ."

T.G. "It's a terrible problem."

K.L. Yes. And, "This helps shed light on the housing problem." You know, if it can do that, in a way it's kind of terribly failed. Not totally, but it's largely failed, because while it gives an impression of the problem, nevertheless it doesn't lead towards an understanding of what causes the problem.

T.G. Or lay the blame or show how it can be solved. I mean, you can put your hand in your pocket and give ten shillings to charity and think that that's it. You know, it's somewhat like saying, "How unfortunate," in a Dickensian way. You weep, if the film gets to you, and you say, "Oh, how unfortunate, isn't it a pity that this sort of thing goes on. It's such a shame." But that's not enough.

G.R.L. What kind of reaction would you want an audience to have? In what ways would you specifically change the film if you remade it? How would you make it more radical?

T.G. Well, I don't know what Jeremy[4] would think about this, but from our point of view, it would be reframed altogether. It's not just a question of adding a few lines. I think one would take that situation and restructure it, tell the story very differently. One would try to avoid the situation where an audience could get out of their moral difficulty by blaming a few local officials on the periphery of the system, by blaming the petty functionaries of the system. You've got to blame the system at its base. So one would have to bring more of that into it, and one would also have to make it very clear what the solution to

[4] Jeremy Stanford, who wrote the script for *Cathy Come Home*.

the problem would be, in terms of a political analysis. This would then engage one not just in a discussion of how many houses should be built to what standards, but what is the political and economic structure that is behind all this.

G.R.L. How do you think that the structure should be changed?

T.G. Well, the structure has got to be changed from a capitalist way of organizing things to a socialist way of organizing things. [Garnett and Loach begin to laugh.] Maybe I'll just have to give a ten-minute Marxist homily on all that.

K.L. The reaction that one would want to lead them to in the end is an understanding of the power situation in which they find themselves, and leave the impetus to them so that they're left with a need for action rather than a catharsis of sitting back with relief and seeing what's on the other channels.

T.G. Which is nonsense. What one would hope to achieve is a greater tension within it so that not only would they have this emotional reaction, but you would also alienate them from this emotional reaction and not let them wallow in it. If people are harmed, tell them what to do about it. But the task is not just to understand the world, but to change it, and to point out how it can be changed.

G.R.L. You intercut a few statistics about the housing problem. And this time you might do more things like that? To break the emotional involvement, in a Brechtian sense.

T.G. Well, I don't know. You can go so far with that, and you're into a cul-de-sac. It's an easy way out to do too much of that.

K.L. It's a usual device.

T.G. A legitimate device.

K.L. A device to involve people emotionally, and then you turn the tap off.

G.R.L. Did you try more of that in the film about the funeral you just made in Liverpool?

T.G. Well, that was tried more in a film that was also done in Liverpool, but a couple of years ago, that Jim Allen wrote; it's a film called *The Big Flame*. The basic situation is a dock strike in Liverpool, which lasted for six weeks. The strike was on an economic plane. For more wages, and better conditions, and fear of unemployment and so on. And then we suddenly changed gears and put the strike onto a political plane. The dockers went back into the docks and took it over and ran the docks under workers' control for some time. And obviously all the forces of the state came in, and the army and so on, and they held out for a few days and of course they were beaten. But one hoped to leave the audience with a number of political lessons from it.

G.R.L. Who was that film made for?

T.G. The BBC.

G.R.L. And they showed it?

T.G. In the end they did, just.

K.L. Yes. We'd just gone ahead of our own feet by giving an announcement to the "Radio Times" before they actually saw it at BBC, so that if they had withdrawn it there would have been . . .

T.G. A public stink.

K.L. I reckon we've gone just as far as we can go.

G.R.L. Is that why you both left the BBC and started your own company?

T.G. No, not really. The reasons for that are quite complicated, and I suppose we don't know all of them, really. You know, things happen. I don't know, Ken's reasons might be different from mine. First of all, I'd been at the BBC for four years. I think the BBC can be rather like Sing Sing. You can get institutionalized in a place like that. I suppose I wanted to do some work on feature films. Kenneth got out the year before and had done a film. We both wanted to work outside and do some feature films. But we still wanted to work in the telly as well, and so it doesn't mean that we won't go back to the BBC and work there. We'd like to continue to work in both, because some subjects are more appropriate to television and others to the cinema. In some ways it's more satisfying to work in the cinema. You have longer to do it, more money to spend on the film, and you're working on a bigger canvas, literally. Nevertheless, I think it's essential to work in television because it's the only time you can get to twelve million people on the same occasion. And certainly some subjects are more appropriate to television—subjects with a very overt, present social content, something more directive. Previously, although we have some fears about this, the regime at the BBC has been much more liberal.

G.R.L. Than the commercial film world?

K.L. Well, of course, all that the commercial cinema is interested in is whether the film is going to make money or not. For them it's a commodity.

G.R.L. Tony, would you say again why you think the BBC is the best television system in the world?

T.G. Ken will share this view. On the one hand I think it's fucking awful; but on the other hand I recognize that it's the best firm in the world. All right now, what are the reasons for that? First of all, because it's a public corporation, so it's not dependent, it's not been created to make profit, so that apart from some administrative fat, every penny that comes in goes on the screen. Second, it is in a country which is quite big, and compared to most countries in the world, very wealthy, so it has a very secure financial base and can spend money on a big range of programs, which many countries can't. Third, as a public institution, although it is tied very closely to the state, and is governed by the state just as is every other public corporation in the world, there is a liberal tradition in this country which is sustained—except in times of danger to the system—and reflects the security that the ruling class in this country has compared with a lot of other countries. Like France, for instance, or the Soviet Union. And therefore part of the genius of the British ruling classes, feeling as secure as they have, is to allow an institution like the BBC to develop, seemingly independent of the executive, although it isn't at all. But in broad cultural areas, it does allow a civilized, urbane, bland freedom which allows people like us to do work—within certain limits. Also there is another liberal tradition in this country, in that we have a number of social safety valves, to allow young people, providing they are not too radical and not revolutionary, or Marxist, to work, and this reinforces their own judgment of their liberalism. It's also a nasty place for buying off any element of protesters, because you can be promoted out of trouble, and cosseted out of trouble, and flattered out of trouble, and materially rewarded out of trouble, and it's a delicate system of checks and balances that works. Only in times of acute political danger to the ruling class, which again usually occurs in times of economic difficulty, are there sanctions imposed on people like this. The iron fist within the velvet glove is rarely seen. But don't underestimate them. I mean that phrase of Galbraith's is often used in the BBC—the bland leading the bland. But in fact, when they move, if they really want to move, they move very swiftly and ruthlessly. They know what power is about. Would you agree with that, Ken?

K.L. Yes, I think you summarized it. Well, one thing really, that there are so many people in the organization that you can go away and get on with what you're doing and nobody knows what you're doing till some months later, and then they notice you in the cutting room and you say, "There it is." A company that is that big can't keep their papers on you. You can just shoot off and cover your tracks.

T.G. This is also true. It's also part of another tradition, provided you're not politically dangerous. It's the extension into the public corporation of the idea that is at the heart of this country, the attitude in the eighteenth century of private patronage. And so the individual producer, writer, director, whatever, is allowed to get on with it. Here is some money, get on with it and let's have your program. And producers are allowed a lot of freedom on the BBC within those limits.

If you're working in one of the categories regarded as culture, you're allowed a great deal of freedom. If you're working in public affairs, in current affairs, you're allowed hardly any freedom at all. The ground rules are very precise in that area, and most of the people who run television in the BBC are ex-television journalists or press journalists, and they know just how far to go. That's why the traditional comment program, like *Panorama* and so on, and all the traditional documentary in contemporary affairs is very severely restricted, whereas drama is traditionally seen as an area of culture that has nothing to do with real life because it's fiction. They like actors to look like actors—it's art and all that stuff—so that you're allowed more freedom there because it's obviously not so dangerous. This is where we came in, because we were able to use traditional fictional, dramatic forms in the departments of the BBC that were long-haired and had nothing to do with the "real world."

K.L. We were always in the drama departments. So we did our plays, but decided to say what we wanted to say. Now if we'd been working in the sensitive areas—public affairs, documentary and so on—we wouldn't have been allowed to do anything like what we wanted to do. There's been a big debate in British television over the last few years about what is a drama and what is a documentary. And we've been criticized by the avant-garde for irresponsibility, because we have confused the two categories. Because for them, drama, documentary, whatever, isn't just an administrative convenience, it's a doctrinal position, and documentary is one thing and drama is another.

G.R.L. So it's a heresy.

T.G. Oh, it's a heresy, because they say, "People might start believing your plays," and we say, "Well, isn't that the traditional ambition of drama, the willing suspension of disbelief? The more people believe in them, the more successful we are." "No," they say, "you're passing opinions," and we say, "Yes, that's what drama is, it's by definition subjective; the writer wants to say something about the world and he has the right to say it." And they say, "Ah no, but that's not a balanced program, that's propaganda. And people might start believing your propaganda whereas our documentaries are balanced and objective. And fair." And we say, "On whose criteria?" And in the end they have to say, "Ours"—their criteria. Then they've got themselves in a hell of a mess. It used to be nice and safe. Richard Cawston, for instance, is a man who does very fair, balanced and responsible documentaries. By that is meant public-relations jobs for establishment institutions like Esso or the Royal Family.

Another thing about the BBC, it works by osmosis: you never have to be told how to behave. You kind of learn how to behave. The people who do well are the ones first of all who want to, and secondly, who learn to assimilate this feeling of responsibility. And they know how to behave. So there aren't any written rules in the BBC. You just learn what is going to be acceptable and what isn't going to be acceptable. And if you learn it well enough, people say, "He's very mature." And, "He's responsible." And, "He can be delegated authority." If you don't learn these unwritten rules and apply them, you are irresponsible and immature and not to be trusted with authority. It does work well.

G.R.L. I think what you're saying is absolutely true. It's true in the States too, even though television isn't a public broadcasting corporation—it's privately owned. I don't think the heads of the three networks meet, let's say in Idaho in a subterranean passage with representatives of the government, and decide on a policy line. They just know how to behave.

K.L. They know which side their bread's buttered on.

G.R.L. Okay, so what do you do? I mean, let's say you remade *Cathy Come Home* or made another documentary which was very radical. Where would you show it?

K.L. That's the problem. They really own it.

T.G. You know what capitalism is about. They own it.

[. . .]

K.L. This is very interesting, this kind of phony debate about the drama versus the documentary—which was how they phrased it. Everybody forgets that many years ago the BBC regulars started a program for farmers called *The Archers*, a fictional story of country folk in which factual hints, information, was peddled by the Minister of Agriculture. Now here is a classic example of drama-documentary, and the BBC was probably then in principle in favor of it. Of course, this causes much embarrassment when mentioned now, and it's very revealing in that their dispute with us was not with the form, but with what we were saying inside it, you know.

G.R.L. *Pett and Pott* by Cavalcanti could be another example. It was made in the thirties, I think, and was really government propaganda to get people to get telephones in their homes. But the film was fictional, a comedy in fact, and done very nicely in a stylized manner. But let's go on to *Kes*,[5] the feature you just made. How does social content come into that?

K.L. It's a story about a lad at school. It's very much a film about the sort of school we have here. It tries to be a film that relates the sort of school in the ghetto to the sort of work and opportunity that society provides for these kids and the kind of role that they will have in society. It's done in the form of a story of one lad; it's not got the sort of broad sweep like *Cathy*.

T.G. It's about this boy's last day at school, and the way he trains a wild hawk, but the whole thing has been informed by a number of social attitudes, and we'd be very distressed, and would think we'd failed, if people didn't take from the film more than just a little about the lad.

K.L. It's one thing to set out with these intentions, and another thing for people to come out with that in mind.

T.G. It's not overtly propagandistic, it's not full of statistics or statements about schools, only what happens within the story.

G.R.L. Do you feel that using fiction is a viable way to say what you want to say? I don't mean documentary fiction in the way *Cathy* is, but fiction in a traditional sense. I'm taking it that you're both dedicated—and correct me if I'm wrong—to social change and to trying to bring this about. Is that fair?

T.G. Yes, that's true.

K.L. It does tend to become a bit portentous.

[Loach and Garnett are laughing.]

T.G. A bit pompous.

G.R.L. Well, I said it, you didn't.

K.L. I think it's a very viable way. Sure, it's a whole tradition of writing, using a fictional form. I mean, the problem is that there are

[5] The film was shown at the 1969 London Film Festival. John Gillett describes it in the festival program as follows: "A simple telling of the story—semi-delinquent boy, oppressed by family and school and the prospects of a glum future, seeks self-fulfillment in training a kestrel—might suggest yet another working class saga. But Ken Loach, in adapting Barry Hines' story, has developed a kind of inner realism, derived from both Truffaut and TV documentary; the result is sad, funny and disturbing in turn. The real Barnsley locations and people help a lot; also the verisimilitude with which the script has caught local speech and a way of living. The influence of *The 400 Blows* may be most evident in the numerous school scenes, yet even here Loach makes his own strongly personal comment in the beautifully sustained episode when the boy (a brilliant discovery, David Bradley) describes his adventures with the kestrel."

only very narrowly defined areas in which you can actually have stories.

T.G. But I take it you weren't talking about the practical problems one has in the writing and the doing, that you were talking about if we had complete freedom to do what we wanted to do, and the money was available, what forms would we choose?

G.R.L. No. What I meant was, given the system that finally controls our TV, or given the fact of commercial distribution, I don't quite see how one can make the films one wants to make. One, just the problem of raising the money, and two, getting the film shown.

K.L. I think you're right. I think to make many of the films we want to make, you're seriously impeded right from the beginning. It's not so that you can't say anything—you hope you can set people's minds thinking along a certain course, but you're not going to dot all the i's and cross all the t's in the way that you'd like. Look, when we made *Cathy,* I think it was very much in our minds that it was sort of apolitical, and it was a conscious decision at that time. It was the only way we could get it on. I think we'd probably make a different decision now. So that was one way that the system limited our program. And in *The Big Flame* there was a big gap in the content of the film in the absence of the role of a political party. We considered putting it in, but we thought, "After we put this in, we just won't get it shown."

G.R.L. Do you know of any documentaries that make as strong a statement as you would like to see made?

K.L. Not that get shown.

T.G. Well, there are some. Kids working in London, underground films, pamphlet films, very short films that are made on shoestring budgets with bits of stock they've gotten from the labs, and by borrowing somebody's cutting room and just knocking the film out, say about a strike or whatever. Although I disagree politically with a lot of their positions, which would be another discussion, they're making very brave attempts to make political films. With direct political statements. But you're left with these two problems if you work in the underground in that way: one is that you're making bad films (and I don't think the film is the better for not having enough money spent on it); and secondly, you've got the bigger problem of who sees it. The danger you're in is that the only people seeing it are your fellow people in the underground or a few left-wing intellectuals in London, because the means of exhibition and distribution are owned by the enemy, and these are very complicated and expensive things to set up. So for as long as we can, we shall work not in the underground, but in the overground. Why should the devil have all the best resources?

G.R.L. What about Godard, for example? Are his films relevant to what you're talking about?

T.G. Well, he's just done a film for our company.[6] He's done a documentary in London, but I doubt if it will ever get shown on television. The money was put up by London Weekend, because they're a bit impressed by his name, and he got some money and they're not too impressed with the film.

G.R.L. How long is it? And what's it about?

T.G. It's around fifty minutes. It's his view of England. His peculiarly muddled view of politics, and the crazy state that he's in, too, in rejecting images and wanting sound, rather like *Le Gai Savoir*. And he's in a raw state as a man; politically, he's all over the place. I think the events in Paris in May '68[7] had a big effect on a lot of people, and I think he's been in a bit of a state ever since. It reflects well enough his own situation. I don't think it'll be shown on television, and that's what it was made for. It's not easily available, it's a very confused, esoteric piece, which is something that we've tried to set our faces against. Our ambition always, not that we've often achieved it, has been to try to do serious work and make the work available to a very large audience. In other words, to try and demonstrate that seriousness and a big audience are not mutually exclusive notions. And so we've set our faces against doing esoteric work. What he's up to, I don't know. It's difficult to say anything about him because he's not in a very coherent state.

G.R.L. This relates to a question that I'm not sure you would find relevant, and is perhaps politically naïve from your point of view. I was telling somebody about this commune I'm peripherally involved with, right? Most people that I've told about it are very interested and want to know the mechanical details, how it works. But this one person I talked to wasn't interested in any of the mechanical details. What he kept asking was, "But how does the commune hope to go about changing its members? If you don't change what's underneath, basic feelings and attitudes towards other people, towards one's self, then all you have is a slightly different mechanical way to live." The point is that one could make a parallel with the work of certain American underground film-makers—though not in any sense directly political, perhaps very radically political. I mean radical in the sense that if you show fucking on the screen for the first time, show two men kissing, or fucking, or whatever they do, or two

[6] *British Sounds.*

[7] The time of the French student "revolution."

women, then in a sense this too is radical. In a sense this is saying, "You, out there, if you have some of these feelings, desires, it's okay; you don't have to be ashamed." It could be genuinely liberating. Is this radical, political for you? Does it have any of the same kind of importance as an overt political statement?

T.G. Well, I don't know. I mean, I think that there's a tendency to a very crude pseudo-Marxist response to these things. Two responses: one is to ignore the importance or even the validity of these psychological realities that you mention, and the second is from the position of their own puritanism, to seem not to care about social and sexual taboos. But really their not caring is a sophisticated and defensive way of saying that they are horrified, because they've got these taboos, right? And so you often get a doctrinaire left-wing point of view which is crudely hostile to both these things that you've mentioned. This is dangerous, because I think both of these things insofar as they are genuinely trying to explore people's psychological realities and relationships with other individual human beings, and in doing that, trying to break down some of the prisons that they've got themselves into, can only be a gain for humanity. The problem politically, it seems to me, is that when these activities aren't a footnote to the main activity, but replace the main activity, you're in political trouble. Because they are based philosophically on an idealist view of the world; what one is really saying is that what I think, and what my psychological realities are, is primary, and the world is secondary, therefore the material world follows from my psychological reality. Whereas, in fact, my psychological reality, speaking as a materialist, follows from the material world, and how our material world is organized, and what we do with it. And the primary thing is the political task, to change that world. Only after that can men change. You and I can have beautiful things going for each other, but it won't change the world. We can change the world, and then there will be a chance that beautiful things will be going for everybody because the relationships between men that we're talking about are fundamentally economic relationships. And behind that, technological relationships, because technology predicates all social change.

FRANCE

GEORGES FRANJU

Georges Franju was born April 12, 1912, in Fougères, Brittany, France. His military service was spent in Algeria; he was demobilized in 1932. He studied theater decoration and then worked as a set decorator. With Henri Langlois, he started the Cercle du Cinéma, directed a first film, *Le Métro*, 1934, started a film magazine, *CINEMAtographe*, 1937, of which there were only two issues, and founded the Cinémathèque Française, also in 1937 (and of which Langlois is still the director).

Franju was also the executive secretary of La Fédération Internationale des Archives du Film from 1938 to 1945 and secretary-general of the Institut de Cinématographie Scientifique from 1946 to 1954.

In 1949 Franju made his first documentary (he discounts *Le Métro*); his first feature was made in 1958. He lives in Paris. (For further information, see *Franju* by Raymond Durgnat, from which most of this information was taken.)

FILMOGRAPHY*

SHORTS

1934: *Le Métro*. Directed by Georges Franju and Henri Langlois. 16mm.

1949: *Le Sang des bêtes*. Script by Georges Franju. Commentary by Jean Painlevé, spoken by Nicole Ladmiral and Georges Hubert. Photography by Marcel Fradetal. Music by Joseph Kosma (*La Mer* sung by Charles Trenet). Production: Forces et Voix de la France.

1950: *En passant par la Lorraine*. Script by Georges Franju. Commentary spoken by Georges Hubert. Photography by Marcel Fra-

* From *French Cinema Since 1946*, Vol. II, by Roy Armes; and *Franju* by Raymond Durgnat.

detal. Music by Joseph Kosma. Production: Forces et Voix de la France. 31 minutes.

1951: *Hôtel des Invalides.* Script by Georges Franju. Commentary spoken by Michel Simon and museum guides. Photography by Marcel Fradetal. Music by Maurice Jarre. Production: Forces et Voix de la France.

1952: *Le Grand Méliès.* Script by Georges Franju. Commentary spoken by Madame Marie-Georges Méliès and Lallemant. Photography by Jacques Mercanton. Music by Georges Van Parys. Art director: Henri Schmitt. Produced by Fred Orain. Production: Armor Films. 30 minutes. With Madame Marie-Georges Méliès and André Méliès. Note: the English version usually seen is dubbed with an inexact English commentary.

1953: *Monsieur et Madame Curie.* Script by Georges Franju, based on *Pierre Curie* by Madame Curie. Commentary spoken by Nicole Stéphane. Photography by Jacques Mercanton. Music: Beethoven (*Les Adieux*). Produced by Fred Orain. Production: Armor Films. 16 minutes.

1954: *Les Poussières.* Script by Georges Franju. Commentary spoken by Georges Hubert. Photography by Jacques Mercanton. Music by Jean Wiener. Produced by Fred Orain. Production: Armor Films. 22 minutes.

Navigation marchande. Scenario by Rodolphe-Maurice Arlaud. Commentary by Georges Franju, spoken by Roland Lesaffre. Photography by Henri Decaë. Music by Jean-Jacques Grünewald. Production: U.G.C.

1955: *À propos d'une rivière,* also known as *Le Saumon Atlantique and Au fil de la rivière.* Scenario by Georges Franju. Commentary spoken by Marcel and Jean-Pierre Laporte. Photography by Quinto Albicocco. Music by Henri Crolla. Sound: André Hodeir. Production: Procinex. 25 minutes.

Mon chien. Script by Georges Franju. Commentary by Jacques Prévert, spoken by Roger Pigault. Photography by Georges Delaunay and Jean Penzer. Music by Henri Crolla. Production: Procinex. 25 minutes.

1956: *Le Théâtre National Populaire.* Script by Georges Franju. Commentary spoken by Marc Cassot. Photography by Marcel Fradetal. Music by Maurice Jarre. Production: Procinex-Antinex. 28 minutes.

Sur le pont d'Avignon. Script by Georges Franju. Commentary spoken by Claude Dasset. Photography (Franscope, Eastmancolor), by Marcel Fradetal. Production: Procinex-Antinex. 11 minutes.

1957: *Notre-Dame, cathédrale de Paris.* Script by Georges Franju. Commentary by Frédéric de Towarnicki, spoken by Marcel Chaney. Photography (Franscope, Eastmancolor) by Marcel Fradetal. Music by Jean Wiener. Production: Argos-Como. 18 minutes.

1958: *La Première Nuit.* Scenario by Marianne Oswald and Remo Forlani, adapted by Georges Franju. Edited by Henri Colpi. Music by Georges Delerue. Production: Argos. 21 minutes.

FEATURES

1958: *La Tête contre les murs/The Keepers.* Screenplay by Jean-Pierre Mocky, adapted from the novel by Hervé Bazin. Dialogue by Jean-Charles Pichon. Photography by Eugen Shuftan. Art director: Louis Le Barbenchon. Edited by Suzanne Sandberg. Music by Maurice Jarre. Sound: René Sarazin. Production manager: Jean Velter. Production: Atica-Sirius-Elpenor. 98 minutes. (François Gérane), Pierre Brasseur.

1959: *Les Yeux sans visage/Eyes Without a Face/The Horror Chamber of Dr. Faustus.* Screenplay by Jean Redon, from his own novel, adapted by Georges Franju, Jean Redon, Claude Sautet, Pierre Boileau, Thomas Narcejac, with dialogue by Pierre Gascar. Photography by Eugen Shuftan. Special effects: Assola, Georges Klein. Edited by Gilbert Natot. Art director: Auguste Capelier. Music by Maurice Jarre. Sound by Antoine Archaimbaud. Produced by Jules Borkon. Production: Champs Élysées-Lux. 90 minutes. *The Horror Chamber of Dr. Faustus* is the title of a dubbed version.

1960: *Pleins feux sur l'assassin.* Screenplay by Pierre Boileau and Thomas Narcejac, with dialogue by Robert Thomas, Pierre Boileau and Thomas Narcejac. Photography by Marcel Fradetal. Decor by Roger Briaucourt. Edited by Gilbert Natot. Music by Maurice Jarre. Produced by Jules Borken. Production: Champs-Élysées. 95 minutes.

1962: *Thérèse Desqueyroux*. Screenplay by François Mauriac, Claude Mauriac and Georges Franju, from the novel by François Mauriac, with dialogue by François Mauriac. Photography by Christian Matras. Edited by Gilbert Natot. Art director: Jacques Chalvet. Music by Maurice Jarre. Sound by Jacques Labussière. Production manager: Robert Vignon. Produced by Eugène Lepicier. Production: Filmel. 109 minutes.

1963: *Judex*. Screenplay by Jacques Champreux and Francis Lacassin, based on the original film by Arthur Bernède and Louis Feuillade. Photography by Marcel Fradetal. Edited by Gilbert Natot. Art director: Gilbert Natot. Music by Maurice Jarre. Costumes by Christiane Courcelles. Sound by Jean Labussière. Production manager: Jean Maumy. Production: Comptoir Français du Film (Paris)/ Filmes (Rome). 95 minutes.

1964: *Thomas l'imposteur/Thomas the Impostor*. Screenplay by Jean Cocteau, Michel Worms, Georges Franju, based on the novel by Jean Cocteau, with dialogue by Jean Cocteau and Raphael Cluzel. Photography by Marcel Fradetal. Edited by Gilbert Natot. Art direction: Claude Pignot. Music by Georges Auric. Sound by André Hervé, Raymond Gaugier. Production manager: Georges Casati. Produced by Eugène Lepicier. Production: Filmel. 93 minutes.

1965: *Les Rideaux blancs* (episode for a planned TV feature, *L'Instant de la paix*). Script and dialogue: Marguerite Duras. Photography by Marcel Fradetal. Edited by Geneviève Winding. Music by Georges Delerue. Production: Régie Française de Cinéma.

December 18, 1969, in Georges Franju's apartment in Paris.[1]

G. Roy Levin: How did you start making films?

Georges Franju: I wanted to make a film about slaughterhouses and I made one. It was my first film, *Le Sang des bêtes,* made in 1949. It was a professional film, about the slaughterhouses of Paris. There was an amateur film that I made before that with Langlois,[2] but that doesn't count. It doesn't mean anything to me.

G.R.L. But when you made your first film you knew how to use a camera?

G.F. No. I didn't know anything at all. I wanted to investigate a particular subject; I didn't want to become a film-maker. It was not only the slaughterhouses of Paris that interested me, but also the surroundings, which make a beautiful setting. Or, to put it another way, I didn't simply make a document, but a documentary. That is, I went far beyond the framework of a document, which was the killing of animals, to show the surroundings, the wastelands around the canal, around the Porte de Vanves, which no longer exist because of new construction. The Porte de Vanves, the location of the slaughterhouses for horses, is a wasteland. That's why I made the film, because they all go together. If it had been only the slaughterhouses, I wouldn't have made the film.

G.R.L. Were you always conscious of the social content of films?

G.F. I was a student set designer; then came the Cinémathèque Française, then I worked with Jean Painlevé at the Institut de Cinématographie Scientifique, and it was during the course of my work at the Institut that I decided I wanted to make *Le Sang des bêtes.* Then I got involved and continued. But I never wanted to be a film-maker at all, I wanted to make certain films. These are people who say, "I want to be a film-maker," but when you ask them, "What films?" they don't know. It's a pity.

G.R.L. In the documentaries you've made, do you do the shooting yourself?

G.F. No, no, never. I make professional films. I've always had a good sized crew, otherwise I wouldn't make films. In my opinion, making films without a crew is amateur film-making. When I made *Le Sang des bêtes,* I had a crew of five—and that was my first film. That was twenty years ago; now times have changed, which is prob-

1 The interview was conducted in French and was translated by the interviewer.
2 Henri Langlois, director of the Cinémathèque Française since 1937.

ably why film has become shoddy. I don't see any documentaries, do you? They're horrible.

G.R.L. Well . . . Chris Marker?

G.F. Chris Marker! Chris Marker isn't young any more; he's been making documentaries for a long time. —Listen to me. I was on the jury at the Festival of Tours, and saw sixty or eighty films, and I didn't see one documentary. I saw art films. But what are "art films?" It's ridiculous.

G.R.L. By "art films," do you mean films about painting or painters?

G.F. About painting, or made in an aesthetic manner, purely aesthetic with absolutely no content but great charm. They're things people did in 1928 and are being rediscovered now. People are rediscovering what I call "perfume photography." There's lots of perfume photography now. If someone did your portrait, they'd put a red filter in front of the camera, which would give a red tinge to your face; no one could say why, but that's the way it is. That's what today is called an "art film." Art films are made with photographic tricks and without any content. So, if you're talking to me about documentaries, I tell you I haven't seen any.

The English are the only ones making them any longer. That's because of their social sense, the respect they have for documents. They don't use tricks. But at Tours I didn't see anything but photographic tricks. Now you have films made up entirely of hop! hop! hop! And taken up by television besides. They do a lot of that on television; it's exasperating, it doesn't mean a thing—pointless photographic tricks. None of it has anything to do with what I call "documentary of content." It ought to have something inside. What's "dynamic photography?" One day someone said to me, "Do you like dynamic photography?" And I said, "What's dynamic photography?" Well, for example, if you're there opposite me, I'm going to shove these damn pencils in front of your face to make a blue shadow—that's "dynamic photography!" I call "dynamic photography" photography with dynamic content, where there's something inside. But trick photography, that's bullshit, it's amateur photography. It's amateurs who started all these tricks which made a splash and came along with art films. At first art films were about painting, painters, the impressionists, the play of light, and afterward the photography itself became impressionistic.

G.R.L. They're not exactly young, but do you know Leacock, Pennebaker, the Maysles brothers?

G.F. No, I don't know them. It's a long time, ten years, since I've made any documentaries.

G.R.L. The style of their films is generally called cinéma-vérité, and—

G.F. Cinéma-vérité! If that's where you set up the camera and go away, then it's the moment when you bug off that everything is marvelous. I know about aiming a camera in the street and leaving it and coming back the next day. You have to at least follow the people. There isn't any cinéma-vérité. It's necessarily a lie, from the moment the director intervenes—or it isn't cinema at all.

I was a member of a jury at a film festival and I saw a documentary, and I was told, "all the characters in the film are drugged." Now, I know mental hospitals and drug addicts (I did a film on mental hospitals, *La Tête contre les murs*). I refused to give the prize to this famous film, because those people were certainly not addicts. Addicts are bad actors, and when the drug addict is no longer drugged, he breaks everything. It was obvious, and afterward I learned that they were actors. Shit!

G.R.L. Do you know the title?

G.F. *The Connection*. Shit!

G.R.L. Who said they were—

G.F. Drugged? Everyone, and all the publicity, otherwise I wouldn't talk about it.

G.R.L. It was a play.

G.F. Of course! But no one said that at the Locarno Festival. I was a jury member, and when they told me that, I told them they were giving me a lot of crap. And I was the only one to perceive it. It's part of a false cinéma-vérité. Nothing happens in cinéma-vérité, or it happens by a miracle when you're not there. Or else, as with Rouch, if it's not directed, the conditions for filming are set up—and it's no longer cinéma-vérité.

G.R.L. When television presents news events and documentaries, they pretend to objectivity.

G.F. For me, television is non-existent, it's sinister.

G.R.L. Why is that?

G.F. Because you don't see anything interesting or passionate.

G.R.L. Is that only since the May Revolution?

G.F. No. I've only had a television since then, and we watch it very little. The material on television drags, it isn't direct, it's contrived. Look, documentaries depend so damn much on the talent of the director. If Joris Ivens has made the most beautiful documentaries that anyone has ever seen, that's because the films are composed, worked out, and they have an air of truth. Sure the documentary part is true, but all around the documentary sections there's an interpretation. And then you can't talk about cinéma-vérité. I don't know what's meant by the term. Like when people talk of the "New Wave," what's that supposed to mean? There are always "waves" —every five or ten years.

G.R.L. Then for you, a documentary is clearly not objective.

G.F. First of all there's a necessity imposed by a documentary. I'm talking about a sponsored documentary, which is very important, because that marks the boundaries of a very limited subject. Then, either you're an ass and everything gets screwed up, or you have a certain amount of talent and you illuminate the subject, go beyond the subject—and that's documentary. It's as useful to have a precise question to answer in a documentary as it is for a fresco painter to have a wall—if there's no wall, what the hell is he going to do with his fresco? Documentary is to the cinema what the poster is to painting. A poster has a clear, precise question to resolve, which is why there are rarely good posters. The narrower the question, the better your chances of going beyond it. In *En passant par la Lorraine* if I hadn't noticed that the factories and steelworks of Hagondange[3] were in the middle of wheat fields, I would never have made the film.

Also, there's a question of conditioning, not so much to condition the audience, but to condition oneself. I've noticed that all the documents—and I'm speaking precisely of documentaries—that I've done have a relationship to subjects I'm afraid of. If I made *Le Sang des bêtes,* it's because I never saw that; if I made *Hôtel des Invalides,* it's because I'm anti-military. If I made *Notre-Dame de Paris,* it's because I'm anti-clerical and heights make me dizzy, and if I made *la Lorraine,* it's because I'm afraid of fire, and I condition myself and stay in the fire. Since I'm afraid, then that makes others afraid, obviously. It's a way of sensitizing oneself by violence, and in doing violence. And at that moment comes the result —but it doesn't have anything to do with truth, not a thing to do with it. There's *a* truth, your truth, the film-maker's truth. It's the only possible truth. There aren't any others. For me, the difference between a documentary and a fiction film is the same thing; if I make one or the other, I've conditioned myself, otherwise I wouldn't make the film.

G.R.L. You don't see any difference between a documentary and a fiction film?

G.F. There isn't any. There isn't any difference between *Hôtel des Invalides* and *Thomas l'Imposteur*. There's no difference between *Le Sang des bêtes* and *La Tête contre les murs,* which is a film that takes place in a mental institution. You'd think there were only

[3] In Lorraine, in the northeast of France.

mental patients in the film, but there isn't one—you don't have the right to use mental patients in a film. They're actors, but you believe them. During the film Aznavour has an epileptic fit; a psychiatrist, a specialist in epilepsy who didn't know anything about music halls,[4] thought Aznavour was epileptic; but an epileptic would never have been capable of doing that; he would have broken everything. That's a certain form of cinéma-vérité or realistic documentary cinema. That's realism. You must re-create reality because reality runs away; reality denies reality. You must first interpret it, or re-create it.

G.R.L. There's a rather famous definition of documentary by Grierson which says that it's the "creative treatment of actuality."

G.F. That's right, obviously. Right, a creative interpretation of actuality.

G.R.L. But isn't there a difference between the slaughterhouses in *Le Sang des bêtes*, which are real, which exist, and treating them in an imaginative way, and treating a fiction that doesn't exist?

G.F. But I do the opposite. When I make a documentary, I try to give the realism an artificial aspect, which is what I did do in *Le Sang des bêtes*. For example, at one point I waited several days, came back over a period of several weeks to get a barge going through a wasteland, because I think that a barge which crosses a wasteland is much more of a barge than a barge which goes over the water. It's therefore a very artificial way of seeing, because a barge is made to go on the water. But I maintain that a barge that cuts a wasteland in half without being able to see the water is much more beautiful, more of a barge than a barge.

If you want to make an object stand out, there are two methods. The surrealist solution is to displace the object by putting it in a place where it wouldn't normally be found, where it refinds its quality as object by being unclassed. For example, if you put a piano in the middle of the street, it's much more beautiful.

The other way to make an object stand out is to strip it, deprive it of all ornamentation—which is more difficult. It's generally what one does in documentary. It's what I do in documentary. It's the most difficult solution, and difficult to use. I did it in three or four films. When I made *Le Sang des bêtes* there was a man with a Louis Quinze table in front of him; he was surrounded by a group of men. I had everyone leave, and I left my man all alone in front of his Louis Quinze table. That way, it was right; otherwise,

[4] Singers in France perform in music halls—a rough equivalent to what our vaudeville was in America. Aznavour, besides being an actor, is a well-known French singer and performs in music halls.

it wouldn't have meant anything. With all the other men, you wouldn't have seen anything. That wasn't by displacement, but by stripping, deprivation.

There are two systems, and I know them well because I think I was the only one to apply them to the cinema. But they're only systems—and therefore artificial.

G.R.L. To take an obvious example, if there's a demonstration, a riot, do you think it's worth the trouble to film it?

G.F. And do what with it?

G.R.L. Let people know what's happening, for example.

G.F. Oh, that! There are reporters for that. I'm not a reporter—it doesn't interest me. There are news photographers who do a damn good job at that sort of thing—and they've gotten their heads cracked open doing it, and they do a better job of it than film-makers.

Listen. We were talking about art films before. Everyone who makes these films with artistic pretensions uses dumb tricks—cutting heads in four as they did in 1925. Listen. There's a guy who's supposedly a TV marvel, Jean Christophe Averty. Now he did a show with Sylvie Vartan, whom I like. But I never saw her in that show. I saw an eye, a lock of hair, or, if I did see her, I saw five of her at one time. It's not exactly hilarious. The old bastards of the French avant-garde did that kind of thing. Méliès[5] used tricks, making people appear and disappear. Cutting heads in four—Fernand Léger did that in *Le Ballet mécanique*. Now they call that the avant-garde!

G.R.L. Do you know any underground films? At least that's what they're often called in America.

G.F. You know, it's been a long time. . . . Once, when I saw *La Bête humaine*, I said to Langlois, "That, my friend, is fantastic. It's been a very long time since I've seen a film without any tricks, straightforward and magnificent." Why? Because it was simple. But no one wanted to do that; they wanted to use worn-out tricks instead. And now it's becoming absolutely monstrous. The way television does things makes me laugh.

I did a show for television on the House of Culture of Grenoble, and the cameraman was a guy who was used to doing variety shows. At one point I had to discuss something with the boss of the House of Culture, and I told the cameraman to shoot this scene. Well, when I saw the rushes, that section was unusable because he was singing with the camera—ta, ta, ta, ta. Ah, you're

[5] Georges Méliès, 1861–1938; a pioneer of the French cinema and one of the first to use camera tricks, his films are full of fantasy.

laughing. The one time I wasn't there, that's what he did. Shit! That's television! Everything's like that on television. They say it's young, spirited—bullshit! that's what it is, bullshit! And the zoom! I use the zoom, but I use it when I can't do otherwise.

G.R.L. Have you had trouble finding money to make your films?

G.F. They were all sponsored.

G.R.L. Even *Le Sang des bêtes?*

G.F. No, that was the only one that wasn't. *M. et Mme. Curie* was for a government agency. *Les Poussières* was a sponsored film, and an important one. The National Institute of Security asked me to make a film for workers to show them the dangers of dust—that's why I say it's important to have a very precise subject—to show workers the dangers of not using a protective mask. They said, "That will bore the hell out of him to make a film like that." But just the opposite. I was passionate about the idea. I read all about it and I said, "It's a fantastic subject. I'm going to show terrifying things, terrifying." And that's what I did—showed terrifying things. If you say to the workers, "It's good to wear masks," you get nowhere. First, they don't wear them because they're too uncomfortable, they can't breathe, they croak under those masks. Okay. I filmed in mines, I filmed the guys who make porcelain and gulp down silica—it's monstrous. These guys are wiped out, wiped out in ten years doing that. I was in a region called "the factories of death" that Social Security doesn't even want to recognize—and I was going to make an optimistic film to say everything was fine! That was the way they saw it. The director of the Institute of Security had said to me, "You understand, dust is the housewife's problem." Why did he come to me if it was to show a housewife sweeping—that doesn't interest anyone. If she wants to shake out rugs, what the fuck has that got to do with me? That doesn't kill anyone. So I begin the film on dust from the sun and end with the atomic bomb. You see, starting with the broom I speak about all the kinds of dust, from the stars, the sun, the atomic bomb—which is the worst. I can't disassociate the notion of security from the notion of danger.

Therefore it's a question of saying first off that dust is dangerous. No one ever makes a film for something that's going well; no one ever puts out propaganda for a product that's selling well; no one ever publicizes a drink or a car that is selling well—never. From the moment you put out propaganda or publicity, then it's not going too well. I understood that very clearly—but it wasn't what they wanted.

G.R.L. Was everyone happy with the film?

G.F. It gets shown everywhere, because it's very, very scary. In effect, when workers see it, they say, "Hey! it's terrible not to wear a mask." It has to be said that they use masks now, and it led to the manufacture of more modern masks, more comfortable than the crap they had before.

G.R.L. Have you ever had any trouble with the government?

G.F. No. But I have with the newspapers, with *Le Figaro*.[6] I haven't had trouble with the government, because there was a good guy in the Foreign Affairs Office—Henri Claudel, the son of Paul Claudel. He directed the film section, and we both agreed that we would make a film against war.[7] When the film was finished, there was an exchange of telegrams between the Minister for the Direction General of Cultural Relations and the Director of the Ministry of National Defense. In this exchange of telegrams, the Minister of National Defense reproached the Minister of Foreign Affairs for having encouraged an anti-war film, and the Minister of Foreign Affairs answered—always by telegram—"The Director General of Cultural Relations is against war." That was perfect.

G.R.L. That's a good trick, to make an anti-war film with government money.

G.F. Absolutely. The best way. Look, to make an anti-Nazi film, that's too easy—even a Vietnam film. What's difficult is to make an anti-militarist film, but against the French army.

G.R.L. When you were talking about the film *Les Poussières*, you said with a big smile, "I'm going to show terrifying things." Why—

G.F. When you see a guy making porcelain, it's really terrifying. I'll be exact: violence will always be violence, but violence is not an end, it's a weapon which sensitizes the spectator and which lets him see what's lyric or poetic beyond or above the violence, or what's tender in the reality. Violence, for me, is a means, like blasphemy for Buñuel. Let's take *Les Poussières*. There's nothing more beautiful than porcelain from Limoges, the kind that's white, transparent. Now, at one point we see this guy working on one of these porcelain plates. He takes the plate, looks at it to make sure there are no particles, specks—to make sure it's impeccably white. The commentary talks about the beauty and the transparency of the porcelain, and there's this lovely image on the screen. Then the commentary says, "He may feel perfectly well . . ." and at the same time we see this guy holding his plate, then just the guy, then the plate, then his hand which is behind the plate, and then we

[6] A conservative Parisian daily.
[7] *Hôtel des Invalides*.

see him again, happy about a job well done. But then we get to his lungs, and though he may feel perfectly well, silicosis is there, detected by X rays—and this guy is going to croak. That's how I did the film—otherwise it wouldn't be interesting. The guy I filmed had silicosis. The result was something that goes beyond documentary.

G.R.L. For you, then, a good documentary is one that goes beyond mere realism?

G.F. It has to, otherwise it doesn't mean anything.

G.R.L. Do you think documentaries can help to change things?

G.F. Not at all. You don't change anything with films. Films never changed anything. Listen. I saw the events of May here, and it's revolting for cops to shoot at people. But when you see cops, whom I detest (and I've good reason to detest them), standing there for an hour and a half and getting spat on, let me tell you it's not exactly hilarious. Like a guy I know said, "I knew the Germans well, and I don't like them, and with good reason, but when I think that people say CRS—SS![8] If you had said that to a German in the SS, you would have been killed on the spot."

So what's cinéma-vérité? You should show all of that, but it's nevertheless goddamned infuriating not to move for an hour and a half and have someone spit in your face. You asked before if I was interested in filming things like that. But *how?* You can always show cops clubbing people, but all the newspapers do that. Why get angry at the cops? They're not the problem. If they're told to hit, they hit; if they're not told to hit, they don't hit—and that gets on their nerves, which is understandable.

G.R.L. In the U.S. television isn't censored, but there's a kind of self-censorship: the networks know what they can and can't show. But in Chicago, when the cops turned on the press, they got angry, and they showed things on television that they don't usually show.

G.F. That's a good thing.

G.R.L. It was reality—cinéma-vérité. And at least a lot of people who don't believe this kind of thing happens could see—

G.F. Right. But the really ugly things go on inside the police stations. That's what's disgusting, not what happens in the street. That's what has to be shown, but how are you going to show that? Guys who are mutilated when they come out of a police station, it's dramatic what's happened—especially during the Algerian War.

G.R.L. Have you ever thought of making a film about the May Revolution?

[8] Compagnie Républicaine de Sécurité, the national French police force used only on special occasions, as for special riot control; the SS was the elite Nazi corps during the war. The French police are being called SS men.

G.F. No, not at all.

G.R.L. It's not possible?

G.F. It doesn't interest me. I don't believe in it, I don't believe in what happened during the month of May—not a bit. When people said to me, "You'll see, nothing will be like it was before," they were right—it's not like it was before, it's worse. No doubt about that.

G.R.L. Don't you believe in the sincerity of the people involved?

G.F. But it's not a question of sincerity, it's a question of effectiveness. A revolution where there isn't a single shot fired isn't a revolution. It's a joke. And at the level of film, it's a country fair. Think about all those guys playing the fool, carrying banners, each with his pet theory on the cinema, and each one taking more than his share: it's clear what came out of it—nothing. Shit! You see guys proclaiming social plans when they're the very ones loaded with money. It's laughable. Believe me, they're guys bored shitless with life. People don't show their sincerity that way. And these fights and disputes between the leftists and the Communists—shit! How's it going to work? I understand damn well why the workers laugh. Students try to win over the workers, but there's no reason for the workers to march with the students. It's not their game, it's not the same problem.

G.R.L. In *Le Joli Mai*, Marker says something like, "As long as there are unhappy people, no one is happy; as long as there are prisoners, no one is free." Perhaps the students see the condition of the workers as—

G.F. But they don't give a fuck about the workers. In the last analysis there's something that's always existed, the class struggle. A student isn't from the working class; there's no reason they should work together—different classes, different problems. There's one thing that interests the workers, their wages, and they're right. I don't give a fuck about universities either, they bore the shit out of me. And a worker cares even less than I do. Shit! You know, I have a holy horror of authority, and I always have. But it seems to me that a professor is more competent than a student—it's indisputable. Listen, at one point a joke was going around from the medical school. The students said the professors didn't matter any longer, and the dean even less. It was the students who counted, and some suggested counting in the hospital attendants, and someone else said, "A mental hospital isn't a joke—perhaps we should count in the patients"—and there were some who said, "Yes!" That's great! Have the patients help run the hospital! That's funny. But finally, you'll have to admit that it's not funny. I know them too well—they're kids' games. So it's the fourteenth of July[9] and they're going to a demonstration. What the hell for? I never believed in the students. I always thought Cohn-Bendit was a maverick, and all those kids who took part in it. So I never took it seriously, never. I was in London when it started. I don't know if you know, but it started at the Cinémathèque, and it was a god-awful joke.

G.R.L. At least in the United States I think students will have an influence on—

G.F. I don't know. I'm not American. I don't know about these things in foreign countries. In any case, here there's absolutely no possibility of any union between the workers, who were behind the gates at the Renault factory and who wanted to get out, and the students, who were outside.

G.R.L. When you shoot a feature, you have a script beforehand. Is it the same when you shoot a documentary?

G.F. Always.

G.R.L. Do things change during the shooting?

G.F. Never. Or almost never—I don't have any reason to change.

G.R.L. And when you edit the film, is that also preplanned?

G.F. That's the way I do it.

G.R.L. Even the sound?

G.F. Of course, since the sound follows the picture. I rarely change things.

G.R.L. Do you know the English documentaries of the thirties, and from during the war?

G.F. Yes, yes.

G.R.L. What do you think of them?

G.F. They were good. The English school of documentary was very important. It was a "new wave," the avant-garde.

G.R.L. But often they're very straight, so to speak, not at all poetic.

G.F. The young Flahertys, Griersons, Cavalcantis, they were very good. The G.P.O. school—the Post Office school—was very good. But otherwise, damn boring—the English are often god-damned boring. But the time of Grierson and the G.P.O., that was very good.

G.R.L. You said before that you don't see many contemporary documentaries. Why is that?

G.F. Because they bore the shit out of me. Besides, they don't show them in many places; you have to go to festivals, like Tours, to see documentaries.

[9] Bastille Day, which commemorates the destruction of the Bastille during the French Revolution (1789).

G.R.L. What do you think of Flaherty, and let's say, *Nanook?*

G.F. *Nanook* is a fiction, it's not a documentary.

G.R.L. But it's called a documentary.

G.F. That's because you see the life of the Eskimos, but it isn't a documentary, it's romanticized. But finally it's very beautiful.

G.R.L. Is *Le Sang des bêtes* your favorite film?

G.F. No. *Hôtel des Invalides.*

G.R.L. Because of the subject?

G.F. Sure. And because of the scope, and because it's obvious that I could never do it in a feature. In a feature it would necessarily be a fiction, and it wouldn't work the same way. As a documentary, you can't attack it; it's respectable because it's a documentary. I didn't make it up, not any of it.

G.R.L. Do you know of any anti-militarist fiction films that you think are successful?

G.F. I haven't seen any.

G.R.L. Do you know this book? *Défense du court métrage français?*[10]

G.F. No, not at all.

G.R.L. It says here on page 103, ". . . Franju knows how to endow reality with an aspect of the illogical, the irrational, the fantastic." And here he quotes you, "In fiction, the fantastic is usually obtained by giving to that which is artificial . . ."

G.F. ". . . an aspect of what's natural."

G.R.L. Bravo.

G.F. And in a documentary, it's the opposite. It's what I was saying before: you endow what's natural with an aspect of the artificial. It's what I was saying before in reference to the barge, because it's a documentary. And when I make a fiction film, I try to make it as real as possible. A studio is full of artificiality, which annoys the hell out of me, and this is why I prefer to shoot in a real setting when I make a fiction film.

G.R.L. Then do you like to be in a studio when you shoot a documentary?

G.F. Not at all. But I find that the aesthetic of a document comes from the artificial aspect of the document. I'm speaking of the lighting, for example. Some of the skies that I waited for in *Le Sang des bêtes* almost seem to be studio skies. One has the feeling that they're very composed, and for them to be composed, they have to be recomposed. It has to be realistic, if you like; it has to be more beautiful than realism, and therefore it has to be composed.

G.R.L. It's to give it another sense . . .

G.F. That's it, to give it another sense. A barge that is more of a

[10] By François Porcile.

barge than a barge that goes on the water. In any case, it's very surprising.

G.R.L. Would you like to make more documentaries?

G.F. Oh, no.

G.R.L. Why not?

G.F. I find fiction films more satisfying.

JEAN ROUCH

Jean Rouch was born May 31, 1917, in Paris. He obtained a Doctor of Arts, became a civil engineer and then became an ethnographer. He presently works from the Musée de l'Homme in Paris for the National Scientific Research Center, as an ethnographer. Also an explorer, he made the first descent of the Niger by dugout canoe in 1946–47.

Rouch began to make films in Africa as a result of his ethnographic studies. Later, he also began to make documentary films in France, and at times has turned to fiction. With *Chronique d'un été* he became one of the first film-makers to be associated with the term "cinéma-vérité." A number of his films have won prizes at various festivals.

FILMOGRAPHY*

1946: *Chasse à l'hippopotame.*

1947: *Au pays des mages noirs.*

1948–49: *Initiation à la danse des Possédés; Hombori; Les Magiciens de Wanzerbé; La Circoncision.*

1950–51: *Bataille sur le grand fleuve; Cimetière dans la falaise; Les Hommes qui font la pluie; Les Gens du mil.*

1955: *Les Fils de l'eau* (feature-length compilation of the last five films); *Les Maîtres fous.*

1955–65: *Mammy Water.*

1957: *Moro Naba.*

* From *French Cinema Since 1946*, Vol. II, by Roy Armes.

1957–65: *La Goumbe des jeunes noceurs.*

1958: *Moi un noir* (feature). Production: Les Films de la Pléiade. Photographer: Jean Rouch.

1958–65: *La Chasse au lion à l'arc* (feature-length documentary). Production: Les Films de la Pléiade. Photography: Jean Rouch. Editors: José Malterossa and Jan Hoenig.

1958–67: *Jaguar* (feature-length documentary). Production: Les Films de la Pléiade. Photography: Jean Rouch.

1960: *Hampi.*

1960–64: *La Punition* (feature). Production: Les Films de la Pléiade. Photography: Michel Brault, Roger Morillère, Georges Dufaux, Music: Bach. Editor: Annie Tresgot.

1961: *La Pyramide humaine* (feature). Production: Les Films de la Pléiade. Photography: Jean Rouch.

Chronique d'un été (feature). Production: Argos Films. Directed with Edgar Morin. Photography: Roger Morillère, Raoul Coutard, Jean-Jacques Tarbès, Michel Brault. Editors: Jean Ravel, Nina Baratier, Françoise Colin.

1962: *Urbanisme africain; Le Mil; Les Pêcheurs du Niger; Abidjan, port de pêche.*

1962–63: *Le Palmier à l'huile; Les Cocotiers.*

1963: *Monsieur Albert Prophète.* Production: Argos Films. Directed with Jean Ravel.

Rose et Landry. Production: National Film Board of Canada. Photography: Georges Dufaux. Music: Maurice Blackburn. Editor: Jacques Godbout.

1964: *Véronique et Marie-France* (sketch in *La Fleur de l'âge ou les adolescentes;* also known as *Les Veuves de quinze ans*). Production: Les Films de la Pléiade.

Gare du nord (sketch in *Paris vu par . . .*). Production: Les Films du Losange (Barbet Schroeder). Photography: Étienne Becker. Editor: Jacqueline Raynal.

December 17, 1969, in the dining room at the Musée de l'Homme in Paris.[1]

G. ROY LEVIN: Let me begin by asking why you began to make films. Was it because you really liked films?

JEAN ROUCH: No. There are two reasons. Before the war, when I was a student in a school for engineers, I used to go to the Cinémathèque Française, which was run by Henri Langlois. So I was passionately interested in film even when I was a student. The second reason is that I studied ethnology. I became a film-maker because I discovered that you have to have a camera to do research. So right after the war I bought an old 16mm. Bell & Howell, and I was very lucky, because it was then that 16mm. first started to be used professionally.

The film revolution in the area that interests me was the one that produced a kind of tool which made the observation of man's movements possible. That was the beginning. Then the illusionists came along and created the fiction film. But the two men who played an essential role [in the non-fiction film revolution] were Robert Flaherty and Dziga Vertov[2]; and both tried to use film to observe the world around them. The second essential revolution took place when the film industry had become very expensive—which was during the war of '39–'45. And what it did was to make it possible for newsreel cameramen at the front to use light, portable 16mm. equipment that cost four times less than usual.

I was very lucky because 16mm. film hardly existed when I began in films—everything had to be invented. And when you have to invent everything, you're stimulated and you try to find solutions. There weren't any 16mm. splicers—I had to splice, to cement by hand. There weren't any viewers—so you had to use a projector and you had to become a projectionist. There wasn't even any way to have copies made. The first film I made, *Au pays des mages noirs,* had to be blown up to 35mm., otherwise you couldn't add sound—there was no way to put sound on 16mm.

Anyway, in terms of my start, the last piece of good luck I had was when I made my first films about Nigeria. I left with an amateur cameraman's manual, and I had the good luck to lose my tripod at the end of a week, and was forced to work without a tripod. That was in 1945, and to work without a tripod was absolutely forbidden!

[1] The interview was conducted in French and was translated by the interviewer.
[2] V. Historical Outline, pp. 8–9.

But I realized that it really wasn't important. So again I had great luck. If you like, that was the beginning.

G.R.L. Accidents, happy accidents.

[. . .]

J.R. I did a series of short films in the beginning, and with an English producer we blew them up to 35mm. under the title of *Les Fils de l'eau*. Here again I was lucky. I thought that the editor was superfluous, like the cameraman, but I realized that I was wrong, because I edited the film with Suzanne Baron, who was Jacques Tati's editor and is now Louis Malle's editor. Suzanne, a wonderful girl, made me realize that what I saw in the film wasn't necessarily what she saw, and that things that I didn't see, she perhaps did see. So I understood the necessity of having a first viewer—or rather a second viewer, because the first viewer is myself looking through the viewfinder and the second viewer is the editor who sees what is shown to him (with the one condition that he isn't there for the shooting).

G.R.L. But you cut your films the way you want them cut?

J.R. Yes. But I cut with an editor at my side, and he tells me what he sees, and if he doesn't see something, then what I wanted to put in isn't there, and if he sees something that I don't, then I have to take that into account—which I find invaluable. But I find the cameraman prehistoric, with no need to exist.

G.R.L. Meaning you do your own shooting?

J.R. Yes—always. And every time I've had to use a cameraman, however good he might have been, I've always had regrets. I admire the things he's done, things that I could never have done; but the film has never been the way I would have made it, awkwardly, if you like, if I had been on the camera.

G.R.L. But in *Chronique d'un été* you couldn't have shot everything yourself.

J.R. No, because there I was faced with a very difficult problem, which was synchronized sound. We were in the middle of experimenting with the material and I didn't know anything about it. I profited from the experience of my friends at the [Canadian] National Film Board—Michel Brault had already done it at least two years before that. And we had Eclair manufacture the first camera we used for that [—for synch-sound filming].

G.R.L. When you go to Africa to make a film, for example, do you make a distinction between yourself as ethnographer and yourself as film-maker?

J.R. No. It's all part of my life. And I look on the human sciences as poetic sciences in which there is no objectivity, and I see film as being not objective, and cinéma-vérité as a cinema of lies that depends on the art of telling yourself lies. If you're a good storyteller, then the lie is more true than the reality, and if you're a bad storyteller, the truth is worse than the half lie.

G.R.L. There are film-makers in the United States who make what are called cinéma-vérité films, and some of them feel that this is the only way to tell the truth, because it's objective.

J.R. That's false. Essentially you have to make a choice: if I look at you, I look here and there; what's behind me is perhaps important because of the woman making noise, and perhaps my attention will be drawn to her, and from the moment that I've chosen to look in one direction or another, I've made a choice—which is a subjective process. All editing is subjective. In brief, I'm one of the people responsible for this phrase [cinéma-vérité] and it's really in homage to Dziga Vertov, who completely invented the kind of film we do today. It was a cinema of lies, but he believed simply—and I agree with him—that the camera eye is more perspicacious and more accurate than the human eye. The camera eye has an infallible memory, and the film-maker's eye is a multiple one, divided.

[. . .]

The one thing I want to say about cinéma-vérité is that it would be better to call it cinema-sincerity, if you like. That is, that you ask the audience to have confidence in the evidence, to say to the audience, "This is what I saw. I didn't fake it, this is what happened. I didn't pay anyone to fight, I didn't change anyone's behavior. I looked at what happened with my subjective eye and this is what I believe took place."

G.R.L. But there are problems. As I'm sure you well know, you can take the same exact footage and make different films from it that will say absolutely different things.

J.R. Right. That's the editing. But personally, when I make a film I edit in the camera. I see the film in my viewfinder—which is why I want to be my own cameraman. The editing is creating the form, but I've never made a film where the editing didn't conform to what I wanted to do. It's a question of honesty. From the moment that a documentary film-maker changes the sense of the film he wanted to make in the editing, it's bad, it's false for me. And generally bad and false at the same time.

G.R.L. Do you think it's better when the film-maker lets the audience know his bias, doesn't pretend to objectivity?

J.R. Of course. That's why a lot of my films are suggestive. For example, the film that I made about lion hunting[3] is much less the lion hunt as it actually exists than myself in face of this

[3] Presumably *La Chasse au lion à l'arc*, 1958–65.

phenomenon. That's the reason that the commentary is very important. I've wanted to, but haven't finished researching this—how to make films without a commentary, which is almost impossible, precisely because of this subjective outlook.

You could say that a particular shot, let's say of a crowd in the streets of Paris, is significant in itself. But it's not true; it's dependent on the context, and therefore there is something to say. The solution is to do what I'm doing now, the fiction film, if you like. This is, invent a story which is also in great part improvised but which is meant to illustrate an aspect of something. Say to people, for example, "You're going to be such a character, a plausible character, and you're going to act as if you were that plausible character in a given situtïon," which is to my mind a psychodrama, if you like, and one of the ways to rediscover the truth. To do that I've made many films, fiction films in fact, on real subjects, and which are much more real than I myself would have been able to make. I did a film called *Jaguar* about migrant laborers who work in West Africa, in Ghana, and at the same time I did a sociological, ethnographic investigation. Well, the only objective document is the film, which is, however, a fiction film, acted by people playing plausible roles. Why? Because they show what an investigation would never show, that is, the context: how it happened, where it happened, the relationships between people, their gestures, their behavior, their speech, etc.

Presently I'm attempting to go in that direction, and above all to create reality by starting from fiction—which is essential for me. That is, I'm making films now like the one I'm finishing little by little. I call it *Parisian Anthropology*. It's the opposite of what I usually do: there are two African anthropologists who discover the tribe of Parisians and the way we live. Actually, I'm the one who provokes it: I ask people I know to come here, to act like anthropologists and to discover the world which surrounds them. And at that moment you understand that by shooting in this way . . . let's call it direct-cinema, meaning that I have a camera and a sound man and we shoot very quickly, and the the presence of the camera is a kind of passport that opens all doors and makes every kind of scandal possible. That is, the quest itself for reality. And I think that that's a method that television should use at this time. Not by means of the hidden camera, of *Candid Eye*[4] or that series, but by means of a much more important kind of provocation—to tell a story with someone who not only feels himself to be a witness, but who is profoundly implicated in it.

[4] Presumably the reference is to the television show *Candid Camera.*

G.R.L. Aren't you concerned that the presence of the camera will influence people's actions? In effect, deform—

J.R. Yes, the camera deforms, but not from the moment that it becomes an accomplice. At that point it has the possibility of doing something I couldn't do if the camera wasn't there: it becomes a kind of psychoanalytic stimulant which lets people do things they wouldn't otherwise do.

For example, while shooting *Chronique d'un été*, I had a big discussion with Edgar Morin[5] about this subject, because I asked Marceline,[6] who had been in a German concentration camp, to talk about her memories of being deported—while she walked on a street in Paris. It's false—no one walks along talking out loud. But I suddenly discovered that this released a series of confessions that Marceline had never made during a direct, face-to-face interview, simply because she was suddenly in a totally different element. So perhaps this was a constraining element in some way, and deforming, I agree, but deforming in a good sense because it stimulated something she would never have said without it. That's what a document does: it reveals these exceptional moments when, suddenly, there is in effect no camera, no microphone. There's a revelation, a staggering revelation because it's totally sincere—and totally provoked. And totally artificial, if you like, because you asked someone to walk in the street and talk. Besides, she was carrying a Nagra[7] and she was wearing a microphone around her neck. So it was totally artificial. And it's in that direction only that I'm trying to go, toward that area.

G.R.L. Would you go so far as to make purely fictional films?

J.R. I've made a few. One, for example, *Gare du nord*, was based on the fictional story of an imaginary suicide and was part of the film *Paris vu par. . . .* It's a completely fictional film.

G.R.L. You said that you never succeeded in making a film without a narration. What do you think of the films of Americans like the Maysles and Leacock?

J.R. I think that these are films where, in spite of everything, there is an element of narration. I think that Leacock's films integrate themselves into an American information system that is totally different from ours, and where people know about things, know Mr. Levine the producer,[8] know what an electric chair is.[9] If you like,

[5] Codirector and coscenarist of this film with Rouch.

[6] One of the people in the film.

[7] The portable tape recorder most often used by professionals in synch-sound filming.

[8] The reference is to the Maysles film *Showman*, which is about the producer Joseph Levine.

[9] The reference is to the film *The Chair*.

that perhaps comes from the fact that in your country information is a kind of voyeur's information. One never sees the corpses of men killed in a gangsters' fight in a French newspaper. An American journalist would immediately question the murderer—and has the right to do so. The relationships of an Indianapolis racing driver, probing his private life—you see it.[10] That doesn't happen here. We certainly still have a great sense of modesty, and because of this, people here in France don't know these heroes filmed by Leacock and the Maysles. We don't know them—you have to show who they are. If you wanted to make a film in France about General de Gaulle, people wouldn't know, in a personal sense, who General de Gaulle was—you'd have to show who he was: you'd have to say it's this, it's that, etc. Leacock and the Maysles take exceptional situations, well-known people. You could only do that in France with famous singers, let's say, or with people who aren't of any real interest.

G.R.L. Do you think these films without narration present a form of truth that's valid?

J.R. Yes. For example, in Leacock's film on the quintuplets,[11] it starts to rain during the parade. Normally you'd be furious that it had started to rain, but Leacock is certainly very happy about it and continues shooting that shabby disaster. This is Leacock's commentary, the commentary of the film-maker himself who's relating to the event and who turns it into ridicule.

G.R.L. Do you know *Pour la suite du monde?*

J.R. Yes, by Michel Brault and Pierre Perrault. It's a film that tries to express itself through itself. Nevertheless, they suppressed the questions, which Perrault asked, but kept in the answers. Why? It would be better to keep in the questions. People don't express themselves that way; they don't express themselves that freely if you don't question them.

I think it's very difficult to have a commentary without narration. When Chris Marker made *Le Joli Mai,* there was also a commentary —as weak as they might have been, you still heard the questions being asked.

G.R.L. You're saying that even asking questions is a form of commentary.

J.R. Certainly.

G.R.L. When you go to Africa to make films, do you get to know the people well, as, say, Flaherty did?

[10] The reference is to the film *On the Pole,* about the race driver Eddie Sachs. V. Pennebaker filmography and interview with Leacock for further details.
[11] *Happy Mother's Day.*

J.R. Yes. Perhaps even better. These are people I've known for twenty years, they're old friends whom I've always known. And I've always presented my films as Flaherty. The great lesson of Flaherty and *Nanook* is always to show your film to the people who were in it. That's the exact opposite of the ideas of the Maysles and Leacock.

G.R.L. In *Moana,* Flaherty showed ritual ceremonies which I believe were no longer part of Samoan life when he made the film. Do you nevertheless see this as presenting the "truth?"

J.R. I'll answer you not by speaking of Flaherty but by giving you an example which is more extraordinary for me. The best film on Mexico is Eisenstein's *Que Viva Mexico.*[12] Now, it happens that this film is completely false—it was all created, there wasn't one real scene in it; and the Mexicans themselves recognize it as the truest film on Mexico, simply because the fiction that Eisenstein reconstructed was closest to the Mexican image. I think that's what we have to do. And Flaherty, who is a poet, not an ethnologist, who thought that everyone in the world had a message which was common to all men, applied this method in all of his films by introducing, for example, a child like the child in *Nanook,* the little boy in *Moana,* the boy in *Louisiana Story,* who have this naïve view of the world, and which is Flaherty's view. If you like, you could call Flaherty a "witty naïve,"[13] which is undoubtedly the summit of art.

G.R.L. According to you then, the truest documentary is the one that's the most false.

J.R. Yes, from the moment that the person who makes the film assumes the responsibility for it and signs it.

G.R.L. Do you think then that an edited film that one finds truthful is more valid than one which an ethnographer makes, for example, by turning on the camera and letting it run for twenty-four hours without cutting anything out?

J.R. Let's say that it's both. It's one of the real conflicts that we have, between the archival film and the edited film. Let's take a period that's going to last ten or fifteen years; finally you have to keep both types when you consider that we're dealing with a civilization that's in the midst of transformations and disappearances. You don't have the right to cut because there are very, very important things which will be worthwhile in a few years; and at this

[12] An unfinished film by Sergei Eisenstein and Grigori Alexandrov, 1930–31. A film made from the original footage by Sol Lesser and the film's backers, *Thunder over Mexico,* and a film compiled and edited by Jay Leyda, *Eisenstein's Mexican Film: Episodes for Study,* are both available from the Museum of Modern Art.

[13] Rouch's English phrase.

moment all the information that we gather is valid, all the newsreels, all the television broadcasts—but the world is going to be inundated by archives and what is the use of that? But let's say that we do keep them for ten years, out of concern; then you have to keep all the broadcasts, television and radio, and then you come to the fact that for each hour of life you would have to inspect twenty-four hours' worth of documents, and you'd never get anywhere. It's not useful for anything. So you have to tell stories.

G.R.L. You work here at the Musée de l'Homme, and in the archives?

J.R. Yes. I put my records on the stairs, and you can see them—they're jammed in and nobody ever uses them.

G.R.L. Why do you do it?

J.R. Because I've been taught that it has to be done. I've been taught that I have to breathe, so I breathe, that I have to make pee-pee, so I make pee-pee. I don't know what use it serves. And I'm sure it's going to change. For example, in my ethnographic research I've done biographies, I've done books; and I do critical biographies which say that this book is a document but it's bullshit, crap, the author is a son of a bitch, etc. and that I don't think it's worthwhile.

G.R.L. Do you like to work here at the museum, besides making your films?

J.R. Yes. First, because I like this place, I like this area, and also because it's here, when I was very young, that I discovered other parts of the world. I came here and learned that there were people other than white people, that there were Indians, black men—and I find man a passionate subject.

[. . .]

G.R.L. Do you use a small crew?

J.R. I'm alone with a sound man, who is an African, and that's all.

G.R.L. Let me ask you what you think about Grierson's definition of documentary: "the creative treatment of actuality."

J.R. I think that to make a film is to tell a story. An ethnographic book tells a story; bad ethnographic books, bad theses are accumulations of documents. Good ethnology is a theory and a brilliant exposition of this theory—and that's what a film is. That is, you have something to say. I go in the subway, I look at it and I note that the subway is dirty and that the people are bored—that's not a film. I go on the subway and I say to myself, "These people are bored, why? What's happening, what are they doing here? Why do they accept it? Why don't they smash the subway? Why do they sit here going over the same route every day?" At that moment you can make a film.

For example, in *Night Mail*,[14] the hero is very probably the train, or the train's battle against the ascent. There's no postal clerk or conductor as hero. That's going the limit. Look at all of Flaherty's films, there's always a hero, there's always someone who is personalized, whom you recognize. If you compare the films of Rasmussen[15] and Flaherty on the Eskimos, the difference is Nanook, who is someone, who is a man. When we meet people, we're men—even if you're doing work in the social sciences, you're someone. And perhaps the best films of the Maysles and Leacock are based on that, the *portrait* of someone in a given situation, whether it be Kennedy who is the hero,[16] the lawyer in *The Chair* . . .

G.R.L. Do you know the films of Fred Wiseman? In *High School* and *Law and Order*, for example, there aren't any heroes.

J.R. Yes, there are elements that one recognizes. The hero is what you might be, if you were the victim of the police or the law. But I think it would have been better if there had been a hero. There are, however, two heroes in *Law and Order*, the policemen in the patrol cars, even if they are odious.

G.R.L. Do you know *Titicut Follies*?

J.R. I like John Marshall[17] enormously, but I must say that I react to this film with horror.

G.R.L. Why?

J.R. Because, if you like, there's no hope. Finally it's a film of despair. There's abolutely nothing positive in it. Nothing. It's a totally negative certified report about a situation.

G.R.L. But if you see it as the truth?

J.R. Then you have to speak, you have to say it. I would like him to say something, say what the thesis is. Does it mean that we have to suppress this police system? That you have to be in a mental hospital? Does it mean that this particular hospital is a disgrace? It's not obvious. Perhaps it's obvious for Americans, but it's not obvious for foreigners.

G.R.L. Perhaps it's not his fault then. He is American, and finally he made it for Americans.

J.R. Perhaps it's not his fault—I understand that. But it's a little as if you went into a hospital for retarded children and showed nothing

14 Directed by Harry Watt and Basil Wright, 1936.
15 *The Wedding of Palo*, directed by F. Dalsheim and Knud Rasmussen, 1937.
16 The reference is to *Crisis*, a Drew Associates film mainly by Leacock and Pennebaker.
17 *Titicut Follies* was codirected by John Marshall and Frederick Wiseman and was photographed by Marshall.

but that. There's a fascination with horror here. For example, a horrible film like *Nuit et brouillard*[18] is a profoundly human film precisely because the commentary is there, because there's a guiding hand. In *Titicut Follies* there isn't any, it's a certified report, which could perhaps be interpreted as a cynical and sadomasochistic report. I asked John Marshall . . . What's the name of the young man with whom he made the film?

G.R.L. Wiseman.

J.R. Wiseman. What was Wiseman's reaction in the face of all that, did he take pleasure in it, was he happy? And John Marshall said that there was a fascination with the place, and that this fascination was a fascination with horror, which is a strange fascination and which should have been expressed.

G.R.L. Are you saying that one has to be human?

J.R. Yes, but it becomes human at the point that he himself becomes visible or says something and puts things in question, even if it's something banal, but which gives you distance in face of this certified horror report. That's what Alain Resnais did in *Nuit et brouillard*, and Chris Marker.

G.R.L. What about *Le Sang des bêtes?* Because that's a horror.

J.R. Franju's *Le Sang des bêtes is* . . . Franjued. Franju and Polanski are devils, angel-devils who want to show horror and are fascinated and drawn to horror. But they rise above it by a personal kind of poetry that I found lacking in *Titicut Follies*. I don't know how to tell you why. I saw the film three times, and it gave me a feeling of horror. And I regretted the impression that there wasn't a subjective camera. There's no one who says anything. The message isn't obvious to me.

G.R.L. I think this is one of the great dangers of television.

J.R. Right, right. I don't think it's possible to be a witness to the things happening around you and at the same time not take a stand. I think one must take a stand.

G.R.L. I really liked *Chronique d'un été* and *Les Maîtres fous*, but I don't think *Moi un noir* worked, and I asked myself why. One thing is perhaps that the actors aren't very good, because they're always acting, so to speak; they're playing at acting, and/or they're really like that, because they seem to be playing a game, as if they were acting out roles in a kind of American film, a Western. And I didn't find it particularly attractive or enjoyable. I'm not sure. But do you think that this reveals a truth about these people?

J.R. Yes, because you're quite right—they are playing a role. They're people who come from the country, from the bush, and who

[18] By Alain Resnais, 1955; about the German concentration camps.

find themselves in a city where they have models they don't understand, where they're obliged to behave in ways that they don't understand—the behavior is in effect Western, it's the behavior of heroes they see in the movies. For them, that's it, they don't have anything else. It would be a little like your asking a bum on the Bowery to tell you about the Louvre.

G.R.L. But it's worse than that because one doesn't see anything real in their lives.

J.R. But their lives are completely stereotyped because they're in a milieu that isn't their own. They're farmers who live in a city and who are obliged to take on these customs and live that way.

G.R.L. That's perhaps why I didn't find the film true.

J.R. Listen, the hero of *Moi, un noir* became a film-maker, and you ought to see a film he made, *Cabascabo*.[19] It's about his life preceding *Moi un noir*. Indeed, *Moi un noir* is false, it's a film that's acted out, an acted-out autobiography, and therefore false.

G.R.L. How did you come to make *Chronique d'un été?*

J.R. We thought that the Algerian War was going to end in 1960.[20] and Edgar Morin and I wanted to make a film that would bear witness to a very important period in French life. That was the point of departure. It was a bet that this was so. A little like Leacock's bet in the film about Indianapolis, that he was going to win or get killed.[21] One doesn't know.

G.R.L. Is it a film that both of you made?

J.R. Yes, yes.

G.R.L. That's the only time that you made a film in collaboration?

J.R. Yes. And it's the last—it's too difficult. You should never collaborate with anyone in the area of film, especially if there's improvisation when you're suddenly there, it's happened, and you're off.

G.R.L. Do you know what's happened to the people in the film?

J.R. Yes, I'm continually in contact with them. Most of them went to work in film. Marceline works with Joris Ivens, Régis Debray went to South America to investigate what was happening—and it turned out badly—and—[22]

G.R.L. Which one was Debray?

J.R. He was one of the students who left for Algeria. Jean-Pierre, another person in the film, also became a film assistant and made a

[19] By Oumarou Ganda.

[20] It ended in 1961.

[21] Eddie Sachs in *On the Pole*.

[22] Debray went to Bolivia to contact and write about Che Guevara and was eventually arrested by the Bolivian government for revolutionary activity and sentenced to jail, where he remained until December 1970.

film about the revolutionaries in Colombia. Edgar Morin is interested in film.

G.R.L. Do you think documentary films can help change society? Do you think that your own work is a way to change anything?

J.R. I'll give you an example. I was involved in what happened during the Month of May,[23] which was something very important in France. A lot of films were made about it, and I saw these films—

G.R.L. Where?

J.R. They're all banned, forbidden. The films are bad, and I think that the best film that you could make about the Month of May would be a fiction film, because the Month of May taught us that what was true one day wasn't true the next. In order to take advantage of the event immediately it was necessary to have a continuing audio-visual element. Instead of having a stupid strike, which they had, in the labs or in the theaters, they should have been able to occupy a movie theater and every day project rushes of what happened the day before. Then you would've had a cinematic reflection of reality that could have modified this reality in that it would have broadcast what happened in one place to all of Paris at the moment when this world was in the midst of searching out its way. That's the example. That was the example, if you like, that made me understand that it wasn't possible to do that, because you would have to do it day after day, immediately, to take advantage of this information. And you couldn't do it because you were involved in this game, and you can't make a film and be an actor at the same time—it's not possible.

I think our duty is precisely to try to make use of these kinds of moments—what's happening now in the United States, in Washington, in Berkeley; not only like the Black Panthers, who, if you like, show films on police suppression or whatever, but to transform these moments.

I don't know if you're familiar with a Canadian film called *Prologue*.[24] It's about a young hippie who abandons the road to Katmandu, hippieism and non-violence. This same film-maker went to Washington at the time of the demonstrations there and made a fiction film based on real events. I think that's very important because there's someone who can draw a conclusion. And it's there that I think that the documentary can add something. That is, if you like, in my domain of ethnography, I've tried to show that civilizations which have been considered primitive

[23] May 1968, the time of the French student "revolution."

[24] Directed by Robin Sprye, 1970.

or have been despised until now did have something to say and that they knew things that we had to learn. That's what I learned in Africa—and I learned a lot more than I taught. That's very, very important. That's what the Peace Corps should learn—that when you go to a country like that, you don't know anything, and it's for you to learn. They come to educate and teach people about the "American way of life"[25] when they themselves, if they've left the United States, don't believe in the "American way of life."

G.R.L. But it seems as if that's going to become the way of life for everyone.

J.R. Right, but it must be denounced. I think that our duty as film-makers is to make films bearing witness to violence. These films ought to stimulate something, ought to be the stimulant to let people reflect on their situation: Does the family still exist? Is money worth something? Things of this kind. Scandalous films must be made. I think Godard is undoubtedly the one who has best understood this, in a stupid way, perhaps, since practically speaking he's stopped making films, but *One Plus One* is perhaps the most naked, the most extraordinary film that he's made if you look at it closely, and the most difficult also. Its fault is that it's reserved for a few intellectuals. Perhaps he'll go further. That's what I'm looking for.

[25] Rouch's phrase.

BELGIUM

HENRI STORCK

Henri Storck was born September 5, 1907, in Ostend, Belgium. In 1928 he founded a film club in Ostend and ever since then has been "involved in the management of film clubs in Brussels and Paris." (H.S.) After making amateur films in his home town, with the help of Germaine Dullac, he got a job as an assistant to an assistant cameraman in the Studio des Buttes-Chaumont in Paris; he then went on to work as an assistant with Pierre Billon, Jean Gremillon and finally Jean Vigo on *Zéro de conduite* (1933).

Storck has directed about one hundred short and long documentaries and several feature films and has won prizes at a number of festivals. Among them are: Le Grand Prix du Roi at the Festival of Belgian Films (1937) for *Les Maisons de la misère*, the Selznick Silver Laurel Award for *The Continental Story* and the Robert J. Flaherty Award, Honorable Mention, 1960, and the Selznick Golden Laurel Award (1961) for *Masters of the Congo Jungle.*

Storck was a cofounder of the Royal Film Archive of Belgium in 1938 and of the International Association of Documentary Film-Makers in 1964. He was also president of the Association Belge des Auteurs de Film et Auteurs de Télévision for fifteen years. In 1949, at the request of UNESCO, he wrote a book entitled *The Entertainment Film for Juvenile Audiences.*

Storck presently teaches at the Institut des Arts de Diffusion (Institute of Communication Arts) in Brussels, where he lives.

FILMOGRAPHY*

1929–30: *Pour vos beaux yeux.* Scenario by Félix Labisse.
Images d'Ostende.

1930: *Une pêche au hareng.*
Le Service de sauvetage à la côte belge.
Ostende, reine des plages. Music by Maurice Jaubert. Sound by Jean Painlevé.
Trains de plaisir.
Les Fêtes du centenaire (and thirty-five other newsreels made in Ostend).
La Morte de Vénus.
Suzanne au bain; industrial and publicity films.

1931: *Une idylle à la plage.* Scenario by Jean Teugels, Cameramen: Gérard Perrin with Raymond Rouleau. Music by Manuel Rosenthal.

Route nationale 13 and *Bombance.* Codirector (films of Pierre Billon, Studios G.F.F.A., Paris).

Dainah la métisse: Assistant to Jean Gremillon (Studio de la Victorine, Nice).

1932: *Les Travaux du Tennel sous l'Escaut.* Cameramen: Boris Kaufman and Louis Berger.

Histoire du soldat inconnu (compilation of newsreel footage from 1928), sound added in 1959.

Sur les bords de la camera (compilation of newsreel footage from 1928).

Zéro de conduite. Assistant to Jean Vigo (Studio G.F.F.A., Paris).

1933: *Trois vies et une corde* (film shot in Chamonix with Roger Frison-Roche). Music by Maurice Jaubert. Cameraman: Georges Tairraz.

Misère au Borinage. Codirected with Joris Ivens. Cameramen: Joris Ivens, Henri Storck, François Rents. Sound added in

* The filmography was supplied by the film-maker. Except where noted, all films were directed by Storck.

1963: Speaker: André Thirifays. Production by Éducation par l'Image at the initiative of the Club de l'Écran de Bruxelles.

1934: *Création d'ulcères artificiels chez le chien* (in 16 mm.).
La Protection sélective du réseau à 70 K.V.A.

1935: *Électrification de la ligne Bruxelles-Anvers.*
L'Île de Pâques. Produced and edited by Henri Storck. Directed by John Ferno. Newsreel material and cameraman: John Ferno. Music: Maurice Jaubert. Commentary: Henry Lavachery. Spoken by Maurice Jaubert.
Le Trois Mâts Mercator. Directed by John Ferno. Music: Maurice Jaubert. Songs: Charles Forat. Newsreel material and cameraman: John Ferno. Produced and edited by Henri Storck.
Cap au sud. Directed by John Ferno. Music: Marcel Poot. Newsreel material and cameraman: John Ferno. Produced and edited by Henri Storck.
Industrie de la tapisserie et du meuble d'art. Cameraman: John Ferno.

1936: *Les Carillons.* Cameraman: John Ferno. With the bell ringer Jef Denyn.
Les Jeux de l'été et de la mer. Cameraman: John Ferno. Music: Marcel Poot.
Sur les routes de l'été. Cameraman: John Ferno. Music: André Souris.
Regards sur la Belgique ancienne. Cameraman: John Ferno. Music: Maurice Jaubert. Musical adviser: Paul Collaer.

1937: *La Belgique nouvelle.* Commentary: Eric de Haulleville. Music: André Souris.
Un ennemi public. Music: André Souris.
Les Maisons de la misère. Music: Maurice Jaubert. Cameramen: Eli Lotar and John Ferno.

1938: *Comme une lettre à la poste;*
La Roue de la fortune;
Terre de Flandre;
Vacances;
Le Patron est mort (about Émile Vandervelde).

1939: *Scénario de Bula Matari* (an evocation of Stanley and Leopold II with Camille Goemans).

1940: *La Foire Internationale de Bruxelles;*
Monsieur Wens en croisière. Producer. Scenario: St. A. Steeman. Directed by Georges Jamin.

1941: *Ces messieurs du Marché Noir*. Scenario, with Fernand Crommelynck.

1942–44: *Symphonie paysanne* (in five parts: "Le Printemps"; "L'Été"; "L'Automne"; "L'Hiver"; "Noces paysannes"). Music: Pierre Moulaert. Cameramen: Henri Storck, François Rents, Maurice Delattre, Charles Abel. Photographs: Raoul Ubac. Commentary: Marie Gevers. Speaker: Marcel Josz. Sound man: J. Lebrun.

1944–46: *Le Monde de Paul Delvaux*. Scenario: René Micha. Poem: Paul Eluard, spoken by the author. Music: André Souris. Production: Séminaire des Arts de Luc Haesaerts.

1945: *Le Mannequin assassiné*. Scenario, with Stanislas-André Steeman.

1945–46: *Le Pélerin de l'enfer* (feature-length film on the life of Père Damien). Assistant to Henri Schneider and Robert Lussac for this film.

1947: *La Joie de revivre*. Scenario: Arthur Haulot.

1947–48: *Rubens*. Codirected with Paul Haesaerts. Cameramen: Robert Gudin, D. and H. Sarrade, Maurice Delattre, Charles Abel. Photographs: Paul Bytebier. Music: Raymond Chevreuille. Speaker: Stéphane Cordier.

1948–49: *Au carrefour de la vie*. Scenario: Stéphane Cordier, Luc de Heusch. Cameramen: Arthur J. Ornitz, François Rents, Charles Abel. Music: Raymond Chevreuille. Commentary: Charles Dorat and Stéphane Cordier, spoken by Jean Davy of the Comédie Française, Raymonde Reynard and Jacques Delvigne. Production: Department of Information, United Nations.

1950: *Carnavals*. With Georges Lust, Paul Leleu and Luc de Heusch. Cameramen: Fernand Tack and Luc de Heusch.

1951: *Le Banquet des fraudeurs*. Scenario: Charles Spaak. Cameramen: Eugene Shuftan and Raymond Picon Borel. Assistants:

Georges Lust and Paul Leleu. Decor: Alfred Butow. Music: André Souris. Editor: Georges Freedland. Production: François Van Dorpe for Tevefilm.

1952: *La Fenêtre ouverte.* (Technicolor). Scenario: Jean Cassou. Music: Georges Auric. Directed by Edward van Beinum. Cameraman: Cyril Knowles. Speaker: Roger Pigaut. Production: Union de l'Europe Occidentale.

1953: *Herman Teirlinck.* Cameraman: Algoet. Musical adaptation: Dimitri Balachov. Commentary: Herman Teirlinck and William Pee.

1954: *Les Belges et la mer* (color) and *Les Portes de la nation.* Cameramen: François Rents and Fernand Tack. Music: Célestin Deliège. Directed by André Souris. Commentary: Jean Raine, spoken by Henri Billen.

Ten newsreels on the Belgian Congo, Argentina and Brazil for Flemish TV. Cameraman: Fernand Tack.

1955: *Le Trésor d'Ostende.* Cameramen: Frédéric Geilfus and J. Moniquet. Music: Joseph Kosma. Dialogue: Charles Dorat. Artistic consultant: Raoul Servais.

1956: *Décembre, mois des enfants* (color). After an idea by Georges Franju and René Barjavel. Cameramen: André Bac, Reginal Cavender, Pim Heytman, Frans Dupont, Wim Gerdes, Hattum Hoving. Commentary: Charles Dorat, spoken by Michel Gudin. English version: John Maddison, spoken by Frank Hawkins. Dutch version: Max Dendermonde, spoken by Wim Povel. Music: Jurriaan Andriessen. Production: Union de l'Europe Occidentale.

1957: *Couleur de feu* (color and CinemaScope). Cameramen: André Bac and Jacques Moniquet. Music: Jacques Lasry on instruments by François and Bernard Baschet. Sound: Paul Leponce and Benoît Quersin.

1958: *Les Seigneurs de la forêt* (color and CinemaScope). Executive producer for the Fondation Internationale Scientifique.

1960: *Les Gestes du silence.* Scenario: Edmond Bernhard. Music: Benoît Quersin. Cameramen: Frédéric Geilfus and Claude Gabriels. Poem and dialogue: Jacques Dormont. Sound: Jacques Delcorde.

1961: *Les Dieux du feu* (color and CinemaScope). Cameramen: André Bac and Jacques Moniquet. Music: Jacques Lasry on instruments by François and Bernard Baschet, and music by Edgar Varèse. *L'Ènergie est à vous*. Codirected with Philippe Arthuys. Cameraman: Jean Rabier. Production: Communauté Économique Européenne (C.E.E.).

Enquête sur les Tsiganes (with Luc de Heusch).

1962: *Variations sur le geste*. Scenario and commentary: Juana. Decor: Corneille Hannoset. Music: Nicolas Alfonso. Cameramen: Paul Defru and Jacques Moniquet.

Le Bonheur d'être aimée or *Félix Labisse* (color) and *Les Malheurs de la guerre*. Cameramen: José Dutillieu, Georges Strouvé, Marcel Weiss. Sound editor: Sylvie Blanc. Music: Philippe Arthuys. Commentary: Pierre Seghers, spoken by Jean Desailly. Poem: Paul Éluard, spoken by Catherine Lecouey. Coproduction: André Tadié and Henri Storck. Dutch version: Karel Jonckheere.

1963: *Plastiques*.

1964: *Matières nouvelles* (color). Cameramen: Jean Rabier, Jean Penzer, Jacques Moniquet. Music: Arsène Souffriau, Benoît Quersin. Editor: Ginette Boudet. Speaker: Roland Ménard. Commentary: Charles Dorat. Production: Solvay and Co.

Enquête sociologique en Yougoslavie (with Lucien Goldman).

1965: *Le Musée vivant* (color, 16mm.). Cameraman: André Goeffers. Commentary: Jean Raine. Speaker: Ph. Dasnoy.

1966: *Jeudi on chantera comme dimanche*. Executive producer. Directed by Luc de Heusch. Scenario: Luc de Heusch, Hugo Claus, Jacques Delcorde. Music: Georges Delerue. Coproduction: Les films de la Toison d'Or (Bruxelles), André Tadié, Les Films de l'Hermine (Paris).

1967: *Forét secrète d'Afrique* (compilation).

1969: *Paul Delvaux ou les femmes défendues* (from an idea by René Micha). Music: Philippe Arthuys. Poem: Henry Bauchau, spoken by Monique Dorsel. Commentary: René Micha, spoken by Jean Servais. Director of photography: Paul de Fru, assisted by

Jean-Pierre Étienne, Pierre Bellemans. Photographs: Charles and Virginia Leirens. Editorial assistant: Alain Marchal. Director of production: Baudouin Mussche.

1970: *Tête folkloriques en Belgique.*

December 13, 1969, at Henri Storck's office in Brussels.[1]

G. Roy Levin: Do you know Grierson's definition of documentary, "the creative treatment of actuality"?

Henri Storck: I find it a bit limiting, because Grierson always, how shall I say it, saw documentary films as a weapon, as a tool for creating a society. He thought film should deal with problems of information, and even of propaganda, in the service of the general public. That is, he didn't see documentary film as a form in itself, a category of film. For him the documentarist is a man who is above all not preoccupied with expressing his own sensibility but with expressing ideas for the purpose of analysis, and disseminating information about problems with a social character. It was only after his sensitivity as a spectator was touched by a number of documentaries that had greater ambitions than simply this service to the community that he returned—no, he came to; he never returned to because he never came from—he came to a conception of documentary as an artistic form of film. Deep down he didn't see films of a lyric or poetic character as documentary.

[. . .]

I think there was certainly an ethnographic approach in Flaherty's films, but also a human approach based on a sensibility which had nothing to do with public service. For me, Basil Wright's *Song of Ceylon* is, for example, above all the film of an artist with a sensibility; it is the work of a poet. So given Grierson's definition of documentary, where do you put lyric films like the ones, for example, that I myself tried to make about the sea at Ostend, or films of social criticism such as Jean Vigo's *À propos de Nice*, which is a satirical film, or certain actuality montage films that are also satirical? Later Grierson understood the importance of this form, and he used it, but in the beginning it was a question of bringing a message to the community, not in a questioning spirit, but rather in a spirit of conformity.

I think he had an idea of education; he wanted film-makers to be teachers—didactic teachers. And perhaps Grierson was before his time in this, because this role has obviously been taken up again by television, particularly in bringing a mass of information to the public.

G.R.L. But there's an important difference between television,

[1] The interview was conducted in French and was translated by the interviewer.

which pretends to objectivity, and Grierson, who, I think, had a point of view that he wanted to express and didn't pretend to be objective.

H.S. I think that the foundation of Grierson's theory—and I could be mistaken—is that first there's the realistic aspect of things, and I think that this was a reaction against film which was solely dedicated to fiction; only studio films were made then. Also, reality still had a certain magic then; to see boats on the screen, the building of a bridge, the working conditions or the misery of certain workers was a cinematic revelation, because for the first time people were astonished to see everyday reality on the screen, enlarged, and in a sharper, more lucid, more penetrating way. But I think there's a difference between this joy in the discovery of reality and the deeper truth of things. I don't think that this profound truth can be reconstituted except through the sensitivity of an artist who, as Vigo said, expresses his point of view about the world.

G.R.L. Is *Zéro de conduite*[2] a documentary?

H.S. For me it's more of a documentary than a fiction film, but with the ambiguity that its form is fictional since it tells a story. But if it had been pure fiction the film wouldn't have had this impact, wouldn't have provoked such a strong reaction, because people saw in it only its documentary, realistic character, and they were shocked by what Vigo showed. It was a truth seen through Vigo's sensibility, certainly, but you couldn't say that it's pure documentary since it embraces fictional forms, since there was a story, and above all because in addition to the reality there was a poetic quality which was Vigo's basic originality.

[. . .]

G.R.L. There are film-makers, especially now in the United States, who do what are usually called cinéma-vérité films, people like the Maysles, Leacock, Pennebaker, Wiseman. And some film-makers feel that the cinéma vérité method is the only way to present the truth, because it's objective.

H.S. No, I think that Leacock and the Maysles start out with a point of view, they're people who have very precise opinions about the event that they're going to film and they choose aspects of the event which will support their thesis; and this choice already exists in what they shoot. They'd have a difficult time claiming that they shoot everything. But there are ways of shooting and choosing details, and this is what touches us in their films, because it's the way one man looks at another man. In my opinion, there is no absolute objectivity, and in reality it's Leacock's truth, it's the Maysles' truth,

[2] Scenario and direction by Jean Vigo, 1933.

but it's a truth which has an influence, an impact, a meaning because it isn't a conformist truth. That is, it's the truth of a man who has his eyes open and who has a precise opinion about the events that he's going to shoot. I don't think that genuine objectivity exists in film, or else you'd have to let the camera run twenty-four hours and leave it no matter where. Real objectivity, for example, is possible in scientific films, but again it would be necessary to see things more closely. When you film an animal, a flower or things through a microscope, you can say that there's a certain objectivity, but this objectivity is always, once again, the result of a choice. The most beautiful scientific films are nevertheless the ones where the scientists who made them (if they were already film-makers, that is, artists like Jean Painlevé)[3] added to the objective truth a way of seeing, a sensitivity and a personal poetic quality. I think that the most beautiful scientific films, like the most beautiful documentaries, are made by men who have an artistic temperament, a deep sensitivity and great culture.

G.R.L. Obviously your films aren't purely objective. There is a personal point of view, there's compassion and—something which is a bit odd. In both *Misère au Borinage*[4] and *Les Maisons de la misère* the people in the film were actors, so to speak, but in *Misère au Borinage* they were men who actually worked in the coal mines, miners, and in *Les Maisons de la miserès* they were the people who lived in the . . .

H.S. The slums. There's nevertheless a difference to which I'd like to draw your attention: *Le Borinage* is a report, if you like, it's not a scripted documentary, it's not a film made on the basis of a study and from a point of view. It's a very sincere and passionate certified report, because Joris Ivens and I were overwhelmed by the misery and the conditions of the life of these people. We were both sons of the bourgeoisie, and we wanted to show the infernal Dantesque vision of this worker's world, how they lived in a kind of unimaginable misery, degradation, resignation, revolt. They weren't really men as we knew them; they were truly the exploited proletariat, the lumpenproletariat who had been harshly punished because they had dared to hold up their heads and take part in strikes. So there was a feeling of intimate participation in the life of these people, and we simply wanted to show what was happening, knowing that the document in itself would be enough to have enormous meaning for most audiences who didn't know about these conditions.

[3] One of the pioneers in science films; he founded the Institut du Cinéma Scientifique in 1930.

[4] Borinage is an area of Belgium where there are large coal mines.

Les Maisons de la misère is another problem. It's a propaganda film which tried to demonstrate that many people lived in slums and the consequences of that. It was the kind of study a sociologist would do to show how disastrous these conditions are for society and for the people who lived in the slums. Furthermore, we wanted to show that these things could be remedied by destroying the slums, and by relocating these people in inexpensive homes built with the help of public funds. The characters in the film were played by actors, with a few people taken from those slums. And the setting was real, but the actors, if you like, were my work, and they completely identified themselves with the people of those slums.

G.R.L. Who exactly was to pay for the new housing?

H.S. The National Association for Inexpensive Housing. It's an association that receives government subsidies and whose aim is to create Associations for Inexpensive Housing throughout the country in order to construct modest houses, to buy land so that they can rent or sell these houses to people with low incomes. But the great difficulty was to get these people to move out of the slums because they had gotten used to living there. Their lives were more and more degraded, less civilized, and they ended up liking these conditions. So, to get them to move and to pay a little more for rent, to get them to work, to get them completely to change their mentality and their way of life, they had to be forced to move; and to do that the slums had to be destroyed, because if you didn't destroy them there would always be people who would move into them again.

G.R.L. Is it possible that these people didn't believe that there would be other, better housing, that work would be difficult to find and that they wouldn't be able to pay the increased rents?

H.S. Yes, the economic conditions were very difficult. There was a lot of unemployment and a lot of these people had lost their jobs or no longer had the qualifications for work, or there were difficult situations such as the father being dead, sickness, things like that. I should say that at the time we made this film, in 1937, Social Security wasn't as developed as it is today, and these people were left to their fates.

G.R.L. Was the aim of the film to influence the government to help with this problem?

H.S. Yes, the aim was very clear. For three years the National Association for Inexpensive Housing had been asking Parliament to allocate a substantial sum of money to construct new housing. They were asking for 350 million Belgian francs and it was the National Savings Bank that was supposed to give the money. But Parliament refused to vote the law allowing the Bank to advance the money.

So the Housing Association came to me and said, "If you made a film, knowing your fiery temperament, etc., your film would make the deputies and senators change their minds." They were right, because one month after the film was shown they got the money. That was the film's only use. It was a film made for a single screening for the benefit of both chambers of Parliament, the King, who came, all the foreign ambassadors and all the newspaper reporters. The morning after the film was shown there were long articles in all the newspapers about how they had discovered that there were a hundred thousand slum dwellings in Belgium and that there were one million people living in them and that it was a scandal that had to be remedied. Parliament was afraid. If you like, the film was a piece of blackmail, but it had results.

However, I was very disappointed, because this money wasn't used to destroy these slums, but to construct housing for the middle class and not for the proletariat. That's life. In the end I was betrayed, and I wasn't very happy about it; but nevertheless, every time the film is shown it reminds people of the reality of the situation in the slums. But I must say that life in Belgium is better now, and I think there are fewer slum dwellings now, even though there are still a lot. The press talks about it once in a while, and even people in positions of authority, like the Queen and the King, say that it's a scandal and that it should be ended, changed. It's a very, very difficult problem because, as you know, slums are an excellent investment. If someone has a large house with a lot of rooms, they end up renting each room to a family. And we now have the problem of slum dwellings again with the immigration of foreign workers.

G.R.L. In *Le Borinage,* were the actors real miners?

H.S. There were no actors in *Le Borinage*. They were all real miners and all the situations were real, as in a news report, as in cinéma-vérité, except that one scene was reconstructed, the scene with the police, because it was impossible to get police to act in the film. We'd been told this story of how the police wanted to take the furniture from a house. There's a law in Belgium that says that if people lean on the furniture, the bailiff can't take it away—which is very funny. So they had friends come and lean on the furniture, so the police couldn't take it. Since obviously we couldn't get the police to take part, we reconstituted the scene with workers dressed like policemen, and that's the reason this scene isn't completely successful.

We did something else in this film. We had heard that on the anniversary of the death of Karl Marx workers had marched in the streets with the portrait of Marx. We thought this would be a great way to end the film and we wanted to reconstruct the scene, so we asked them to take the portrait of Marx and march in the street with it. Well, instead of becoming a cinematic event it became a political event. People thought it was a new demonstration in honor of Karl Marx and they came out and cheered and again it had the same impact. The proof is that the police took it as a demonstration; they didn't know it was for a film, they chased us, they wanted to stop it. In any case, it was a forbidden demonstration. You couldn't parade with the portrait of Karl Marx because it was Communistic, and in Belgium at that time it wasn't completely accepted as a legal party.

G.R.L. That's interesting, because it raises a question that's often asked: if there's a demonstration, for example, does the presence of photographers, of television people, influence what happens?

H.S. Partially, yes, I think.

G.R.L. Who paid for *Le Borinage?*

H.S. There was a cinema club in Brussels and they wanted to make a film, and the secretary of the club, André Thirifays, asked me if I wanted to make a film about the consequences of strikes. He'd heard about the misery of the Borinage workers and asked if I wouldn't like to make a film about it. I said yes, but that I didn't know very much about social questions, that I was the son of a merchant, that I didn't know the world of workers. But I remembered my friend Joris Ivens, who had just made a film about youth in Russia, so I said, "He knows these problems better than I, and we'll do it together." I asked him, and he was eager to do it. And for him, as for me, this film was a great step in our lives, because even he didn't know the conditions of the workers in industrial Europe, and that let us both ignore all of our aesthetic theories about film. At that point there was no longer a question of beautiful angles or beautiful lighting. Besides, there was no electricity and we had to use acetylene lamps, which gave off a light like gas. Also, I remember that the lamps gave off a lot of heat, and when we put them in the houses where there wasn't any electricity, the cockroaches, all the bugs that were in the walls came out by the thousands. It was really terrible to see.

So the secretary of the film club, with the consent of the president of the club, Pierre Vermeylen, asked a few rich friends for some money. So it was a group of friends who paid for the film. Then, there wasn't enough money, and a retired industrialist, who seemed to feel remorse for having exploited workers all his life, gave a little money to pay the rest of the expenses. He lived a hundred kilometers from Brussels, by the sea, and when we showed the film for the first time, in Brussels, we invited him since he was a backer—but an anonymous backer; there was only one person who knew his name; I never knew who he was. When he came to Brussels he took the train, but we never saw him arrive because he died on the train. It's not a story, but the truth, and rather romantic.

G.R.L. Did *Le Borinage* change anything?

H.S. No, I don't think so. First of all, the film was strongly opposed by the Socialist Party because it was made with the most advanced elements of the strike, who were Marxist workers. The Socialists, who had all of the Borinage under their political jurisdiction, were furious that someone had dared to attack their region by showing the misery there, because they wanted people to think that where you had socialistic politics there wasn't any misery; so they attacked us. Because of that the film was less widely distributed. I don't think it had any political or social consequences, except that Ivens took it to Moscow and the Russians made a propaganda version for the Russian miners, saying to them, "Look, here miners have good working conditions, they're happy, they have a good life, while look at what it's like in Belgium." They generalized; it wasn't really honest. On the other hand, I think the film had a great influence on certain other film-makers, especially in England. The film was shown there almost in the same year it was made, in 1933 or '34. I remember Grierson saying that the film really impressed many young English film-makers at the time. And I know that in France it had a certain effect, and a little before or after the war (I don't remember which) Joris Ivens showed it to some American film-makers, who were also impressed by the film. I also remember that after the war Italian film-makers of the "new wave," the neo-realists, saw it, and they said, "That was the beginning of neo-realism, in '33." Finally, I think that its sincerity, its rough documentary quality and its truth were what impressed documentary film-makers.

G.R.L. How did you come to begin to make films? Was it a passion? By chance?

H.S. No, no, not at all by chance. I think it's because I lived in Ostend, in a milieu of painters. Naturally it was by chance that my family and I knew a lot of painters, because at that time three important Belgian painters lived there. First, there was James Ensor, whom I saw a lot of, a great expressionist Flemish painter named Permeke—you see one of his paintings over there—and another painter named Spilliaert—you can see one of his paintings over there. So, if you like, I was very sensitive to imagery, everything that was visual, and since these people painted everything that was in the city of my birth—fishermen, the port, the sea, everything that surrounded the city, the country, the peasants—I too wanted to describe the same things with a camera. But that came afterward, because I did quite a bit of still photography, and I worked with an amateur camera called a Pathé-Baby, 9 1/2mm., and I had already done a film to amuse myself and to express the vision I had of my city, a poetic vision and a very fresh look at it to rediscover the city and above all nature.

G.R.L. How old were you?

H.S. At that time I was between fifteen and twenty years old.

G.R.L. Does the film still exist?

H.S. Yes, it's called *Images d'Ostende*, and I made it at first with a Pathé-Baby. Then, when my friends saw it, they said I ought to make it in 35mm.

But that's not the way it began. I came to Brussels one day to see a film at a film club, and I saw Flaherty's *Moana*, which greatly impressed me, precisely because of the beautiful images of nature, of men. At that time I wasn't thinking of making films, but I wanted to start a film club. I returned to my native city of Ostend and we started a film club to see beautiful films. I suddenly had the revelation that there were beautiful films, because the only films that you saw in Ostend were commercial films, except for a few documentaries and the films of Chaplin. So we started a film club which was very successful and we showed many of the masterpieces of the cinema, particularly, for example, Buñuel films like *Un chien andalou*, films of René Clair, of Eisenstein, for example, *The General Line*, *The Battleship Potemkin*, films which could only be seen in film clubs, and films from the beginnings of the cinema, the films of Delluc, etc. Also, films by young Belgian film-makers, because there were already some who were making avant-garde films. Then, after two or three years, as often happens with young people in film clubs, we said, "We're going to try to make films ourselves," and so, with friends, I started to make films, and I continued. And that's the beginning.

I should also say that this beginning was in good part due to the use of the portable hand camera, a small camera that the Germans had made called the Kinamo which used a seventy-five-foot magazine and which was the camera that Joris Ivens had used to shoot *The Bridge* a few years earlier. It permitted you to leave the studio and to go outside into the country and film everything you saw.

G.R.L. Is there a reason why you started to make documentaries rather than fiction films?

H.S. Yes, because I liked documentaries better than anything else. I wasn't very responsive to fiction. I like the poetry of reality. Have you seen my film *Symphonie paysanne?* It was my dream to make films like that. Nevertheless, in 1931, I did make a fiction film, rather poetic, not very structured, called *Une idylle à la plage.* It wasn't very successful at the time it was shown—the public didn't like it very much; but it's still shown in film clubs, so it has survived the disfavor of the public. But it discouraged me to see that I was not able to please. I think that with fiction films you have to be immediately successful or it's very difficult to continue. Documentary is different because I think it gives you more profound satisfactions.

G.R.L. But you've been able to earn your living.

H.S. Yes, I've been able to earn my living because I've done many, many films on commission. Not having a personal fortune to make films, I've really done very few films on my own initiative. Most of the films I've done have been commissioned by official or private organizations. When the subject interested me, like the slums in *Les Maisons de la misère or Le Borinage,* I put all my heart into it. Obviously there are a certain number of films that I did without very much conviction, without much sincerity because they were subjects that didn't interest me, subjects dealing with tourism, things like that. But *Symphonie paysanne,* for example, on the four seasons and showing the life of the peasants, is a film that I conceived myself, and if I'd had the money, I would have paid for it myself.

Sometimes I look for money to do a film, as I'm doing now, for example. I want to do a film about folklore here in Belgium, on popular traditions, and I've proposed the subject to official organizations, to ministries which are giving me money to do it, but who are also giving me complete freedom to do the film as I wish. Obviously it's not a controversial film, or a film of social criticism.

G.R.L. Films like *Rubens* or *Le Monde de Paul Delvaux,* were these films you wanted to make?

H.S. *Le Monde de Paul Delvaux,* yes. He had done a great deal of very beautiful work just before and during the war, which the Germans didn't like very much at all. He wasn't able to exhibit—the Germans didn't want any abstract or surrealist art. So when the Germans left, one of the first things done was to organize a retrospective exhibition of Delvaux's works; that was December '44 here at the Palais des Beaux Arts. It produced a real shock. I went to the exhibition. I've always been a bit of a surrealist since my youth. I've always marveled at the surrealist movement and I had many friends who were surrealists—and the exhibition gave me a shock. So with some friends of Delvaux we found money to film it. It cost very little since I had the film and the camera, and I did the work myself. Afterward we waited for the money to add the sound.

Rubens was also a commissioned film; I was asked to make a prestige film for Belgium. It's a film that I'm not completely satisfied with because the conception is in great part due to M. Paul Haesaerts, who did a book that I admired very much[5] [. . .] especially the layout, the technique. I did a lot of work in Paris with specialists in animated design, in animation, to try to give movement to the pictures, and it was rather new at that time, this didactic manner of presenting a painter, of analyzing the structure of his work, the composition. But I think the film at times lacked a lyrical quality and a genuine sensitivity.

G.R.L. I haven't been able to see *Rubens* yet, but *Le Monde de Paul Delvaux* seems to me to have a value in itself that goes beyond the paintings. You don't see the paintings in a museum the way you do in the film; I think the details and the camera movement add a great deal.

H.S. Very simply, I think it's a kind of sincerity. First, I believe a great deal in the sincerity of sensitivity and the freshness of how one sees. Discoveries; you must not have opinions on the paintings. You have to be in front of the paintings—the actual paintings, not reproductions, because reproductions are already an image to the second degree—because the material of the painting, the canvas, the paint itself, even the odor of the painting has a magic value. You have to put yourself in front of the painting like a child and go toward the discovery of this painting with great sincerity—and that's very difficult. But since these paintings were not yet famous at that time, it was still easy enough to do. There wasn't this distance between the masterpiece and the film-maker; it was still a living work.

I've had a curious experience. I've just redone a film on the same paintings by Delvaux in color.[6] It's a completely different approach, because since then I've reflected a great deal on Delvaux's art, on the subconscious Freudian meaning of the work, and all these preoccupations come out in this film. I think it's a sincere film, but less poetic, more intellectual, more elaborate, which perhaps lets you know Delvaux better than the first film. I think part of the charm of the first film was that all of the parts form an ensemble. Besides, I think that when a film is a success it's because there's harmony

[5] *Flandre* by Paul and Luc Haesaerts, Éditions des Chroniques du Jour, Paris, 1931.

[6] *Paul Delvaux ou les femmes défendues*, 1969.

among the collaborators. I think it's very rare that anyone makes a film alone.

G.R.L. But it's you who finally decide on all the aspects of the film.

H.S. No, no, I give a lot of freedom. For example, I didn't intervene at all with the music. Every time I have it's been a catastrophe. Musicians know much more about those things than the film-maker. Where I have the last word is in the shooting of the film; that is, I have cameramen but I want them to understand me, to do as I want them to do. *Le Monde de Paul Delvaux* I shot myself, awkwardly, because I'm not actually a cameraman, and that's why there are some rather jerky camera movements. But that's not serious for me because it's like the movement of an eye—but that's something else. For the new Delvaux film I've found a cameraman who feels things as I do and we work well together. He did a very good job. But it's a little more academic than the first film.

[. . .]

G.R.L. Did you ever paint, or did you ever want to paint?

H.S. No, I don't think I'm a painter at all and I've never been tempted to be one. But I like painting very much, and because of having been with painters a lot and having discussions with them, I've understood their profession, their difficulties, their struggle. Besides, we have the same difficulties in film. For us it's also the problem of reconstituting an atmosphere, a light. In *Symphonie paysanne* I was very sensitive to the passage of the seasons: going from the extraordinary darkness of winter here in Belgium to the beginning of spring when the light is clearer and clearer, to the marvelous light of summer, and then autumn, when you have wind and the light diminishes. It's these perpetual changes of weather here in Belgium that oblige the peasants to be flexible in their agricultural work. They must also be prescient about the weather and live with the clouds and the sun, so that the crops aren't destroyed; they must know how to make use of the weather in the most efficient way possible. That's what I was preoccupied with, and I think that I rendered it in this film. At a particular moment in the film it rains, and you really have the feeling of rain, you feel the humidity, the cold. That's what I wanted. So that's almost the same as a painter's problem, although I wasn't thinking at all of imitating painters. When the film was finished, there were Belgian critics who said, "The director has unconsciously represented a whole period of Belgian painting, the schools of impressionism and expressionism."

G.R.L. Is it your favorite film?

H.S. I think it is my favorite film, along with another, also commissioned, which is the biography of a famous Flemish writer who was also very influenced by nature. *Herman Teirlinck* is the name of the writer and the title. There's a sequence in the film on the mystery of the forest, the trees—I'm very fond of trees. It would be very difficult to express those things in a fiction film, because I'm afraid it becomes a little artificial and literary then, while if you express it as a documentarist you touch people's sensibilities with the things that you care about.

G.R.L. The country, the climate are influences.

H.S. Oh yes, I really like to work in Belgium. I need this environment, this climate, these changes of weather, this rain, and I love the sea, the movement of the waves. My very first film, *Images d'Ostende,* is devoted entirely to that.

G.R.L. From films like *Le Borinage* and *Les Maisons de la misère* it's obvious that you're concerned with social questions. Do you think that documentary films can help change social conditions?

H.S. I think that the documentary film has played and continues to play a very important role in our society. And now you have with television a formidable means of broadcasting, and many documentaries are shown, nevertheless. And I think that young people will more and more seek out information and the secrets of life and society in films. I think that young people see documentaries, cinéma-vérité, scientific films, films on art as much as they see fiction films. It's in commercial theaters that you see very few documentaries, but I think that in the non-commercial sector, in 16mm., short documentaries have vast distribution.

G.R.L. It's a very difficult problem. Television, for example. The establishment, the government, directly or indirectly, finally controls it. And the documentaries that I think should be made and ought to be shown aren't shown on television, at least not in the United States. They're shown at times in England.

H.S. Listen, at Leipzig[7] I saw a new group of American documentaries called American Documentary Films, from San Francisco. Not only do they produce films, they distribute a complete series of films that are important from a political and social point of view. I was told that these films are shown in many American universities and in many clubs, churches and communities which show 16mm. films. That's nevertheless fantastic because he told me that they have a public of twelve million. And in Europe we have a circuit of film clubs. In France there are several federations which have hundreds of film clubs. Also in England. Finally, I'm nevertheless surprised at the distribution. You can't, when you make a documentary,

[7] The reference is to the film festival at Leipzig, in East Germany, which is devoted to documentaries and shorts.

hope that a lot of people will have seen it one year afterward, but at the end of ten, twenty years a lot of people will have finally seen it because there are retrospectives, festivals, etc. And documentary goes all over the world. There are retrospectives of Joris Ivens' films throughout the entire world. As for my own films—I don't have much to complain about; they're shown here and there, and sometimes to the general public. Fifteen hundred copies of my film on landscape painting[8] have been made—it's exceptional, but it's a lot, isn't it?

I was also surprised to learn that the Minister of Foreign Affairs had fifty copies made of the film I just did on the educational resources of museums here in Belgium,[9] which is also a commission. The ministry had twenty color copies made of my film on landscape painting, and they had eight copies made of *Le Borinage* because they distribute films free to the schools, and they told me that the eight copies circulate every week. Well, that's not so bad, because even with big fiction films here in Belgium there are only eight or ten copies made, even with the biggest. And eight or ten copies of my films are made, and they circulate, they don't stay in the can, so I'm happy enough. Now, lots of documentaries have to be made, because it's not the work of one man.

G.R.L. In spite of all those showings, documentaries are often shown after the fact, so to speak, when it's really too late for them to have an influence on changing things.

H.S. That's something else. I think that film has become a cultural arm which will be able to play a very important role in the changes which are going to take place. For politically conscious films there are those people in America, because they make films about the Black Panthers, Black liberation, on Vietnam, on Cuba, Spain, Latin America, capitalism, domestic protest, imperialism, war, Africa, China —there are a lot of titles. And all that's happening now. And Chris Marker has arranged for the creation of film groups in certain French factories. Just the discussion of a documentary film scenario in a factory is an important question of consciousness about the problems of the working class, if the workers learn that they can use film to understand and express themselves about their situation. Besides, it's a revolution from a cinematic point of view—it's a completely new use of film. I'm a professor at a school here in Brussels, and I see all these young people who are going to make films as they do in America without any money. I think young people are going to express themselves now by writing letters with the camera instead

[8] *La Fenêtre ouverte,* 1952.
[9] *Le Musée vivant,* 1965.

of writing letters with a pen; instead of writing newspaper articles or books, they're going to write films.

G.R.L. Chris Marker said yesterday, in effect, that he wanted to write letters in Super 8.

H.S. Why not? I think it'll be possible when there's sound with Super 8. And in the past few years we've been moving very quickly toward a magnetic film that will be a lot less expensive. [. . .] Yes, it is becoming less and less expensive, and young people have more and more money.

G.R.L. A personal question. You don't have central heating here. . . .

H.S. No, I don't have central heating, but I'm not cold.

G.R.L. But is it a question of habit, or of money?

H.S. It's a question of money. I don't own this house, and since there's no heat, the rent is very cheap, and I need room for my books, my machines—I have an editing room upstairs which I can show you. It would be very expensive if heat was put in—I'd have to pay three times the rent that I pay now, and I don't earn enough money from my films because I'm a one-man concern. My organization is one person, myself. I have an assistant, a secretary who comes in two or three times a week. I can't do more. If I grew I would be lost in business matters and administration and I'd no longer have time to make films. So I have to be very careful to remain small, artisanlike, or else I should change professions and work as a director for a producer, and that I've never been able to do. I can never agree with anyone on the conception and the direction of a film. It's a weakness, and I don't advise it for anyone else. I tell my students that they must work with producers, but me, I'm too old to change. Starting at a certain age you don't have the flexibility to collaborate with someone else. And I'm too sensitive to being contradicted, it upsets me.

G.R.L. Working with producers is apparently a common enough problem for film-makers. Chris Marker was saying that it was one of the things that he found difficult, and now he's starting to work with a co-operative in Paris.

H.S. But even in a co-operative there are still all kinds of problems. Now if a co-operative was being formed in Belgium with people I was friendly with, it's very possible that I would willingly collaborate with them. But film is a very individualistic profession. All directors are individualists, and producers also. It's very difficult to unite them because each one thinks he knows better than the other, and each wants to preserve what he thinks is his personality, his originality. It's as if you gave a painter a producer and the producer said, "You have to use such and such colors, do paintings of certain dimensions because that's what sells." The painter wouldn't be able to do it; he would no longer do anything sincere.

G.R.L. That's a funny comparison, and a good one. Obviously one of the reasons is that compared with making a film, it's very inexpensive to make a painting. In reference to the Festival of Leipzig, I have a general question about documentary films from the Communist countries. Are many of them purely propagandistic, or are they documentaries that tell us something true about the world?

H.S. I think that there are documentary films in Communistic countries that are completely objective—scientific, didactic films, industrial films for workers, and now, films on art, biographies of famous people. Propaganda plays a role in political films, but I think there aren't many of them. They make films that deal with external problems, and they're beginning to make films, in Hungary, for example, of social criticism about everyday life, but on small problems; that is, the young film-makers essentially ridicule the bourgeois tendencies found in most of the socialist countries. From a cultural, economic point of view it's the petit bourgeois mentality of the socialist countries that strikes you. You don't have this freedom of behavior, of thought, of dress, of how you amuse yourself that you have, for example, with the working classes of industrialized countries. You have the feeling there of discipline, of authority, of surveillance; and the people are looking for intellectual, political and material security.

[. . .]

Obviously the young film-makers try to break through this kind of mentality. Most people are obliged by circumstances to trust the directives of the people who finally think for them, while here, little by little, especially with young people, everyone tries to understand the world by himself and to avoid listening to what's said on television, in the newspapers or what the politicians say. In those countries this isn't permitted—it's almost impossible to express personal opinions, and if you do, you have to do it in a very discreet manner or in a satirical form.

You can see the problems of youth very clearly in Jancso's film *Ça ira;* that is, for the young, not knowing the capitalist world, they can only learn about it through rumors from the outside. They completely accept the Marxist, collectivist ideology; for them there is no other solution. The remedies that they want to apply and the criticisms that they make are really criticisms of details against the petit bourgeois mentality, against the excesses of the bureaucracy, like the satirical films that have been made in Poland. But the morals remain very traditional: all the education is still very bourgeois, the relations between the sexes, the lack of sexual liberty—all that is still forbidden, and by youth as well as by the adults and the authorities.

G.R.L.—In general, do you find that their films are as truthful, so to speak, as films in the West?

H.S. That depends on the film. Critical films or films that want to express a truth that doesn't conform to the official truth are prohibited. And in the vaults of their production houses are many films that have never been shown, or else they're banned for one, two, three years. There was the famous film, *La Fête et les invités*, by Němec, from Czechoslovakia, which was held up by the censor for three years. Obviously, when you see the film you understand why. It's a film that attacks more than the bourgeois mentality; it attacks the methods of the police, the spiritual tyranny. But with the spiritual liberation of last year, these films have finally been able to be shown in festivals outside the country, but not always within the country.

You can't say that there isn't any truth in their films, but you can say that films that demonstrate a truth that doesn't conform to the official truth aren't distributed. I think that's a fairly honest statement about their problems. And it's obvious that in periods of tension certain subjects are taboo. At Leipzig you couldn't show a film that said something about present-day Czechoslovakia. Also, for example, there were films on Biafra that couldn't be shown because the Soviet Union supported Nigeria. You couldn't show pro-Israel films because they're on the side of the Arabs, etc. There are all sorts of political forces at play, and you couldn't say that the choice of films shown at the Festival of Leipzig was very honest or very complete. On the other hand, you see films there about Vietnam and about other countries heading toward revolution or in revolutionary evolution that you couldn't show on our Occidental television, and that wouldn't be shown in commercial theaters here.

The difficulty of distribution exists here also, but it's because of self-censorship by television and film distributors. It's more subtle, and it's private instead of official, and the public here wouldn't understand these films. If the public is conditioned in the socialist countries, it's also conditioned here; we also have taboos. For example, for many people who are still under the influence of anti-Communism, if you show them a Soviet film or a Chinese film, they'll look at it with distrust or with hostility.

UNITED STATES

WILLARD VAN DYKE

Willard Van Dyke was born December 5, 1906, in Denver, Colorado. After a career as a still photographer with one-man exhibitions at a number of museums he began working in film as a cameraman on Pare Lorentz' *The River* (1937). With *The City* (1939) he established himself as a film-maker. During World War II he was a producer for the OWI Overseas Motion Picture Bureau and acted as liaison officer between the OWI and a group of Hollywood writers who were providing scripts for the bureau's production unit.

From 1946 to 1965 Van Dyke made many films for television and other sponsors, among them the Rockefeller Foundation, The Ford Foundation, *Omnibus* and the CBS programs, *The Twentieth Century* and *The Twenty-first Century*. He has won awards at a number of film festivals.

In 1965 he was appointed director of the Department of Film at the Museum of Modern Art, a position he still holds. He is now president of the Robert Flaherty International Film Seminars, a vice-president of the International Federation of Film Archives and a member of the Advisory Board of Learning Corporation of America, a division of Columbia Pictures.

Van Dyke is married and lives in New York City.

FILMOGRAPHY*

1937: *The River.* A story of the Mississippi River basin and flood control by the Tennessee Valley Authority. Made for the Farm Security Administration. Written and directed by Pare Lorentz. Photographed by Willard Van Dyke, Stacey Woodard and Floyd Crosby. Music by Virgil Thomson. 27 minutes, b&w.

* From *Film Comment*, Spring 1965, vol. 3, no. 2, pp. 35–37, and the last listed film from the film-maker.

1939: *The City.* The classic film on city planning and the problems of uncontrolled urban growth. Produced, directed and photographed by Willard Van Dyke and Ralph Steiner. Written by Lewis Mumford and Henwar Rodakiewicz. Music by Aaron Copland. Narrated by Morris Carnovsky. Additional photography by Roger Barlow. 44 minutes, b&w.

1940: *Valley Town.* A study of the human consequences of automation in a steel town. Produced by the Educational Film Institute of New York University and Documentary Film Institute of New York University and Documentary Film Productions, Inc. Directed by Willard Van Dyke. Photographed by Roger Barlow and Bob Churchill. Edited by Irving Lerner. Music by Marc Blitzstein. Written by Ben Maddow, Spencer Pollard and Willard Van Dyke. 27 minutes, b&w.

The Children Must Learn. The story of an experiment in education in the Kentucky mountains. Written and directed by Willard Van Dyke. Photographed by Bob Churchill and Willard Van Dyke. Music arranged by Fred Stewart. Narrated by Myron McCormick. 12 minutes, b&w.

Sarah Lawrence. The experiences of one girl at Sarah Lawrence College. Directed by Willard Van Dyke. Photographed by Roger Barlow. 15 minutes, b&w.

To Hear Your Banjo Play. An analysis of several folk songs by Pete Seeger. Directed by Willard Van Dyke. Written by Alan Lomax. Photographed by Richard Leacock and Peter Glushanock. Edited by Irving Lerner. 20 minutes, b&w.

Tall Tales. Three songs by Josh White and Burl Ives. Directed by Willard Van Dyke. 10 minutes, b&w.

1942: *The Bridge.* A study of the economics of South America, particularly its trade relations with North America, and the importance of communications and aerial transportation during the war. Produced for the Foreign Policy Association. Directed by Willard Van Dyke. Written by Ben Maddow. 27 minutes, b&w.

1943: *Oswego.* A small American city through the eyes of French visitors in wartime. Produced by the Office of War Information. Directed by Willard Van Dyke.

Steeltown. How American steelworkers live and work. Produced by the Office of War Information. Directed by Willard Van Dyke. Written by Philip Dunne. Photographed by Larry Madison. Music by William Schumann.

1944: *Pacific Northwest.* A film about Oregon and Washington. Produced by the Office of War Information. Directed by Willard Van Dyke. Written by Ben Maddow. Photographed by Larry Madison and Willard Van Dyke. Narrated by Walter Huston.

1945: *San Francisco.* The official film on the establishment of the United Nations. Produced by the Office of War Information, Bureau of Overseas Motion Pictures. Directed by Willard Van Dyke. Photographed by Larry Madison. Edited by Sidney Meyers.

1946: *Journey into Medicine.* For the U. S. Department of State, about the education of an American doctor. Directed by Willard Van Dyke. Written by Irving Jacoby. Photographed by Boris Kaufman. 30 minutes, b&w.

1947: *The Photographer.* A film about Edward Weston. Made for the USIA under Hamilton McFadden. Directed by Willard Van Dyke. Written by Irving Jacoby and Ben Maddow. Edited by Alexander Hammid. 30 minutes, b&w.

1948: *Terribly Talented.* A theatrical short for Pete Smith, featuring a girl who plays a tune by knocking on her forehead and opening and closing her mouth as a resonating chamber; also, a man plays *The Volga Boatman* by controlling the tension on the neck of a balloon. Produced by Willard Van Dyke. Directed by Alexander Hammid. Photographed by Boris Kaufman.

1949: *This Charming Couple.* One of five films for McGraw-Hill on courtship and marriage. Shot at Stephens College. Produced by Irving Jacoby. Directed by Willard Van Dyke. Photographed by Peter Glushanock.

Mount Vernon. The story of George Washington's home in Virginia. Directed by Willard Van Dyke. Photographed by Richard Leacock. Written by Howard Turner. Music by Alex North. 14 minutes, b&w.

1950: *Years of Change.* Made in Latin America, this USIA film deals with U.S. technical aid to foreign countries. Directed by Willard Van Dyke. Written by Irving Jacoby. Photographed by Richard Leacock.

1952: *New York University.* A film about New York University. Produced by Irving Jacoby. Directed by Willard Van Dyke. Photographed by Richard Leacock and Kevin Smith. Music by Mel Powell. 20 minutes, b&w.

1953: *Working and Playing to Health.* Characterized by Amos Vogel as deceptively simple, this film is set in a mental hospital and deals with recreational therapy. Acted by the hospital staff. Directed by Willard Van Dyke. Photographed by Kevin Smith.

There Is a Season. Made for the Ford Motor Company Labor Relations Board; about three men in the changing automobile industry. Directed by Willard Van Dyke. Photographed by Kevin Smith. Music by Mel Powell. 20 minutes., b&w.

1954: *Recollections of Boyhood: An Interview with Joseph Welch.* An interview with Joseph Welch by Alistair Cooke. Made for the *Omnibus* television series. Directed by Willard Van Dyke. Photographed by Richard Leacock. 15 minutes, b&w.

Cabos Blancos. A dramatized documentary in Spanish on farm co-operatives in Puerto Rico. Produced for the Department of Public Education of Puerto Rico. Directed by Willard Van Dyke and Angel F. Rivera. Photographed by Kevin Smith. 30 minutes, b&w.

Excursion House. Two half-hour films for Saudek Associates, for television. Directed by Willard Van Dyke. Photographed by Kevin Smith. Narrated by Burgess Meredith.

Toby and the Tall Corn. Also Saudek Associates, for *Omnibus.* About a tent show in the Midwest. Produced by Willard Van Dyke. Directed by Richard Leacock. Photographed by Kevin Smith. Reported by Russell Lynes.

1957: *Life of the Molds.* The life cycle of fungi, for the Pfizer Company. Directed by Willard Van Dyke. Written by Jack Churchill. Photographed by Robert Young. 20 minutes, color.

1958: *Skyscraper.* A fanciful look at the changing face of New York City, with emphasis on the construction of 666 Fifth Avenue. Directed by Willard Van Dyke and Shirley Clarke. Photographed by Kevin Smith, Wheaton Galentine and Donn Alan Pennebaker. Edited by Shirley Clarke. Music by Teo Macero. 15 minutes, b&w with color sequence.

Tiger Hunt in Assam. One of the *High Adventure* television series, with Lowell Thomas. Directed by Willard Van Dyke. Photographed by Robert Young. 1 hour, color.

Mountains of the Moon. Again *High Adventure,* with Lowell Thomas. The story of four white settlers in Africa, with glimpses of Pygmy life, an African secret society and a hunting camp. Directed by Willard Van Dyke. Photographed by Fred Porret and Graeme Ferguson. 1 hour, color.

1959: *Land of White Alice.* Radio communication in Alaska, as seen during a day with an Alaskan bush pilot. Produced for Western Electric. Directed by Willard Van Dyke. Written by Graeme Ferguson and Norman Rosten. Photographed by Graeme Ferguson and William Jersey. Music by Daniel Pinkham. Narrated by Shepperd Strudwick. 27 minutes, color.

The Procession. The problems of Protestant clergymen in ministering to a rapidly changing urban community (Chicago). Made for the United Church of Christ. Directed by Willard Van Dyke. Photographed by William Jersey. 25 minutes, b&w.

1960: *Ireland, the Tear and the Smile.* A two-part essay for television, on Ireland today. For *The Twentieth Century,* with Walter Cronkite. Produced by Isaac Kleinerman and Burton Benjamin. Directed by Willard Van Dyke. 1 hour, b&w.

Sweden. A two-part examination of myths about Sweden's welfare policies and their effects on morals. Made for *The Twentieth Century,* with Walter Cronkite. Produced by Burton Benjamin and Isaac Kleinerman. Directed by Willard Van Dyke. Photographed by Rune Ericson. 1 hour, b&w.

1962: *So That Men Are Free.* A film on a distinguished American anthropologist, Dr. Allan Holmberg, and his work with an Andean Indian community. Made for *The Twentieth Century,* with Walter Cronkite. Produced by Burton Benjamin and Isaac Kleinerman. Directed by Willard Van Dyke. Written by Earle Luby. 30 minutes, b&w.

Search into Darkness. A film on how a large company uses the brains of its scientists and engineers. Made for Schlumberger Limited. Produced by Willard Van Dyke. Designed and directed by William Jersey. Music improvised by Lukas Foss. Narrated by Joseph Julian. 20 minutes, b&w with color sequences.

Harvest. The story of maize improvement in Mexico and Colombia through the aid of the Rockefeller Foundation. Directed by Willard Van Dyke. Written by Howard Turner. Photographed and edited by Dave Myers. Narrated by Joseph Julian. 27 minutes, color.

1963: *Depressed Area, U.S.A.* An examination of a county in Appalachia and the reasons for its poverty. Made for *The Twentieth Century,* with Walter Cronkite. Produced by Isaac Kleinerman and Burton Benjamin. Directed by Willard Van Dyke. Written by Earle Luby. Photographed by Jess Paley. 30 minutes, b&w.

1964: *Rice.* A film on the growing imbalance between population growth and rice production in Asia, and the work of the International Rice Research Institute. Made for the Rockefeller Foundation. Directed by Willard Van Dyke and Wheaton Galentine. Written by Howard Enders. Music by Irwin Bazelon. Narrated by John Connell. 26 minutes, color.

Frontiers of News. A year of strife, seen through a dramatic treatment of still photographs made by the Associated Press. Directed and photographed by Willard Van Dyke. 11 minutes, b&w.

1965: *Pop Buell, Hoosier Farmer in Laos.* The story of an American farmer's dedication to his job for the U. S. Agency for International Development—helping the Meo tribesmen of Laos. Made for *The Twentieth Century,* with Walter Cronkite. Produced by Burton Benjamin and Isaac Kleinerman. Directed by Willard Van Dyke. Photographed by Merle Severn. 30 minutes, b&w.

Taming the Mekong. The co-operation between four countries in Southeast Asia in beginning to control one of the great rivers of the world. Made for *The Twentieth Century.* Produced by Burton Benjamin and Isaac Kleinerman. Directed by Willard Van Dyke. 30 minutes, b&w.

The Farmer: Feast or Famine. A look at the changing farm situation in the United States. Made for *The Twentieth Century.* Produced by Burton Benjamin and Isaac Kleinerman. Directed by Willard Van Dyke and Roger Barlow. 30 minutes, b&w.

Frontline Cameras 1935–1965. A filmic treatment of the great news stories of the past thirty years as depicted by photographers of the Associated Press. Produced and directed by Willard Van Dyke. Assisted by Hugh Johnston. 16 minutes, b&w.

1969(?): *Shape of Films to Come.* Directed by Willard Van Dyke. Produced by Isaac Kleinerman. Narrated by Walter Cronkite.

May 21, 1970, in Willard Van Dyke's office at the Museum of Modern Art.

G. Roy Levin: Let me start by asking about your time at the Office of War Information during World War II. What was it like working there?

Willard Van Dyke: Well, we welcomed the opportunity to gain experience in making films we believed in. We believed the war was a just war, and we had a great deal of freedom. One frustrating thing was that there was a group of writers in Hollywood who were anxious to help us, to write scripts for us, and we were unable ever to get a script from any of them that we could make a film about. And the real reason was that they approached film-making by sitting down at a desk with a preconceived idea and writing a script which would illuminate that idea. We went to the subject and let the subject dictate its own form to a large extent. It was a very frustrating period because they wanted very much to make the kind of films that we were making, and we very much needed help in terms of ideas and in terms of shooting outlines, and so on, and we just never could quite get together. But it was different with the documentary unit in New York with Irving Lerner, Roger Barlow, Frank Beckwith, Robert Riskin, Joe Krumgold, Philip Dunne, Sidney Meyers, Irving Jacoby and myself. And Alexander Hammid, who came in rather late, but he was very important in working there. (He was then known as Alexander Hackenschmied, but he changed his name at the end of the war under the prodding of Maya Deren, who was then his wife.) In any case, two of the best films we made were his, *Toscanini: Hymn of the Nations*,[1] and the film on the TVA.[2]

Our films really went through two phases. The first was to say to our allies, we're stepping up our production, hold on, we're coming with the materials of war. The second phase was, this is the nature of the American people, this is the way we live, this is the kind of people we are and so forth. Those films were designed for Sweden and Switzerland, as neutral nations, and later, to be shown in the various countries in Europe that we began to occupy. The films were designed to make them feel that we were pretty nice people after all. At the end we all began to look for that ideal little American town that was pristine and lovely, and to look for those idealized situations

[1] 1945.
[2] *Valley of the Tennessee*, 1944.

in those small towns. Somebody once called them the East Toilet Ohio Films.

G.R.L. I take it you feel these films were successful as propaganda. But do you feel that they still remain valid as films today, or, rather, are valid mainly as historical examples of a particular time and purpose?

W.V.D. I think they are valid mainly as historical examples, although I saw *Hymn of the Nations* not too long ago and . . . It's a film about an orchestra and about a great conductor, and, as such, it's as good as any other film of that kind that I've ever seen. It was very beautifully photographed by Boris Kaufman and very well directed by Irving Lerner and Alexander Hammid. It remains valid not only as a document, but it is also moving in its own right. Aside from that one I don't think they are very good. I recently looked at *San Francisco*, which I directed in 1945 and—incidentally, Waldo Salt wrote the commentary (Waldo Salt, of course, got an Academy Award for *Midnight Cowboy*). It was edited by Sidney Meyers. Well, the film has a kind of sterility about it that comes from our having set up certain kinds of situations outside of the United Nations conference itself. The acting and directing now look very false, and by present-day standards, I think most of the films would suffer from that kind of thing. There's one I also directed called *Steeltown* that has one sequence in it that I think still holds up. But most of the films don't. By the way, Von Sternberg[3] did one of those films, a film called *The Town*, about a little town in Indiana and the way the people lived there and so on. Larry Madison was his cameraman (he was usually my cameraman, but he was Sternberg's at that time) but Sternberg couldn't stay away from the camera when they went inside, and he usually pushed Larry away and began to do his own lighting. Well, the first rushes that came back were embarrassing, but as the film developed it became quite a respectable movie.

G.R.L. I've been looking at films here in the Museum, and among them were a number of wartime propaganda films. The ones that struck me most, probably because they were the most irritating in being the most blatantly chauvinistic, were ones like *The Battle of Russia* and the whole *Why We Fight* series.[4] *The Battle of Russia*

[3] Josef von Sternberg, the feature film director.

[4] "The famed 'Why We Fight' film series, produced by Frank Capra for the War Department in the belief that a man who knows whom he is fighting, what led up to the conflict, and what he is fighting for, makes the best kind of a soldier." (The Museum of Modern Art Department of Film Circulating Programs catalogue, p. 43.) It should be noted that these films were primarily produced as propaganda to condition feelings and attitudes toward our enemies, and were hardly meant to be objective information films.

was one of the best that I saw: the use of good animated diagrams and maps, some powerful footage and good editing and excellent use of sound; but they're very hard to take now—they're so jingoistic and smug. I understand that there was a war going on then, and that people weren't interested in being reasonable. But a film like *The Battle of San Pietro,*[5] also a wartime propaganda film, is different. It isn't jingoistic, and it doesn't falsify the facts—and it's still a moving film. I think it's because Huston wasn't trying to say how great we were, how bad the Nazis were; it was straightforward, honest. He was simply telling this story of how difficult it was to take the hilltop of San Pietro, and something about what it was like to be a soldier in such a situation, perhaps being wounded or killed, and something about the Italians of that town, to whom he was sympathetic. And he himself narrated, with his dry, cracked voice in a quiet, understated manner. There was no screaming or false passion. A touching film still, and at least from the point of view of 1970, much more effective than the blatantly propagandistic ones. But he had trouble getting it released, didn't he?

W.V.D. Yes. Because it showed American soldiers being killed.

G.R.L. Did that automatically make it bad propaganda?

W.V.D. The film came very late in the war, and when we saw it at the OWI, we jumped up and down with glee. We thought, this is really it, this is a fine film. We felt the same way, to a lesser extent, but still strongly also about *The Battle for the Aleutians,* which was also a Huston film. Those, and then subsequently *Let There Be Light,*[6] came right at the end of the war. Well, Huston was alone from our point of view. He was the master of the thing. But also let's not forget that his films came late in the war, he had the advantage of seeing the mistakes all the rest of us had been making from the beginning, besides just being a master film-maker. He taught us the lesson we should have known and did know but didn't follow through, which was to let the reality speak, let the actual situation speak, don't try to impose your ideas on it, don't mold it according to your own concepts—which is what we were doing all through the war. But Huston didn't. The Capra films of the *Why We Fight* series were synthetic; they were made in the cutting room, and they were skillful at that time, and their blatancy matched

[5] Directed by Major John Huston in 1944 for the Army Pictorial Service.

[6] Also directed by Huston; 1946. It is about U.S. soldiers in a mental hospital after the war and the way their illnesses were successfully treated. The film was banned by the War Department and has never been publicly released, because, says Huston, "They said that they felt it was unfair—to the patients, to the men." (Quote from an interview with Huston in *Film: Book 2, Films of Peace and War,* edited by Robert Hughes, p. 32.)

the feelings we had that we were in the middle of a war. We felt strongly about that war, and patriotism at that time was not a chauvinistic thing; it was something that we drew strength from.

[. . .]

G.R.L. In a note to one of your letters[7] there is a reference to *The World Today.* Were you ever involved with that?

W.V.D. Yes. It was a left-wing newsreel, a kind of progressive *March of Time*—if there is such a thing. Many of us felt that *The March of Time* was not frank about issues, that very often it covered up things that needed to be talked about, needed to be exposed. So we, a group of us, got together in 1936 and conceived this idea of a magazine, a screen magazine such as *The March of Time,* to be called *The World Today.*[8]

The group consisted of Ben Maddow, Sidney Meyers, Irving Lerner, Ralph Steiner, Paul Strand, Leo Hurwitz, and, for part of the time, Henri Cartier-Bresson, and myself. We put out two issues. One was about a rent strike in a middle-class community in Queens, and the other one was about the Black Legion. The Black Legion was a kind of offshoot of the Ku Klux Klan which was organized in Detroit; there was an oppressive thing against Blacks, against labor organizations, etc. It was like the old Know-Nothings of the beginnings of our country, when anything that was moving toward change was repressed. They used the same scare tactics that the Ku Klux Klan did. It didn't last very long, but there was a feature-length motion picture made about it, and we re-created an incident when a labor organizer was kidnapped and taken out and tortured by members of the Black Legion.

G.R.L. Do you know the name of the film?

W.V.D. No, I don't. I don't know whether there are prints of these films still in existence or not.

G.R.L. Who financed them?

W.V.D. Thomas J. Brandon.

G.R.L. Out of sympathy or for business reasons?

W.V.D. I think that he was a businessman, and he felt the films would have an audience among the then sort of budding film societies, and among left-wing groups. They did not get shown in theaters. Actually, I don't really know how much release there really

[7] This is a series of letters Van Dyke wrote to his wife from October 1936 through February 1937, while working as one of the cameramen on Pare Lorentz' *The River;* long excerpts from these letters were printed in *Film Comment,* Spring 1967, vol. 3, no. 2.

[8] The "parent" group was called Frontier Films, which then made *The World Today* series.

was. I left to go away on *The River* about the time they were being finished. I was a cameraman on these films.

G.R.L. Do you remember the problems in trying to get them distributed?

W.V.D. No. Brandon had a distribution company, and we assumed he would do the distribution.

G.R.L. Was there ever any talk or hope of producing more issues for the series?

W.V.D. Oh yes, there was talk about it, but then this group of film-makers[9] got involved in the making of a film which had a long, sad history but eventually emerged as *Native Land*.[10] It was then that Ralph Steiner and I left the others because we felt the thing was moving away from good film-making into direct propaganda, and I think neither one of us was particularly interested in making propaganda films. So when a chance to make *The City* came along, we left Frontier Films. And besides, at that point, we were a group of unorganized people, working together at night, weekends, just out of the pleasure of it, and then somebody—I don't know who it was—came up with some money and I think several people were paid fifty dollars a week, for full time. I had a wife, and I couldn't live on fifty dollars a week; and besides that, it went against the grain to be hired to make propaganda films. Then I would have to make whatever film came along and I was not interested in that.

G.R.L. In another interview[11] you mention a film you made for the U. S. Information Agency and which they refused to release. Were all of the films that you've made sponsored by some organization?

W.V.D. Yes. I never had money enough to make the films that I wanted to make. The USIA film was about Blacks in this country, and probably made in '63 or '64. I don't know that there was a title.

G.R.L. Has that been a source of frustration?

W.V.D. Yes, it has been a source of frustration. Not frustration. That's too big a word. I've been extremely lucky that I could always find something that interested me in almost any film that I worked on, to a greater or lesser degree, of course. I really enjoy the process of

[9] i.e., Frontier Films.

[10] Made during the years 1939–42, it was "based on the report of the Senate Civil Liberties Committee, which had been investigating violations of constitutional liberties throughout the country. Financed from small contributions by thousands of people, *Native Land* was a series of episodes dramatizing representative instances of terrorism in a variety of styles, not all of which marched harmoniously together. . . . When it appeared in 1942, it passed almost unnoticed." Rotha, *Documentary Film*, p. 322.

[11] *Film Comment*, Spring 1965, vol. 3, no. 2.

making movies, over and above the content. The process itself has always been a very satisfying thing for me. I've worked as a cameraman, obviously, I've worked as a sound man, I've worked as an editor and I've worked as a writer; there isn't a part of the process that I don't know and know well and enjoy doing. And I really wouldn't mind in the least just recording the sound on a picture. It was just part of a whole process, so frustration is too big a word. There are things I would like to have done and didn't do, but then who doesn't feel that way?

G.R.L. Do I take it correctly that the films where you're listed as director you always kept a close hand over the editing?

W.V.D. Yes, except for the television films such as *The Twentieth Century*.

G.R.L. Let me quote a paragraph from one of the letters you wrote while working on *The River*. It's from Helena, Arkansas, and dated February 10, 1937. You start the letter saying you've been studying maps, and make a long list of place names, American and Indian—it's a very evocative list; you call them "long rolling names for the great plains and wild sweet rivers." Then you say, "How are we to make real the dreams of the men who made this country? What can we do to justify their heroism? How shall we carry on the work of John Brown, Bill Hickok, Daniel Boone? This is no country for scheming merchants and grocery clerks. We have a bigger destiny. Our lot crawls not between dry ribs, but past them, over desert to a rich land where the sun shall rise forever. How to re-create the vision of the pioneer?"[12] A very passionate statement. You were a young man.

W.V.D. Yes, I was a young man, and I was quoting, drawing on a lot of things. On Eliot, on Whitman, on my own background. My father was a pioneer. He left home at the age of seventeen and was in charge of a section gang laying the half-mile stakes on the railroad from New Orleans to El Paso, Texas, along the frontier. Subsequently he became an itinerant photographer along the Mexican border, and in New Mexico, Arizona and Texas. But in any case, he used to tell me a great many stories. I had malaria when I was a kid, and when I was sick in bed, my father used to come and talk to me and tell me long and very moving stories about his life and about the early days in the West. He photographed people like Buffalo Bill and Annie Oakley. He was an extremely good pistol shot and he'd lived through a period when the West was very wild. His older sister went out to California in a covered wagon. It was very close to me when I was just a little boy in Fort Collins,

[12] Quoted in *Film Comment*, Spring 1965, vol. 3, no. 2, p. 54.

Colorado. There were still Indians there, and my father took me to see Buffalo Bill's Wild West Show, and introduced me to Buffalo Bill. So there was this kind of marvelous feeling that I was living through a part of the development of the country, in a very real sense. So when I first came to New York I felt that it was somehow a little effete, a little too intellectual, that the true source of American strength lay in the heartlands. I have long since outgrown that romantic notion, and I feel very much a New Yorker. But at that time in my youth, these memories were very, very strong.

G.R.L. *Skyscraper*, on which you worked, is in some ways an enjoyable film, but what bothers me is that if one makes a film about building a skyscraper in New York, there are all kinds of implicit social comments to be made, and these seem to be ignored. What mainly comes across is how nice it all is. So what I'm asking is, were you concerned about any of this, or had you simply decided that you were making a film for a sponsor and wouldn't bother about any of the possible social implications?

W.V.D. Well, that film has a very curious history. First of all, let me say straight out that that's Shirley Clarke's film basically. The way it came about was that when 375 Park[13] was going to be built, the daughter of the man who headed the Seagram Company decided to hold a competition for the plans for the building, and that was won by Miës van der Rohe and Philip Johnson. She then held a kind of competition for a film to be made, and some film-makers were chosen to submit ideas. I wanted to make that film in the very worst way because I loved the plans for the building and I could see that the building was going to have real distinction. So Wheaton Galentine and I submitted a plan, but the plan submitted by Leacock and Rodakiewicz won. In frustration then, one day I happened to say to a man who knew John Tishman that I was not working and that I would love to make a film about a skyscraper, and that I had not been able to get to make this one, and I'm sure Rodakiewicz and Leacock would make a great one but I wanted to make this kind of film. And he said, "Well, I know John Tishman. Maybe he'd like to make one about a building he's making." So it turned out John Tishman indeed was interested in making a film about the Tishman building and tried to get the suppliers—the elevator people, the air-conditioning people, the Bethlehem Steel people and so forth—to put up the money for the film. Well, they put up most of it, but not all of it, and we started to shoot over about an eighteen-month period—before you could begin to edit very much you had to get what was happening in the building of the

13 The Seagram Building.

building. About this time, I decided that my association with Irving Jacoby in Affiliated Film Producers was at an end, and I got an offer of a job to go to India to make an adventure film, which intrigued me, and I asked Shirley if she would edit the film. To edit the film really meant to supervise some additional shooting and so on, and it was Shirley's idea for the script, and she worked with the man who wrote it and so on. Shirley intended it as a kind of satire. It doesn't quite come off that way, but she hoped that you would see underneath the surface of such things as the band playing, the mayor talking, etc. I would say that I enjoyed it. I didn't feel very involved in it, very committed to it, and I was moving on to other things when that film was made, and I really don't take very much credit for it.

G.R.L. In the interview I mentioned before, you say that one of the main influences on your work was John Grierson. When you made *Valley Town,* which uses a voice-over, first-person narrator, were you aware of other films which had used that technique? *The Saving of Bill Blewitt,*[14] for example?

W.V.D. I've never seen that film. Let me say that with the commentary on *The River,* Lorentz posed all of us a tremendous problem. What do you do about the soundtrack? Lorentz did a thing that I would love to have done. I didn't know he was going to use the names of the rivers[15] when I wrote that letter to my wife.[16] There was no script for *The River;* but this was the way in which I would have been impelled to do it, and so it seemed to me absolutely apropos. But now as a film-maker, what do you do? How do you overcome the problem of that voice from on high? Well, in *The City* for instance, the way we did it was to use it very sparsely, and use great blocks of music and let the visual images carry you. In *Valley Town,* it seemed, I was very interested in Marc Blitzstein and *The Cradle Will Rock* and *No for an Answer,* and the way in which he used recitatives and songs. Then the problem was, who is the person who is looking at this? Well, there was a radio program in which the mayor of a town was played by the man whom I chose as narrator, and it was one of those soap opera kinds of things, but he had this commanding, sympathetic voice, so I conceived of the idea of the mayor talking about the problems in his town. It came directly out of radio soap opera. I hope that the script for it is a little better than the radio soap opera. But nevertheless, that was the origin of it. In that film, I was not influenced by British films, but

14 Produced by John Grierson, directed by Harry Watt; 1937.

15 In the narration of *The River* there is a list of American rivers.

16 One of the letters referred to in note 7.

again was trying to get a fresh approach. As a matter of fact, it seemed to me very far from what the British were doing.

G.R.L. You mention *The City*. At last year's Flaherty Seminar,[17] I remember you saying that the film was as applicable today in its presentation of urban problems as it was when it was first made; and I certainly agree. The cars and clothes are clearly from an earlier era, but the same basic problems remain. I think it's a very good film. The only part that bothered me was the end, where this supposedly ideal community is presented as a kind of antidote to urban problems, but everything is so supernice that it doesn't ring true. Was it an actual community?

W.V.D. It's a composite of four locations. The main location is Greenbelt, Maryland, which was just outside Washington and made for government employees; Greendale, Wisconsin; and Greenhills, Ohio—I think it's Ohio, but I'm not too sure now. Then there is a public school in Long Beach, California—there are a couple of public schools out there in Los Angeles. All of those were put together to make a synthetic community. And the ending is far too long. It was never conceived of that way at all. We had planned it to be very short. When the city planners said, "Oh, come on, you've had your fun, this is our time to say what we really want. You have to spell it out." And so we spelled it out. But you're quite right, it is much too long, And besides, as Grierson said, it lacks the smell of fish and chips. It's antiseptic.

G.R.L. When you made that film, was there ever any question of talking about why cities were like that?

W.V.D. No, no. The city planners simply insisted there be no sociological or political or any kind of examination of the reasons behind, but simply that this is what exists and this is what it could be. Not "how do we get there" or "how did we get here." We posed those in the commentary, you know, a couple of times, but they're rhetorical questions.

G.R.L. Did you have any feelings about wanting to or caring to talk about causes?

W.V.D. Yes, but we simply couldn't.

G.R.L. What are your feelings about cinéma-vérité and film-makers like Leacock, Pennebaker, the Maysles, Wiseman, Rouch and Marker? Would you say that cinéma-vérité is objective or subjective?

W.V.D. Leacock says it began in this country with *Toby and the*

[17] The annual Robert Flaherty Film Seminars, begun in 1955, emphasize the viewing and discussion of documentary films, though other works of contemporary and historical significance are also included. In the words of the Seminars' brochure, the emphasis is on "films that draw their inspiration from life and reflect the spirit of Robert Flaherty's explorations."

Tall Corn. Well, I was the executive producer, and looking at it, all I can say is that as far as that film is concerned, it may have generated something in Leacock, but that film is very far from being what I would think of as cinéma-vérité. Leacock and Pennebaker and Al Maysles all worked for Drew.[18] They all had arguments with Drew, based on differences in aesthetic values. Drew insisted many times on the use of a commentator. They didn't want a commentator. They felt that the film had to speak for itself, but if you had to have commentary, the less the better. At the beginning there was a belief that if you just shot the material and put it together, you were not imposing any of your own feelings on it.

Well, I think that we've moved away from that now, thank God, because it is, in my opinion, ridiculous. When you press the button on the camera, you press it for a reason. Something has triggered it and you've recorded something. The angle that you took, when you chose to zoom in, when you chose to zoom back, or if you did, the move that you made, all of these things affect what is going on. Without any doubt your presence affects what is going on. So the idea of objectivity is nonsense. What I think really comes out of it finally is a greater flexibility, a way of putting the people in front of the camera at ease because you're not cluttered up with the kind of things we used to be cluttered up with—rigging lights, a completely immobile camera and the recording equipment we had to use. To make a very long story short, it seems to me that what the cinéma-vérité people in this country were looking for was an aesthetic, and that aesthetic grew out of two pieces of apparatus: the Kudelski tape recorder[19] and the mobile hand-held camera. Now I think they found that this was an extremely interesting and useful and valuable way of approaching social documentation. Of all of them, I think the person who comes closest to being that non-existent objective ideal is Wiseman, because in none of his films does he have commentary; in all of his films he has managed to penetrate into his subject to an extraordinary degree, and one feels in his films the lack of camera relatedness, or awareness, to a greater degree than any of the others.

G.R.L. Would you say he is objective in his cutting?

W.V.D. No, no, of course not. Of course, as soon as he's faced with all of these materials, then his choices come into play and he emphasizes certain things and de-emphasizes others. He's a film-

[18] The above-mentioned film-makers worked on a series of television documentaries Robert Drew produced for Time, Inc., including *On the Pole, The Chair, Petey and Johnny, Primary, Football* and *Crisis.*

[19] i.e., the Nagra tape recorder invented by Stefan Kudelski, which is the standard professional tape recorder used in cinéma-vérité filming.

maker, and at this point he begins to put it together. Basically I think it's a way of shooting that we're talking about, and that shooting has been adopted by all the television people now—nobody shoots any other way except with this kind of equipment and this kind of approach. But I don't think there is this objective truth that they were searching for. The film *David Holzman's Diary*[20] is a marvelous example of the fact that there is no such thing.

G.R.L. I agree. But what bothers me is when documentary films pretend to objectivity. This false pretension to objectivity seems to me of real concern, and with television, a real danger.

W.V.D. I feel very strongly about this and I therefore welcomed the statement on the part of NET that they were going to make a series of documentary films that took a point of view, the point of view of the film-maker, and I think this is an extremely healthy thing. Jack Willis' film on the farm problem,[21] for instance, is perhaps a little too discursive, perhaps it covers too much territory, but it is Jack Willis as a reporter going out there and really trying to find out what is happening. There is no question about his point of view in that film. Now, for the film-maker, it seems to me extremely healthy if the networks, or for that network, to begin to say, "Well, this film-maker has as much right to his point of view as Reston has when he does something on the editorial page of the New York *Times*. And we don't have to balance it, we don't have to give it equal time. This is a statement that this man has to make, and it's a thoughtful statement, and it is worth listening to." It seems to me that that's the way we have to go. We have to forget the whole business of objectivity.

G.R.L. One of the problems that seems to be universal is finding money to finance documentary films.

W.V.D. Oh, come on, there are more documentary films being made today than there ever have been in the whole history of the world. When you get a film like *Ice*,[22] which is sponsored by money from the American Film Institute, a film that is reputedly a film about revolution, I just don't see it. There are films about all of the problems that we are facing at this moment. Where the money comes from, I don't know, but I know very well that there's money for films. Now it doesn't mean that everybody who wants to make

20 Directed by Jim McBride, 1967; every shot in the film could have been shot by the leading character, David Holzman, whom we are led to believe is a real person and has actually made the film; only when the credits are shown at the end is it revealed (admitted?) that the film is a fiction.

21 *Hard Times in the Country*, 1969, for NET.

22 Produced by David Stone and directed by Robert Kramer, who formerly made films for the radical film group Newsreel.

a film is going to find the money to do it, but there are more being made.

G.R.L. I guess there are. But still, people like Bill Jersey, Leacock, Pennebaker, all say they have difficulty finding money to make films. And these are established film-makers, not unknowns. You certainly quoted examples of worthwhile films, and on TV there are some good documentaries. But doesn't the problem remain that if you make documentaries, having them shown on network TV is almost impossible?

W.V.D. Yes, it is. It's almost impossible, and you have to find other ways of distribution. De Antonio's film, *Year of the Pig*, is getting around. He found the money to make a film which at that time was about a very unpopular subject.[23] But he found it, and it's still getting around. It's always difficult to get money, also difficult to make movies. But the fact is that more concerned movies are being made now than have been made in the past. For the first time in the history of this country you've got what seems to be a viable, working left-wing distribution outfit. American Documentary Films seems to be existing, operating, run by Jerry Stoll.

G.R.L. Do you think that documentaries can influence our opinions?

W.V.D. Not very much.

G.R.L. Okay. How did you come to take this job here at the Museum? You were a working film-maker and then . . . well, this is a different kind of job. Why did you decide to change?

W.V.D. Well, first of all, the first person that I came to see when I came to New York in 1935 was Iris Barry, who was the director of this department at that time. I have been close to the Museum all through those years. When it became apparent that Richard Griffith[24] was not at all well in 1963, Iris Barry asked me to help her find a successor to Mr. Griffith as director for this department. I made a number of suggestions and I kept trying to sell people on the idea, and trying to define what the job should be, and finally one day Rene d'Harnoncourt[25] said, "Why don't you take the job?" And other people began to say, "If it is as good as you say it is, you better do it." Well, I had also reached a point in film-making where I was doing a good many things that I was really not very happy doing. I had two sons who were still in school, and a wife, and I was shooting programs for *The Twentieth Century*,[26] so I had no control over the editing and this was enormously frustrating to

[23] About the Vietnam War.
[24] Curator of the Museum of Modern Art Film Library, 1951–65.
[25] Director of the Museum of Modern Art at the time.
[26] For CBS.

me. The idea that somebody else would shape it without even conference most of the time was frustrating in the extreme.

Then there was the enormously disappointing experience of the cancellation of the film that Ed Murrow asked me to do on American Blacks. It reached a rough-cut stage and was taken away, in pretty fine cut. It was a very mild, very honest film in which the Blacks spoke for themselves, and I didn't attempt to impose my own ideas on it. It would have done us an enormous amount of good overseas, I believe, but someone, and I'm pretty sure it was Ed Murrow himself, made the decision that the film would not be finished and they took the negative and the print and handed it over to Jim Blue, who couldn't or didn't want to find a way to finish it, and he made *The March*[27] instead. This was very disappointing, and I felt as if I were in a period where I had earned the right to make a movie my way. If I hadn't, I thought, then I had better find something to do where I would have less supervision over what I did, but where I could say what I have always believed, that film-makers are artists—some of them—and some films are works of art, and that in any case it's a lively, exciting, marvelous medium and this is the showcase for it. So that's why I took it.

G.R.L. Is there a chance of expanding the Film Study Center, or expanding the distribution of rental films? Or are those mainly problems of trying to raise money?

W.V.D. Yes, yes, it's primarily that. I should say that when I came here, the trustees agreed that I could take time off to make films. I have taken time off to shoot one film for *The Twenty-first Century* called *The Shape of Films to Come*, which explored film formats basically. But I don't really have the time, and when I was offered four documentaries to do in Yugoslavia, I couldn't find the time to get over there and do them. But I really do miss film-making, and I want to try now to organize my life so I can get away and do it.

27 Made for the USIA on the Civil Rights March on Washington in August 1963.

RICHARD LEACOCK

(The following material was written by the film-maker.)

[Born July 18, 1921, in the Canary Islands.]

"Educated in England. Came to America 1938; attended Harvard University—class of 1943—major, physics.

"Four years in the U. S. Army.

"Combat photographer W.W. II, 1942–46.

"After war was associate producer and photographer for Robert Flaherty filming *Louisiana Story*, which won British academy award and the Golden Lion of Venice. Worked on numerous documentary films with Louis de Rochemont, John Ferno, Willard Van Dyke.

"With Robert Drew of Time-Life a group of us made a series of experimental television documentaries which formed the style known as cinéma-vérité. Among these films are *The Chair; Eddie Sachs* (also known as *On the Pole*); *Crisis*, which won numerous prizes all over the world. Subsequently I went into partnership with D. A. Pennebaker. Made *The Invisible Empire* for CBS, which won an Emmy; A *Stravinsky Portrait; Happy Mother's Day* (an account of the birth of quintuplets in a Middle Western town, which won the Silver Medals both in Venice and in Leipzig—on both sides of the Iron Curtain). After completing *Chiefs*, a short film study of a convention of three thousand police chiefs and their wives at Waikiki Beach, I was offered a unique opportunity to found and head up a Department of Film at MIT."

Condensed Dogma of One Film-Maker
by Richard Leacock

(Written for a series of screenings of ten of Leacock's films at MIT in 1969.)

"Having grown up in the documentary film tradition of Flaherty, Grierson, Elton et al., I believed that we should go out into the real world and record the way it really is. Without sound we were limited largely to processes—this is how we fish, this is how we blow glass, make boats, build dams, etc. With the advent of sound, far from being freed, we were paralyzed by the complexity and size of equipment. We still went out to the real world and proceeded to destroy, by our own impact, the very thing we went to record.

"After much experimenting and some wonderful failures we managed to put together a portable, quiet synch-sound camera and recorder in 1960. *Primary* was the first film that our group (Bob Drew, Pennebaker, Al Maysles, Macartney-Filgate and myself) made where the new equipment worked; where two people made up a whole film unit; where we could walk in and out of situations without lights, tripods, cables and all the other impedimenta which had shackled us before.

"We now subjected ourselves to a rather rigid set of rules. If we missed something, never ask anyone to repeat it. Never ask any questions. Never interview. We rarely broke them and when we did we regretted it.

"*On the Pole, The Chair, Petey and Johnny, Primary, Football* and *Crisis* were produced by Bob Drew for Time, Inc., as an experiment in TV journalism that really never got on the air. They are group film works with often as many as six teams shooting, and many are group-edited. I had very little to do with *Football,* for which Jim Lipscomb, who attended Miami High, was most responsible.

"The other films* are entirely shot by me and for better or for worse are entirely my responsibility."

FILMOGRAPHY†

1935: *Canary Bananas.* Director and Photographer: Richard Leacock. Sponsor: Dartington Hall.

1938: *Galápagos Islands.* Director and Photographer: R.L. Sponsor: Dartington Hall.

1940: *To Hear My Banjo Play.* Photographer: R.L. Director: Geza Karpathy.

1946: *Louisiana Story.* Director: Robert Flaherty. Photographer: R.L. Editor: Helen Van Dongen. Sponsor: Standard Oil.

* *Happy Mother's Day, A Stravinsky Portrait, Hickory Hill, Chiefs.*
† The filmography was compiled by the film-maker.

1947–49: *Geography Films Series.* Photographer: R.L. Producer and Director: John Ferno. Sponsor: Louis de Rochemont Assoc.

1949: *Pelileo Earthquake.* Photographer and Director: R.L. Editor: Leo Horowitz. Sponsor: United Nations.

1950: *New Frontier.* (Also known as *Years of Change.*) Director: Willard Van Dyke. Photographer and Editor: R.L. Sponsor: USIA, HEW, NIH, NIMH for Affiliated Film Producers, Inc.

1951: *The Lonely Night.* Director: Irving Jacoby. Photographer: R.L. Sponsor: USIA, HEW, NIH, NIMH for Affiliated Film Producers, Inc.

1952: *Head of the House.* Director: Irving Jacoby. Photographer: R.L. Editor and Producer: Jacoby and R.L. Sponsor: USIA, HEW, NIH, NIMH for Affiliated Film Producers, Inc.

195–? *Jazz Dance.* Producer (Director?): Roger Tilton. Photographer: R.L. Editor: Roger Tilton. Sponsor: Roger Tilton.

195—? *New York.* Based on story by E. B. White. Director: Bob Sharpe. Photographer: R.L. Sponsor: CBS.

195—? *The Lonely Boat.* Producer: Ed Foote. Photographer and Director: R.L. Editor: Shirley Clarke. Sponsor: Ed Foote.

1954: *Toby and the Tall Corn.* Director, Photographer, Editor: R.L. Sponsor: *Omnibus.*

1955: *How the F-100 Got Its Tail.* Director: R.L. Sponsor: *Omnibus.*

1958: *Bullfight at Málaga.* Photographer: R.L. Editors: Bob Drew, Pat Jaffe. *Bernstein in Israel.* Director and Photographer: R.L. Editor: Pat Jaffe. Sponsor: *Omnibus.*

1959: *Balloon.* Photographers: R.L. and Pennebaker. Editor: Bob Drew. *Bernstein in Moscow.* Director: R.L. Sponsor: Ford Motor Co.

Science Films: *Coulomb's Law; Crystals; Magnet Laboratory; Frames of Reference.* Director: R.L. Sponsor: Physical Sciences Study Committee of ESI.

LIVING CAMERA SERIES

1960: *Primary*. Film-makers: R.L., Al Maysles, Pennebaker, Terry Macartney-Filgate. Producer: Bob Drew. Editors: mostly R.L., Drew. Sponsor: Time, Inc. *On the Pole*. Producer: Bob Drew. Photographers: R.L., Al Maysles, Pennebaker. Editors: R.L., Pennebaker, Drew, and others. Sponsor: Time, Inc. *Yanki No!* Photographers: R.L., Maysles, with Drew. Sponsor: Time, Inc.

1961: *Petey and Johnny*. Photographers: R.L., Bill Ray, Jim Lipscomb, Abbot Mills, etc. Sponsor: Time, Inc. *The Children Were Watching*. Film-makers: R.L., Abbot Mills, Greg Shuker, with Drew. Sponsor: Time, Inc.

1962: *The Chair*. Film-makers: R.L., Drew, Pennebaker, Shuker. Sponsor: Time, Inc. *Kenya, South Africa*. Film-makers: R.L., Maysles, Shuker, etc. Sponsor: Time, Inc.

1963: *Crisis*. Film-makers: R.L., Pennebaker, etc. Sponsor: Xerox.

1963: *Happy Mother's Day*. Film-makers: R.L., Joyce Chopra. Editors: R.L., Joyce Chopra, Nancy Sen. Sponsor: *The Saturday Evening Post*.

1964: *A Stravinsky Portrait; Portrait of Geza Anda; Portrait of Paul Burkhard*. Photographer and Editor: R.L. Sound: Sarah Hudson. Sponsor: Norddeutscher Rundfunk. *Republicans—The New Breed*. Film-makers: R.L. and Noel Parmentel. Editor: Nick Proferes. Sponsor: CBS.

1965: *The Anatomy of Cindy Fink*. Film-makers: R.L. and Nick Proferes. Editor: Pat Jaffe. *Ku Klux Klan—The Invisible Empire*. Director of photography: R.L. Sound: Noel Parmental. Sponsor: CBS Reports.

1966: *Old Age—The Wasted Years*. Photography: R.L. Sound and Editing: Nell Cox. Sponsor: NET. *Portrait of Van Cliburn*. Director, Photographer and Editor: R.L. and Nell Cox. Sponsor: Bell Telephone Hour.

1967: *Monterey Pop*. Photographer: R.L. one of seven (including Pennebaker, Maysles). Editor: primarily Pennebaker. Sponsor: ABC-TV. *Lulu* (mixed media). Director of photography: R.L., with Roger Murphy and Don MacSorley. Sponsor: American National Opera for Sarah Caldwell.

1968: *Who's Afraid of the Avant-Garde?* Part of Photography and Editor with Pennebaker et al. Sponsor: PBL. *Maidstone*. One of six photographers. Sponsor: Norman Mailer. *Hickory Hill*. Photographer and Editor: R.L. Sound: Sandra Bramhall.

1969: *Chiefs*. Photographer and Editor: R.L. Sound: Noel Parmentel. Sponsor: PBL.

1970: *Queen of Apollo*. Photographer and Editor: R.L. Sound: Elspeth Leacock. Sponsor: Mrs. John B. Hobson III.

August 13, 1970, on the back porch of Richard Leacock's apartment in Cambridge, Massachusetts.

G. Roy Levin: I looked at the *Show* magazine article[1] and at the interview you did with James Blue[2] a few years ago, and I have questions about what you said in these pieces. But if you think you're repeating yourself, just yell—we'll leave it out. For example, in *Petey and Johnny* there are a number of scenes with cross-cutting: a fist fight intercut with shots of gang members; early in the film, Petey's pregnant girlfriend is dancing in the apartment and it's intercut with a man dancing in the street—things like that. If you were making the film today, for yourself, would you do things like that?

Richard Leacock: Probably not. All of those films[3] are very hard to discuss because they weren't anybody's films, they were a mishmash. This became more and more of a problem. That particular film was shot by innumerable different people, and sometimes they were learning. It started out with an idea to follow Johnny,[4] the teen-aged kid, but this wasn't possible, because if you go along with a gang of kids, inevitably, they're not going to do anything. They just take advantage of you and freeload. Finally I shifted it to Petey, because he was at least doing something, and then things started to develop. The shooting went on for a period of about nine months, and it was then that Drew needed terribly to structure it in order to make a presentable work out of it. And in my view it got too structured. There were nice things in it, using sound effects, a police car. . . . It got a little hokey at times.

G.R.L. I think there are good things in all those films. But, and I would guess that you'd agree, they finally don't really work. For one thing, the narrator plants the argument, tells us too much, and parts are too hoked up.

R.L. At least in that particular one the narration was by Petey, so it had a certain validity.

G.R.L. He wrote that narration?

R.L. He did.

[1] *Show*, January 1970, vol. 1, no. 1, "Leacock Pennebaker: The MGM of the Underground?" by Robert Cristgau.

[2] *Film Comment*, Spring 1965, vol. 3, no. 2, "One Man's Truth, an Interview with Richard Leacock" by James Blue.

[3] Films made by Drew Associates.

[4] Briefly, as Leacock noted in a mimeographed sheet for an MIT showing of ten of his films, *Petey and Johnny* is "the result of months of filming Piri Thomas, ex-con turned religious social worker in East Harlem."

G.R.L. Then let's talk about *Eddie Sachs.*[5]

R.L. There was narration in all the rest of them, which is awful. We got into terrible fights about them.

G.R.L. At the end of *Eddie Sachs,* when he goes to the car in the empy lot, and the empty track—

R.L. No, that happened. What went wrong in that scene was one of the assistants opened a reel of film and it got exposed to the light, an essential piece of film when he was puking in the waste-paper basket in the garage. I must give Drew credit. I would have thrown it away. I'm rather fond of that ending.

G.R.L. How long did you work for Drew—or with him?

R.L. Well, it shifted. I first met Drew . . . I made a film called *Toby* which was made with classic 35mm. equipment. It was sort of a cyclical story about a traveling tent theater show in the Middle West. By just sheer hard work, in spite of this impossibly heavy equipment, we were able to get things—and we did use synch-sound even though it's clumsy. But it has a surprising feeling of just being there. Drew was with *Life,* but he had taken a Nieman Fellowship at Harvard. He was studying what television meant to journalism and vice versa, and he saw this film, came roaring down to New York to find out who had made it. He eventually got together with me and we talked a lot and then I made another film for *Omnibus* about testing an F-100 jet airplane,[6] and Drew is an old jet pilot. Not a very good film, but it has certain elements . . . this feeling of being there. Again Drew flipped out; so he came down to New York again. Then he came back to *Life* and he started getting drips and drops of money from *Life* to buy equipment, and we developed this idea of getting very portable equipment and he managed to get enough money to try to have some made up for us. Which didn't work, and then we kept changing it. And we did a film on a bullfight (*Bullfight at Málaga*) but the camera didn't work. It was still a pretty good film of a bullfight, but nothing was really working. I remember we had a brand-new camera, and we were just taking it out of the box, and I was festooned with cables and all this crap, and we were connected by cables and could barely walk with them. I think after the second bull the camera just stopped working, so we had to grab an old spring-wind camera and make the movie with that. We did have a tape recorder, and by a lot of tricky cutting and faking we managed to make it look like it was working. But it

[5] "A result of filming the Indianapolis 500 race two consecutive years. We did not film the third year when Eddie was killed within moments of the start of the race." (Richard Leacock)

[6] *How the F-100 Got Its Tail,* 1955.

wasn't until *Primary* that the equipment was working, and even in *Primary* it really wasn't working, but it was close enough. I mean we got the first taste of being able to walk into a room shooting.

It gets to the silly business of who did what first. Morris Engel was trying to do the same thing in theatrical filming and someone else had built a sort of synch-sound 35mm. rig he could barely stagger along with; but this idea has been around for a long time.

I had a lovely quote from Tolstoy, in 1904—it's up in the office; but in 1904 he looked at movies and said, "With this we can go out into the real world and photograph Russian life as it is. We have no need to invent stories." Then Vertov in 1920 came out with this whole list of slogans which is saying essentially the same thing, only with revolutionary zeal tagged onto it. Everybody had this notion, or a hell of a lot of people did; the problem was you couldn't do it. I differ, I think, with most people's view of that, though—of Vertov. The view that he was sort of suppressed I don't think was all true, because to me the original Kino-Eye films, which were really newsreels, did as much as you could do in this direction. I mean they recorded famine, disaster, but in this very superficial way, and then he went on to film *The Man with the Movie Camera*, which was accused of being formalistic, blah, blah, blah, and to me it was. It was tricks, games, and I don't see that it really has any connection with his expressed desire to show life as it is.[7]

G.R.L. Not the newsreels either, his early ones?

R.L. Yeah . . . but somehow there's something immensely unsatisfactory about those. They simply didn't say enough, because all you could do with the silent camera was what we were stuck with. You could deal with processes but you couldn't deal with communication and so this was the very problem, right there. I guess I'm always being accused of putting overemphasis on technology, but it couldn't happen until the transistor came along. This is a silly idea, but had Vertov had that possibility, he would have gone in a very different direction. But then I wonder. . . . As far as I can see, Godard is totally uninterested in this aspect of film-making. He sort of recognizes that this kind of film exists, but he's not the least bit interested, insofar as I can see, in observing. To me he's essentially theatrical. Maybe a sort of uncontrolled theater.

G.R.L. I don't see Godard as a documentary film-maker.

R.L. No, he's not.

G.R.L. But as far as truth goes, in other words his perceptions of

[7] For a concise discussion of Vetow, v. Rotha, *Documentary Film*, pp. 88–91, and Historical Outline, p. 7.

the world, they generally coincide with mine, so I see more truth in his films than I do in most so-called documentaries which give us reality, but which, for all kinds of reasons, don't tell me as much about the reality of the world as some of Godard's—

R.L. You've got the problem of observing. It's extremely difficult. I think in works that I've had to do there are only tiny moments of revelation, when you really find something out. At the moment we've reached a point where I think people tend to mistake the technique for the result. Just because you go film people with this equipment and don't intervene doesn't mean it's going to be interesting, revealing or true. I guess where I'm at now—and I may be begging the question—is that I think it's got to be 8mm., or something much, much cheaper and smaller, because to get these moments is extraordinarily difficult and rather expensive, and there are incredibly few moments of what I call revelation. And I'm talking about my own work. It's very, very rare. Most of it is sort of padding what is already there, to justify having people sit down at all.

G.R.L. I don't know which films you really consider yours. I read something that said *Happy Mother's Day*[8] was one.

R.L. Yeah.

G.R.L. And *Football*—[9]

R.L. *Football* I had almost nothing to do with. This is Jim Lipscomb's, basically.

G.R.L. Of that whole series of Drew films that I've seen, I think *Football* was one of the best, because of the inherent drama, social implications, because it's so flamboyant. And I think *Happy Mother's Day* is so good, works so well—at least in part—because there was an implicit comment, because you manipulated that material in an illuminating and revealing way.

Two or three years ago I met Al Maysles for the first time and he was like a maniac, a zealot: you shot, you couldn't touch or change anything, he wasn't any part of it, it was reality, he wasn't really mucking around with it. Fiction films could never be as good. I exaggerate, but not completely. And it's not even necessarily a criticism—I'm sure that that zeal is an essential part of what lets him make the kinds of films he makes.

R.L. The thing about Al is, he refuses to do his own editing.

G.R.L. So David does it. But I talked to him again a couple of months ago, and he's not quite so adamant about the purity of

[8] "Describes what happened when Mrs. Fischer had quintuplets in Aberdeen, South Dakota. Commissioned by *The Saturday Evening Post*, the film was rejected by them. I made this film with Joyce Chopra." (Richard Leacock)

[9] "(Meaney vs. Fowle) tells of the annual game between Miami high schools." (Richard Leacock)

cinéma-vérité. I think one of the things that makes *Salesman* good is the fact that they have edited; even so, there are times when it's slow, but if it hadn't been edited and gimmicked up if you like, using cross-cutting for example, it would have been deadly dull. And I don't think it would have been as revealing.

In that interview with James Blue in *Film Comment* you talk about realizing that you were part of the problem that you were trying to film in *Happy Mother's Day*—the Fischers being exploited commercially by everyone around them.

R.L. You are exploiting them. You're down there to make money out of their predicament, just like everybody else.

G.R.L. Did you ever think of putting that in a film?

R.L. Not at that time.

G.R.L. Would you now?

R.L. Yeah, I think so. I'm not quite sure how, but I certainly would want to bring it up—the pretense of our not being there.

G.R.L. Right. I want to see the microphone, the tape recorder, a shot of the camera—

R.L. That too becomes a cliché. I mean . . . we've done it several times. In the stuff we did with Godard,[10] Penny and I were constantly filming each other. That was a strange situation, because we really had no idea of what was going on in Godard's head. I was trying very hard to oblige the man, but he would always give you these very inhibiting injunctions, like don't zoom too much, don't do something else too much. He was sort of director, but then you're in a half-assed position—it's the impossibility of the cameraman. You're sitting there thinking instead of saying to yourself, "Wow! Look!" You're thinking, what does the man want? Does he want this, does he want that, and what am I supposed to do? The only reason you go on shooting is not because you're interested in what's going on, but because the man said shoot. You may be bored stiff, but you're in this ridiculous position, so I tend to think in my mechanical way that if you're going to direct a film, for Christ's sake direct it, and tell the cameraman exactly what you want. In the scene where I went up the elevator on the skyscraper, I became a human bipod, which I find rather silly. Why the hell doesn't he hold his own goddamn camera? I'm not that much stronger than he is. He would push me forward, and I'd bend down, he'd pull my hair, and I'd stand up, he'd turn me this way and turn me that way. That's what tripods are for—it gets silly. I enjoyed it. I sort of like the guy, but at the same time I found it grotesque, and sort of goofy. Sometimes when I did shoot what intrigued me, like the

[10] *1 A.M.* (*One American Movie*). For further comments v. pp. 235–39.

little girl running down the street with a Victrola, a record player, there were marvelous reactions from people on the sidewalks, and I diligently filmed those because they were fabulous. So with great pleasure I said, "The reactions are marvelous," and he said, "Oh no, no, no. That is completely irrelevant. I do not want the reactions, I want merely the street." So, hey, hold your own bloody camera! Don't hide behind other people's follies. Now the way he films in *La Chinoise* or *Weekend*, the camera is a colossus. It's completely controlled. It's completely automatic. It's just like a great big shotgun. Fine, but then in a sense he's controlling it. Being the cameraman—someone says start and stop, and I don't like being a cameraman. When you're making your own film, it's different. But this, you're second-guessing somebody else. You're an engineer, or something.

G.R.L. Did he never really talk to you about what he wanted, like in the scene in the garden with Tom Hayden?

R.L. He said follow each other around, photograph each other; and even during the scene he told us, photograph this or photograph that. The result is amusing.

G.R.L. Did he never get in contact about coming back to edit the film or anything?

R.L. Oh, he came back. I wasn't there, but apparently he had some theory that he didn't know enough about American politics to deal with the subject.

G.R.L. Who paid for it?

R.L. We did. I guess it's part of Leacock-Pennebaker's gigantic debt.

G.R.L. Let me go back to that *Film Comment* interview. You talk about "the formation of self-perpetuated cultural myths, which can get more and more inaccurate." This is in reference to fiction films. You say that you think you know about certain things—like the law courts, Pearl Harbor, the Nazis coming to power—when actually you may not know a bloody thing about these things but think you do from films—made by people who don't necessarily know any more about these subjects than you do. You also talk about this being true in documentaries because of the demands of commercial television. You mention the version of *Happy Mother's Day* which ABC insisted on and which you thought had nothing to do with anything, and the idea in *The Chair*[11] of will he or won't he be executed? So that in the end, to build up that tension, a

[11] "An account of the last desperate efforts of lawyers Donald Page Moore and Louis Nizer to save convicted murderer Paul Crump from the electric chair in Chicago." (Richard Leacock)

month later, you take shots of the lawyer walking up and down the hall. Were there other examples of this in other films?

R.L. Yes. Eddie Sachs is worried—what sort of information is that? I think there's a real danger, a real temptation if you have the need to grab an audience, hold an audience and to hoke it up and conform to the audience's expectation—it's a real danger.

G.R.L. Were there problems with political aspects, either direct or indirect? Was there the same kind of censorship?

R.L. No, there was no censorship, just kind of trying to make it "work"—that is, make it fascinating. The need to make it attractive to an audience. You know, personally, I don't think it's necessary. I remember this was a big problem in a rather strange film we did called *Portrait of Nehru.* To me the most fascinating aspect of that film is the boredom of being Prime Minister—inspecting guards of honor, shaking hands with visiting Prime Ministers from Christ knows where, drinking tea with conventional schoolteachers, and the scores of mumbo-jumbo political things you have to go through. But if you're fighting for prime time on television, you can't get away with much of that. It's always got to be *important.* That word "important" is a very bad word.

G.R.L. What about a film like *Primary,*[12] or others that had political implications?

R.L. No problem except total censorship at the source. *Primary* in no way achieved what I at least wanted to achieve. I wanted to see the political process at work, and we saw only the public aspects of the problem. There was no chance of our being privy to the real discussions that took place with the statisticians, with the public relations people, which is where modern politics operates. No one has ever got that on film or, with our present system, ever will. There's much more chance of getting somebody fucking on film than of getting politicians being honest. It might have been thought before that this was a bigger problem, but people are much more open about sex than they are about politics.

G.R.L. Are you interested in making films with political or social implications?

R.L. That presents the problem of what's an important film. It's hard to deal with. You mention *Football.* Can you imagine a serious executive of a TV station or a TV network agreeing to make a film about two high schools he never heard of having a football game he couldn't care less about? Whereas if you go to him and say, "We should do a film on air pollution or old age or ecology,"

[12] "Senator John F. Kennedy and Senator Hubert H. Humphrey and Wisconsin, 1960." (Richard Leacock)

World Without End by Basil Wright. Photo credit: UNESCO. Courtesy Basil Wright.

Song of Ceylon (Part I) by Basil Wright. Photo credit: John Taylor. Courtesy Basil Wright.

The Immortal Land by Basil Wright. Photo credit: John Anderson. Courtesy Basil Wright.

The White Bus by Lindsay Anderson. Courtesy Lindsay Anderson.

Thursday's Children by Lindsay Anderson and Guy Brenton. Courtesy Lindsay Anderson.

Every Day Except Christmas by Lindsay Anderson. Courtesy Lindsay Anderson.

The Pilots by Richard Cawston. Courtesy Richard Cawston.

Royal Family by Richard Cawston. President Richard Nixon (center, right) and the Royal Family. Photo credit: Joan Williams. Courtesy Richard Cawston.

I'm Going to Ask You to Get Up Out of Your Seat by Richard Cawston. Billy Graham in Hyde Park. Courtesy Richard Cawston.

Kes, directed by Kenneth Loach. David Bradley, left, star of film, and technical adviser Richard Hines. Courtesy United Artists.

Hôtel des Invalides by Georges Franju. Courtesy Georges Franju.

Mon chien by Georges Franju. Courtesy Georges Franju.

Le Sang des bêtes by Georges Franju. Photo credit: Patrice Molinard. Courtesy Georges Franju.

Chronique d'un été by Jean Rouch and Edgar Morin. Courtesy French Cinema Office.

Misère au Borinage by Joris Ivens and Henri Storck. Photo credit: Willy Kessels. Courtesy Henri Storck.

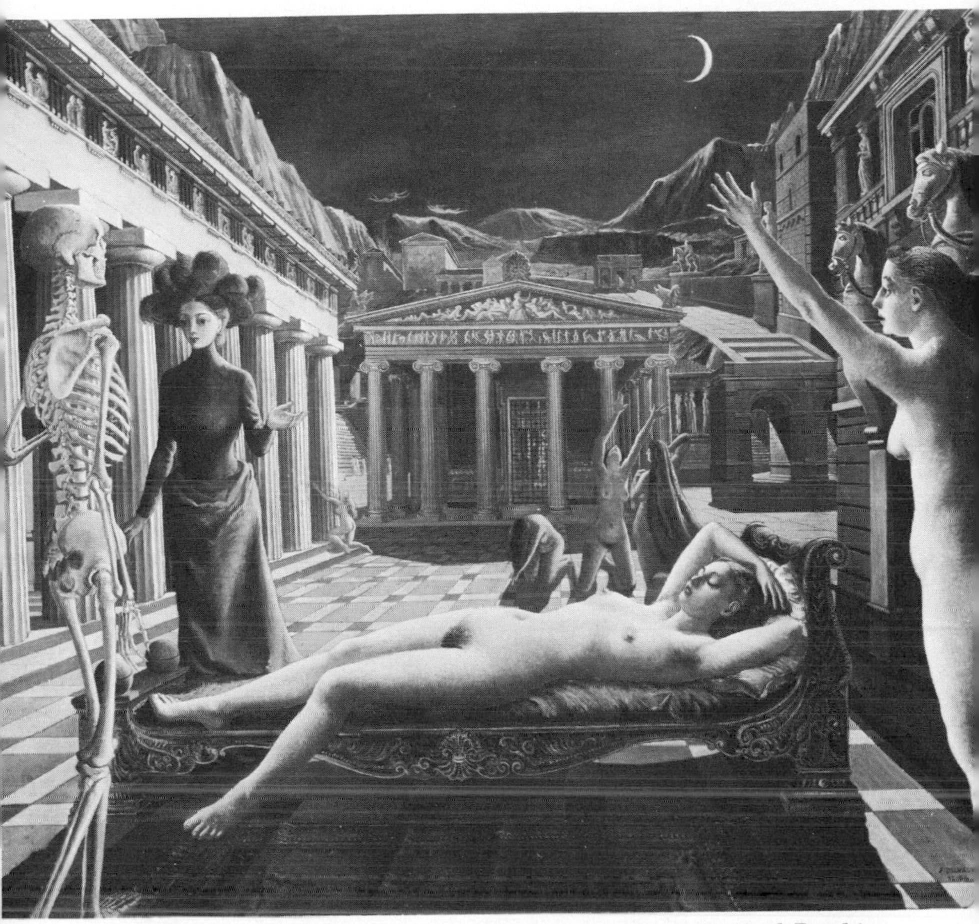

Le Monde de Paul Delvaux by Henri Storck. Photo credit: Paul Bytebier. Courtesy Henri Storck.

Symphonie paysanne, "Noces," by Henri Storck. Photo credit: Raoul Ubac. Courtesy Henri Storck.

Valley Town by Willard Van Dyke. Courtesy Museum of Modern Art/ Film Stills Archive.

The City by Willard Van Dyke. Courtesy Museum of Modern Art/Film Stills Archive.

The City by Willard Van Dyke. Courtesy Museum of Modern Art/Film Stills Archive.

Happy Mother's Day by Richard Leacock. Courtesy D. A. Pennebaker.

The Chair by Drew, Leacock, Pennebaker and Shuker. Photo credit: Richard Leacock. Courtesy D. A. Pennebaker.

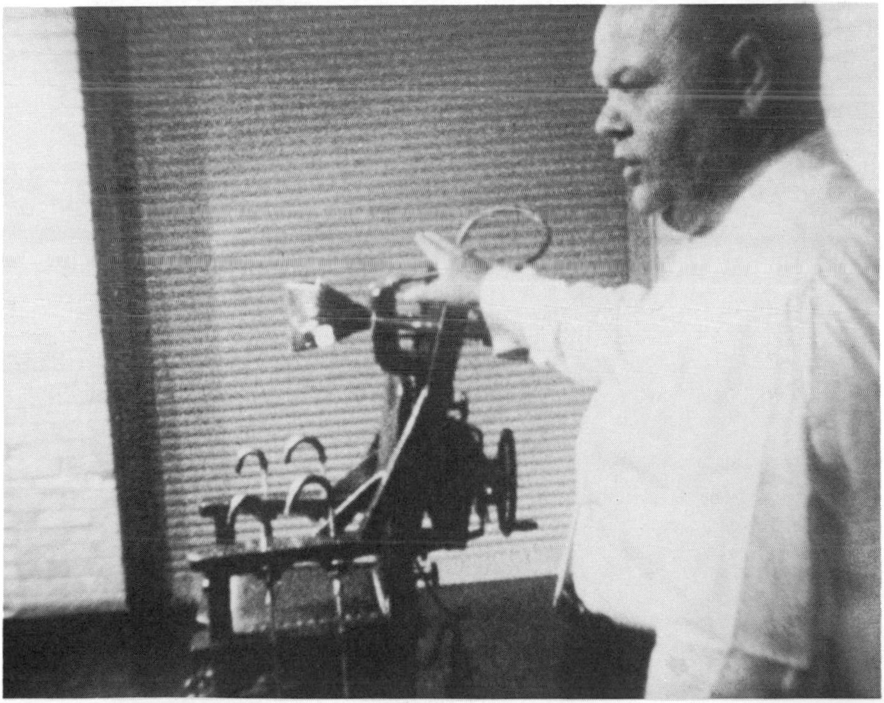

Toby and the Tall Corn by Richard Leacock. Courtesy Richard Leacock.

Monterey Pop by D. A. Pennebaker, Richard Leacock, Al Maysles and others. Janis Joplin. Photo credit: Jill Gibson. Courtesy D. A. Pennebaker.

Don't Look Back by D. A. Pennebaker. Bob Dylan. Courtesy D. A. Pennebaker.

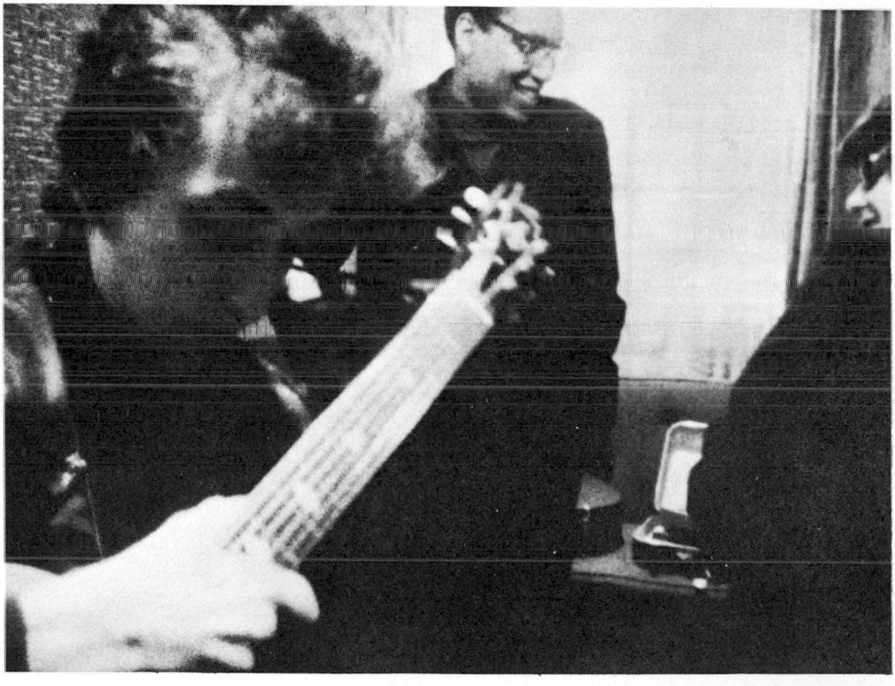

1 P.M. by D. A. Pennebaker. LeRoi Jones. Photo credit: Kate Taylor. Courtesy D. A. Pennebaker.

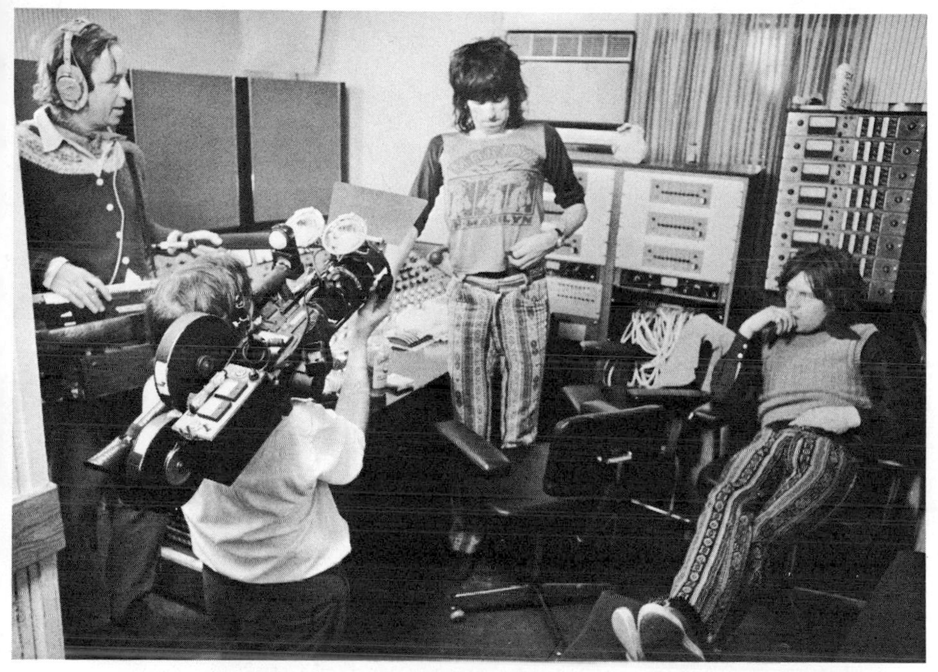

Gimme Shelter by Albert and David Maysles and Charlotte Zwerin. Left to right: David, Albert Maysles, Keith Richard and Mick Jagger. Photo credit: Stephen Goldblatt. Courtesy Maysles Films.

Salesman by Albert and David Maysles and Charlotte Zwerin. Standing: David, left, and Albert Maysles; sitting: Paul Brennan, left, and Ray Martos, two of the salesmen. Photo credit: Bruce Davidson. Courtesy Maysles Films.

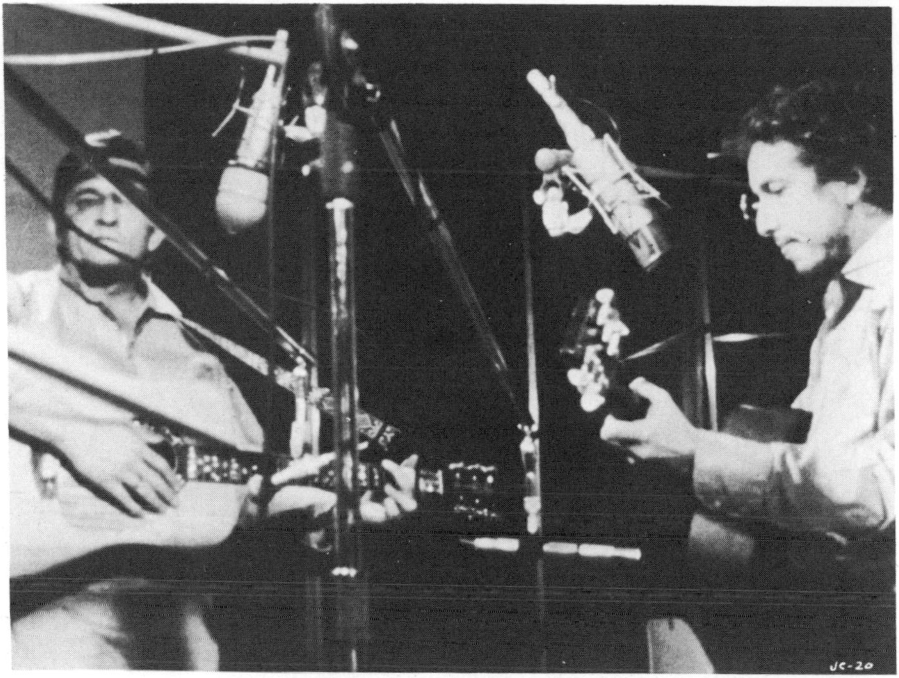

Johnny Cash by Arthur Baron. Cash and Bob Dylan. Courtesy Arthur Baron.

High School by Frederick Wiseman. Courtesy Frederick Wiseman.

Law and Order by Frederick Wiseman. Courtesy Frederick Wiseman.

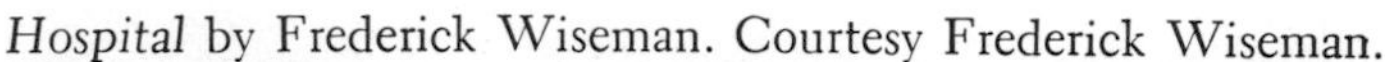

Hospital by Frederick Wiseman. Courtesy Frederick Wiseman.

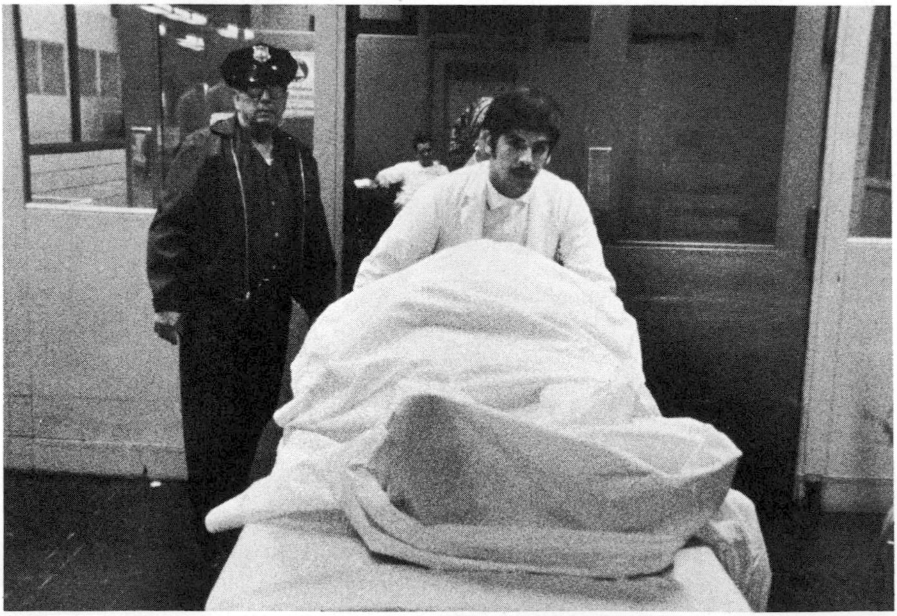

Black Natchez by Ed Pincus and David Neuman. Courtesy Ed Pincus.

One Step Away by Ed Pincus and David Neuman. Courtesy Ed Pincus.

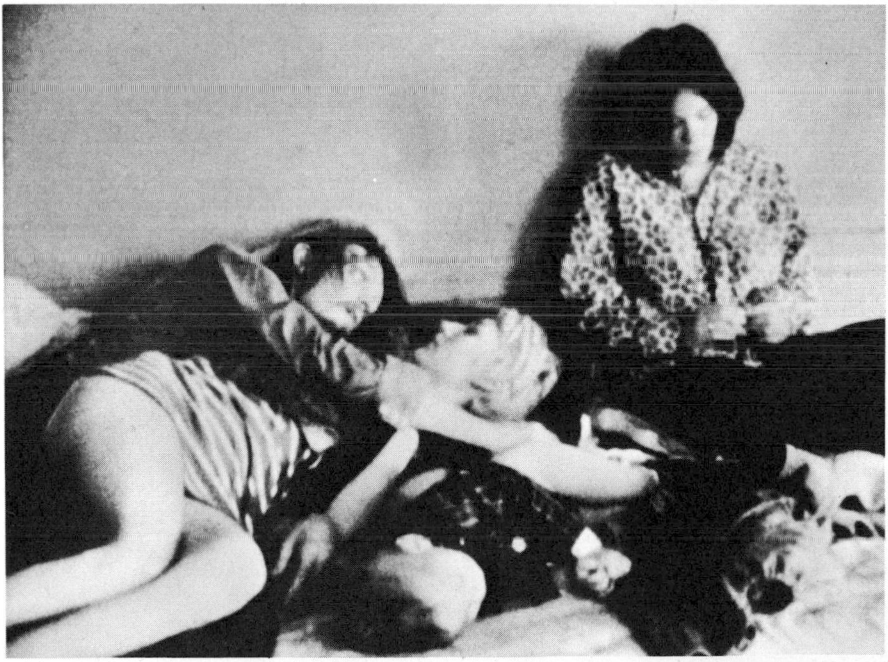

Videofreex control room. Chuck Kennedy, left, and Bart Friedman. Courtesy Videofreex.

Raindance video tape. Abbie Hoffman interview produced by Ira Schneider. Courtesy Michael Shamberg.

that's virtuous. But I always had this dilemma. It seems to me that the best films we've ever done have been on almost idiotic subjects, supposedly. But you find something out in those situations. What you find out in *Football* has nothing to do with football. What you find out in *Happy Mother's Day* has nothing to do with having quintuplets. *The Chair* and *Crisis*[13] both had obvious socially virtuous, acceptable subjects. Oh, the silliest one I'd made was *Hickory Hill.*[14] It's about a children's charity pet show held at the Robert Kennedy home in Virginia every year, and I guess it was about a cat who ran up a tree and wouldn't come down and a dog that peed on a lady. This is the subject matter.

G.R.L. What was it really about?

R.L. A strange look at a little place of upper political snobbery and their children in Washington.

G.R.L. When you were working with Drew, when you chose a subject for a film, did you have to clear it with the network first?

R.L. No. That was an extraordinary situation. It was paid for by Time, Inc., and they decided to make something like twelve pilot films, and it was really up to ourselves and Drew if we could do it. We had some real disasters. I mean, you're bound to. Like we went down to film a flood that we were sure was going to happen in the Mississippi basin, and all our diligent little minions went scattering off with their cameras and thousands of feet of film, and the water came up, and up, and up, and up, and suddenly started going down, and down, and down, and down. That was a total disaster.

[. . .]

R.L. Sometimes I think maybe I'm just as glad. The idea of making fifty-two of those a year? No, no, no. And the more and more it became a possibility, a reality, the more and more you got to see the division of functions. You know, you're a cameraman, you're a recorder, you're an editor, and this film has to be made in a rush—and that's not film-making to me.

G.R.L. You obviously didn't have personal control over the films.

R.L. No.

G.R.L. Was it Drew who finally had control?

R.L. Yes, he ultimately had the control, but this shifted when we made *Primary*. The people who shot it sat together in a room in a hotel with Drew and we all edited it together, but more and more it shifted. That's the problem. I don't know how you solve it. I'm

13 "The day of the confrontation of the Kennedy administration and George Wallace during the integration of the University of Alabama." (Richard Leacock)

14 "Made with George Plimpton for Public Broadcasting Laboratory, but they lost interest." (Richard Leacock)

not criticizing Drew. If you've got to make fifty-two one-hour films a year, you can't do it any other way. Unless you choose people to make one film a year.

G.R.L. Which of the films that you've made would you consider your own—the way you want them?

R.L. Oh, *Happy Mother's Day* and *Chiefs* are really my own. *A Stravinsky Portrait* is my own, but I wish we had been able to spend more time with Stravinsky and not had these questions being asked; but it's still very much my film. *Hickory Hill.* I had a tremendous amount to do with *Primary.* I had a great deal to do with the second half of *Crisis,* nothing to do with the first half. *Toby* is mine, and *Canary Island Bananas,* my first movie. Very few.

G.R.L. *Canary Island Bananas* is the one you made when you were fourteen years old? Where did you learn how to use a camera at fourteen?

R.L. I'd been doing a lot of still photography, and at the school I went to, we would go camping in small groups, and they gave me a movie camera to shoot some pictures of it. I had a curious difficulty filming people. I filmed miles and miles of waves, wakes of boats, moving clouds, very seldom people. I think it was because of the sound problem. I only photographed people if they were doing something.

G.R.L. Did it have anything to do with an inhibition about getting close to people?

R.L. I don't think so. I think it was the impossibility of getting them whole.

G.R.L. You mean at fourteen you were somehow aware that you didn't want to film people unless you could hear them talking?

R.L. No, there just didn't seem to be much point to see people talking without being able to hear them. It didn't seem to make much sense to me, so I tended to photograph people if they were doing something. If they were wrapping bananas, or nailing boxes together, or running a machine, then you photographed them. I think most documentaries of that period showed processes you can deal with. If you go all the way back to *Nanook,* you see Nanook catching a seal, Nanook building an igloo and so forth.

G.R.L. When you made the *Banana* film, had you seen a lot of other films?

R.L. Yes. The *Banana* film was a direct take-off of a particular film that I saw when I was eleven or twelve, called *Turksib,* a Soviet silent documentary about building the Trans-Siberian Railroad.

G.R.L. How long is *Canary Island Bananas?*

R.L. Oh, about sixteen or eighteen minutes.

G.R.L. Had you always wanted to make films?

R.L. Oh yes.

G.R.L. Were you always interested in documentaries rather than fiction films?

R.L. Yes. At this point I've managed to rationalize that. I don't know how true it is. You always wonder about these things, but I think this probably has to do with the fact that I grew up in a strange place. I grew up in the Canary Islands.

G.R.L. From what age were you there?

R.L. Oh, from when I was born. So when I went to school in England—in that horrible cold climate—how could I explain to people what the Canary Islands were, you know, my home, where I came from. It's very different, and people do different things, and when I saw *Turksib*, it was the obvious solution. Now here was a way of telling people where I came from, what we did, and this is what it looked like.

G.R.L. Is that what your father did? Run a plantation?

R.L. Yes. Still does.

G.R.L. From what age did you start getting sent back to England to school?

R.L. Oh, I was about nine.

G.R.L. But until then you had been strictly on the island?

R.L. Pretty much.

G.R.L. Was being in the Signal Corps during World War II and shooting what I presume was straight documentary newsreel, was that a reinforcement of all that?

R.L. No. As a matter of fact, I tremendously enjoyed the Army—it was sort of a lark. I enjoyed being a private in the Army.

G.R.L. Where were you during the war?

R.L. I was sent to the Alaska highway—which was fascinating—and then I was sent out to India, and I spent a lot of time in Burma and ended up in China. But the frustration was you were filming and you kept handing the film in and that was the last you ever saw of it. So for three and a half, four years, whatever it was, I had no idea what I was doing. The stuff just disappeared.

G.R.L. You were always just a cameraman, never had anything to do with editing?

R.L. No. I was a combat cameraman. Photograph this, and photograph that. Sometimes I'd get a little crazy. I remember in Burma there were some marvelous festivals, and I photographed yards and yards of these marvelous dances, and then I'd get rather irate telegrams, you know, What in the name of God did I think I was doing? I didn't know what I was doing. It made just as good sense to me as photographing people being put on stretchers and carried away, and people shooting guns.

G.R.L. Did you shoot a lot of battles?

R.L. Yeah.

G.R.L. Was that scary?

R.L. Oh yes, very scary. Very scary. But that doesn't make it uninteresting, especially in retrospect. But I enjoyed it at the time. I found it extremely interesting. It's a crazy business. What on earth makes people do these things? I wasn't terribly militant, I must say. Never fired a shot in anger at anybody.

G.R.L. Is that where you learned to be a cameraman?

R.L. No. I don't think I learned a goddamned thing there except how to be a racketeer in the Army. No, I learned before that on my own, and then I learned, I think, a tremendous amount with Flaherty.

G.R.L. Why is that?

R.L. Because it was a very, very close relationship. From Flaherty I really learned almost feeling things instead of looking at things with a camera, and before I had been somewhat mechanical in my camera work; but he conveyed to me what it's like to discover something visually with a camera. They're very, very subtle things, extremely hard to talk about meaningfully. Flaherty had a little line he was fond of: How in the world do you teach somebody to smell a rose?

G.R.L. You were very much involved in the whole process of *Louisiana Story?*

R.L. I wasn't involved in the structure of the film; this was strictly Flaherty.

G.R.L. I mean you weren't just the cameraman who pushed the button?

R.L. Oh no. This was inconceivable. Flaherty was a superb photographer, and often we would both shoot. He just really enjoyed shooting, and we were tremendously close. It sounds sort of pretentious, but our aesthetic sensibilites were extremely close, and he was enormous fun to work with, although we didn't always agree about everything and he had a marvelous bite. I'll tell you, there was no one in the world more fun to shoot for, because if he liked it, oh God, he liked it! He also realized that you had to have the freedom to goof. Both of us would shoot perfectly awful things and we suffered through them together—and what in the name of God were we shooting all this junk for? You know, it didn't work the way we thought it would work.

He had the extraordinary ability to look and look and look at stuff when he had something in mind, and if it wasn't there . . . We shot the whole drilling sequence in daylight—seemed to be the sensible way to do it—and he looked and he looked and looked and it was fine, nothing wrong with it; it wasn't very interesting, wasn't very exciting, but it was fine, technically beautiful. And he suddenly said, "We've made a terrible mistake," and I thought he was crazy. He said, "We're going to reshoot it at night." I said, "We don't have any lights." He said, "Get some lights." "We don't have any money." "Well, never mind, we're going to do it anyway." And we did. And my God, was he right. It eliminated all the cruddy details that were distracting, that were carrying your eye away from the central action. But we didn't know that. We had to find out the hard way. He was an absolutely extraordinary man.

G.R.L. Had you known him before?

R.L. He had seen the *Banana* film.

G.R.L. Wasn't that kind of a stroke of something that he would hire you to be cameraman on that film? You hadn't made any professional films before that, had you?

R.L. I'd done a few, but he didn't care about that. He liked me and he didn't have to worry—he was a superb cameraman. As long as I wasn't a complete moron, I could at least be used for carrying stuff. It turned out marvelously, but I could have been a half-wit and it wouldn't have made a hell of a lot of difference to him. And we'd talk in a way about film that I don't think he did with hardly anybody else. In a sense he seemed very conscious of certain techniques that he had developed. An obvious one is, how do you make a tree tall? or a cliff high? And his solutions were purely cinematic solutions. They weren't compositions, they weren't from paintings or stills. The obvious one is in *Moana* where the kid climbs the tree and he goes way the hell down the beach with a long telephoto lens. No cameraman in his right mind would have done that, and it's just a question of the time it takes to make the tree tall—there was no shot of that whole tree. He had all sorts of interesting notions. The standard thing in film school is you must have an establishing shot, a medium shot, a close shot. Flaherty didn't care for this. Why do you want an establishing shot? What's that all about? You want to puzzle the audience, you want to intrigue them, you want to give them a little bit at a time and let them construct what they have in their minds. It's a different kind of film. It takes forever before you get a long shot of that oil rig, and by the time you do get it, you've already decided that it's very tall. I find very, very little of this kind of thinking and feel in film-making. I think until film-makers start playing with cameras themselves you're not going to get it. This is an extraordinary man. Almost no film-maker bothers to handle the camera himself. He really enjoyed it. I've never known anybody who enjoyed shooting more than he did. I mean, he just would go crazy looking through that viewfinder.

G.R.L. Shooting in cinéma-vérité style, or whatever you want to call it, one really doesn't have time for that kind of thing. Does one? I'll make it a question.

R.L. Well, there is a problem. At first we got so hung up on sound, and all of us were very aware—I know I was very aware—that the images were suffering. Then it became sort of a two-way thing. The last thing I did with Pennebaker, the film on the Toronto festival[15]—I've never seen it—but I know I had enormous fun sitting in the audience trying to get a visual feel of those kids, and a lot of it was almost abstract.

G.R.L. Do you know how much of the footage he used?

R.L. I think he used a surprising amount of it. It's hard in this kind of shooting, but to me there are, in *Happy Mother's Day*, moments. To me, a miraculous shot of the parade at the end, the American Legion Band. There are shots of Stravinsky with the orchestra, at the rehearsal, that to me are lovely. There are continuous long pieces, image, image, image. . . . But they're extremely difficult to get.

[. . .]

A real problem is no outlet—there's no way to show film.

G.R.L. What about the college market?

R.L. Bullshit. Everybody talks about it, but nobody has made any money on it yet.

G.R.L. Lots of large companies, including Hollywood companies, are trying to sell to the college market. They charge a lot of money and every school has at least one film program. Is this not viable?

R.L. I don't think it is—so far, that is. They're peddling films, so I guess it's a little extra money for them. But I don't see anything in it, especially for short films. I mean a hundred years of college market won't ever pay for *Happy Mother's Day*. Or even *Chiefs*.[16]

[15] *Sweet Toronto*.

[16] "P.B.L. commissioned this film along with five other film-makers of different attitudes. I was asked to make a film of less than twenty minutes on anything I chose that was to be my 'personal cinematic view' of where America was at in 1968. The only condition was that it must start on the steps of the Capitol in Washington, D.C.

"I chose to visit a convention of some three thousand American police chiefs and their wives at Waikiki Beach with my friend Noel Parmentel, Jr." (Richard Leacock)

Chiefs was paid for by television, but it ran in theaters, everywhere that *Monterey Pop* went; but it gets fifteen dollars a week. It's meaningless. Doesn't even pay for the prints. It costs you five thousand dollars to make the prints for the goddamn thing, but we needed the film to lengthen the program a little bit, so it was okay, but as far as paying for anything, it's meaningless. There's no way at the moment to get shorts around except little tiny film clubs and the college market. At the University of Wisconsin in Madison there are some thirty-five thousand students. I bet you no more than fifty people come for the screening. If you have a personality like Bob Dylan or Janis Joplin, then you can probably reach more people, but the real problem is to arrange it. I said this in an article the other day: If five people in Abilene, Kansas, want to read a book, they can buy it. No problem. If five people want to listen to a record of some strange, idiosyncratic music, they can get it. But there's no way that five people in Abilene, Kansas, can see a movie that way, short or long.

G.R.L. Unless the local library had a copy.

R.L. It's too expensive, it's too much trouble, dragging around 16mm. reels of film and getting them checked—it's a little too complicated. Until we get some form of cassette . . . it's too expensive. The prints get ruined—it's a nightmare, distributing film.

G.R.L. Have you ever thought of television?

[. . .]

R.L. The trouble with television is that we're dealing with awful numbers. What makes a successful book? How many do you have to sell? A hundred thousand? Or records. It's unbelievable—a hundred thousand is great; a million is extraordinary. Do you remember *Omnibus?* That was deemed total failure, disaster because it only reached nine million people. That's bloody crazy.

G.R.L. Do you think cable TV is a possible answer?

R.L. I don't think so. I think cable TV is going to mirror commercial TV pretty much, at least to start with. Maybe a little bit better. You'll get an occasional Swedish film on instead of *Who Loves Lucy?* or something, but I don't think it can handle it—especially the idea that I want to see what I want to see when I want to see it. I may want to look at a long, long film by Jonas Mekas and I may want to start looking at it at one o'clock in the morning, and maybe there will be somebody with me, and we'll have a marvelous time looking at Jonas' crazy notes on his visit to Stan Brakhage, which may take three hours. We may look at it in pieces, or we may go fast forward and skip most of it.

G.R.L. But you don't see that being possible?

R.L. Oh, I think it's possible. I keep having these ideas that everything is going to change with the next technological jump, and of course it doesn't. So maybe I am a technology freak, but I don't see any other solutions.

G.R.L. It is depressing sometimes—New York City recently granted the cable TV rights to two companies without any competitive bidding. The companies said, "Well, obviously we have the public interest at heart," which is questionable, to say the least. Yet what happens when all these freaky kids grow up—get to be twenty-five, thirty, forty? Let's say that the family structure doen't fall apart completely and that the world doesn't consist of a series of communes, will these freaks be different enough to create a genuine alternative media outlet?

R.L. Oh yeah, at least. They've created the pop festivals, but the moment they create something, someone comes along and takes it over and makes money out of it. But there is a shift, and people do get together on a lot of films, even though it's very difficult. Most of what we've been talking about is the commercial world, and we all really want to get away from that because we want to communicate. Now it's still very difficult to make films, but it could be a lot easier. And when I say films, I don't exclude video tapes—I mean the visual medium and recording medium. It's a hell of a lot easier than sitting down and writing a book, I think. More fun, anyway, for me. I guess the nasty questions are do people want to communicate? I've always assumed that they do. Sometimes I think maybe they don't.

Oh, we do have an example of somebody stubborn enough to make it work—the Cinémathèque Française had a fantastic period after the war. Night after night Langlois showed films, films, films, without being too picky and choosy about what he showed, just showing them, and he had enormous audiences. There have been a few cases, and we'd like to get something like that going here. We'll have our own projection rooms.

G.R.L. You mean at MIT?

R.L. Yeah, just keep running things, our own things, other people's things.

[. . .]

G.R.L. What kind of films are you working on now, or hoping to work on?

R.L. I'm pretty vague at the moment because we're sort of getting set up, and I'm just getting around to really thinking about it. I'd like to do some highly theatrical things. Mixed media is a sort of crummy word now—like all these things get beaten to death; but using, creating—I guess you get all these phrases now—creating an environment for an audience. I think there's a tremendous amount that can be done in this area. I'm interested in why most teaching films are so bloody dull. We're really tackling that problem. At the moment we're trying to make physics films that aren't as boring as most physics films, gummed up and sticky. We're starting out pretty open-minded to see what we get. It doesn't cost a hell of a lot of money to do it. We're not hiring great big crews, or professionals—that's baloney. Very soon I would hope to be able to do this in 8mm., and not just because it's cheaper, but because it's a nice thing to take around with you. It's even smaller, the setup, than the video camera. We've got one almost ready to go. It'll be noisy. We've got a lot of problems to solve.

G.R.L. Will it be a separate tape recorder with a synch signal?

R.L. Yeah, the whole thing. What makes it attractive to me is that especially in the sort of observational, observing films, you're much more liable to take it along with you, whereas no one in his right mind would drag one of those 16mm. camera rigs around with him unless he's paid. It's just too much of a pain in the neck—all those cans of films, magazines, black bags and things. They're antediluvian, those things.

G.R.L. How will you edit it?

R.L. Well, we've got to build editing equipment.

G.R.L. Would it be the same kind of double system editing as with 16, using 8 mm. sprocketed tape?

R.L. Yes. I hope that we can build synch-sound 8mm. equipment that, if manufactured, could cost less than 16mm. by a factor of ten. That is, the camera is five hundred instead of five thousand. The editing stand is five hundred instead of five thousand. Maybe you can go even further, I don't know. But you reduce the cost, especially the equipment. I want to be able to give a camera, a tape recorder to someone who's into something, working on some project, heaven knows what, who's really involved in something they want to communicate, and give it to them for a year. Say, "Here, keep it. Put it in your own locker," so that when something strikes them as extraordinary and they want to record it, there it is. Fantastic! And they don't have to have all this garbage.

G.R.L. You would show it on a projector that has magnetic sound?

R.L. Yeah, presumably. But there's a long way to go in the technology. Oddly, the industry doesn't seem to want to solve the problems. They don't believe that people are serious about this. Now,

I think that when every high school in the country has film courses, let alone the elementary schools, that they're going to change their minds. It doesn't make you tired to carry it, either. You go out with my camera, and everybody asks that dreadful question, "Who are you from?" I'm from somebody? They see you with an 8mm., they don't ask a damn fool question like that.

But there are problems coming up already. When we first started cinéma-vérité, whatever you want to call it, that kind of shooting, we were the only ones. Now you've got all these bloody newsreel men from ABC, CBS, CBC, NBC, BBC, all of them, blah, blah, blah, companies. You've got millions of these creeps all over at every public event, so let's get away from public events. I like the idea of the Videofreex, whom you mentioned before, that if you're with somebody and you're having a nice time and feel it's worth filming, I shoot a little bit, you shoot a little bit, and like you were describing it. It still isn't that easy. To get anything good out of a situation means a lot of work. It's very easy to make a very bad film, whereas it takes a hell of a lot of work to write even a bad opera.

G.R.L. In an interview in *Film Comment,*[17] in reference to *Chronique d'un été*, Rouch says that he thinks people are more real, in a sense, in front of a camera because they learn that they can do and say things they normally wouldn't do or say, because afterwards they can claim it was just for the camera. In a certain way, they're playing a role for the camera. Does that seem valid to you?

R.L. I think I'm shifting on that. When *Chronique d'un été* was made, it bothered me very much that, very clearly, the only important thing that was happening to these people that summer was that they were being filmed. Now when this started to distort the situation in *Petey and Johnny,* we took very stringent measures to stop it, because I personally found what was happening was very uninteresting. I still tend to think that way, but then when I see the kind of thing the Videofreex are trying, I'm not so sure any more. Really depends on what you're after.

G.R.L. In that interview with Blue, in reference to *Happy Mother's Day,* you say you wanted people to talk about the film—what it was about; you got them together, they talked and it was their discussion. This is obviously hindsight on my part, but in that kind of situation, would you now think of talking to the person directly and you yourself perhaps becoming a character in the film? You could simply ask a fairly objective question, but you could also say how you felt.

[17] *Film Comment,* Fall/Winter 1967, vol. 4, nos. 2 and 3, "The Films of Jean Rouch" by James Blue.

R.L. I haven't done it. I'm not sure why not. I guess it's usually because I've always been doing the filming and that's enough. I can't. Also, my mind is so full from absorbing what's going on, that I would find it very difficult to.

G.R.L. Then let's say the sound man, which I guess would be more feasible.

R.L. Well, in *Happy Mother's Day*, Mrs. Fischer, in answer to a question, actually does say, "We're never going to be on display to anybody as far as I'm concerned." And Joyce, who did the sound, said, "To anybody?" and she said, "To anybody."

G.R.L. That's nice. I've got to remember that line.

R.L. It's just in there. But I guess I have a real fear of . . . You see, when you ask questions, one of the main problems is that people would like to be friendly and nice to you and they would like to do what it is you want. The danger is that when you ask questions you in effect tell them what you want, because almost all questions are leading questions. Then they start doing what it is they think you think they ought to do and we spend much more time trying to get out of that box. Sometimes it's ridiculous. By like not shooting, and not shooting and not shooting until they give up. And they decide you're a complete idiot, a moron, a nuisance, a something. Not that far—I'm overstating it; but they sort of give up and say, "Okay, I must do what I have to do. This guy isn't responding." And you're making terrific judgments all the time. We have asked questions at times, great big open-enders, like, "Mr. Nero, what do you think of your life?"

G.R.L. I agree. For example, in *Happy Mother's Day*, when Mrs. Fischer gets her coat fitted, if you said almost anything then, even boo, you would have been interfering, and you wouldn't have gotten the same kind of thing you did get.

R.L. One might have said at that point, "Don't you think this is pretty silly?"

G.R.L. If you did, you'd be taking a real chance—you might have gotten something extraordinary, but you certainly wouldn't have gotten what you got.

R.L. I agree, I agree. This is a real question.

G.R.L. Suppose you said to Mrs. Fischer afterward, after the coat fitting, "What did you think of that?"—Basil Wright told me about a Canadian film—*The Things I Cannot Change*. It's about an Irishman, who's a drunkard, and his family, and there's a scene where he gets drunk and is arrested, or almost arrested, and he doesn't want to go to the police station, he hides in the john, and then afterward the crew asks him about it. He talks about it and they intercut the interview with the actual scene with the police—which sounds exciting. I think generally I'm not in favor of an absolute cinéma-vérité, but somehow that you illuminate something. You say, this is my bias, this is the way I feel, this is my view. At least the viewer knows where the hell he stands and that he's getting a particular person's perception, which is not the way cinéma-vérité has been defined, not the way cinéma-vérité films have been made or presented in the past. That's not the way you've worked. But you seem to be . . . I guess not knowing exactly where you're heading, going off somewhere else.

R.L. I guess. We started out in the whole tradition of the television guy asking the questions. We really tremendously wanted to get away from that. It's so easy to fall into the interview thing, such an easy way to get out of a hole. And our refusal to ask people to redo things, which Shirley Clarke used to kid us about, it wasn't because of any great virtuous feeling. It's simply because we found it didn't work. We tried it lots of times and it was grotesque. I remember howling with laughter: In *Happy Mother's Day* we were filming in some newspaper man's office or the local radio station or something, and this secretary came in saying that the local senator was on the telephone from Washington. She did it so beautifully, and I had just run out of film. I asked her to do it again, and it was grotesque. She came on like something in *Who Loves Lucy?* It was weird. But there are whole other areas. I think I said earlier, I'm not even sure what I mean by highly theatrical. I mean abstract, I mean poetic. You can do all sorts of things with this equipment. It doesn't have to be this observing business. That's just one aspect of film-making. Some people are beginning to do it. I haven't seen too much that excited me, and I have a general feeling that I'm getting bored with that screen up front there. We've been playing with multiple projectors. Usually it's used just as a gimmick, but we want to try to get it to make some sort of real sense, do something that can't be done any other way. I've been intrigued by some of the light shows. They have a tremendous dependence on music, which isn't necessarily bad. I guess a Wagnerian opera without music would be pretty dumb-looking.

G.R.L. Then you're not sorry you left the Leacock-Pennebaker office?

R.L. No, it couldn't cope with me. I made two short films in a period of about three years, *Chiefs* and *Hickory Hill*, both for television. Everything else I was doing . . . I was shooting for Norman

Mailer, I was shooting for Godard. It didn't make any sense to me. I enjoyed them, but it had nothing to do with me.

G.R.L. Are you still interested in the possibility of cinéma-vérité films?

R.L. Oh lord, yes.

G.R.L. I didn't know how bored you were with that screen up there.

R.L. I'd like to think of multiple screens. We've done some trivial things so far—lots of it has been done. We're just beginners at it. We did some things for Sarah Caldwell last year for an opera here. It's all kind of fun. There were segments on film, multiple screens, which were part of the opera, including people singing.

G.R.L. So that if you do go on to do cinéma-vérité films, you would like to extend it in some way. Is it fair to say that?

R.L. Yeah.

G.R.L. In other words, you wouldn't be particularly interested in just doing what you'd done before?

R.L. I guess I'd gotten into sort of a rut too. My nasty camera-eye view of what goes on in this world. Another thing that's been bothering me—not bothering me—something I've been thinking about is this whole question of the social impact of a film—this is a big issue of revolutionaries. I'd like to see more of what people in Newsreel and things are doing. I hope to this year. *Chiefs* is amusing and it's obviously got a fairly clear moral; it has an attitude actually, but it's an attitude that was at the time acceptable to the chiefs of police. I think the *New Statesman* review in England pointed out that they thoroughly accepted it as their own home movie of what happened in Hawaii, and they did in fact. Now they've seen it with young people looking at it and realize that it's bad public relations. I don't know what in the world they would think was good public relations.

There's a lot of talking going on, and it's back to Vertov. I'm really not clear. I just read the latest statement by Godard on revolutionary film-making, and I really don't understand it. This was in a little English magazine. There was a whole list: one, to make revolutionary films; two, to make films in a revolutionary way, and that if you do one it cannot be two. It was that kind of reasoning, and I don't really understand it.

G.R.L. But who's going to finance them? And even if they get them made, where the hell are they going to show them?

R.L. Big problem. They don't discuss that.

G.R.L. The few Newsreel films I've seen have been so strident that they're difficult to take—even when you're very sympathetic.

R.L. I think of myself as being sympathetic. But finally they're not very revealing, except for the opinions of the film-makers. I want to do certain things myself, but what's more important to my way of thinking now is why aren't Africans making movies? There are one or two, but there's a whole bloody continent. That's crazy. Why aren't black Americans making movies? It is beginning to happen, but these are the things that are important. I care, but that's not the issue. The problem is to get people doing it and to find some solutions to this confusion. To find ways of showing these films. I keep coming back to that.

G.R.L. Here you are, an artist, who finds, to a certain degree, the medium insufficient unto itself and that unless you concern yourself with, in effect, the business and economic aspects, the political and social aspects, it's not satisfying. Is that it?

R.L. Well, it's just that there isn't enough being done. All I really see are these commercial enterprises, the entertainment business, show business. I'm really not interested in *Catch-22*—it cost something like twenty million dollars. In fact, I think it's downright immoral and not political. I mean, it's a goddamn crime when you spend twenty million dollars on something like that. I think it's asinine.

[. . .]

G.R.L. I saw an ad in *Life* from Kodak, Eastman Kodak, which said, "Take your Instamatic to the next demonstration." I'm not sure how one is to cope with all of that.

R.L. Did you see the little peace film we were making? I did a day's shooting last fall. It's rather like *Chiefs*. I went and filmed because I thought I was getting into a rut; I filmed a meeting of the United States Army Association in Washington. It's all these generals and people instead of police—riot control systems, the latest thing in weapons. In the end we simply intercut this material with a sit-down peace demonstration at the U. S. Army base in Boston. Seventy kids got arrested for obstructing traffic in the process.

G.R.L. Did MIT pay for the film?

R.L. No, I got some money from a friend of mine. It was very cheap.

G.R.L. How long is it?

R.L. Oh, it's about six minutes, eight minutes. You see intercut these two guys with short haircuts selling weapons and those things and the guys with long hair and beards getting arrested for trying to stop the war. At the end there's simply a question, you know, who, question mark, crazy. That's all. It was sort of nice. This next term we want to start with a course in graphic design, posters, a still photography course and my course. We're going to get all three groups together and we're going to ask the students, "Do you want to do something about the present situation? Either in ecology, peace, whatever. In which case, who are we going to talk to? How are we going to reach them? What are we going to say to them? How are we going to do it? And let's do it." They're going to make some posters, still things and some short movies like this, and find ways to use them. Even one-minute commercials, I don't care what. Work on the form. Let's make some! It doesn't cost much money.

DONN ALAN PENNEBAKER

(The following material was written by the film-maker.)

"I was born in Evanston, Illinois, which is really Chicago. I went to a Catholic school there, a large public school in Richmond, Virginia, a Christian Science school in Elgin, Illinois, a military school in Abingdon, Illinois, an Episcopalian school in New England, and graduated from Yale University as a mechanical engineer [1947]. The only things I can remember studying there were music with Hindemith and philosophy (Kant). Spent a year at MIT, allegedly in naval architecture.

"After two years in the Navy I moved to New York, where I worked as an engineer for about six months. Since that time I have started and abandoned an electronics company, written technical books for an advertising agency, helped Francis Thompson finish *N.Y., N.Y.* (I used to drive the car), produced affectionate documentaries for the YWCA and the Girl Scouts, and helped Gypsy Rose Lee put together old home movies to make her life story.

"I [. . .] spent three months in Moscow with Al Maysles making a film about Russia and there encountered Ricky Leacock, who was filming Leonard Bernstein and the New York Philharmoic. In return for twelve rolls of badly needed film we agreed to help Ricky with his film. Ricky had brought what he called a portable synch-sound rig (it took the three of us to carry it), and I got the first inkling of what could be done with a really portable sound camera.

"Earlier that year [1959] Ricky, Shirley Clarke, Willard Van Dyke and myself had started 'Filmakers,' a sort of co-operative arrangement designed to share space and equipment and even occasionally films.

"Bob Drew, an editor at *Life*, appeared. He had gotten Time, Inc., to put up money to develop a dream of his own: a film journal for prime-time television that would support itself financially. Then, as now, the bulk of public affairs programing on television was put on as a public service by the networks with sponsors paying only a part of the actual production cost. This made possible a kind of film-making that Ricky and I had been trying to do on our own, and it was a chance for a market that simply had not existed outside of a few specialized programs such as *Omnibus*. It also meant money to tackle the equipment problem. [This corporation, called Drew Associates, produced a number of films.]

"When Time, Inc., was unable to sell the shows to television, Drew Associates began to split up, right in the middle of our last, and in many ways our best, film—*The Crisis*. I departed Drew Associates and again set up my own company, determined this time to have all the equipment and facilities necessary to produce a complete film—except for actual film processing. I believed then, and still believe, that to compete with the well-financed theatrical and television producers and distributors I must have the ability to initiate a project instantly and the facilities to complete it without dependence on expensive outside sources or investments. It was in this way that I was able to shoot films like *Lambert, Elizabeth and Mary*, the film on Tim Leary's wedding and, in fact, *Don't Look Back* (Bob Dylan) when the chance came along.

"Leacock joined me, and with his quintuplet film (which was later renamed *Happy Mother's Day*) and some of my old films we decided to become distributors. I still feel that that was the second most important move we made. I think it is essential for the film-maker to own some part of his work—not for money alone, although that's an important part of it, but to ensure its life as an entity and not to have it fall prey to the David Wolpers. I did a few commercials, which I still think were interesting.

"In the spring of 1965 Bob Dylan's manager, Albert Grossman, wondered if we would be interested in making a film of Bob's tour in England. So, with nothing more than a handshake, I set out with Dylan and Joan Baez to make *Don't Look Back*. Subsequently, the next year and the next tour, I agreed to shoot another film—this time for ABC, and Dylan was to edit the film himself. That film has never been released for a number of reasons: Bob's accident, too long a delay in the editing. But it's film history of sorts and eventually, I am certain, will be shown.

"I have a wife, four children, a small sailboat, an old house in the country, several cats, completely delightful business associates and a conviction that if I couldn't make films I would be completely unemployable."

FILMOGRAPHY*

"The following credits and attributions are made mostly from memory and often may seem surprisingly informal. Remember, these were not Hollywood movies and were made without the hierarchy those films required. Almost every one was a personal journal, a personal obsession, either of mine or someone else's. I've tried to indicate the person responsible in each instance by using the term film-maker. Occasionally there was no single film-maker, but rather a consortium of talents that fused for some brief period and resulted in a film. If I have left out or misplaced any contributions herein I do apologize."

1953: *Daybreak Express.* 16mm., color, 5 minutes. Distributor: Leacock Pennebaker, Inc., 35/16mm. This was my first film and was made while heavily under the influence of Francis Thompson's *N.Y., N.Y.* It was shot in two or three days with a few rolls of drugstore Kodachrome.

Baby. 16mm., b&w, 8 minutes. Not released. A home movie, watching my daughter Stacy take her first ride on a merry-go-round.

1954: *Indifference.* 16mm., b&w, 8 minutes. Not released. Another home movie, this time friends were actors and I directed.

1955: *Storm.* 16mm., color, 10 minutes. Not released. An experiment in filming a Florida thunderstorm, which turned into a gale.

1958: *Yorktown Coker.* 16mm., color, 10 minutes. Not distributed. This was made for the Lummus Co. Shot and edited by me, it was about a coking furnace they wanted to show to engineers.

Brussels Film Loops. 16mm., color, 15 loops about 2½ minutes each. Not distributed. These were part of a project commissioned by the State Department through Willard Van Dyke's urging. They were shot by myself and an assistant, Derek Washburn, as we drove about the U.S. over a period of 6 months. There was no sound track, and the loops were intended to show visitors to the Brussels World's Fair what America was like. Shirley Clarke helped me edit some of them, as did Lenny Mandlebaum and Leon Prochnik. As far as I can remember, I was the producer, but Willard may recall that he was.

* The filmography and notes were compiled and written by the film-maker.

1959: *Opening in Moscow.* 16mm., color, 52 minutes. Distributor: LPI. I went to Moscow and lived for three months at the request of a group of sponsors who wanted me to make a film on the American Exhibition that opened that spring. It was a fantastic experience. Unfortunately, synchronous filming equipment for this sort of film-making did not exist, so that the result was a very beautiful film about Russia with an attempted "real" sound track made up of live interviews. It was a sort of long *Daybreak Express.* In the end the so-called sponsors, except for two or three heroes, refused to pay for the film and I was left holding the bag. Lesson: Get your money in front. But I've always loved the film, flawed though I know it to be. Al Maysles helped me and did some of the filming and sound. Later Shirley Clarke started the editing, which I finished.

1960: *Primary.* 16mm., b&w. Distributor: Time, Inc. In many ways this was the most important of the Drew-Time, Inc., films. For Ricky, Drew, Maysles and myself it was something of a religious experience. I think Terry Filgate, who shot quite a bit of it, felt less communal than we did, but he still sensed something new. Now seeing it after all these years, I suspect the reason for its importance was not just the cinéma-vérité technique which got most of the attention, particularly in Europe, but the fact that it was a kind of news about JFK that everyone wanted to know. There are no credits on the film, other than Time, Inc., but the filming was done by Ricky (the Kennedy hotel room and Humphrey TV interview) Filgate, Maysles and myself, with a section in the voting booths provided by a local TV cameraman. Drew was the only sound man, except for some migitape recordings Ricky and I did by ourselves. All of the above edited, with the addition of Bob Farren.

On the Pole. 16mm., b&w. Distributor: Time, Inc. Something of the spiritual energy of *Primary* persisted in this film which has as its protagonist a most incredible person, Eddie Sachs. It was split in the editing into three sections, one of which I did, one Ricky did, and one Drew with Farren and Posner did. The shooting was done by Ricky, Maysles, myself and Bob Galbreth. Drew took sound and with Time, Inc., was producer.

Balloon. 16mm. b&w, 28 minutes. Distributor: Time, Inc. In 1959 Ricky Leacock and Bob Drew had begun a film chronicling the adventures of a scientist and a Navy balloonist who were going to take a huge telescope into the stratosphere to look at Mars. Unfortunately the balloon was disabled and the project put off a year. Then the problem became finding out whether there is water on Venus. Derek Washburn, Bob Drew, the photography class from

Rapid City High School (about twelve in number and an average age of twelve) and myself spent nearly three months getting up every morning at three o'clock and waiting in 30° temperatures for the balloon to go. When it finally did we pursued it for several states until it finally crashed, nearly killing the pilot. It was a good story, but the equipment was still too unreliable and bulky so it ended up a rather conventional documentary. It was edited by Anita Posner and Bob Farren under Drew's direction.

Breaking It Up at the Museum. 16mm., b&w, 8 minutes. Distributor: LPI. Under my instigation an army of film-makers tried to record Jean Tinguely's self-destroying machine when it was turned loose at the Museum of Modern Art. I recall giving cameras to Graham Fergueson, Shirley Clarke, Stan Vanderbeek, Ken Tynan, Al Maysles, and just about anyone else who would promise to give me back the film. The film is crazy, but so was Jean, and the machine did grind itself to death noisily enough. Tony Schwartz recorded some of the comments and I edited the whole thing with Maria Winn.

1961: *David.* 16mm., b&w, 54 minutes. Distributor: Time, Inc. This was the first of what I call the theatrical story films, and it was produced for Time, Inc., and Bob Drew by myself, operating under the flag of Filmakers, which was a loose association of Richard Leacock and myself. Greg Shuker, in his capacity as reporter for Time, Inc.–Drew projects, had come upon the story of the Synanon House, an addict rehabilitation center, and the attempts by local residents to dump it. We started, "we" being Greg, Bill Ray and Nell Cox, who took sound for Bill. What we found or what I found was not so much a documentary of a social problem, but an ongoing personal story of a particular person, David, who was about to come to a turning in his life. I suddenly had a vision that that was exactly what I wanted to do with this new kind of film-making. Later there was a difficult struggle with the forces of reaction, in the person of Bob Drew, who had the responsibility of making films appetizing for television. As I saw it, it was a struggle between real life as re-enacted by soap opera and real life itself; between narrators, contrived editing and superimposed explanations and the straight reporting of an event as it took place. There were numerous editors: Nell Cox, Betsy Taylor, Mike Jackson, Hope Ryden, and plenty of in-fighting. In the end it was Drew and Shuker who wrote the narration and to a great extent determined the outcome. But the original vision had been mine and I clung to it. Somewhere in fact there is a work print of *David* that is feature-length and quite different from what can now be seen. Of course, the final irony was that none of these films ever got on the network show they were intended for. Instead they were dumped ignominiously onto the syndication circuit and so interlaced with commercials and station breaks that they all became more or less unintelligible. Joe Jullian narrated.

1962: *Susan Starr*. 16mm., b&w, 54 minutes. Distributor: Time, Inc. This was another in the same vein. Hope Ryden was correspondent and additional cameramen were Jim Lipscomb, Peter Eco, Abbott Mills, with Pat Jaffe shooting a hand-held Kodak K-100 from the orchestra pit. I did most of the shooting and editing with Hope Ryden. The sound was recorded by Bob Van Dyke and the story was supervised entirely by Drew. Joe Jullian narrated.

Jane. 16 mm., b&w, 54 minutes. Distributor: Time, Inc. Yet another. Probably the best shot but somehow lacking in synthesis. It revealed for me the desperate importance of the major characters and their ability to project spiritual energy. At this point we saw every human situation as a ripe fruit for our picking. In fact we described the two kinds of films possible as 1) the personal film in which a single person was closely shadowed and 2) the event film in which many cameras recorded a single event simultaneously so that the final edited version was the view no one person could ever see. I shot most of *Jane*, Ricky Leacock filmed Walter Kerr, Abbott Mills the performances, and Al Wirthimer the audiences. Hope Ryden, Ricky and I edited the film with assistance from Betsy Taylor, and a few others I can't recall. Greg worked with Ricky and I worked with Hope or by myself. Jim Lipscomb narrated.

1963: *Crisis*. 16mm., b&w, 55 minutes. Distributor: ABC and Drew Associates. I was the cameraman with Bob Kennedy, the President, and for two days with Vivian Malone and the boy—I've forgotten his name. Greg took sound with me and managed to get us into everywhere we weren't supposed to go. Jim Lipscomb was the cameraman with Governor Wallace, Ricky with Nick Katzenbach and General Abrams. Pat Powell worked with Ricky on sound and I believe Hope with Jim. The editing was difficult. I was quitting, mostly because of the unfortunate press agentry in which certain of the principals of Drew Associates were nimbly engaging, and which resulted in the film being censored for its showing on the air. The only person who stuck with the real problem of the film was Ricky. He put all the phone conversations together, and they represent the only part of the film that today has any historical or artistic significance. The conference in the President's office is a scene that I'm sure will never again be filmed. It was unfortunate that this scene was finally emasculated by removing the sound track and replacing it with narration. The narrator was Jim Lipscomb.

Mr. Pearson. 16mm., b&w, 60 minutes. Distributor: Intervideo, Canada. I was the cameraman, and to a certain extent the film-maker since the sound man, Dick Ballentine, had really never worked as a sound man before or filmed in this fashion. He felt, unfortunately, that the life process could be improved upon by conspicuous editing. The result is slightly mishmash, but not unamusing. I think it was Dick's sense of humor that made this film work. Dick was the editor and the producer and generally takes credit for the film.

1964: *Lambert & Co.* 16mm., b&w, 15 minutes. Distributor: LPI. This very informal film was Bob Van Dyke's idea. Dave Lambert was going to have an audition; let's shoot it. That's all there was to it. Nick Proferes, Jim Desmond, Nina Shulman, Bob Van Dyke and I spent an afternoon at RCA. It was an attempt to make a minor film that would record something that had happened musically, with the least amount of editing we could get by with. When Dave was killed, the film took on a different significance, but that did not affect the initial concept, let's shoot it. I edited it with Nick and Nancy Sen. Leacock Pennebaker was the producer.

Michèle et Michèle. 16mm., b&w. Not released. This was the first of an entirely new sort of film: films made by their own subjects. It was entirely my own film except that the persons the film was about helped shoot it. It was not unlike sections of 1 P.M., the film I later made with Godard. I think the idea for this one was good, but I needed money, which the Ford Foundation was not about to expend, and it was never finished. I'm sorry because in many ways it was the most interesting film I've ever gotten in to.

You're Nobody 'til Somebody Loves You. 16mm., b&w, 12 minutes. Distributor: LPI. Another let's-shoot-it film. Nick Proferes, Jim Desmond, Michael Blackwood and I went off to Tim Leary's wedding with a friend, Monti Rock III. I filmed it as a kind of pageant and edited it as a mystery. Sometimes I think it's beautiful, sometimes I wonder why I did it. (It ran as a short with *La Chinoise.*) LPI produced it. Monti Rock sang the title song (the film actually has no title) and the rest of the music was indigenous.

1965: *Elizabeth and Mary*. 16mm., b&w, 60 minutes. Distributor: LPI. This film was made expressly for medical purposes and yet it is one of my favorite theatrical films. The purpose was to spend a day with a pair of twins, one of whom was partially sighted and the other totally blind and brain-damaged. The difference between the children was predictably interesting, but not at all in the way I expected. The film was an incredible lesson in looking and expecting. It never fails to astound me. Nick Proferes was the other cameraman; Nina Shulman and Nancy Sen took sound. I edited with the expert psychiatric help of Dr. Arthur Gillman, who was at that time connected with the Jewish Guild for the Blind. He and they produced the film. The original version was eight hours long, a truly pure film, but unwatchable. No narration, hardly any editing and no preaching.

RFK-*Two Days*. 16mm., b&w, 60 minutes. Unfinished. This was the start of a project I intended to do with Bobby Kennedy, a sort of ongoing theatrical history of a man who would have to be President. I shot it myself with the aid of Michael Blackwood. It's tampered with very little and the time is real. It would have been a fantastic project. I'm sorry I didn't go along with him on his last campaign.

1966: *Richard Avedon*. 16mm., b&w. Unfinished. A disaster. Dick and I agreed to drop it.

Herr Strauss. 16mm., b&w, 30 minutes. Distributor: LPI. This film is most remarkable in that I do not understand a word of it. I hope Michael Blackwood, who helped me, does. I did it as an experiment along the lines of *Elizabeth and Mary* to see if I could make a film about someone whose language I don't understand. The shooting was surprisingly simple, and with Michael (who was born in Germany) beside me, the editing also seemed easy. However, I am forever frustrated by the film since I don't know what it's about. Produced by LPI for German TV.

Don't Look Back. 16mm., b&w, 95 minutes. Distributor: LPI. This film was begun with no particular outlet in mind and no financing, but with total conviction that it must be done. I filmed all of it (except for a short piece from Dylan's younger days supplied by Jack Willis) with Howard Alk and his wife, Jones. Bob Van Dyke taped the concerts and Jones took sound for me. I edited; LPI, Albert Grossman and John Cort produced.

Rookie. 16 mm., color, 20 minutes. Distributor: CBS. This was made for a TV sports show. It never really had much potential because the rookie, as nice a guy as you'd want to know, had no real crisis of interest I could get into. I filmed and edited with the help of Jim Desmond. Produced by LPI for CBS.

1968: *Goin' to San Francisco*. 16mm., color, 2½ minutes. Distributor: Columbia. A prelude to *Monterey Pop*. I shot it and Scott McKenzie sang the song. A piece of dessert if you don't take it too seriously. Produced by LPI for Columbia Records to help sell the record of the same name.

Monterey Pop. 16mm., color, 82 minutes. Distributor: LPI. From the beginning I saw this as a theatrical film. It was intended to be a TV show, but it didn't take much imagination to know that Hendrix and Joplin were not TV fare. Cameramen were Richard Leacock, Al Maysles, Roger Murphey, Jim Desmond and myself, with some spectacular audience wide-angle shooting by Barry Finstein. Wally Heider did the sound on 8 track and Bob Neuwirth got everybody's head straight. John Phillips and Lou Adler put on the show, which was what made the film interesting, ABC (reluctantly) put up the money, and LPI distributed the final film. Nina Shulman, the only girl on the crew, edited with me. Others on the crew: Brice Marden, Tim Cunningham, John Maddox, Baird Hersey, Peyton Fong, Larry Mong and John Cooke.

1969: *Awake at Generation*. 16mm., color. Unfinished. One night at a club called the Generation, which has since folded. It was a wake held several days after the shooting of Martin Luther King, Jr., at which appeared Janis Joplin and the Big Brother, Joni Mitchell, Buddy Guy, BB King, Jimi Hendrix, Richie Havens, Paul Butterfield. They played all night. I was simply recording musical history, with no customers for the film in sight. John Cooke, Robert Leacock and Kate Taylor went along. An extraordinary film, but what do you do with it?

Moscow—Ten Years After. 16mm., color. Unreleased. One day in Moscow, ten years after *Opening in Moscow* was made. This was the day the astronauts landed on the moon. Not a spectacular film, but all synch-sound at least.

ONE P.M. 16mm., color, 90 minutes. Distributor: LPI. This is the salvage of a project Ricky Leacock and I filmed with Jean-Luc Godard. It was to be about revolution, and included such media heroes as Eldridge Cleaver, Tom Hayden, the Jefferson Airplane, LeRoi Jones—and Rip Torn as the protagonist. It even had a genuine bust by the New York Police Department. Unfortunately, Jean-Luc never completed the film. I put together some of the rushes with a few filmed notes of my own and released it. LPI produced.

1970: *"Original Cast Album," Company*. 16mm., color, 53 minutes. Distributor: Talent Associates. The recording of the original cast album of the Broadway musical. It was a very simple situation. The photography was done by Ricky Leacock, Jim Desmond and myself; Robert Van Dyke recorded and mixed the track during the shooting. It was produced by Talent Associates. I edited it, and the title was shot on the Bulova Accutron sign on Broadway.

Sweet Toronto. 16 mm. blown up to 35mm. stereo, 120 minutes. Distributor: LPI. An incredible concert of rock 'n' roll music, filmed at the Toronto Rock 'n' Roll Revival of 1969. It features Bo Diddley, Jerry Lee Lewis, Chuck Berry, Little Richard, John Lennon, and in a science fiction ending, Yoko Ono. Cameramen were Jim Desmond, Dick Lieterman, Ricky Leacock, Roger Murphey, Barry Bergthorsen (who filmed a really marvelous motorcycle beginning), Randy Franklin, Bob Neuwirth and myself. In some ways, it finishes what *Pop* began. Like *Pop*, it is another giant new film, but it concentrates totally on the performance and the immediate audience response. The film was partly financed by some of our subdistributors and produced for distribution by ourselves.

Other films that Pennebaker has worked on are listed below. Pennebaker's role in the making of each film appears directly after each film title.

1955: *N.Y., N.Y.* Drove car. Sponsor: Francis Thompson.

1956: *Widening Circle*. Writer/Assistant. Sponsor; YWCA.
Wider World. Writer/Assistant. Sponsor: Girl Scouts.
Suez. Writer/Producer. Sponsor: Julian Bryan.

1957: *Your Share in Tomorrow*. Cameraman/Assistant Director. Sponsor: N. Y. Stock Exchange.

1958: *Gypsy*. Editor/Cameraman. Sponsor: Gypsy Rose Lee.
Highlander. Editor. Sponsor: Highlander School.

1959: *Skyscraper*. Cameraman. Sponsor: Tishman Reality.

1960: *Christopher and Me*. Writer (song for titles). Sponsor: Edward Foote.

Demolition of Western Electric. Cameraman. Sponsor: Western Electric. Not released.

Mardi Gras. Cameraman. Sponsor: Walt Disney.
Yanki No! Editor. Sponsor: Time, Inc./ABC.

1961: *Adventures on the New Frontier*. Cameraman. Sponsor: Time, Inc.
Football. Cameraman. Sponsor: Time, Inc.
Blackie. Cameraman. Sponsor: Time, Inc.

1963: *Eddie*. Cameraman/Editor. Sponsor: Time, Inc.
Road to Button Bay. Cameraman. Sponsor: Girl Scouts.
Aga Kahn. Cameraman. Sponsor: Time, Inc.

1964: Goodyear Snow Tire Commercials (2); Green Mint Commercial. Cameraman/Editor. Sponsor: Young & Rubicam.
Timmons. Cameraman/Editor. Sponsor: Granada TV.

1965: 8 Experimental Commercials with Second City. Cameraman/Editor. Sponsor: Group.

1966: *Casals at 88*. Camera and Sound. Sponsor: CBS.

1967: *Van Cliburn*. Cameraman. Sponsor: AT&T.
Industrial Commercials. Cameraman. Sponsor: J. Walter Thompson.
Dylan Color Special. Cameraman. Sponsor: ABC.

1968: *Wild 90*. Cameraman. Sponsor: Norman Mailer.
Beyond the Law. Cameraman. Sponsor. Norman Mailer.
McCarthy. Cameraman/Editor. Sponsor: McCarthy Headquarters.
Two American Audiences. Cameraman. Sponsor: L.P. Inc.

1969: ONE A.M. Cameraman. Sponsor: L.P. Inc./Godard.
Maidstone. Cameraman. Sponsor. Norman Mailer.
Lindsay Commercials. Cameraman/Editor. Sponsor: Lindsay for Mayor.
Ramblin'. Cameraman. Sponsor: Lindsay for Mayor. Not released.

1970: *Eclipse*. Cameraman. Sponsor: Pennebaker. Not released.
John Glenn. Cameraman. Sponsor: Glenn for Senator.
Robert Casey. Cameraman. Sponsor: Casey for Governor.
Lampman's Boogie. Cameraman. Sponsor: Lampman. Not released.

September 2, 1970, in D. A. Pennebaker's office in New York City.

G. ROY LEVIN: On the phone you said that you don't make documentary films.

D. A.[1] PENNEBAKER: Well, I try not to. I can't help it if you call it that. I mean, if somebody paid me, I'd just make anything. You know, just a working man.

G.R.L. You're willing to make any kind of film? You really don't care at all?

D.A.P. That's what I'm told by everybody else.

G.R.L. I don't believe that.

D.A.P. You do what you're told. You want to see documentary films, somebody pays you to do it, right?

G.R.L. There aren't any films that you want to make?

D.A.P. Oh sure. God, yes. But when you work here, you work. If you're a cameraman or a film-maker, you're committed to making films people want to pay for, most of the time. I've got seven or eight films in the back room. Hour-length, hour-and-a-half, half-hour-length films that I can't sell to anybody. What does that prove? That I'm virtuous? That I know something nobody else does?

G.R.L. What kind of films are they?

D.A.P. Oh, they're just films about people, but they don't have any particular form to them. A film of Jack Elliot and people like that. I made it in a nightclub one night with Janis and some people singing in there.

G.R.L. Janis Joplin?

D.A.P. Yeah. They're not documentaries. They weren't intended to be documentaries, but they're records of some moment. I've got a film I made in Russia, a film I made of the eclipse. They're just films that I made because something happened that interested me, but I can't make a living off these kind of films. Not for a minute. But I don't call them documentary films. When people come to me, they've already got a sense of what they want to call the film they want me to make. If they want to call it documentary film, that's their problem.

My definition of a documentary film is a film that decides you don't know enough about something, whatever it is, psychology or the tip of South America. Some guy goes there and says, "Holy shit, I know about this and nobody else does, so I'm going to

[1] Donn Alan.

make a film about it." Gives him something to do. And he usually persuades somebody to put up the money who thinks this is the thing to do. Then you have the situation where this thing is shouting on the wall about how you don't know something. Well, I think that's a drag. Right away it puts me off. There are a lot of things I don't know about, but I can't stand having someone telling me that. That's what the networks do: "Ah, you don't know about dope. We're going to tell you about dope today. Here is an interview with Mrs. Jones. She knows about dope." And Mrs. Jones, gee, she's a billion people around—I mean, how can one or ten or even five hundred people know really what's going on? Then five minutes later it's all changed anyway. So the whole basis for this kind of reporting is false. It pretends to be reporting but it isn't, most of the time.

On the other hand, it's possible to go to a situation and simply film what you see there, what happens there, what goes on, and let everybody decide whether it tells them about any of these things. But you don't have to label them, you don't have to have the narration to instruct you so you can be sure and understand that it's good for you to learn. You don't need any of that shit. When you take off the narration, people say, "Well, it's not documentary any more." That's all right, that's their problem. That's why I say that films that interest me to do, I wouldn't consider documentaries.

If I was going to make a film on dope, let's say, if I made one this week, it might say one thing. If I made it next week, it might be quite different. But you couldn't call that documentary film. It's not very analytical. I don't know what it is, but I've got to be absolutely prepared that that's the way it's going to go, that there isn't a thing to say about dope that's going to be universal and I'm the one that's got the message to do it. So you pay me a little money and you tap me on the shoulder and I'm blessed. And I get to do it. Ah, that's bullshit. I don't trust people just because they have a camera. I don't even trust people who write books, and that's a lot harder than shooting a camera.

G.R.L. You spent a long time working with Drew.[2] How long?

D.A.P. Two or three years. That's not a long time. A long time just getting into the camera.

G.R.L. In that time, were the films you made what most people would call documentary?

D.A.P. They are half and half. They are kind of half soap opera,

[2] For other comments on Drew Associates, v. the Leacock interview, pp. 195–96 and 200–1.

half documentary. The part that interests me, that I like about them, is the soap opera, I suspect. The parts where they failed are probably as documentaries. They probably weren't quite objective. I don't know, they were different. Which ones have you seen?

G.R.L. *The Chair*, *Susan Starr*, *Football*, the one—

D.A.P. *Football* is, I'd say, one of the good documentaries. *Yanki No!* is a good documentary. They were good documentaries in that they had a measure of unpredictability and life that made them interesting, just as I guess *Target for Tonight*[3] was documentary and so was *Night Mail*.[4] But there was a kind of freshness and excitement in them that pulled them out of that, so you remember them. You don't remember them for their marvelous insights into the mail service or anything; you remember them for their poetry, or whatever it is. I think that *The Chair* is abominably edited, that it was reduced to a kind of straight-line plot analysis when in fact what is most interesting about the story in the film was the people involved, the characters, and the problem was they kept shifting their positions; these were people who were supposedly guided by the majesty of the law, who supposedly proceeded straightforward, but they didn't, they jumped around. Well, we ended up with just a rinky-dink plot, and in the end nobody remembers a thing—but Drew was always persuaded that the plot carried. He edited it, actually. Ricky[5] and I shot it, but we were out on something else when it got edited; when we saw it later, we were both quite shocked.

As for *Crisis*, I think part of it was badly edited and part of it was marvelously edited. And it makes a difference; the halfway point in that film is fantastic. The first half is sort of a paean to Kennedy—it has a statue of Lincoln; it was just filled with the worst kind of prosaic, predictable bullshit. The second half was marvelous. Ricky sat down—I'd quit by then, kind of over that film—and found both ends of the telephone conversations. It really opened up. So in fact there is a great deal to be learned by looking at it. There's nothing to be learned from the first half, it simply summarized your position.

I just glanced at something on television the other day. CBS is doing something on Africa. First the cat goes down there, he gets off the plane, he's in Africa, right? He's going to dig black faces and bizarre things. He's got his camera out and there's a guy doing traffic. In any English place or most of the East, traffic is a

[3] Direction and script by Harry Watt; 1941.
[4] Direction and script by Basil Wright and Harry Watt; 1936.
[5] Richard Leacock.

marvelous thing. Well, the cat gets carried away, so for the first four minutes some cute editor in New York decides this is a wonderful insight, and it's bullshit. So we're all treated to what some editor and some cameraman—neither of whom know anything really, about Africa or about anything, other than to get the film into a bag—take a cute shot. Well, in the end, you just have to think, if they're looking at the wrong things, where are the right things? How do you see the right things? And who is doing that? You never see it in documentaries, so I don't know. I'm actually more interested in somebody's bullshit Hollywood film. At least when I go see it, nobody's bullshitting me. They're doing what they know how to do, and most of the time it's boring too, in a sense, except if the story happens to be good or if it's just the animal, simple thing, at last you see something that's alive. I can't stand dead films, I guess. And my sense is that most documentaries, by their very nature, the minute they're conceived, become dead.

G.R.L. Are there any documentary film-makers that you like?

D.A.P. I don't know what you call documentary film-makers. I was quite surprised, in fact I was knocked out when I saw *Warrendale,* because I'd seen some films that Al[6] had done before, and I thought they were terrible. They used to be dead alligators lying there, perfectly exposed and set. But in *Warrendale* he had the wit to see that it was drama and to go for the drama and get that. He isn't a cameraman. I was surprised, because normally I can hardly conceive of anybody making a film without a camera. I mean, what is it you do? It's an easy thing to say, but it means that later he just picks up and kind of summarizes somebody else's intuitions. It's like two people painting a picture. I'm sure you could do it if that's the way it had to be done, but it seems a strange and incredible way to do it, and it's hard for me to imagine it coming out. Well, he did it. *Warrendale* is an honest film. It's not the greatest film ever made.

In a way it doesn't have anything like the excitement of *Target for Tonight,* which I'm sure is fake. It was all shot in a studio, though some of it in planes, but everybody doing lines. They're all actors. But it had a kind of excitement, because at the time everybody was going to war, or because the people who did it, Grierson, or whoever was pushing the buttons on the thing, they had a kind of excitement. I don't care whether it comes from real people reciting lines or actors reciting lines. Lines are lines.

G.R.L. Have you ever seen *The Battle of San Pietro?*

D.A.P. Sure. A Huston film. It's a good film, although if you see it

[6] Alan King, director of *Warrendale.*

a lot of times you realize what a total amount of fakery went on in the editing of it. He's using shots from all over the place, so it isn't really . . . It looks on first viewing, or second viewing, to be just some cat with a camera watching everything go to pieces, but in fact it's incredibly put together, and after you've looked at it a lot of times, and I have, you begin to see the cheating that took place in the editing. But you accept that because you know that Huston came out of that kind of film-making, and to him that wasn't cheating. Only cheating let's say to Al Maysles, who thinks it's cheating—but that doesn't make it cheating. Of course, the film is going to be here a hell of a lot longer than Al Maysles is, so in the end, cheating is a misnomer. But if I was going to make a battle film, I wouldn't do those things. I'd be afraid to. That's because everybody is smarter now, but it took that film to get us smarter, so it doesn't take anything away from the film. In fact, it gives something to it because the evolution had to be toward more truth, not less. And if that was true, how do you get more truth? Well, you find out what in it could be more true, and that takes looking and thinking, so that it does a lot of work. Just as another Huston film did, *Let There Be Light*, the one about shell-shocked soldiers. That's probably got less contrived editing.

G.R.L. I've seen both of them only once, and on first viewing it seemed to me to be the opposite, that *Let There Be Light* is more gimmicked up.

D.A.P. Maybe it is. I've only seen *Let There Be Light* once, a long time ago, and it's fuzzy in my mind. *San Pietro* I looked at a lot because it has a lot of vitality to it, a lot of excitement, and he throws away a lot of form—and that passes for excitement too. If that film were made now, it would create a lot of excitement. That's as up to date a film as is being shot around now. There's nothing around now that's as well done as that.

G.R.L. I've looked at a good number of the wartime documentaries, and a lot of them were really well made, exciting in the editing, but they were often offensive, infuriating, because they were so chauvinistic.

D.A.P. Actually I have a lot of Signal Corps films. They didn't even bother to do that. They just show endless landings. Of course, the great final travesty on all war films is the film that wasn't about any war at all, which was *Victory at Sea*. It was just stock shots. It was the thing that NBC did on television. A thirty-two-hour show with that mellifluous voice of what's-his-name? The guy, the announcer. Well, you know, he's got the terrible, very English accent? and he's announcing all these battle scenes. Then there's a shot, there's just long, black cannon shooting at each other. Everything could be anything. It gives you a terrible feeling that there was no war at all. It's all somehow out-takes, and edited versions. I never sensed I was in a place when they told me I was in a place. I'm sure somebody tried to—they must have. There are some pictures from Kwajalein, but in the end it didn't matter. That's what's fearful. You could have taken Kwajalein and put it with Tinian and nobody would have cared. It was just people doing the same thing in the same shot to the same music. It was just an endless kind of tapestry of no place, no time.

G.R.L. That kind of thing seems most dangerous to me in television documentaries where it's done in part by the voice-over commentary that changes the sense of what you see.

D.A.P. Scourby. Did you know Alexander Scourby? He does some Band-Aid commercial now. I can just hear him saying, "Three hundred fifty thousand were killed at Tarawa Beach," you know, but with this kind of meticulous accent like a man selling you a brooch at Tiffany's. Terrifying. So out of sorts with what he's talking about. But it didn't bother anybody. People just accepted it—"That's nice." Somehow it upgrades war. Sort of makes it a noble enterprise, I guess.

G.R.L. What I liked about *San Pietro*, contrary to all those others that were so harsh and chauvinistic and shrill, is that there's a humanity there.

D.A.P. Yeah, that's true, but the thing about *San Pietro*—and this is my personal feeling—is that all those things are his style. He's one of the great stylists. People, I think, make the wrong assumptions about Huston. Most of the time I don't think he is a very good storyteller. He has the reputation for being a good storyteller because he's gotten some good writers, but he really was a great stylist. He put the mood of a place marvelously down, very toughly, very ruthlessly. *San Pietro* was a terrific story and I think his style is the thing that made it real. But the story is what it's about. It's just like *Breaking the Sound Barrier*,[7] It was about something. It was about a lot of people trying to take a place and finally saying, "Fuck it," and it didn't matter. It still ends in hopeless, impossible slaughter. I mean that incredible thing where the tanks go down the road, each one at a time, and get blown up. But they have to keep doing it. There's a fantastic story there about what people have never shown in a war film, because it has taken itself away from Rock Hudson going down in a tank. It was just some slob you'd never seen before—you're never going to see again—so you had to

[7] Directed by David Lean; 1952.

put it together: what is this about? are they going to take the town? That was the story. And in terms of that, it was hopeless, because in the end it didn't matter if they took it or not. The Germans just left finally. Well, that's a fantastic story, and I think it was so subtle that in the end you went away still working on it.

If he'd applied the same style, the same kind of compassion, whatever else, to a bad story, you would have hated it, because it had to have that underlying corridor. The opening thing with Clark—wasn't it Mark Clark?—saying, "We have this problem," and he goes on and he sounds just like your school instructor telling you there are too many bikes being stolen, he wants you all to smarten up and no more bikes be stolen, and in the end he says, "Well, we lost this one," he says, "but that's war for you." If you listen to what he's saying, it's horrifying. Yet he's just saying a straight thing that he didn't see as horrifying, and suddenly Huston translated that into a real thing: a lot of people trying to cross that river and most of them don't make it, but that's war for you. Which people don't have any sense of—that isn't war for most people. War is something removed. We win. Or, If we win; that's what war is. Not, We lose. And that film is about We lose. It's pretty important.

Breaking the Sound Barrier was the same way, was a first-rate movie in that it was a terrific story, and you were surprised. I was, anyway. You didn't think there was going to be any story. That's what documentary should be. You really care about that fucking plane. They were all actors, everything was fake—it's just fantastic the way you really care about the plane. You make an hour-and-a-half documentary on some airplane, I'm not going to look at it. I don't care about airplanes.

[. . .]

I don't happen to make fiction films. I might start tomorrow. If they paid me enough, I'd probably try. I'd probably make a terrible one. I'm willing to do it, but I don't make that kind of film. I'm actually drawn into a peculiar kind of genre which is a semimusical reality thing. I don't know what it is. I know how to do it, I know how it begins and I know how to edit them pretty fast. I'm good at it, I guess, but I didn't think that's all I was going to do all my life.

G.R.L. What about *Don't Look Back?* How do you feel about that? Is it a documentary?

D.A.P. A guy acting out his life.

G.R.L. Weren't they real situations?

D.A.P. It doesn't matter. Would you care if I told you it was all fake? What if I told you it was only a script?

G.R.L. I'd feel cheated.

D.A.P. Michael Pollard wants to do it with a script. Get all the same people, have them play different roles, but all learn the lines —he learned the whole thing by heart, he knows every line in it. He can recite it. Someone performed part of it onstage. Like a play. He learned all the lines and just did it as a play. Does it matter? If it works, I don't think it matters. It shouldn't. But I'd agree with you, I'd probably feel cheated too.

What happens is that when you watched the film, you withheld an enormous amount of technical criticism because you felt the other had too much run; and if at the end I said, "Hah, I fooled you, it was all fake," you'd say, "Like fuck you did, because I'm going to let loose to hell with technical criticism now. I don't have reason not to any more." Well, that's the style. That is just saying, "What's this fucking Cezanne doing?" It's just that you're used to one thing and then got used to another. We all have that problem. I'm about in the middle of it. [. . .] It shouldn't matter if it was scripted, but I agree with you, it does.

G.R.L. I don't think it's true that if you made a fictional film in that style it would necessarily have to be good or bad.

D.A.P. You couldn't fake it in a hundred years. You'd know it and you'd say, "What's this guy doing?" That's what happened to Norman[8] a little bit. They're interesting in that they're kind of rough. I mean, they're rough to the cob, and they sure as hell aren't documentaries, but they're not fiction either. I don't know what they are. They're about a guy defining himself as he goes along. The last he made, *Maidstone*, was a pretty good film. It hasn't been released.

The things that are interesting . . . Like if you happened to really want to know what was going on in the Hollywood dope scene, fag scene, everything else, you'd go to see *Myra Breckinridge*, and you'd find out a lot of things. Whether it stands up as a story or as a drama is something else again. I can't answer that, but in a sense, if you were really interested in that world, that is documentary. In the right sense of documentary, you do find out something. If it interests you.

Information outside of what is needed to fulfill the plot. Fiction films have this problem. They have this big urn they have somehow got to fill, and as they get closer and closer to the end, you have fewer and fewer possibilities, and you know finally that it has to end a certain way, he's got to be killed, he gets the girl—whatever

[8] Norman Mailer. Pennebaker was the cameraman for Mailer's *Wild 90*, 1968, *Beyond the Law*, 1968, and *Maidstone*, 1969.

it is—so that the filling of that urn gets less and less interesting. Then comes the problem, why do you deal with the plot? Well, it's because we're caught in a transition. Like you're frustrated if I tell you it was documentary and in the end I tell you it wasn't. There's no reason why you should be. That's what plays do all the time.

G.R.L. No.

D.A.P. Well, they try to. Let's say *The Connection* tries to. There are guys running around saying, "This is really going on on the stage," and you know it's not going on on the stage.

G.R.L. But that was the part that didn't work.

D.A.P. Then why did they get into that bullshit? Why is there a need for it? Why not just eliminate it? Why not say, okay, if you don't need the urn, let's get rid of it. There is still some peculiar compulsion to hang on to this strange little starveling called the plot. So now you have Hollywood going through numerous tortures trying to get new and interesting plots that won't seem so draggy that people will walk out on them.

G.R.L. Outside of some Broadway movie houses they have small screens where they show scenes from the films being played inside, okay? Now one of the things I saw was a Western, but what you saw was a shot of the camera filming a big action sequence. You also see commercials on TV which are about the making of the commercial.

D.A.P. But people aren't really interested in how the play got made, how the movie got made.

G.R.L. But they're not interested in plot, at least not in what used to be called the "avant-garde" of the arts. No one considered a serious playwright writes straight, realistic plays now. Nobody paints straight, realistic paintings, makes straight, realistic sculptures. Contemporary dancers who are considered good—whatever that means—don't—

D.A.P. What you're talking about now is fashion. I happen to like plot, and I like realistic art and I don't like abstract art too much.

G.R.L. Where do you go, to Broadway?

D.A.P. No. I don't even go to movies, for God's sake. I don't have time to go to the movies. I have a six-month-old child. Actually, movies don't interest me that much.

G.R.L. Is film-making just a trade, the way a blacksmith would have a trade? Do you have any particular kind of feeling, for example, about *Don't Look Back*?

D.A.P. Yeah, I like it, it's an interesting film, it's easy to watch. I haven't looked at it for a long time, but it was interesting to me to make and to watch because I learned a lot. I learned something about Dylan, about myself, I guess. I don't think much about it now—it's left my hands. Dylan was doing his thing and we had to make something that would work theatrically. Well, that was kind of hard at the time. All experience told everyone you couldn't do it. The problem was to make that into a really working musical, not a documentary. Most people look at it and say it's documentary. It is not documentary at all by my standards. It throws away almost all its information and becomes purposely kind of abstract and tries to be musical rather than informational. Many people complained about the movie—it didn't tell about the life-style of the hippies or dope or something like that; that's what most complaints are. Especially the people who were in it. They felt it wasn't informational, although I broke my neck trying *not* to be informational. I never felt any reason to be informational because it wasn't something that I should tell you about. What I want to tell you about is the mood, I guess, not the information.

G.R.L. The documentaries I like best are ones that have a very personal point of view, that are subjective—documentaries that don't pretend to be objective.

D.A.P. Yes, but it can't be done obviously. The trouble with a documentary is it really requires a lot of artfulness, and most people making documentaries, for one reason or another, feel embarrassed at being artful. Or else they're artful in a totally obvious way, which is not artful. You know, like they shoot their reflections.

I'd like to see a good documentary on Nasser. That really interests me a lot. And I'd like to see a good documentary on Cuba.

G.R.L. Have you see Marker's film *Cuba Si!?*

D.A.P. Yeah. I thought it was kind of bullshit—he was so caught up with that French love of the liberal. I know that's not right from my own firsthand information. I'm not looking for somebody to give me a cause to follow. That's not the purpose of film, although that's what it seems to be used for. It's such a fantastic flag, it's so persuasive. There you are, your eyes glued to one end of a room, you can't look anywhere else—anyway it's all dark everywhere else—and the music is crashing around you. My God, it's like a moonbeam. So whatever it says to do, for a minute you feel like doing it; but at the end, the more it turns you on, the more you flip the other way later. It kind of sets up its own battle. I wouldn't mind seeing a film about Nasser in Egyptian. It doesn't have to be English. And I can tell a lot.

I would have loved to have made a film when Donovan Avis went down with his kid to give Castro those Red Cross trucks. Castro was going to let the people from the Bay of Pigs go and he demanded a whole lot of Red Cross stuff in return, and Donovan went down, and he was kind of the in-between guy. He took his son along, just to take him along. And the son just went out and stayed and hung out with Castro for a week. I think he said they fished a lot. That was a great makings of a film. It wouldn't have to have a personal point of view. Just have it so that he was there and interested in everybody who was interesting. You don't have to be slanted toward or against it. Either way, it doesn't matter. It's no help. The mood of that moment, in that man's time, in the young American kid's time, would have been a fantastic thing just to be on film. I don't know what you would have learned from it, but I'm sure you'd know more about something you need to know than you knew. But that's exactly the kind of thing the networks wouldn't dream of doing. They are so terrified of a non-oriented position in a so-called documentary, they never would just let that go.

Did you ever see a film I made on Timothy Leary's wedding called *You're Nobody 'til Somebody Loves You?* Well, I'm not for or against Leary, but it was just that afternoon, what happened there, the mood of that place, and it's kind of not what you would expect to see. It lasts about fifteen minutes. We ran it with *Chinoise*. In a sense that would be a documentary for me. That is about as close as I come to it.

G.R.L. One reason I like documentary is that you get moments that I don't think you can get in fictional films—even though I can't think of many. Do you know *No Vietnamese Ever Called Me Nigger?*[9]

D.A.P. I haven't seen it, but that is true. And I think Al does it in *Salesman*. Al has some marvelous moments in that. But moments are like aesthetics, really—they're putting you off. Moments are cheap now. I'm looking for a longer line than moments. We all know moments are going to happen. You can stand out on the corner here and watch the soliciting on Broadway. You'll see marvelous moments. But you don't do it because you want something a little bit more substantial. It's like aesthetics—they're for women and children, really. You want something more coming out of it. Moments are the cop-out. It's like after the film: the people who go away and they've got nothing to lose, and they say, "Oh, what marvelous faces." There is always some line that they've got. That doesn't mean anything.

[9] By David Loeb Weiss, 1968.

G.R.L. Why did you make *One Parallel Movie?*[10]

D.A.P. Oh, you saw it?

G.R.L. Yeah.

D.A.P. Did you like it?

G.R.L. Some of it I liked a lot. Some of it I didn't.

D.A.P. I don't know. I got dragged by shooting Jean-Luc's[11] film after a while. I liked Jean-Luc, we got along fine, but I thought he was crazy. I had no business making his movie. We trusted each other about as much as Chinese pirates, for God's sake. So after Ricky and I both did just what we were told in the beginning, I started to branch out. I got more interested in the effect he had on people, in his machinations, and I just started to shoot . . . kind of notes. I do it all the time when I can afford it. I film notes on something that is interesting, people hanging out, going to sleep. His relationship with people, the way he maneuvered them, the way it didn't work finally, and his attempt to come to grips with what he considered to be the American Revolution, which I don't think he has the foggiest notion about. None. Particularly the Panthers. None. And there was a total lack of comprehension among all the people involved. It intrigued me. The lack of communication by people who all got put in the same boat. They all signed the same anti-Vietnam War manifesto and they were all saying quite different things. In fact, if it really came to blows, they'd probably be on different sides.

When I got it all shot I had it hanging around awhile; I didn't know what to do with it. We'd talk a little about it. I said, "Maybe I'll shoot a film," and he said, "Okay, you shoot a film," and then, "Can I have some of the footage?" I said, "Yeah, you can have everything. We'll just use each other's footage if you want, or whatever," and then he went away, and I got kind of dragged because there was this fucking film we had, just sitting there, gathering dust. So I said, "All right, I'll put it together the way he said to put it together." I had a ten-minute reel in which he outlined the thing to us all. So I put it together to see if it worked, but instead of

[10] "In early 1969 Jean-Luc Godard approached Pennebaker and Leacock about making a film called ONE A.M. This film was never finished. According to Pennebaker, shooting was completed but the material was never edited. Pennebaker says, 'I assembled the rushes trying not to edit them too much and added a few other scenes—notes I filmed during [Godard's] shooting. LeRoi Jones's street Mass just happened. It was not part of the script. This is not the film Jean-Luc intended as *One American Movie* (ONE A.M.) nor is it a substitute. It's a parallel movie. ONE P.M.' " (From program notes, Cinémathèque at the Metropolitan Museum, 1970)

[11] Jean-Luc Godard.

putting it together the way he suggested, I put it the opposite way, because you could see right away that he intended first to have the reality and then the art, and the art wasn't on par with the reality. It worked the other way around really; to see Ricky first doing the so-called art and then see the reality, it pulls you into the reality, which to me is vitally more interesting in the end. So I flipped the order a little bit, but I left them just as hunks, and when I got about halfway through . . . Well, after a while it wasn't that interesting. So what I got into was making a movie, and I got through it somehow and it got finished. I still don't know what it is. Henri[12] liked it, Jean-Luc hated it, but then he reluctantly decided it was okay. I don't know what it is, but that's documentary.

G.R.L. Then a lot of that footage you purposely shot for your own reasons. Not for Godard?

D.A.P. Right. Toward the end especially. Like the stuff with LeRoi.[13]

G.R.L. But he was around when you shot it?

D.A.P. Yeah, he was standing there watching, but he didn't want that. He had it in his head what he was interested in and wanted. I don't see how you can find out what's going on if you have it in your head what you're really interested in. But he's that type; he says, "You're just fucking around. You're not coming to grips with anything." But I suspect I'm wronger than he is. So I said, "Sure."

G.R.L. In the version I saw, there were lots of shots of Ricky shooting, but I don't remember seeing any shots of you shooting.

D.A.P. He didn't use any of Ricky's material, which has got me shooting too, I guess. I didn't use it either. The only one I did show was the one in the mirror. It's very easy for me to criticize Jean-Luc. Where he's listening to the interview with Eldridge,[14] and Eldridge says, "We really don't trust you fucking film-makers around here because you're only out for yourself," it's meant to be cute, to show Jean-Luc sitting there, thumbing his cigarette, and being guilty about it.

I didn't mean to be in any way critical of Godard. . . . That's not quite honest either. I certainly meant it to be critical of him, but I wasn't trying to put him down. I mean, I don't feel in any way superior to Godard, either as a film-maker or a revolutionary-

[12] Henri Langlois. The film was shown for the first time publicly on July 30, 1970, as part of the Cinémathèque at the Metropolitan Museum, "An exhibition of films presented by the City Center of Music and Drama and The Metropolitan Museum of Art, conceived by Henri Langlois, Director, Cinémathèque Française."

[13] LeRoi Jones.

[14] An interview with Eldridge Cleaver in Oakland, California.

watcher or anything else. In fact, I feel that Godard probably knows a lot of things I don't know at all. So I didn't want it to be a put-down of him at all, and I felt it was very important at that instant that I show myself—the shot of myself in the mirror—and I remember when I shot it thinking, I'm not blameless, I'm not removed from this at all. Everybody was going over the thing about we were part of the system. So there were things that I didn't plan a lot. It just seemed to me something that fell into place, and then at the end I shot the kids in the street.

G.R.L. What about the Jefferson Airplane?

D.A.P. That he set up.

G.R.L. And the cops coming?[15]

D.A.P. No, that wasn't set up. That happened.

G.R.L. Does he have any intention of coming back to edit the film?

D.A.P. Well, he tried it. He came back, spent a couple of days here, went through it and then he sort of gave up. He's into something else. It didn't interest him any more.

G.R.L. Who paid for it?

D.A.P. NET paid for part of it, and we paid for the rest. We're out about fifteen grand, probably.

G.R.L. Do you hope to release *1 P.M.* as a commercial feature?

D.A.P. I'm not sure that chick will ever give a release on it.

G.R.L. Who is that chick?

D.A.P. That lawyer, the lady in the film gobbling about curing the business. It comes after the Eldridge thing, where she's in an office. Well, there's a little bit that she cut off the head of that roll that actually makes the reel more intelligible. I don't know how you could make any sense out of the whole end of the film without seeing it, but she insisted that be cut out of the film. Well, I won't cut it out. She's a lawyer, and she could sue us. She's just a sorehead. That she ever got put into the film really enrages me, because she is absolutely unnecessary to the film. We thought any business lady would have done, but we had to have this one, and somebody gave her a contract which allowed her to censor the whole film if she doesn't like any part. I mean it's a really bullshit, dumb story —I feel ashamed to tell you about it. So I said, "Okay, we're going to run the film up there,[16] and you can stand in front of the projector and what you don't want in, you can hold your hand in front of the projector." If the chick has the balls, with a room

[15] There is a sequence in the film where the Jefferson Airplane plays on the roof of a building, in Manhattan, and the police arrive, stop their playing and make them leave.

[16] At the Cinémathèque at the Metropolitan premiere.

full of people, to blot out a part of the film, that takes a lot of something. Well, she went and did it, and the opening of the second reel is very important, and should never have been cut. I'm not going to cut it out, so at this point we're at a standstill. I'm not going to have anyone tell me how to edit a film—it's crazy. Even Godard was outraged when he knew about it.

G.R.L. Has *Don't Look Back* made money for you?

D.A.P. Yes. Not really very much. Mostly because we're so little. Like there are about ten thousand theaters in this country, and a reasonably good Hollywood movie is going to get into half of them, a third of them, without too much trouble, but we're lucky to get into five hundred. It's very hard; we're very inefficient. We don't have too many movies, we don't have too much muscle, we don't have an operation that's able to put together a selling operation that can hustle a film into the last nickel and dime, so we're probably operating at about 5 per cent efficiency where everyone else is operating at about 75 per cent. The theaters and a lot of people make money out of the film, but we don't make much money. Our total profit right at this point is probably about a hundred thousand dollars, of which we owe Dylan maybe half.

G.R.L. How do you keep going?

D.A.P. It's tough. In the end, what's going to keep us in existence is 16mm. distribution of films that we release theatrically.

G.R.L. In the college market?

D.A.P. In the colleges, and probably that is going to expand. Those theaters out there are going to run *Tom and Dick and Alice and Bill* till their roofs fall in. And the other films, like *Chinoise*, have no chance unless some alert person says, "Okay, let's do it a different way." At that point you might as well do 16. You can get really good 16 projectors now, and 16 sound. There's no need for 35 in that market. So it means we can compete a little bit. It's hard for us to compete with 35. We're doing the same thing everybody else is, but maybe dumber, a little slower, a little more expensively, probably. So the fact that we're small should help, but it doesn't really.

G.R.L. The films that are being released to the colleges, is that through other distributors?

D.A.P. No, no. We do it. We have this great big room in there and letters come in and come out. We may have half a dozen films that other people have done that we're distributing, but not too many. I'd like to end up with films that I've made that aren't readily distributed. I've got maybe a dozen films like that.

G.R.L. Mainly feature-length films?

D.A.P. Well, maybe not feature films. Some of them are only an hour, some of them thirty-five minutes, some of them are like short stories, but you could band them together in programs. I haven't got a prayer for any of these theatrically. It just doesn't pay. The cost of opening a film theatrically in the city is between thirty and fifty thousand dollars. That's quite an investment, to me anyway, and it hasn't got much chance of making it back in New York. You don't start to make it until you get into those other ten thousand theaters, and we aren't going to get in anyway, so our best bet is to go right into that 16 market. Forget the 35. And if you want to show it in New York, get a theater and put a good 16 projector in there and just run it for a while, in 16. I wouldn't even blow up those things. The only reason to blow them up is if you're going to really go for a wide distribution, then it pays you, because the prints hold up longer and the system is geared to 35 and maybe it looks better in most theaters. But any film we've made we could have opened in 16. *Don't Look Back* played for six months in San Francisco with the answer prints.[17] Never had a 35 print—they were all 16. Nobody ever knew it.

G.R.L. Have you ever shot any films in 35, or have they all been in 16?

D.A.P I did one—a dumb film called *Skyscraper*.[18] That's "documentary." That's a dumb, dumb picture. It's a bullshit documentary. It's just pretty pictures.

G.R.L. One could say the same thing about most features, that they're really just bullshit, that they're not about anything.

D.A.P. No, no. I'll tell you why. You know why? I mean, sometimes I feel this way. I might not tomorrow. There's a difference, because a feature film is like a major job, like building a ship, a boat for a fisherman. Every decision, everything you do is made with one intent, that somebody is going to make a living out of it, that a whole system is going to be supported by it. Now a little thing like *Skyscraper* was made as a kind of dig at that system, so we're trying to show off a little bit, show that we can be cute too. But in fact nobody gets any benefit out of that film, except Tishman, who owns the building, gets the publicity. We don't make any money for doing it, the distributors don't make any money distributing it. It's a gas. It has no real purpose in life. It's floating around pretending it's ready for the party, but doesn't even know where the party is.

17 The first print made for projection from a finished film. From examination of this print, changes in black and white gradation or color balance are made for subsequent prints.

18 About the building of the Tishman building in New York City. V. interview with Van Dyke, pp. 177–78, for further details.

Take the dumbest film you can think of coming out of Hollywood, the worst film you can think of. That thing was made fantastically, right? I mean those guys hammered every nail in there in perfect style and fashion. When it's all together, a lot of people live off it for a long time, even if it's not very good. They support their families, they buy cars. That's not unimportant. Maybe it's not artistic, maybe it's not a lot of things, but it isn't unimportant. A lot of people, that's what they know how to do, and they're not going to stop. Just like building a boat to go out fishing with, what's that to fish? Who needs the fish any more? They're all loaded with strontium 90 anyway, and yet every fishing boat that is built in Japan, it takes those cats one day to get down a forty-foot plank and saw it lengthwise. You can't tell them that's not important. That's the only thing they know how to do and they're doing it.

So I don't put down any of that Hollywood thing on an artistic level because I don't feel strong enough on that. It's because we're in business too, just like everybody else. We have to make a living, keep it all alive and pay the rent, and if I can do anything else that interests me on the side or in addition, that's great. If I can do it and have it succeed, it's fantastic. But I don't care if I don't. I'd like to get feedback, but on the other hand I've got to survive. I mean survival, keeping my family alive, my kids fed, that's as important as making a movie. I don't knock that. Even what the mailman does isn't less than what I do. Mailmen, really, they're very talented, and they're very good at what they do. But there's nobody guiding it most of the time. It's like missing the moon with a ship full of people. It's a terrible thing, but that's the way most things go. In the United States there's nobody to help. Floating endlessly around. Everybody wants to blame somebody for the horror show. There is nobody to blame, because nobody knows how to stop it or control it or do anything with it. It's just floating, knocking people down in the streets. What do you do with it? And Hollywood is just the same syndrome, just this great machine going berserk, but it is marvelously attended. It's really fantastically mad, what it's about.

G.R.L. People do what they do. I come here and I talk to you and I do this book. I don't know how worthwhile it is, okay? It started somehow, and I'm doing it, and that's nice, but finally it doesn't matter to me terribly. I think it's worthwhile in that there's some information that people will be interested in, some—

D.A.P. Hey, you'd like some feedback, even if it's only your wife.

G.R.L. There's some information that I think will be useful to people, so I'm going to do it, I'm—

D.A.P. Mostly to you. I mean you'll find out something.

G.R.L. I'm finding out more than anybody.

D.A.P. That's right. That's the thing you dig most or you wouldn't do it.

G.R.L. Right, and that's one of the nicest parts.

D.A.P. You'd hate to do five of these books.

G.R.L. I would.

D.A.P. Right. You see? What's wrong with the fifth one that is not wrong with the first one?

G.R.L. I guess it would just bore me.

D.A.P. Yeah, so you wouldn't be finding out anything, and maybe by then your audience will be finding out more, because you'd have the whole thing all down pat, so in fact your audience really doesn't preoccupy you very much at all. It can't.

G.R.L. But let me try to go ahead. Perhaps there is nothing wrong with the guys in Hollywood doing what they do. They're earning a living, and it's a trade, but they monopolize things, the whole system—

D.A.P. They don't. That's the thing. You say "they." Who's "they"? Gulf and Western? Kinney? Here's this fucking Warner Brothers controlled by a parking lot company. What do you think motivates a parking lot company to make a movie? It isn't just money. They all want to go fuck the stars, they want to get in on the action, right? And they think the action has got to be with movies, and they meet all those girls and all that shit goes on. They want to get into it too. Now, somewhere in the back of the building there's a controller who says, "Profits are down. Quick!" and somebody starts to rustle papers and they all begin running in different directions. Next thing you know a supermarket, Gristede's, will be running Warner Brothers. Well, what really runs it? What makes the changes? What determines what happens? I don't think it's anybody.

G.R.L. Well, there is a System somewhere.

D.A.P. Well, of course, there's a System. Everybody spends his whole life looking for it, and the System seems to be that it's devoted to going onward, crushing as it goes whoever wants to stop it. But it's not anybody. I refuse to believe that there's a creature sitting on top saying, "What else can I fuck up today? What is there I haven't got into yet to really put to the wall?" Nobody's got that control.

G.R.L. Obviously there's not just one cat, but don't you ever get angry or frustrated that you can't do the kind of film that you would like to do?

D.A.P. All the time. No, no. I don't, because I honestly don't feel that I should make films all the time. I'd like to go a year without making a film. Does that sound terrible? I don't care. I don't mind going sailing on my boat for a whole fucking year. That's as interesting and amusing as making a film. It could be. I happen to know how to make films. I can earn a living making films. I even like making films, and when I finally reluctantly get dragged into starting a film, I usually end up getting interested in finding out something about it that I didn't expect to. But if I could avoid it I wouldn't pick up a camera. It's funny, but I don't feel that my whole purpose in life is turning out films. I don't feel indispensable to the film industry at all.

G.R.L. The Maysles, for example, would probably say that they—

D.A.P. The Maysles are quite different. They do what they have to do, but they're interested in something different. I'm not interested in that. They've got a kind of artistry of their own that they're fabricating, and in a sense—not in a depreciatory way—it's a kind of Hollywood artisan concept in that they want to be the best in their field, making a certain kind of film. They want to put their stamp on it, they want to get into whatever is hip, whatever is going on, and somehow we'll all get it, you know? To depict it, film it in their way. Well, I don't feel any particular compulsion to go make a film about the Vietnam War. I don't think I can bring anything to the Vietnam War that just knowing that it's going on doesn't bring to most people. I don't have any philosophic insights into the war. I don't know anything about it. I wouldn't mind making a film with General Giap if I could, because I think he's an interesting man. I wouldn't mind watching Westmoreland during the Tet offensive—that was an interesting time. Those are instances when it occurred to me that I might have been able to do something that nobody else was going to bother to do. But most of the time everybody is doing it ten times over, and I don't feel any need to just do it again. And I don't. Proliferating films isn't a big deal. I mean what are you going to do with them? I've got these films in there. You should see them. Racks of them.

G.R.L. They're cut?

D.A.P. Some of them are, in a way. I've got a whole color film, a feature film of Dylan in there going to waste. Fantastic. I've got the most fantastic music performances that you've ever seen in your life. There's nothing ever that even comes close to them.

G.R.L. That obviously has commercial value. Why is it not released?

D.A.P. I don't know. I haven't quite finished it yet.

G.R.L. And Dylan has the right to say yes or no?

D.A.P. Oh, yeah.

G.R.L. Did he pay for it?

D.A.P. Yeah.

G.R.L. Is he interested in seeing it?

D.A.P. I don't know.

G.R.L. He doesn't call you on the phone?

D.A.P. No, I haven't seen him in a long time. I'm still working on it actually, a little bit, but I don't think that if it's not out this month or this year we're in trouble. In about ten years it'll be just as interesting, Dylan will be just as interesting as he is now. I don't mean to seem like a dilettante about it, because the films do mean something to me once they're born; then they're real people. But I've got a lot of just raw material, and I just don't see any point in manipulating it in some momentarily fashionable form, copping it together and trying to get it into a theater. We have films in theaters. That doesn't bring any money. It doesn't bring any instant change or karma or fame or anything else. It's just like doing anything else. The filming of the thing is the least important. It's knowing where the thing is happening and having some access to it. Whether you film it or not is your own problem, my own problem. Sometimes I can't stand it, I have to film it; sometimes I just let it go by. That's what you're doing with your life. You try to be where you want to be. If you feel the need to have that camera proceed every place you want to be, there's something very bizarre about that.

G.R.L. Gets to be a way of life.

D.A.P. Well, in a way, but that's not the way I want to live. I don't take the camera on picnics with me. And the trouble with documentaries is that they presuppose that the film-maker is really recording his life. And in most instances he's not. He's recording some kind of venture. He's probably using somebody else's venture, like *Salesman* was a venture for Al. He thought about it for a long time before it appealed to him.

G.R.L. Do you worry much about or get involved much in the business structure of Leacock-Pennebaker?

D.A.P. I have to sometimes, but I try not to. It doesn't interest me much. I ran it for many years. I ran it before Ricky came in. I ran it by myself. It was just like shaving a lot. In the end it was just a drag to have to do. I find no excitement consummating a business deal or making money out of a deal. I just like to get paid regularly, and I'd like to be able to get films out of the labs. I never expect to get rich making films.

G.R.L. There seems to be a kind of ambivalence or self-deprecation about your work, because sometimes when you talk about it you sound genuinely interested and concerned, and other times—

D.A.P. Obviously there are things that interest me. The film is just a little piece of shit that you end up with, and if it's 10 per cent of what happened it's a lot more than most things get. If you just see what is going on all around you all the time on every level . . . It's lethal what's happening in the world. The feedback is so incredible now. Just generally through various media, the rate of increment of energy output is staggering. And what's a film? It's just a little window someone peeps through. The fact is that what really film could do and should interest me to do, is try to break through that increasing area of what's going on and try to get involved in that feedback. I mean now it's so delayed.

G.R.L. What about TV? Does that interest you?

D.A.P. TV is pretty much closed off to us. Sure TV is very interesting. I haven't got many ideas about TV. I don't see how to make it more interesting than it is. I know that it's pretty lame most of the time, just because it's so dead. I don't think *Sweet Toronto,* for instance, would be a big hit on TV.

G.R.L. *Sweet Toronto,* is that *Toronto Pop?*

D.A.P. Yeah, it never was *Toronto Pop.* I don't know where that name popped up. That's a fantastic film.

G.R.L. You talked about feedback. You said that the increment of the knowledge that we're gaining is so enormous that really one can't comprehend it or cope with it.

D.A.P. Well, look. At the very moment that you, let's say, are putting on your hard hat and are running out screaming, "Up the war, down with students," at that very moment, if something gets through to you or not, you just see something you didn't expect to see that would snap your head. I don't know what it would be. That would be interesting, not because it's going to change either one of us, but because it's going to entertain you. That is what art should do. It should snap your head, suddenly. You're all set, and you knew you had it all figured out and there was no problem. Now all the people on this side of the wall go down with the tide, and suddenly, bang! it isn't that way. That's entertaining. That's tremendous. That's what people's heads are for, maybe. That's what they go out and hope will happen. Only they are so protected, it's hard to make it happen. Well, that's what I'm trying to do, except I don't see it as making the world better for anything. I can't make that judgment or take that responsibility. But the problem of being able to do that, that interests me, I have to admit. How would I be able to do it? I'd persist.

G.R.L. What about the possibility of going into video cassette or cable TV?

D.A.P. I don't know. These are just disseminations. I don't care about that. Like *Sweet Toronto,* I don't know how we're going to get it out. We can't even get John Lennon to look at it. He's closeted out there in Los Angeles, and I don't want to do anything until he's seen it. I only want him to look at it, then we can talk. There's no money problem at this point on releases or anything. It's just that I want him to see the film and see his old lady[19] perform, and if he digs what she does as I do, that's good. If he doesn't, then I don't know what we'll do. But I know that it's a fantastic film. Those guys in there will never do it better. In a sense, it's the definitive performance of certain extraordinary rock 'n' roll guys, and I wouldn't even try to do it again.

I just have to be persuaded that sooner or later that news is going to get out one way or another and that film is going to get released. That's what happened to all the others, to *Don't Look Back* and *Monterey*. They sat on the shelf, no way of getting them released. That finally gets through to the mechanism that gets things released and oils the wheels; whether it's money or pressure or power, it happens. And I don't do it. It does it. If the film is a dog—and I can be persuaded that it's great, but in fact it could be old fashioned. And the fact is, if a film doesn't have any news, then nobody is going to carry it. If it has news, it'll get out. I may be dead before it gets out, but it'll get out. I'm persuaded of that. So I don't worry about it. I've done all I can do. I'm not a hustler, really.

We set out to do something in *Sweet Toronto* five days before it happened. I didn't care about shooting a lot of that. I didn't even shoot The Doors, I didn't even put a camera up. I was just interested in the first four people on that poster. I didn't even know John was coming. I went up there to film those guys because they knock me out, and nobody had ever done it and I really wanted to do it. I just felt that was just right, and I don't regret an instant. The film is fantastic.

G.R.L. Let me read these four names from the poster: Bo Diddley, Jerry Lee Lewis, Chuck Berry, Little Richard. That's it. You didn't care particularly about Eric Clapton?

D.A.P. No, no. I didn't even care about Lennon. I didn't go to film Lennon. Lennon and Clapton and Yoko showed up, and did this ending, and the ending is fantastic, and I wasn't prepared for it. It's beyond anything that the first four guys do. The first four guys are going to be a movie, a perfectly transforming movie. What John does is extraordinary, him and Yoko. You can't believe that. In the end it really puts you through a change you didn't expect. So that's a great movie. That's really what movies should do. You go in one

19 Yoko Ono.

way and come out another. People would go in who hate rock 'n' roll and come out just knocked out. That's good.

G.R.L. You do the editing of all these films yourself?

D.A.P. Yes.

G.R.L. Are you politically concerned?

D.A.P. I'd say I'm politically naïve. I hear it all and I can return it all to you, but I'm not too smart about it. It's like anything else, it's a business, and I'm not in that business, so whatever I hear is already old. It's like I can't read *Variety*. It's like Greek. It would drive me crazy to have my life contained by that newpaper. And in politics it's the same way.

I've been to Russia a couple of times. It always makes me laugh, because people I know in Russia are about as concerned about their politics as I am about ours. They don't know what's going on in Moscow. They don't know who's running, or why, or how. Somebody says, "Jesus, you just invaded Czechoslovakia." "Czecholo-what?" It's just like me. I don't know what we're doing in Watts. And I'm damned if I'm going to let anybody put the whole weight of America's political ventures on my back. I just say, "Yeah, I just can't carry that." So it's ridiculous for me to be half-assed into it, but I do get into it. You read the papers, like everybody else; you get into the ball game sooner or later, but that doesn't guide what I film, particularly, I'm not into political films. Look, I was not interested in shooting Johnson in the last two months in the White House.

G.R.L. Are you interested in making features?

D.A.P. Yeah, I'm interested in feature length because it's just sort of a good length. People have adjusted their time spans to get into that, whereas in fifteen or twenty minutes, they're not. Fifteen or twenty minutes is like reading an article at the bottom of *Reader's Digest*. You get about that much interest. A feature-length film merits a certain kind of attention, a certain kind of interest, and I think it's a good length.

G.R.L. And fiction?

D.A.P. It just never happened.

G.R.L. You're not pushing to make it happen?

D.A.P. Not particularly. I think people are pushing me to do it, but I'd rather not. I'd rather make films about things that really happened, if I had my choice.

G.R.L. In working with Drew, are there any stories about how the network censored things that you did?

D.A.P. We weren't into the networks very much. Most of our stuff got syndicated, never went on network. But in the final cutting of the film, it was Drew. Drew was the hand that guided the way those films looked. Like *David*, which was one of the most interesting films I did. About the dope addict. *Jane* was maybe the most competent, most professional, but that really wasn't much of a film, it wasn't about much, in a way. *David* was the most interesting film, the first whole film I did really. The film that I'd like to have made was quite different from the one that was cut. The film that was cut reduces something that is actually very complicated to a rather prosaic, dull story. And the story in fact was false as it was finally made.

G.R.L. Things were set up in it?

D.A.P. No, but in the way it was edited—not the way it was shot. The narration and scenes were put together, were constructed with false voices and this bullshit stuff. Looking at it now, that stuff there just screams of its wrongness. And it isn't just me. I show it to people who wince at some of the things that were stuck in there, which at the time everyone thought were very well concealed within the fabric of the film. But the film itself still contains an interesting dramatic idea: a place where you can go, stay as long as you want to and leave any time you want; but once you leave, you can't come back.

G.R.L. When you shoot now, are you concerned with getting some kind of truthful reality and using it that way in the editing, or do you not mind juggling?

D.A.P. I see what you mean, but I don't think of it quite that way. Usually the first cut of anything, the first thing I do is assemble, which is in time order. I would never violate time unless there was a good reason to, but I wouldn't feel constrained not to if I wanted to. I have no rules about it at all. I think the main thing that keeps me honest is the absolute conviction that I'll get caught out. It's very hard to fool people's eyes. They're smart. Even people like your old grandmother who you think, "Gee, she's so dumb, she really doesn't know the commercials from the program," they see everything. They're just trained all their lives to seeing what the bullshit is and what isn't. And most people are like that, so I think you give it up. They may not be able to explain it, never quite be able to tell you why, or they may tell you the wrong thing. But if you fuck around, and you say this is real and then it isn't, people find out, they lose interest. If you say this isn't real, this is all pretend, this is the Forest of Arden, people will go along with that too. You have to be consistent, then people will accept it.

G.R.L. You have no particular moral compunctions about using footage however you think it will work best?

D.A.P. I sort of do, but I'd probably violate them if I felt strongly enough that the results justified it. I think in the end the film justifies it.

On the other hand, I feel very strongly about what Guggenheim did. I didn't see it, but he did a film on Kennedy,[20] and he took some footage that I shot in *Crisis* of Bob Kennedy who was on the phone trying to deal with that Tuscaloosa problem, those kids in the middle of the university, and he just happily lumped it into the film and said, "Cuba crisis." He had a narrator saying what was going on in the Cuban crisis over this silent picture. Okay, it's just Kennedy on the telephone, but I do feel morally it is wrong, and for this reason: you have a situation where you've got entree to a politician in a hard situation, where he's giving you a kind of license —he may be giving it to you for the wrong reasons, to get a little publicity, but if he's an interesting person, he's not. This is the way I felt always with Kennedy, both Kennedys, and particularly with John Kennedy, that in the back of his head was the idea that someday, somebody who understood better than I did what was going on, who understood the whole problem that he was facing, was going to look at that and find out something, and it wasn't for me to get too smart with what was important, what meant something and what didn't.

Actually, I find that films that I make for myself I edit very little, I only edit them if something goes wrong with the camera or I make some terrible mistake that you can't stand to look at, but generally, if the thing is at all well shot, I feel no need to edit at all. Only reason to edit is if something has to be an hour and it happens to run two. In which case, you've got to edit. And that requires a whole different set of skills. But most of the films shot which are lying back there as just things, I don't feel any compulsion to edit them at all.

G.R.L. Let's say that completed they're an hour and a half. Presumably you shot much more than an hour and a half of film.

D.A.P. No, no. I shoot films one to one, just the way they come out of the camera.

G.R.L. Which ones?

D.A.P. I did a film long ago in Russia.[21] I spent three months on it, it was a long, hard film, one of the first films I ever did. Well, it's a lame, little child. It's a beautiful film, but it's just lame. It's got fake synch-sound, stuff like that. So I went back and Henri was there—Henri Langlois. He's one of the people I knew, and I said, "Okay, this time I'm going to do it the easy way. We'll just shoot

[20] *Robert Kennedy Remembered,* 1968.
[21] *Opening in Moscow,* 1959.

for one day." I had synch-sound, a rig and somebody to do sound, and we shot one day. It's an hour-and-a-half film that's not cut.[22] How can I cut it? It's like a journal, and how do you cut a journal? Who's to say what's the most or least interesting? And film-making for me really has that kind of journalistic quality.

Now later there may be reasons to cut it. Like I had a lot of footage on Dylan, and you don't want to look at all the concerts. And I'm stuck with a different discipline, which is the theatrical discipline. Probably two hours would have been just too much. Even though, who's to say? If you were really interested in Dylan, two and a half hours wouldn't be too much. If you were interested in pop, two hours of *Monterey Pop* wouldn't have been too much. But my feeling was that two hours was too long. It was just a feeling. I could have been wrong, and I felt when it came down to an hour and a half, it was right. It could work and the theatrical audience went away still a little hungry. Which is right. So you just make those decisions. That involved editing, but if you don't have those decisions to make, there's no editing.

G.R.L. Are most of those dozen unreleased films journals shot at a one-to-one ratio?

D.A.P. Some of the early ones are more experiments, like a little short story I did with a girl in Ottawa,[23] and that might have to be edited, although I don't know how. I never knew how to quite finish that, but that's about an hour film. I took a situation where I knew something about the girl—I knew that she'd been through an extraordinary tragedy and that she was about to have a child. I tried to film one day with her—there were several of us involved—in which I was never going to explain what the tragedy was. But it just didn't come out. I felt that everybody involved understood without having it explained to them what I wanted to do, that in some way or other it would come out that this girl had been through some enormous tragedy. And it sort of did come out, but I've never been sure because I've never quite finished the film. It was just an idea to see if you could do something like that. I let people enact their own thing of what they wanted you to know. It's the same in *Don't Look Back*. I never gave Dylan any kind of directions as to what I thought was right or wrong. I never asked any questions. It was entirely up to him the way he wanted to present himself.

G.R.L. Are you concerned about what influence the camera has on a person?

D.A.P. I kind of like to deal with people who are actors and per-

22 *Moscow—Ten Years After*, 1969; not released.
23 *Michèle et Michèle*, 1964; not released.

formers because they are sort of protected. Sometimes I'm concerned with people who aren't protected against the camera, but in the end I guess I've never tried to make a film about anybody that I really felt hostile to. It would be hard to do. Some people could probably do it and do it well. It's hard for me because I have this terrible feeling that afterward, having observed somebody going through that vulnerability, and then to come back with a film that really hit on them, the first question anybody asks is, "What the fuck's this cameraman doing? What kind of a thing is that to do?" You don't know if you're going to put down more of yourself than the guy you're after. But I'm not certain. That's just the way it seems to me. I'm sure there are people who will come along with a very acid camera and be able to really make it, make everybody be happy about it too.

G.R.L. I was also thinking of, say, somebody like Dylan, who is a performer. If one is concerned with getting some sort of reality about the person, the essence of the person, are you concerned then that he might perform for the camera, hide himself from the camera?

D.A.P. No, because I'm in no better position to judge Dylan than anybody else. I'm not a psychologist or anything. I don't have any particular qualifications for making any judgments of any interest, of any value. All the judgments I make about Dylan are based on my reactions to his music, like everybody else, so when I film Dylan, if he chooses to put on an act for the camera, I assume everyone looking at it can instantly tell as well as I can that it's an act. I don't hold any special abilities to determine valid action from invalid action, and I'd just assume that everybody is looking for him to make a break, and if he makes a break, some people will see it, some people won't. I don't feel that because I'm there with a camera I have any special privileges, and I don't feel I should exert any. I don't feel that I particularly have any right to ask him any questions, to have him explain anything. What's an explanation? If I need an explanation, you can only assume that I think the audience does, and then what am I doing? I'm just making a rinky-dink film to get ahead, make a little money.

G.R.L. But if the film gives us—and I think it does—certain perceptions about Dylan, some sort of feeling about him, why shouldn't I think that you had something to do with that?

D.A.P. Well, I would think it's Dylan.

G.R.L. Do you believe any cameraman could have gone there and shot that and got what you got?

D.A.P. It's like . . . how can you imagine somebody in bed with your wife? [. . .] If you sent me out to film some cat that's really not interesting, all I'd show you is a modestly well-done bit—but zap! it's nothing. A lot of people really resist wanting to know about Dylan—he's hard work. The first problem they have is, is he valid, is he a poet, is this young Byron on the loose? And most people want to say no. They want them dead. They don't want to have them alive and around, troubling them. So a lot of people are going to resist, and I can break through that. That's just a thing I know how to do—construct a dramatic thing in which I'll find a way to make Dylan break through. But it's Dylan that breaks through, not me. I just do the thing to make it work. Now maybe the thing needs both, because everything Dylan is about is right there in his music, which he's written. It's not easy to read it. Maybe I've made the mood a little more real, make people want to read and think about it; but I haven't brought any great truth about Dylan to the stage. I just haven't done it—Dylan does that. So if there is any artistry in what I do, it is deciding who to turn this fearsome machinery on.

G.R.L. That's a great deal of it.

D.A.P. If Al Maysles had been there he would have shot a totally different film, but I think a lot of Dylan would have come through, and it still would have been fantastic, see? I can believe that.

[. . .]

Happy Mother's Day. Extraordinary, fantastic insight by an Englishman into America, and it's horrifying. It's an extraordinary film. I could never make a film like that.

[. . .]

G.R.L. But Ricky Leacock might not have been able to do *Don't Look Back*.

D.A.P. Because Dylan didn't interest him. Sure. But if he had made a film of Dylan, it would have been interesting because Dylan is interesting. Now that's the thing. If I had made *Happy Mother's Day*, it probably wouldn't have been a good film, because the situation really wasn't that interesting. It took a different kind of art to make that film work. It took a kind of introspection, it took that irony that Ricky has, the way of making a thing seem slightly ridiculous when in fact it's quite real. The guy climbing a ladder to take a picture of the prizes. Beautifully done. It's so understated. You have to decide in advance that you're going to deal with irony, and irony is hard for me to deal with. I don't shoot that way. So it would have been hard for me to make that film, you see? If Ricky made *Don't Look Back*, he certainly wouldn't do the same film, but it would have been carried through since Ricky would have been open to all the emanations and the things that were going on. Dylan would have come through some way, differently, but in some way. And probably it would have been fantastic. I don't know that it would have quite the chemistry that's in it, but *Don't Look Back* has a kind of responsiveness that I have to Dylan, born of Dylan's coming very close to things that I've been thinking about for a long time. It's sort of an epiphany that took place. And I think that some of that probably does come through in the film.

I've gotten so I'm wary. Someone comes and says, "I've got a great idea for a marvelous film about the marshes in New Jersey." I'd be very quick to say, "No, I'm not going to do it. Don't talk any more about it, I'm going to eat," because you'll get drawn into things and you get persuaded.

I really have to be very tough with myself. I just have to know what it is, where I can go and where I shouldn't go—and I'll make a lot of mistakes. Actually, I'm probably more willing to go into left field than Ricky is, or than most people, because often the best things I've ever gotten into have come that way. But it's very tough, not so much with the situation as the kind of emanations from it, the overtones of a situation, the people involved, and if I feel that it's just not right, it's murder—I've just got to avoid it like the plague. So I don't try to fool myself about it.

I don't think I could make a film about anything. I used to, but . . . The first film I ever made, a thing called *Daybreak Express,* is a very pretty film, a musical film. It's like a five-minute version of *Monterey Pop.* To see it would make you laugh.

G.R.L. You're not concerned with things like trying to make documentaries that will be on TV and reach a much larger audience and perhaps influence more people?

D.A.P. The audience doesn't attract me that much. I like the feedback, but not necessarily from the audience. I don't know what that audience is. I have no real affiliation with a TV audience. I've never been exposed to it very much. There are a couple of things on television, but they fall like stones into a well. You never hear a word. God, you work for four months on some thing, for some prime time, nothing! Wanda Hale says, "The other night . . ." and that's it. Nothing. You can't. Your mind protects you against getting too involved in that emotion. The most feedback I get is actually from people who just walk in here. They see mostly *Don't Look Back* or something that they dug, and they just kind of want to see if there's something else here, if they can get into anything here, you know? That's the most interesting feedback. Occasionally we get some critical feedback. Most of the time they're not too interesting. You'd like them to say real good things, but only a couple of people ever wrote anything particularly perceptive about *Don't Look Back.* I was sort of surprised.

G.R.L. Who were they?

D.A.P. I thought Penelope Gilliatt got into something that I hadn't thought about, but I think she was right on: that one of the things that comes through in *Don't Look Back* is the quality of hanging out, the friendship involved with the people, a quality I guess I've never seen in the movie. In fact, the more I thought about it, the more I guessed that was one of the most compelling reasons for me to do it. And she caught that. And a couple of people out West. Most of the New York critics, they just saw this Dylan Unmasked or something, here's a documentary film.

G.R.L. So the documentary is a dead genre? And you make films to make a living and that's it?

D.A.P. Well, it may not be dead. It may be resurrecting. Maybe it'll get interesting. Television is killing it. It's murder now. I can't get my children to watch a documentary—they go to sleep. "There's a very exciting documentary on tonight's show." Wow, I mean, whew, they don't want to see it no matter what it is. "It's about Black Panthers." That's not the way you want to find out about the Black Panthers. You'd rather see a movie with . . . I don't know who . . . yeah, with Cassius Clay playing the part of a Black Panther, yeah, playing the part of Fred Hampton. The whole plot, you know? and it's documentary, but . . . That's the trouble now. It's not that it's better, it's just that people have been so put off by the bullshit that they get in the documentary.

G.R.L. But with Cassius Clay we'd think about the Black Panthers the same thing we think about war. We'd think it was Brian Donlevy again. That's one of the real dangers.

D.A.P. Sure. That's true. I agree, I agree. There's no answer to this, it jumps back and forth. But what you really are looking for is somebody somewhere along the road that knows something. Now the trouble is the road in films is such a peculiar one. Like the editor that knows something, he hasn't got too much access to make use of it. All he can know about it is how to make a cut work, or how to do this or that. His political knowledge isn't called for. Nobody has a chance. The only person who really has got any chance to put out what he knows is the writer, and then that's very tough too. That gets so butchered up by the time it gets through, that that's lost, so that there isn't really much of a place for a person who knows anything really of interest to get it out as there is in, let's say, a book. That's the only interest you really have in any artist, in how much he knows. Or anybody. That's the basis. They find ways of concealing it, dressing it up and filming it, making it come at you a different way, but in the end that's really it. If Jackson Pollock hadn't known something, then nobody would be looking at his pictures at all. It wasn't the colors or the way he jumped around; it was because he knew something was happening and he was there a little bit before everybody else. And if you wanted to know what was happening, which people do have the need to know, you could find out from him, if you knew how to do it. Same with film. That's why the personal film does have a possibility now. Imagine if you could get Johnson interested in making films, if he made a documentary film about the presidency. That would have to be an interesting film.

G.R.L. I'm not sure of that.

D.A.P. Because you're convinced as I am that he is never going to deal with film, that he is just going to sit there and say, "All right, turn the lights on, I'll talk now." But if he could really get into film the way he's going to try to get into writing . . . Like he's going to sit down and write journals, right? He's got a secretary there, and at first maybe he figures somebody's going to do the work for him, but ultimately he's going to get interested and say, "God damn it, I do want the truth of what happened that day to come out. I want everybody to know what Kennedy said and what I said." So he's going to write it the way he remembers it happening. He may lie, but probably he won't. Probably, in the end, whatever it is that got him will force him to make those journals true. Truth does have some compelling quality about it that makes you want to try to adhere to it.

If, instead of doing journals, he would make a film . . . You can't film things after the fact, but if he could figure out how to tell what it is he knows about it—that man knows something that not many people know. But to have Walter Cronkite tell me about what Johnson knows is bullshit. Walter Cronkite doesn't know any more than I do really, and I like Cronkite. He is better than most of them, but he doesn't know. He doesn't know anything about film either. They just run some pictures and he talks. That's not film. That's not movies. That's bullshit.

G.R.L. Have you ever heard of the Videofreex?

D.A.P. No.

G.R.L. They're into television and they're sort of freaks. Among other things, they want to make these informational videotapes to send around to a kind of underground or alternate network. Like they made one on the pouring of a particular kind of concrete.

D.A.P. What do they use them for? Just look at them?

G.R.L. Right, so if you wanted to know how to do this kind of concrete, you can look at the tape and find out. There's a commune in northern Vermont building this big dome with parts of cars, right? So one of the Freex, a guy named David Cort, has been going up there all summer taping this dome going up. And he's doing one on growing herbs, right? You want to know about herbs, you look at the tape. And Ricky has a similar idea, but using Super 8 cameras. He wants to give it to people who know about specific things—not necessarily film-makers—give them cameras and let them make films about the things they know about.

D.A.P. The people who know about the thing already know two things: how the thing works and also how it doesn't work, and they'll be less susceptible to the kind of easy bullshit that will find its way into most films on how something works. People find it obviously easy or they try to find the excitement because they are afraid to lose their audience. It's all always premised around some hoked-up thing. But if you took scientists, my God!

Like for instance, there was a guy who went down to Mexico to study meteorites. And suppose he chopped one open and he found evidence of a life molecule. Supposing you were going to make a documentary about that. The thing is to make a film about this guy who is interested in this and see it over his shoulder. The fact of finding the thing and the life form is the way *Argosy* magazine would play it up, right? He's just a cat whose name they use, and they say, "There's life on Mars!" and it's that bullshit. But here's a guy who knows as much about meteorites, as much about life forms as anybody alive and you're going to be there the instant he first decides that it's happening. That's a fantastic moment.

How about being in the room when Urie[24] watched, on television, watched the guys landing on the moon? Or Gold?[25] Both of them had said opposite things. Gold had said, "You're going to fall into sixty feet of graphite," and Urie said, "Bullshit, it's hard as a rock." One of them was going to have to revise his whole concept of physics in about two seconds—and these are the two most eminent physicists in the world. What a thing to watch on film. There's nothing like that. Nobody is going to write about that. That's something just unbelievable. That's film. We went to NET, we went to about ten people trying to get the film. Nobody is interested. I almost wanted to do it anyway, just to see, because the idea just struck me. I don't even care about the fucking machine on the moon or anything else. What I finally did is I filmed a bunch

[24] Harold Urie.
[25] Thomas Gold.

of Russians watching it on television. That's in the Russian film. A whole roomful of them, laughing, having the best time, saying, "This will show our fuckers, this will really put their noses out of joint. Now they're going to get to work and get something up there." They were just having the best time, they just loved the idea that the Americans were getting on the moon. Something like that is fantastic.

What you get now on film is bottled and long digested. It's like the guy said, "The trouble with movies is by the time you see them, they're old-fashioned," and that's absolutely true. That's truer in my head than anything McLuhan says. Anything on television is now. Movies, the minute you see them, they're old-fashioned. They're about something that went on yesterday, and the end is calculable. You know where they're going to end. But it doesn't have to be that way. Movies could be the other way, open-ended. I don't know how. That's going to take real playwriting to figure out how to do it, and that of all things interests me now in films, this trying to get past that problem, because that's what movies need.

Right about now there is no movie playing in New York that having seen halfway through you don't know how it's going to end. And it's sad. It should be the opposite. The movies should open up. I've seen only two or three in my life that ever did. A movie made in France called *La Vie commence demain* (*Life Begins Tomorrow*).[26] That film really knocked me out. When I saw that film, God, I just felt sooner or later that is what television should be, because you never forget it. Gide sits there and smokes a cigarette, and you can't take your eyes off the cigarette. It just disappears. He just sits there, and he's marvelous. He really talks about things. Up to then they were just names, suddenly they're absolutely real. I have the feeling I know them, that I've spent weekends with them. That's incredible that somebody could do that.

The film that would have really interested me to do as much as anything, and I'd still love to do it if I could find a way, was that period in Italy when Byron and Shelley went down and hung out in Pisa which was just fantastic. That was a turning point, that was a center, this enormous maelstrom, and Italian people worked off of what took place that summer for the next hundred years. Hemingway was still working off the Byronic legend. It's a fantastic story even in the ending. The carabinieri threw them out—they were firing through the windows of the house. It was a crazy thing. But at that point Byron suddenly decided and realized that the play

[26] By Nicole Védrès, 1950; with the actor Gérard Philipe, and includes interviews with Sartre, Gide, Picasso and Le Corbusier.

wasn't the thing. The act was the thing. He wrote maybe two or three lines of any interest, but in fact the real thing was the gesture. That's fantastic. When a man who has had that incredible effect on the world, you watch him go around the corner, find out something . . . That would have been the most marvelous movie. You could look at that movie for all time. And you couldn't do a documentary about that. You'd do it just like *Don't Look Back*. You just hang out.

G.R.L. How would you do it?

D.A.P. My idea always was to do it with Dylan. To me Dylan is the Byron legend. There's pretty good documentation of a lot of the things that Byron really thought about, then there are the things that nobody quite knows about. Get people in those parts and let that take place. Enact what you know, and let the rest be filled in, let it happen, and see if one part doesn't make the other part.

G.R.L. They would improvise?

D.A.P. No, I don't think improvisation is it. I think you get too much bullshit in improvisation. I wouldn't do it with actors. I'd do it with real people. I'd do it with people that have been there. Most actors haven't been there.

G.R.L. But it would still be improvisation even if they weren't—

D.A.P. Oh no. It would be like this. Let's say that Dylan had a script and was acting, pretending that he was, let's say John Barrymore on tour, or somebody. In other words, that he had a role that he was consciously playing, with words that identified him, kind of a little play within the story. Now you filmed it and he did that. Now let's say that would have been a fatuous exercise in something. It might have been interesting, but only because Dylan was interesting. But let's say that your purpose in the thing is you want to know first of all what happened to Byron, what made him go to Greece, when did he come to the realization that he wasn't the world's greatest writer?

But let's say you assign those roles to people. It could have been Brando in his prime, it could have been anybody that really has been there—you have to have someone that's been there, who has been on the top of that thing and assessed himself in terms of being on the top. And that's a hard thing. You know right away who has it and who hasn't. You can smell it. That's what Hollywood actors, who stars are. Some of them have been there. Well, you put these people into it, and you work out a story line, work out a plot of what you know happened. Trelawny arrives, and Caroline Lamb comes through and throws a scene—whatever it is. You have the situations, you have four or five people who have each written their view of them, so you can pretty much put it down on paper and have people say the lines. But there are a lot of things you don't know about, so you just let it happen—if it's going to happen. They all know. You don't have to explain. Everybody knows what the problem is without your even telling them, because if they're interesting, the same thoughts have gone through their heads.

I don't quite know how to do it yet, but that would be worth doing because what you're after is interesting. Putting together what happens when an atom bomb hits a town, it's not interesting to me. I don't know why; maybe it should be. But I've already seen it, I've seen the bomb go off, I've seen the pictures of the houses burned, I've seen the pictures of Hiroshima, I've seen all of that and he's not doing anything except somehow martyring himself. He's making himself the precursor of the cause.

G.R.L. You mean Peter Watkins' *The War Game?*

D.A.P. Yeah. And it's bullshit. You know what I mean? He's not making me more antiwar. His ideas are all bullshit ideas. The fact is if you really wanted interest in the bomb, the story to make is the one about Stinky Groves and Oppenheimer. Now that's a fantastic story, and it's never really been done.

[. . .]

In terms of playwriting, in terms of film-making, you can't just go for the effect. That's like a little thing they do out at UCLA, for their film theses. They're little impressionisms or something. Film-makers aren't immune to the pressures on playwrights or authors. They've got to think, do their homework, and decide what matters, what they should put their efforts to, and why. They can't just create a little reality, a little subcosmos that is so real that for a moment people will be totally affected by it and be persuaded of film's power. The film's power is vastly overrated that way. It may have a very overwhelming effect on you at the time, but its persistence is very low. Much less, let's say, than a good play. Or even a good book. You don't agree with that?

G.R.L. No, I don't.

D.A.P. I think the persistence of the film is very overrated. I think it tends to fade very fast, except for some extraordinary film-makers who understand imagery.

G.R.L. But our whole conception, image of the West, for example, of war, of—

D.A.P. It's drummed into you a million times, but that's not through any art, any artistry. That's because you never see it any other way. The cowboy, he's just *endless.* You don't have any alternative. But how many movies have given you one tenth of the work for your head to do . . . let's say, that *Man and Superman* does?

G.R.L. I used to feel that way. I wrote plays for a long time, I went to the Yale Drama School for three years. I saw and read hundreds of plays, literally. But I don't believe it any more.

D.A.P. I agree that's not all there is. I dig Shaw—he just knocks me out. To see *Man and Superman* played, it's like a marvelous machine with everything working. It's just beautiful when it's well done, but it's old, it has nothing to do with what's going on now. The theater is gone. It's just the economics of theater. There can't be enough people to see the play so it's got to be film, or it's got to be television. The thing that interests me in film is mood, see? Which is what dreams are. The reality of dreams always fades, but what you do remember—but you never put words to it—is mood. You remember very definitely what the mood of the dream was, usually. If you were happy or unhappy or lost or something. You describe events and the things you saw, but the thing that really holds you was that mood. Well, that's what film has—and people very seldom describe mood in a film. But the mood is what really compels people, what they really love about a film. The thing you loved about *San Pietro* was that strange mood of that terrible range of violence and then those children. The mood is what interests me solely in film. I'd throw away all information. But I don't see it as a turning away from Shaw, I see it as kind of coming out of Shaw. And I still love Shaw.

G.R.L. It's really contrary to Shaw.

D.A.P. But it isn't really, because I don't have either the kind of mind or the abilities Shaw had. I couldn't create that kind of play in a million years, but I feel that if I make a good movie, it's just as valid as his play. I don't think it's as good as his plays, but it's just as valid in terms of the work it does. I don't feel frustrated. I know that I'm a different kind of person—all my reactions are visceral.

[. . .]

G.R.L. Do you like Godard's films?

D.A.P. Yeah, I do. Godard's films are not mood. Godard's films are closer to Shaw, because he's burning with that religious conviction, and they have a very tough logic working through them. But again, my favorite film of Godard's is *Chinoise*, which is just the mood. I guess that's the thing that persuaded me most about it. The early films I don't like much. I like them, but they're not . . .

Godard wants his films to be really hard-line. He's like Shaw. He's got that message, and he wants you to get it because it's a hard message, and he knows most people don't listen to it. I don't listen to it. I don't even know when it's coming on, and I know it makes him so furious. . . . The idea of being able to work on a film purely non-pragmatically really intrigued him. But he said he'd never be able to do it as long as he lived.

G.R.L. You're not really interested in just shooting somebody else's film?

D.A.P. No, not particularly, but I don't preclude that at all. I might if it were interesting. You know when you're interested in something, you don't have to really sell yourself. A film could follow out of that. It doesn't have to. I don't feel bereft if it doesn't, but if I'm going to go anywhere, that's where I'd like to go. I can't stand the idea of making a film that I'm not interested in.

ALBERT AND DAVID MAYSLES

Albert Maysles was born November 26, 1926, in Brookline, Massachusetts. He attended Brookline H.S., received his B.A. from Syracuse University, in psychology, and his M.A. from Boston University, also in psychology. He served in the Tank Corps during World War II; after the war he taught psychology for three years at Boston University. In 1955 he went to Russia, where he made his first film, *Psychiatry in Russia*, which was shown on U.S. and Canadian TV.

David Maysles was born on January 10, 1932, in Brookline, Massachusetts. He attended Brookline H.S. and received his B.A. from Boston University, in psychology. He served in the Army at Headquarters, Military Intelligence School, Oberammergau, Germany. In 1956 he worked as assistant to the producer on *Bus Stop* and *The Prince and the Showgirl*.

In 1957 Albert and David made their first film together, *Youth in Poland*, which was televised in the United States. Albert then worked as one of the principal film-makers on *Primary* and *Yanki No!* for the *Living Camera* series produced by Robert Drew for Time, Inc. David worked as a reporter on *Adventures on the New Frontier* and other films in this same series.

In 1962 the brothers formed their own production company and did the film *Showman*, a portrait of the film producer Joseph E. Levine. In 1965 they received a Guggenheim Fellowship in experimental film. Besides the films listed in their filmography, they have made numerous industrial and corporate promotional films which have helped them pay for their own films.

Albert and David are both single and live in New York City.

Note: Charlotte Zwerin, who collaborated with the Maysles on all their major films after *Showman*, was born in Detroit, Michigan, received a B.A. from Wayne State University and did graduate work in film at C.C.N.Y. Previous to her work with the Maysles she worked on documentary films at the three networks and won an

Academy Award for a feature documentary on Robert Frost, *Lover's Quarrel with the World,* which she produced with Robert Hughes.

(The above material was taken from the filmography in the book *Salesman* by Albert and David Maysles, and Charlotte Zwerin, pp. 125–26, and from conversations with the film-makers.)

FILMOGRAPHY*

1955: *Psychiatry in Russia.* Documentary record of mental health treatment in Russia. Filmed on location in the Soviet Union.

1957: *Youth in Poland.* Shot in Poland during a period of political ferment, this film predicted much of the student revolution of the late 1960s.

1959: *Primary.* The first major cinéma-vérité film made in the United States. Details the dramatic primary election battle in Wisconsin between Jack Kennedy and then Senator Hubert Humphrey. Won the Flaherty award in 1960. (Albert Maysles a major contributor.)

1961: *Yanki No!* A film of the Castro revolution. (Albert Maysles responsible for all filming in Cuba.)

1962: *Showman.* A candid film portrait of movie magnate Joseph E. Levine. Film editors: Dan Williams, Tom Bywaters, Betsy Taylor.

1964: *What's Happening! The Beatles in the U.S.A.* An hour-long behind-the-scenes documentary of the Beatles' first visit to the United States.

1965: *Meet Marlon Brando.* An off-the-record view of Brando—in which he, at times, interviews the interviewers.

1966: *With Love from Truman—A Visit with Truman Capote.* Produced for National Educational Television, this half-hour-long documentary examines the man and the motivations behind the author of the first major non-fiction novel.

1969: *Salesman.* By the Maysles Brothers and Charlotte Zwerin. Contributing editor: Ellen Giffard. Assistant editor: Barbara Jarvis.

* From *Salesman* by Albert and David Maysles, and Charlotte Zwerin, pp. 127–28.

1970: *Gimme Shelter.* By the Maysles Brothers and Charlotte Zwerin. Film editors: Ellen Giffard, Robert Farren, Joanne Burke, Kent McKinney.

Also among the Maysles' work during this period are several major corporate and documentary films, including *IBM: A Self-Portrait* and *Bill Blass: Portrait of a Fashion Designer* (for Allied Chemical).

May 13, 1970, in David Maysles' apartment in New York City.

G. Roy Levin: Is there any connection between the fact that you both studied psychology and now make documentary films?

Albert Maysles: I don't think so. But I can answer this question better now since our films have developed more and more into autobiographical expressions. We've taken another look at our family and our backgrounds in order to make our films and I see very clearly what a great influence our family life has had on our work. They're people with very warm connections with those around them. They believe in life and that's why we went to life itself—common people like our parents to film "the facts" of life. And that, I'd say, is the origin of our interest in films of fact.

David Maysles: I could have just as well majored in English literature; in fact, I wish I had. It would have given me a better education. Reading books is the best education you can get outside of experience itself, I think. Great books are more about life. Psychology is more about technique.

A.M. Well, there are different schools of psychology, but generally one is more inclined to come out of psychology with a technique of analyzing human behavior, whereas the greatest influence on our movie-making was an interest in discovering what people are like as we're filming them and editing the material.

D.M. None of our influences are from the movies. They're more from our experiences on the road, hitchhiking across the U.S. and Canada when Al and I were very young, our family and literature perhaps. We're more moved and interested in scenes that we've experienced or read about in books and plays than we are in the movies we see. I don't think we ever got excited about a movie to the extent that it motivated us in our work.

A.M. It would be appropriate if someone like Chris Marker were a psychologist by training. I would suspect that being French, he starts out with a theoretical point of view, but that's quite the opposite of us.

D.M. For example, Paul Brennan[1] comes from the kind of guys we grew up with, the Irish Catholic guys that we grew up with in Boston, that we knew in school and after school when we were working. Maybe we're also influenced by having read Irish plays and about those playwrights, and novelists, much more. In fact, we

[1] The major character in *Salesman*.

think of film much more as a novelist does as a personal work, as a work of art rather than as a show or piece of entertainment.

G.R.L. Were either of you film buffs when you were kids? Did you go to movies a lot?

D.M. No, not especially.

G.R.L. So here you were, neither of you particularly interested in films, and you both go into film-making. Why?

A.M. Well, I'd say that it seemed natural that we would pursue our interests in exploring life in the world by this new means of movie-making. If the only way we could make movies was with scripts and actors, we would never have gotten into it. But with this new way, in which we could use portable cameras with synch-sound that we could carry about and discover things simultaneously as we are putting them on film . . . We must have felt that that's the most direct way to experience and to report our experiences immediately.

D.M. Maybe there is an association with psychology if you're putting it to use to study human behavior. In our work, we're interested in filming human behavior and getting our own insights out of it instead of the insights of other people. For example, I doubt if you'll ever see a film by us "based on the book by——."

A.M. We rejected that. It didn't start with psychology as a necessary step before movies. If psychology didn't exist as a study, we would have gone right along directly to making movies because of our interest in experiencing life and telling exactly that experience to the world.

G.R.L. But David worked on some Marilyn Monroe movies, started out working in features that were not documentary.

D.M. Yes, but that's because that was available, and it was good, because I could get it out of my system. It was a terribly boring thing to be on a feature film. I don't know if you ever have. But it can be very boring to wait for someone to set up something, and then just to repeat it twelve times. To try to approach that kind of reality . . . just to move that camera on all the fancy racks, dollys and cranes.

A.M. Actually the kind of creative activity that we were interested in, if at all in that kind of movie-making, probably would have been in the writing of the script.

G.R.L. Did either of you want to write? Like fiction or poetry?

A.M. No.

D.M. No, no.

A.M. Actually, where I have been interested in writing has always been in diary form, which is similar to a factual style of making movies. You experience something, and without pressing much of a form on it, you immediately set it down—in this case in print. In other words, a form of expression that comes as directly from your feelings as possible. At least in the film-making part, our style of making movies is totally spontaneous in the photography and in the event that we're filming. People are doing something and there's no time lag between the events and the photography of it, except maybe in the passage of light and sound, which moves pretty fast.

G.R.L. Are you interested in fiction?

D.M. I'm interested in fictional technique as it relates to factual material. I mean, in a sense, editing is a fiction, really, because you're putting it together, you're taking things out of place. They're all real events, but when the salesman might be in a hotel in Florida and you're representing it as in New England perhaps, if you have to, it's the same thing, it's not really a distortion. It could be anywhere. So in a way you're called upon to make some kind of fiction in the end. It's hard to explain, but it's a fictional kind of attitude. In other words, you're not saying this is the truth, this is exactly what happened the way it happened. What we're trying to do is make a development that gives you a sense of truth which will keep the audience interested, will tell them something about the subject that we're filming, will show them something that will intrigue them and get across what we're trying to get across. So the effort to do that is a fictional effort.

G.R.L. I think editing is a kind of fiction. You can even take it back to, you know, Kuleshov and Pudovkin, and the idea that all shots take their significance from their juxtaposition with another shot—not that each shot doesn't have a certain meaning in itself, but, for example, if you take a close-up of a gun, and then juxtapose it with a medium shot of a little kid in a cowboy costume, you have one meaning, but if you juxtapose it with a shot of Richard Widmark with a sneer on his face, the gun obviously takes on absolutely different connotations. And I think this is true in *Salesman*.

D.M. Then you can go back and say *Salesman* is fiction, because when Al shoots Brennan in the last shot of the film, the fact that we stay on it is significant. Also he's practically in tears in that shot and there's a fear in his eyes, but it wasn't long enough, so in the end they made it into an *optical*—freezing and zooming in on him—lengthening the scene. So there is fictionalization there, of the shot itself. I'm not saying it makes it any less truthful, because certainly even Brennan himself, who saw it, and other people who were there thought it was very representative of what happened. It's a hard thing to explain exactly how you feel about it. Neither one of the words is satisfactory, fiction or fact. I guess the best expression of it is "artistic truth." And I don't like the word "artistic" either. Or the word "creative." It's truth, the way we see it—in the shooting and the finishing. And in amost every case, that truth is shared by the people, by the subjects who see the film afterward. I can't even remember a case where anybody ever said that we distorted what happened—even if we changed a hotel room or something like that.

A.M. We can see two kinds of truth here. One is in the raw material, which is the footage, the kind of truth that you get in literature in the diary form—it's immediate, no one has tampered with it. Then there's the other kind of truth that comes in extracting and juxtaposing the raw material into a more meaningful and coherent storytelling form, which finally can be said to be more than just raw data.

In a way, the interests of the people in shooting and the people editing (even if it's the same individual) are in conflict with one another, because the raw material doesn't want to be shaped. It wants to maintain its truthfulness. One discipline says that if you begin to put it into another form, you're going to lose some of the veracity. The other discipline says if you don't let me put this into a form, no one is going to see it and the elements of truth in the raw material will never reach the audience with any impact, with any artistry, or whatever. So there are these things which are in conflict with one another and the thing is to put it all together, deriving the best from both. It comes almost to an argument of content and form, and you can't do one without the other. So I think a film like *Salesman* really works, and is very truthful because somehow the kind of usefulness and veracity in both the editing and the filming were combined to get the best out of both. In editing you've got to have respect for the truth that's in the material.

D.M. And the content does dictate the form. A lot of people think that we have to make a film that doesn't have narration, or that we have some kind of rules that we can't do this or that. I can give you examples later, but it's very much a day-to day process, and what happens and what we're interested in can take all kinds of forms.

If there's a weakness in *Salesman*, it's a sort of monotone. You know, that sort of a steady thing, very few ups and downs, which is one of the things we really have to work on. The same with *Showman*. That flat level, you know, is interesting, but I think it a certain failing.

A.M. I think one of the best things that can be said for *Salesman* is—and I think you'll know what I mean when we can talk about it a little bit more—is nobody dies in the film. And if anyone were doing *Salesman* in fiction he would absolutely insist that somebody die.

G.R.L. He does in the play.

A.M. Yes, yes, Arthur Miller.[2] In the play he does, and if somebody else were doing it in non-fiction he would hope like hell that the guy would die.

D.M. It *is* the death of a salesman—he's gone somewhere else, he leaves Florida, and that really is death in his face, which may be more important than any kind of actual physical death.

G.R.L. That's a nice point about the film. Something else though. I found parts of *Salesman* boring. Personally, I'm perfectly willing to be bored sometime for the kind of truth or perceptions you might get without superficial gimmicks; but I think it's a failing if one is concerned about getting to a large audience. And if one does a cinéma-vérité film—or direct cinema or whatever you want to call it—one usually hopes for dramatic events, for an inherent dramatic structure so that one doesn't have to artificially create the drama in the editing. I don't know if it's less truthful for being so, but the dramatic structure in *Salesman* is at least in part artificial, created. For example, the way in which you present Paul Brennan.

D.M. Well, artificial . . . yes. Artificial in the fact that we're not chronological to start with.

G.R.L. Well, like Paul driving along, and as he thinks of each salesman you cut to that salesman; Paul in the train going to the sales convention, and cutting back and forth from the train to the convention.

D.M. Very fictional devices.

A.M. Actually, and I think David would agree, we're both a little nervous about both of those devices.

G.R.L. If I had brought up examples such as these when I talked to you a couple of years ago, I think you would have said, "No, you can't do that." At least back then.

D.M. They're not the ideal thing, but the content dictated it. There's a scene in *Salesman* where a fictional device worked rather well. Paul being reminded of the sales manager's, Kenny's, words on the train happened in another situation, but we needed to get him moving at this particular time, so we took the incident in the hotel room when he's frightened or challenged by the sales manager and put the sound behind Paul's serious face when he's on the train going to Chicago for the sales meeting.

A.M. The kind of thing that appeals to us more as a way of telling a story, that excites us more as a means of discovery (more so than in

[2] The play *Death of a Salesman* by Arthur Miller.

having to do it in the editing) is what we got of the relationship between Paul and the Bull. For example, in the room where Paul is pouring his heart out: because of the nature of the game of selling and the human relationship between those guys, the Bull could only try not to listen and not to relate to Paul, whom, if he could, he would like to help; but because of the nature of the thing, helping him in that situation would only mean ruining his own sales.

D.M. Al is referring to the time when the Bull is counting his orders.

A.M. So in the same shot we catch the contrast of one guy pouring his heart out and the other guy not being able to relate to him. This is the kind of material we're much more pleased to get, much more so than having to do the train thing.

G.R.L. As objective as *Salesman* might be, you're still making choices all the time—what you shoot, the angle, who is in the frame, the editing, etc. It would have been easy to have gone on that trip and made those guys look like fools, for example, or to have been very sentimental about them. These are my objections to TV documentaries. They pretend to be objective when it's clear—at least to me—that they're not. I think this is dangerous because of the enormous audience they reach and their influence on that audience. If someone were able to inspect all the TV coverage of the Vietnam War over the past years, I suspect we'd find an incredible amount of manipulation of what was presented as objective fact to get across a very subjective point of view, which was essentially that of the conservative wing of the establishment.

D.M. We want to put the relevance of *Salesman* to a test in a way by showing it, say, in Fayetteville, North Carolina, or some town in Ohio, to see if it really is relevant. I'm beginning to wonder whether it's just New York intellectuals that can really understand it. This film is about the emptiness in life. The expression on the Bull's face when he is winning—Beatles' music is playing—and he goes back to the motel and he's the winner, he's made the sale, and Paul hasn't made the sale. But their whole life is so empty, because it just means sales and having exhausting days and making money to live. Now I wonder if people outside of cosmopolitan cities will understand that. I think they may say, "Well, the guy's just doing his job." I wonder if they'll get the message. I'm not sure they will.

G.R.L. They may not, but I don't think that makes it less valid.

D.M. Well, it doesn't make it useful to the people that it really should be useful to. In other words, we're directing it in a way to all these people who are doing the same thing, whether it be manufacturing or anything in selling, anything where the goals are purely materialistic. That's where we're directing this in a way. But —*and this is all afterthought*—I'm sure we were doing the film because we liked doing it; but when you go to college campuses to speak or when you talk to interviewers, you start finding reasons why you're making films and what your message is perhaps, and what you think people should get out of the film. But I'm wondering if people who come off the street in Fayetteville, North Carolina, and go into the movie house, whether they're going to get this. I think it's just going to reconfirm what they already believe. You know, "It's good that the guy goes out and makes a buck. If the guy worked a little harder he would have made it, see?" I think that's what they're going to think.

A.M. But there's so much more in the film than that, that I think that by and large what people derive from the film is a greater understanding of the world in which they live. Everyone gets that out of it.

D.M. I don't. In other words what you're saying is that they don't think it's wrong to sell Bibles, for example, for fifty dollars to people who don't have any real interest.

A.M. That can happen, but they get a hell of a lot more out of it than that.

D.M. I don't see, frankly, trying to make a film to create better understanding. Our motivations for making films aren't intellectual ones. We're not trying to pick a subject and say, "Gee, wouldn't this be interesting for people." It's intersting to ourselves, first. Then, hopefully, to other people.

G.R.L. Perhaps it goes back to what you said before, that in a sense it's like a novel for you—you want to say how you feel about something.

D.M. But remember that the criteria for a movie and for a novel are completely different for most people, and we don't think there should be any difference. There's a novel right now by Wilfrid Sheed about a critic called *Max Jamison*. Well, if you pick that for a movie, that kind of a subject, they'd say, "Well, who the hell can possibly be interested in it?" But why should it be any different?

A.M. "Only critics would want to see it. So you've got five hundred critics seeing the film. You're spending half a million dollars and five hundred people see the movie," they'd say.

D.M. But if that were a subject we were interested in, we would probably do it. You know, make it interesting, I think, to a lot of people, but maybe not enough people to support it, that is, to reimburse the cost. But I think we'd probably do it anyway.

A.M. I'd like to explain it in a more analytical way. Our films very much proceed from particulars to generalities. We don't know, when we get into a film, what the particulars are going to be, or, if what I said a moment ago is true, we don't really know what's going to be derived from the film later on. We start out in *Salesman* with Paul Brennan and the other three, unknown to us except for some kind of feeling we have for them. And also a feeling that there's a film there. Anybody else would say, "You mean you're going to make a film about them?" When you look back at it, if you were there with us and you saw those four guys, you—and we too—would say, "My God, are we going to make a film out of these four guys?"

D.M. That was their reaction. They couldn't believe it either. They couldn't believe it until they saw it. When you have subjects who are just ordinary people, that is, non-actors, the way these guys are, no one believes it will ever be finished and be a film. What could possibly interest anybody in their work?

G.R.L. How many salesmen did you meet and talk to before you chose these four guys?

D.M. Maybe fifteen guys; if you counted long, long telephone conversations, maybe twenty-five or thirty. A lot of sales managers and so forth too.

G.R.L. Did you have a feeling about these four guys? That they had a certain kind of potential as compared to the others?

D.M. Yes; probably because it was New England where we grew up, in Boston, and they were Irish and we could make a very strong identification.

A.M. Also the Bible selling was virtually uncontaminated. By that I mean a lot of other guys will sell Bibles with *Look* magazine and it's a package deal. This was rather pure.

G.R.L. Presumably you were also aware of the social implications of filming a salesman and what he represented and the symbolic nature of selling the Bible.

D.M. Yeah, but I think more than anything that the motivation in this film was sort of romantic. The guys going out on the road, coming home at night to the motel and talking among each other. That really has to be the strongest motivation of all. It's just like when we used to hitchhike at night and go into a cafe and talk to waiters and truck drivers, be out on the road, not knowing exactly what town you're going to—they just knock on the door. They have leads, but they don't ever know what they're going to encounter. That's what you do when you're hitchhiking, and that has always been something we've gotten a lot of enjoyment out of. That really is the motivation—no, not so much the social significance in the Bible.

A.M. My main interest stems from something way back in my infancy, or whatever. I've always been interested to see what happens when two strangers meet. To put it in even more romantic terms, when two people meet and fall in love with one another that first day, it's more than what happens, sometimes, any time after that. So the guy knocks on the door to sell a Bible, and it's going to be two strangers meeting: watch what happens. Of course, what happens is exactly the opposite, it's the degeneration of that possibility. Charles Lamb said that one of the sweetest sounds, whether in the country or the city, is the knocking on the door. Why is it? Because who is it? What's going to happen? Is it going to be a thing of beauty, somebody with a gift, somebody they haven't seen for a long time? All of the possibility of life is represented by that knocking on the door, and the guy who knocks on the door to sell the Bible represents himself as somebody who is going to do something awful good. And he does. Because most people do believe in the Bible somehow or other. That really is the irony. And the irony of ironies is that the salesman is trapped by that misconception too. He thinks there's something good about what he's doing. It is the Bible and it's not a refrigerator, you see? But by the time you see all the film, you see really that it could have been a refrigerator, and, as a matter of fact, it probably would have been better for that person had it been a refrigerator.

G.R.L. Don't I get a feeling of a real identification with those salesmen?

D.M. Oh yes, because our father used to tell us Irish stories, worked among the Irish—one of two Jews in the Boston Post Office, he and one other guy—and he was working for his pension. But Paul coming from an Irish family, one would think that he would be the one looking for a pension. What Paul is doing, though, is out of resentment for his family. He looks down on people who work in civil service, at a nine-to-five job; he's more in the role of perhaps what a Jewish family would want for their son if he couldn't be a doctor or a lawyer. He didn't have any education really, and he's going to make himself something in the world of salesmen. You mentioned the sweetest sound, the knock on the door. I think I can put it in literary terms for you. One of the most exciting scenes for me ever—and I think it was for Al too—was the opening of *The Grapes of Wrath:* Tom Joad gets picked up by this truck driver—two strangers, right?—and he's dropped off at the cafe and he observes and listens to the truck driver talking to the waitress about the state of the country, the state of relationships.

A.M. If you read that book today, you'd be so disappointed. It's out of date. Not because it was written in the thirties, but because of its style. You read it now and you see that it's full of fakery. If that book had been written as a non-fiction film, it wouldn't have suffered from that. I say that because both of us, when we read *Grapes of Wrath* some time ago, took it as one of our very favorite of all books.

D.M. You mean it has a lot of false contrivances?

A.M. Yes, ones that you couldn't get away with today. Especially in our way of making movies. I really think that *Salesman* is going to last a hell of a long time longer because of the people in it. For example, in *The Grapes of Wrath,* remember that scene when the guy on the tractor is coming along, and Steinbeck is saying that he's making these rows neat, that they have to be neat, and he's wearing goggles so he can't see the people? That's a lot of bullshit. He's talking about mechanization of life. He's got to write it this way in order to make it more dramatic. All the facts, the little facts of that book, are chosen and put in the way they are in order to convince you of certain points that he's trying to make. He's got the thing turned completely around. As *Salesman* was being filmed we had no way of knowing how the data would fit in later on. We didn't have that kind of purpose in putting it on film at that moment, so it originally gets onto the film in the purest of ways, and though there are fictions that evolve in the editing, still there's a truth there that you can't tinker with.

D.M. Yes, but we're looking for the most dramatic things when we're filming it too. The fact that we're looking for the most dramatic things to film and not so much the ordinary dull things that happened during the twenty-four hours, in that sense we are contriving. I don't think Steinbeck is the best example of that.

A.M. He's not the best example; it's a work that we respect a great deal. We found a great deal of truth in it.

G.R.L. I have no idea if this is pure rumor, but somebody told me that the opening sequence, the title sequence, and the motel in the rain were staged. Is this true?

A.M. No.

D.M. No. Well, the motel wasn't shot exactly at the same time, we reshot it. The same motel. I can tell you, it wasn't easy to get that shot. Maybe someone else doing it would go to just any motel, but it's the exact same motel they were in. It's only a pan from the street to the motel's neon sign. There was a feeling about it. It was the right one too; it looked right, somehow—and there's something interesting about this. I always think of it, especially when editing. There's a great feeling of security, on any project that you work on when you work in this style, whether you're in the production, the shooting or the editing, because what you've done in a sense can't be faulted—it's all real, so you never have to worry about whether it looks real or not.

A.M. Another way of putting it: no one in the world can tell the truth as well as the truth can tell itself. In this sense, no one doing a film or book of a salesman selling Bibles would dare call the company Mid-American Bible.

D.M. Yet maybe at the other extreme they would. If they were making a camp movie. Or even some of our playwrights—why would Eugene O'Neill call this guy "Jimmy Tomorrow"? You remember, the ex-newspaper writer in *The Iceman Cometh* who can never get out of the bar because he's going to do everything tomorrow.

G.R.L. Do you ever think of making fictionalized documentary? Making up a story, or using actors? Perhaps something like Haskell Wexler tried to do in *Medium Cool.*

A.M. No, not at all. It's funny; some people have said in the course of our career, and they do it now too, "Well, gee, you guys have really made it now. Now go ahead and make a fiction film."

D.M. If I were going to write, if I were going to paint, instead of making films—and I feel good about this too—it would be from the same source. If I were going to write, a lot of it would come from tape recordings, the same way you make films. If I were going to paint, it would be of real situations. One of the painters that I have a lot of respect for is a guy named Al Leslie. I remember he told me about this project he was going to do, and I thought it was so fantastic. There was a guy named Frank O'Hara, a poet, who was killed on a beach on Fire Island by a kid who was driving one of these beach buggies in the middle of the night, and Al Leslie was studying the light at that time of night, and, I expect, several months later he'd done a painting about this killing.

Now that to me is the kind of painting I would do if I was going to do a painting. And the same with writing. It would come out of things which are just as real as anything that we film. It would be close to the same reality. So there's a certain continuity there. It would be like a polished version of the diary I was talking about.

A.M. The exercise for me, in whatever the artistic medium, would be an exercise in memory, trying to remember what my father did with me at such and such a time, what Dorchester[3] was like, the streets and places and events, and the closer the recall, the happier

[3] A section of Boston bordering Brookline, a suburb of Boston, where the Maysles were born.

I would be in retelling the story. And of course the best memory is the immediate one, and that's the one thing the camera can do. For Christ's sake, why not use it where it's at its best? And that's the film of fact. Fiction films with actors and such try to recall memories that are so far away from one another that—to me at least—the truth vanishes. They don't have the immediacy of the thing, they have to make up for it in some other way, so they choose dramatic concoctions where people end up dying, where they take you to strange places and peculiarities of experience. People complain that movies use too much sex and violence and all of that; well, in a way you can't blame the fiction movie-makers, because they don't have the advantage of the truth of the immediate event.

D.M. Do you know what the irony is? Think of all the man-hours spent in the production of a fictional film to imitate reality, all the time the art department alone spends in making all the sketches in trying to re-create a room, a period in time, and all it takes to get a take that is believable before the director is satisfied. We don't spend any time on that. What we have is real; but we spend time in, perhaps, if you can use the word in this way, in "fictionalizing" the finished form. And that's oversimplification, because it isn't fictionalizing; let's say it's fictional technique.

G.R.L. But in a sense you do a lot of takes too. Like what was your shooting ratio in *Salesman?*

D.M. Say about thirty to one. Something like that. But every film is different.

A.M. They're not repeated takes.

D.M. Never the same thing. I think it's less than in Hollywood, too. Maybe the same. But take *Easy Rider,* which is a fictional film. I'm sure their ratio is greater than thirty to one. I heard it was at least thirty to one just on the motorcycle shots alone. The new Hollywood type of film, if you can call it Hollywood, I'll bet their ratios are higher than ours.

G.R.L. I never would have thought that.

D.M. I think they are.

A.M. This thing about ratios, there are a number of factors there. It is not that simple a thing. Someone will say, "What's your ratio?" and you'll say, "One hundred to one, or five to one," and then they derive a lot of conclusions from that, relating it to what Hollywood does. In the film *Salesman* the ratio was higher than it usually is for us because we were filming whole sales pitches. The guy would come in and we would film the pitch all the way through. Also because of the way our equipment is made—which is probably more advanced than anyone else's; but it still would be much more advanced if we could turn the camera on and off like that and still remain in synch. Our ratio, just by that stroke alone, probably would have been cut down to twenty to one instead of thirty to one.

D.M. But you know, it really doesn't make any difference, one hundred to one or eight to one. You just stop shooting when you think you have all the material. You never question a writer on how many notes he has or how long he worked on a book. Truman worked, I think, for five years on *In Cold Blood*, and created a masterpiece. Yet if he had done it in two years, I wouldn't think any differently of the book.

A.M. We invite the question because we speak of our films as being so truthful, so then people will jump back and say, "What is your shooting ratio?"

D.M. A larger ratio might be more truthful. Then they could say you worked that much harder at getting the truth.

A.M. But then they say, "Well, you have more material to select from." The ratio of thirty to one could have been twenty to one or even five to one in *Salesman* if, as we were shooting, we were able to turn the camera on and off all the time, so that if we were trying to prove a point we could have shot it at four to one with practically as good a film.

G.R.L. I'd agree that the shooting ratio is hardly a basis for making a judgment about a film. Again, the thing that still bothers me is the claim that direct-cinema films present an objective truth. I don't know if you say that any more, but I think you were saying that the first time we met.

D.M. Well, we get carried away sometimes.

A.M. There's a hell of a difference between a photograph by Henri Cartier-Bresson and Richard Avedon. And that's where we stand. If you'd seen *Primary* at the time that film was made, there was a kind of truth that came on the cinema screen that no one had ever seen before. Don't you believe that, David? You know what it is from the experience of having seen the film—but I can't explain it; well, it was so exciting to watch. I remember when you came to Minneapolis, David, and you saw some of that stuff. You knew that all of a sudden something new was born. And I think the newness of it is that it's more truthful. It's like when *Life* magazine came into being.

D.M. Like what Godard's *Breathless* was to the conventional feature film when it came out. I think it was the first film I ever saw twice.

G.R.L. Do you know Jim McBride's *David Holzman's Diary* or *My Girl Friend's Wedding*, or Agnès Varda's *Lions Love?* All of them, in a way, are mixing a direct-cinema method and a fictional element, and, at times, as in *Lions Love,* it gets very confusing as to what is straight up and what isn't. Like there's a scene with Varda getting Shirley Clarke to play a suicide scene; Varda walks into camera range and says, "Play the scene like this," etc., and Shirley Clarke doesn't want to but finally does. Now, I've heard that Shirley Clarke actually did try to commit suicide while making that film, though I'm not sure it's true, and this was then incorporated into the film. Varda also used the Robert Kennedy assassination; they got tapes from TV and showed them on a TV set as if the events were actually happening while the film was being made. It's rather confusing to distinguish between what's documentary and what's fiction.

In *My Girl Friend's Wedding,* McBride, the director, has an English girl friend who will be deported if she doesn't marry an American; a guy agrees to marry her as a political act, or for the gesture, and the wedding and party afterward are filmed, and she goes off to again live with McBride. One obvious question is, why doesn't McBride marry her? It's never explained in the film, but I think the reason was that he wasn't legally divorced and couldn't marry her. But I think the other events in the film were real, actual.

D.M. It's very hard to mix those things, isn't it?

G.R.L. It is, but I think maybe it's one of the possibilities available now. Does that interest you?

A.M. No, it doesn't interest us. I feel that when the kind of truth we're talking about is mixed with the other form within a film, it may make the other part of it more believable, but it makes the pure truth part of it less believable. And it's one of the reasons why people seeing our film *Salesman* come out of the film saying, "Gee, it's a terrific movie, this guy is a terrific actor." They cannot appreciate the full truth in this.

G.R.L. I can understand that as you got to know the salesmen they could learn to ignore you and the camera and go on with their work; but what happened when they knocked on a door, did they explain who you were and what the deal was?

D.M. They explained their own purpose, why they were there; and then usually the salesman would sort of defer to us. And we wanted to be separate—there's a history of all kinds of gimmicks in selling like bringing in still photographers to make a big show. "This house is being chosen for special . . ." you know. Anyway, with us, the salesman explained what he was doing and they would maybe look at us aghast and say, "Who are these people with a camera and a recorder?" not really knowing, because the camera looked so odd.

In fact, when it was all over, they would say, "Where is it going to be published?" People right here in Washington Square say "What newspaper is it going to be in?" when they see our camera. I think people are getting a little bit more sophisticated about that now. So we would explain to them what we were doing very quickly, that we're making a film about this man and his colleagues, we've been in New England, now we're down here in Florida to film a human interest story about them, their work and their lives, in motels and in different people's homes, their presentation of the Bible; and they would say, "Oh, it's a human interest story." That would do it. No more questions. We would be filming in the next few seconds.

G.R.L. Did any people object?

A.M. Some people would react, but it would be in the nature of, "Gee, my hair's not done," or, "My house is a mess."

D.M. Then we'd say, "It doesn't make any difference to us, if it doesn't make any difference to you." I would say honestly that the turn-downs, if there were any, were one out of thirty, at the most.

G.R.L. Did you get releases from these people?

A.M. After we filmed them.

G.R.L. You didn't give them any money?

A.M. A dollar. To make it legal.

G.R.L. Let me read you a quote from an interview with Rouch in an old issue of *Film Comment*.[4] He's talking about *Chronicle of a Summer*. He says that people's reactions are "infinitely more sincere" when they're being recorded or filmed, and that when they see the character on the screen they involuntarily represented, they're very surprised, and then "they began to play a role, to be someone different!" They had the opportunity of saying "something in front of the camera and afterwards to be able to retract it," of disavowing the role they played on the screen by saying it was only an "image" of themselves. All of which I find very interesting.

D.M. You're talking about subjects that would be interesting to him, for one thing. It heightens the drama. And with the tape recorder running, it makes you think only of relevant things. We'd be less likely to tell anecdotes than we would in general conversation.

G.R.L. Now, I'll ask whether the tape recorder makes any difference in this conversation—which is what we're talking about.

A.M. Most people who talk about the mechanics of making a movie or taping as interfering with what's going on and changing the reality of, in this case, the discussion, forget one important thing,

[4] *Film Comment*, Fall/Winter 1967, vol. 4, nos. 2 and 3, "The Films of Jean Rouch" by James Blue, pp. 84–85.

and that is, it's more difficult for us to maintain an awareness of the recording process than it is to forget it and to keep our memory and attention on what we're trying to say, so that between those two things, the influence of the taping process and the influence of our own concern to express our own feelings, the balance is so overweighed by our own self-interest that the recording process has no effect.

D.M. Maybe the question is whether you have turned on the recorder or not. When you're not sure it's on you may act differently.

A.M. I went through psychiatry at one stage where every single session was recorded. I'd sit down, he'd put the tape in and say, "Okay." This was the ritual. I've also been through sessions since then without tape, and I don't think it made any difference, really, whatsoever.

D.M. But it made no difference because it was completely confidential. And now, are we talking about a tape recorder or filmed interview? They're quite different. When someone comes in to do a film interview, you are self-conscious—a lot of people will see you. You can't help but be self-conscious. Now, after a certain amount of time, you may not be. I don't think the salesmen are self-conscious after a certain amount of time, or maybe even the very first time, because if they are selling something, they can't afford to be. Their attention has to be on what they're selling. They're salesmen, and their attention has to be more on what they're selling than on the camera.

G.R.L. Do you think that Paul, for example, played a role and that making a film perhaps influenced him in leaving Bible selling? That's what Rouch was talking about, playing roles and doing things for the camera that you perhaps wouldn't ordinarily do; and when I read that, it struck me that maybe making a film hastened Paul's departure.

D.M. Yes, because I think it was sort of an education for him, and being with us was an education. Paul was very rarely with any people that gave him a challenge. In fact, he picks for friends people that he feels are below him. His roommate, for example, whom he lived with subsequently. They're never his peers. However, he idolized us—put us on a pedestal. And he learned a lot just by our being together. He learned something from the film, and that made him someone different.

A.M. In a way Paul is exceptional—and I have to word this very carefully—in that Paul played a role in the film. He is role-playing. He's an actor in the film in a sense where no one else is.

G.R.L. Was he different off-camera than he is on-camera?

A.M. No, but I think that Paul is more aware of the film being made than anybody else. But since that time, other people have filmed *us* and we had an opportunity then to see that material on screen, so I'm aware myself of what I was thinking at the time, and I discovered things about myself on the screen that I never knew.

G.R.L. Do you think the camera influenced your actions while you were being filmed?

A.M. You can't rule that out. I mean, if you sat here and instead of using a tape recorder you made notes and worked on it from memory, you might get something a little bit different from us. But then it goes all the way from taking notes to using a tape recorder to using a camera to using a synch camera to having the camera right here rather than over there and all that sort of thing. What I'm saying is even if you go all the way up the ladder to the point of using a synch-sound camera and having it right here, the way you would use it is very important. If you used it properly enough, the interference and the influence of the camera would still be pretty small.

D.M. Paul, I think, for example, if he knew he was being filmed, wouldn't talk about certain relationships he has with women. That's true.

G.R.L. Another thing that Rouch talks about in that interview is that he began to feel somewhat responsible for what happened to the people he filmed, especially in *Chronicle of a Summer*, where he filmed a group of people over the period of a summer. He began to feel responsible and concerned about his influence and the influence of making a film on the people in the film.

A.M. That's interesting because this spells out the difference between Rouch and ourselves, and also somebody like Arthur Barron. I remember once I was talking to Barron, and he said, "Jesus, don't you sometimes get awfully disturbed that you might hurt somebody when you film, and don't you sometimes question the morality of what you're doing, that you don't have a right to film people at certain times?" And all of a sudden I discovered something about him and about ourselves that really sent shivers up and down my spine—that that's the kind of fear that guy has, and I almost never feel that fear myself.

D.M. Here's another example. We had a meeting at NBC a few years ago and they wanted us to do a film about the Black Muslims, and we said, "Wonderful." But they decided against it finally because they were afraid it would be bad for the black people—if you did a film about Malcolm X, especially when Malcolm X was so violent in the beginning, that you would hurt the black people's cause, and they didn't want to do that. They (NBC) were very wrong, because the more information, the more communication the better—especially if it's done honestly. They were afraid to do that, and I think that kind of censorship is more harmful than it is helpful.

A.M. Arthur was saying, "Aren't you afraid that you're exploiting people when you film them?" and that has never occurred to me as something to be afraid of. I think—and this may be some kind of immodesty—that when David and I make a film, more than anyone else in this medium, we don't have the fear of exploiting anybody. If you look at any one of our films, and they are on pretty goddamn touchy subjects—like *Showman* and *Salesman*, for example—there is not a shred of exploitation in them. Even when a guy has just been fired, and we had to get that guy's release after he saw the film.

G.R.L. I wondered about that scene in *Showman*, whether the phone conversation of the guy who Levine fired would have been different if he hadn't been filmed. Perhaps he would have been cursing Levine.

D.M. I doubt it. I doubt if it would have been much different; at the time it felt spontaneous. It wasn't set up at all, and he was in a tough situation—there was a passion there at the moment that he had to express. He wanted to get to lunch with this guy, who was sort of an old friend, almost like a father figure to him. It's like when Paul is selling a Bible, he has to express something, and tell them why they should have this Bible, and nothing can interfere with that.

A.M. I'll carry it even further. It suddenly occurred to me, we have on film a murder in the Stones film and that's supposedly the ultimate exploitation. A murder on film.

G.R.L. Do you know who the cameraman was?

D.M. The cameraman? Yes. We didn't do it. I was with the guy who filmed it.

G.R.L. Did the cameraman know?

D.M. No.

G.R.L. But that's a real difference, isn't it?

D.M. He didn't know he was filming it, that's true.

A.M. Part of your question can be answered by the fact that even if he knew it, he was still on a staging far enough away that he couldn't have prevented the murder, couldn't have controlled that in any way whatsoever. But anyway, we've got that footage, we're using it in the film. Isn't that the grossest kind of exploitation? People will ask it, they have asked it, and it never occurred to me as that.

[. . .]

G.R.L. Are there documentaries or documentary film-makers whose films you like, other than yourselves?

D.M. I can't think of any.

G.R.L. Are there any feature directors that you like?

D.M. Yes, for individual films.

G.R.L. Who, Godard?

D.M. There's always something good in every Godard film. I've walked out of a lot of Godard movies, but there's always something redeeming, a fresh technique, or some scene of his like you've never seen before, but I don't think I'd ever go to a Godard film again, except *Sympathy for the Devil* . . . and I'm sort of interested in seeing that because the Stones are in it.

G.R.L. In what way do you think the Stones film, which you're working on, will be different than, say, *Woodstock*?

A.M. One thing is that *Rolling Stone*, the magazine, in comparing the two events, said that Woodstock was the myth and Altamont the reality, and I think we had more of the reality in Altamont. Had we done Woodstock instead of Altamont, I think we would have been at a disadvantage. I think there's a myth among all of us, that's in our culture now, that the sadder the fact, the more truthful it is. And Altamont was a tragedy and Woodstock was a more hopeful thing. In any tragedy, as in any lighthearted experience, there's both tragedy and the opposite, but Woodstock didn't have much in the balance of things. I think we have more of the balance.

D.M. *Woodstock* is a show, our film is a film. *Woodstock* is a piece of entertainment mixed between performances and sort of human interest things of people. There's a section for swimming and there's a section for rain.

A.M. *Woodstock* is an interesting comparison for you on many levels. It's a documentary in the old-fashioned sense, very old-fashioned. When we read the critics' reviews and they talk about how *Woodstock* is so new and so exciting, they're not up to date at all with what has been going on in documentary film in the last ten years.

G.R.L. Who financed *Gimme Shelter*? Whose idea was it?

D.M. Theirs to begin with, but really it's more our idea, because they just wanted some footage from Madison Square Garden, and we were contacted by them to do that. Then we filmed just on our own at our own expense, and continued to travel with them, and only for about five days, including Altamont. We thought we had enough material for a feature, which they didn't believe. I had to go over there and convince them.

G.R.L. Do you look upon *Gimme Shelter* as a personal film in the way *Salesman* is, rather than something to simply make money so you can make other films?

A.M. No, in between.

D.M. No, it grew out of an assignment, and has become something that we're very, very interested in. You can't put it in the same category as *Salesman*. *Salesman* is a monumental lifework that's very, very personal, and about everyday people, and the Stones certainly aren't everyday people. Although, they almost are, in a way. I mean, they are very down-to-earth guys.

A.M. I disagree. David liked them an awful lot, so he's willing to say more for them, more than what they are or what we got.

D.M. You get a guy like Charlie Watts, and he doesn't seem to be any different when you're relating to him, filming him than any guy that you could practically pick up in the street.

A.M. But we don't have Charlie or any of those guys the way we have the salesman. We have Paul, but we were disappointed when we didn't get the other salesmen the way we got Paul. We can say in truth, however, that you can't get the other salesmen the way you got Paul because the other guys are the other guys.

G.R.L. Did you personally finance *Salesman*?

D.M. Yes, almost every penny our own money. We raised some of it, we raised about thirty thousand dollars.

G.R.L. Have you gotten your money back?

D.M. No, not at all.

G.R.L. Have you been able to get national distribution?

D.M. We distributed it ourselves in half a dozen cities. The big cities.

G.R.L. If somebody gave you a hundred thousand bucks, would you be interested in making a film about the strike going on now?[5]

A.M. Yes, but we'd have to find within it a human story that interests us.

[5] The interview took place shortly after the U.S. invasion of Cambodia and the killing of four students at Kent State and shortly before the killing of two students at Jackson State. Strike actions were taken by many students and other groups throughout the country to protest these events.

ARTHUR BARRON

Arthur Barron was born in 1929 in Boston, Massachusetts. He grew up in Somerville, Massachusetts, went to Brookline High School, and then spent a year in a prep school. He received his B.A. and M.A. in sociology from Tulane University in 1950, and his Ph.D. in Russian studies from the Russian Institute, Columbia University.

Barron worked for the Research Institute of America designing and conducting opinion surveys. He came to films as a writer; his first job was researching and writing a scenario on the life of Eva Perón for David Susskind. He worked at NBC as assistant to the producer Irving Gitlin, then became a producer himself at WNEW-TV, where he made his first film, *The Rebirth of Jonny*, 1963. Barron then went to CBS, where he made six films (1964–69); he has also made films for Public Broadcasting Laboratory and NET and his films have won a number of prizes. He is scheduled to start *Orville and Wilbur*, a feature film about the Wright brothers, in January 1971.

Barron is now Chairman of the Film Division, School of the Arts, Columbia University. He lives with his wife, Evelyn, in New York City.

(For further information, see "The Self-Discovery of a Documentary Filmmaker," an interview with Barron by Bernard Rosenberg and F. William Howton in *Film Comment*, vol. 6, no. 1, Spring, 1970, from which this information was taken.)

FILMOGRAPHY*

KEY: T: Theme; R: Released in the U.S.A. by; P: Producer; D: Director; S: Script; C: Camera; b&w: black and white; M: Music; F: Festivals.

1960: *The U2 Affair.* T: A historical evaluation of the U2 Affair, the downing of a U.S. spy plane in Soviet territory; and its repercussions. R: NBC (an NBC White Paper). P: Al Wasserman. Exec. P: Irving Gitlin. Assoc. P: Arthur Barron. D: Al Wasserman. S: Al Wasserman and Arthur Barron. C: Joseph Vadalla. Narrated by Chet Huntley. 60 minutes, b&w (tape and film).

1963: *The Rebirth of Jonny.* T: Childhood mental illness. R: Metropolitan Broadcasting Television, Division of Metromedia, Inc. P: Harold Mantell. Exec. P: Arthur Barron. D: Don Horan. S: Harold Mantell and Arthur Barron (based on an article by Mira Rothenberg). C: Ernest Neutranen. M: Tony Mottola. Narrated by David Wayne. 60 minutes, b&w tape. Nominated for New York Emmy (Best Program, documentary category).

China and the Bomb. T: First in-depth study on U.S. television of the Chinese People's Republic as a nuclear power. R: Metropolitan Broadcasting Television, Division of Metromedia, Inc. P: Arthur Barron. D: Don Horan. S: Arthur Barron. 2 parts, 60 minutes each, b&w.

Songs of Freedom with Bob Dylan. T: Folk music as a tool in the civil rights struggle. R: Metropolitan Broadcasting Television, Division of Metromedia, Inc. P: Arthur Barron. D: Don Horan. Shot in a television studio. M: Bob Dylan, Odetta, The Freedom Singers. Host: Alan Edward. 30 minutes, b&w.

The Rise of Labor. T: The struggles and growth of the American labor movement after World War I. R: Metropolitan Broadcasting Television, Division of Metromedia, Inc. P: Arthur Barron. D: Don Horan. S: Arthur Barron. C: Ernest Neutranen. Narrated by Arthur Kennedy. 60 minutes, b&w.

1964: *Tuberculosis: Again a Threat.* T: An examination of the controversy about BCG, the anti-TB vaccine used all over the world except in the United States until New York City decided to use it to fight the new epidemic. R: Metropolitan Broadcasting Television,

* From *Film Comment*, vol. 6, no. 1, prepared by Jonathan Hoops, pp. 24–25; last two films, *Essay on Loneliness* and *Orville and Wilbur*, from the film-maker.

Division of Metromedia, Inc. P: Helen Winston. Exec. P: Arthur Barron. D: Don Horan. S: Arthur Barron. C: Ross Lowell. Narrated by Earl Ubell. 60 minutes, b&w.

My Childhood: Hubert Humphrey's South Dakota and James Baldwin's Harlem. T: Two unique Americans recall their childhoods as voice-over to contemporary footage. R: Metropolitan Broadcasting Television, Division of Metromedia, Inc. P: Arthur Barron. D: Don Horan. S: Arthur Barron. C: Ross Lowell and Ernest Neutranen. M: Tony Mottola. 60 minutes, b&w. Emmy, 1965; National Conference of Christians and Jews Award, 1965; Superior Merit Brotherhood Award in Television, 1965; Annual National Mass Media Brotherhood Award, 1965.

The Burden and the Glory of John F. Kennedy. T: A dedication to the late President and his quest for peace. R: CBS Television. P: Arthur Barron. Assoc. P: Beatrice Cunningham. D: Arthur Barron. S: Arthur Barron. C: Ross Lowell (JFK photos by Jacques Lowe). M: Tony Mottola. 60 minutes, b&w.

1965: *The Berkeley Rebels.* T: The story of four students at the University of California, who with others focused national attention on the resurgence of political activism on campuses across the United States. R: CBS Reports. P: Arthur Barron. Assoc. P: Peter Davis. D: Arthur Barron. S: Peter Davis. C: Walter Dumbrow. Narrated by Harry Reasoner. 60 minutes, b&w.

1966: *Sixteen in Webster Groves.* T: The attitudes of sixteen-year-olds in a wealthy St. Louis suburb toward their parents, education, marriage and their futures. R: CBS Reports. P: Arthur Barron. Asst. to P: Paula Kaplan. Assoc. P: Paul Asselin and Barbara Connell. D: Arthur Barron. S: Charles Kuralt. 60 minutes, color. Ohio State Award (Social Sciences category), 1967; Ninth Annual American Film Festival Blue Ribbon for Best Social Documentary, 1967.

Webster Groves Revisited. T: An examination of the reaction to and impact upon teen-agers, parents and teachers in Webster Groves, Mo., to the previous month's nationwide telecast *Sixteen in Webster Groves.* R: CBS Reports. P: Arthur Barron. D: Arthur Barron. S: Charles Kuralt. Narrated by Charles Kuralt. 60 minutes, color. Ohio State Award (Social Sciences category), 1967.

1968: *Birth and Death.* T: A study of the emotional experiences surrounding birth and death. R: Public Broadcast Laboratory (Vérité Productions). P: Arthur and Evelyn Barron. D: Gene Marner.

Sound: Carol Marner. Actors: real people, not actors, are in the film; Debbie and Bruce North; Albro Pearsall. 2 hours, b&w. Nominated for Emmy as Best Cultural Documentary, 1969.

The Great American Novel: Babbitt and The Grapes of Wrath. T: Focus on the contemporary relevance of two socially and politically significant novels. R: CBS Reports. P: Arthur Barron. Exec. P: Perry Wolff. Assoc. P: Barbara Connell. D: Arthur Barron. S: Based on Steinbeck and Lewis. C: Walter Dumbrow and Jerry Sims. Narrated by Eric Sevareid, Pat Hingle and Richard Boone. 60 minutes, color. National Emmy (Best Social Documentary), 1969.

1969: *The Great American Novel: Moby Dick.* T: Life-style at sea today compared with Melville classic. R: CBS Television. P: Arthur Barron. Exec. P: Perry Wolff. D: Arthur Barron. S: Based on Melville. C: Jerry Sims. Narrated by George C. Scott. Reporter: Charles Kuralt. 60 minutes, b&w.

Johnny Cash! T: A *cinéma-vérité* profile of country-western singer Johnny Cash. R: Public Broadcast Laboratory; theatrical released by Continental for Walter Reade Organization. P: Arthur and Evelyn Barron. D: Robert Elfstrom. C: Robert Elfstrom. M: Johnny Cash, June Carter, The Carter Family, Bob Dylan, Carl Perkins, The Tennessee Three. 96 minutes (theatrical version), color. F: Spoleto, 1969.

Factory. T: A *cinéma-vérité* study of an American factory worker—his fears, frustrations, hatreds—using a real worker and his family and circle. P: National Educational Television. D: Arthur Barron. C: Mark Obenhaus. 90 minutes, b&w.

1970: *Essay on Loneliness.* "An evocation of various forms of loneliness in New York City." (A.B.) P: Arthur and Evelyn Barron. Assoc. P: Anne Boggan. C: Paul Goldsmith. Editor: Muffie Meyer. Sound: Peter Hleil. 22 minutes, b&w and color.

1971: *Orville and Wilbur.* Production scheduled to start in January 1971; a feature film about the Wright brothers.

May 28, 1970, in Arthur Barron's office at Columbia University.

G. Roy Levin: Casting seems to be crucial in certain kinds of films. How did you choose the couple in *Birth?*

Arthur Barron: That's very interesting. We started about it in a very wrong and inefficient way. My wife and I went to our gynecologist and asked him if he had any patients who were expecting. He said yes, and we saw them. It was very inefficient because we could only see one or two a night; we invited some for coffee. It was terrible. Then we started going to hospitals and getting permission to see patients. We would wait in a room and the doctor would ask the patient, and if the patient agreed, we would meet her. That was very dull. Finally, we hit upon another idea. There were two natural-childbirth teachers in New York, Mrs. Bing and another woman, so we hit upon the idea of going to those classes, and that enabled us with a great economy to see many couples, husbands and wives together. Very quickly and efficiently. So we went to those classes.

Originally we had no idea of making the film on a natural-childbirth situation, but out of a question of logistics and efficiency we found that was the best way to see a lot of couples quickly. We'd go to those things and then we'd interview the ones that we were interested in afterward. We came down eventually to a list of about ten couples, and these we narrowed down to two couples. The other couple was an interracial couple, and we decided against them at the last minute because we felt it wouldn't be as universal with an interracial couple. Logistically that's how we did it.

In terms of the actual choice of these people, that's an almost subconscious, intuitive process. The wife didn't want to do it at first. He wanted to do it for two reasons. First, it would help his career. He's an unknown artist and this would help him, which it did, enormously. And secondly, because he thought it would be great to have a filmed record of the birth of his child. So he talked her into doing it.

Finding the guy for *Death,* that was a real tough problem, largely because the hospitals were generally opposed to the project, because the PR departments of each hospital felt they would not want people to associate their hospital with death, and also because of the general uptightness of our society about death as a subject to be swept under the rug, not to be explored, and so forth.

G.R.L. I haven't been able to see that. Did the man die?

A.B. Yes.

G.R.L. Did he know that you were going to make a film, and did he agree to it?

A.B. Oh yes.

G.R.L. Why did he agree to that?

A.B. He said that it would be a legacy. In effect, what he said was that his life didn't add up to very much, that he had wasted his life and that he hadn't really lived, and in effect he said he hoped the film would be like a warning to people to live. It was a fantastic kind of thing. He said he would leave something behind worthwhile and important.

G.R.L. Were there many people who were dying who would have been willing to make this film?

A.B. Well, yes and no. We went to a terminal cancer hospital, finally, where no one lives—where everybody dies. It's Calvary Hospital in the Bronx, and only the most desperate terminal cases come here, and yet I would say that 90 per cent of the people denied that they were going to die. I mean, I remember an Irishman who looked like a plucked chicken. He was maybe down to seventy or eighty pounds and obviously dying. He said to us, "Why do they have me in this place with all these sick people? I've just got influenza or something." We had a very hard time finding somebody who was psychologically strong enough to confront his own death rather than try to do everything to avoid confronting that reality.

G.R.L. Getting back to *Birth* for a minute, were there a lot of people who were willing to be filmed?

A.B. Yes. I find that it's very hard to find someone who does not want to be in a film.

G.R.L. What do you make of that?

A.B. Well, it's complicated. I think people find it very flattering. The surface thing is the attention, the excitement, the glamour of being the center of the film. People just find that irresistibly romantic and appealing. Secondly, there's the curiosity about oneself, the kind of psychological thing of seeing oneself as others see you on film, you know, this tremendous curiosity. I think a very important reason is, especially the way we work in cinéma-vérité, people generally are quite eager to talk honestly and to reveal something meaningful about themselves and to enter a process in which they can make a statement.

G.R.L. There was an interview with Rouch[1] about five years ago

[1] *Film Comment*, Fall/Winter 1967, vol. 4, nos. 2 and 3, "The Films of Jean Rouch" by James Blue.

in *Film Comment* where he talks about people in this situation, how they will be more truthful in front of the camera than they are when they're not because they can then say afterward, if there's a problem with what they said, that it was really just for the film, that it wasn't really that way.

A.B. I think that's true. I think also another point is, people always say, "Well, how do you get honesty? How do you get stuff out of people?" In a funny kind of way, film-making is such an extreme situation that people are very vulnerable, very defenseless once the lights and the cameras are on them.

G.R.L. Did you ever see *Showman?*

A.B. Yeah.

G.R.L. He certainly kept his defenses up.

A.B. But he was revealed. Joe Levine was very revealed in that film, in spite of all his defenses. I mean, he came across as a very torn individual. Sure there are people who are very concerned about their image, you know, powerful people, politicians, entertainers, but ordinary people, I think, are very vulnerable.

G.R.L. What was the ratio on *Birth?*

A.B. Oh, very high. We shot a hundred and twenty thousand feet to get two hours. Well, four thousand feet is about two hours. That's about . . . thirty to one.

G.R.L. In *Babbitt*—I may have missed this—but when Hingle reads Babbitt's speech to that group, does the group know it's Babbitt?

A.B. Yes. If you listen carefully to the man making the introduction, he says, "We will have, verbatim, a passage from *Babbitt* read by the actor Pat Hingle." Even so, I was knocked out by the reactions to the speech. I mean, they lived through it as though it were not fiction. They said those things about Barry Goldwater and about those pink old professors. That to me was quite exciting.

G.R.L. I either read or you told me, but tell me again a little bit about what the people thought about that film in Duluth, where you filmed it.

A.B. They liked it. By and large, they liked it. We were very worried about the two guys who have the conversation about mistresses. They're both married men, and they indicated on film a yearning for sexual adventure and all the things that were going on just below the surface. We were very apprehensive about their reactions, but they actually liked it. In fact, one of those guys wrote me and said how much he enjoyed the film. I think the Duluth businessmen saw the film in a kind of Babbittlike way and thought it was marvelous, that it would put them on the map, merely because it was about them and mentioned Duluth, and showed them singing and everything else. I mean, I think they never got over the ego trip of CBS having chosen the Lions Club in Duluth for this film, and I don't think they saw what the film was really saying.

G.R.L. In any of these films—let's just take *Birth and Death, Babbitt* and *Grapes of Wrath*—did any of the people in the films ever see any of the rushes?

A.B. No. I would never do that unless I wanted to incorporate them into the film as Rouch did in *Chronicle of a Summer.*

G.R.L. Did you get releases from them?

A.B. Yes. I always do. We get releases from any person who is in the film. My recollection is that in that opening scene in *Babbitt,* we got a release from every single person in that room.

G.R.L. How did you choose the man in *The Grapes of Wrath?* It seems to be a really crucial process, choosing the right person. I think you chose well.

A.B. Well, there's a little bit of trickery in *Grapes of Wrath.* When we found that man, he was already in Chicago working for an OEO group helping Appalachian people find employment. He had in effect already made the journey. At one time we thought of using migrant workers in the South, and we even thought of doing it with a Spanish-American family, the César Chavez kind of thing. We decided to stick with the Appalachian people. And we said, let's go to Chicago and enter that milieu and get the feeling of what these people are like. And we went there and said we're going to make a film, and everybody said to us, Chuck Geary, and that's how we found him. He's a very charismatic, marvelous man. I wish I could make a whole two-hour film on him alone. And he just had an extraordinary reputation for being a charismatic and beautiful person, and that's how we found him. By the way, Haskell Wexler saw this film and cast Chuck Geary as the father in *Medium Cool.* Then we had him go back to the farm and visit his family and play horseshoes and drive and do all those things, and then we just inverted the order.

G.R.L. What about when he buys a car and it breaks down?

A.B. He bought the car in Chicago. You see, he said to me, "I want to go back to Kentucky to visit my folks, maybe I'll even go back to the land if I can because I hate the city." So we said, "We'll go with you." And he bought the car in Chicago.

G.R.L. Was he paid anything? Did he ever ask?

A.B. No. Now, another thing, it should be clear we didn't feel terribly bad about this ethically, about this inversion, because this traveling back and forth is very constant. They do it all the time. They go to Chicago and they go back, come back to Kentucky and spend a year there and fail again and go back to Chicago. So we felt we weren't doing anything unethical; we were taking a little bit of license to fit this particular man at this particular moment of time in his life within the plot structure of the novel. We didn't pay him anything. We did buy that secondhand car for him.

G.R.L. I would find that a difficult question to decide, whether or not to make any mention in the film of the fact that he really was in Chicago beforehand.

A.B. Well, when the film went on CBS we did something which was done either in the voice, you know, by the announcer at the end of the film, or was actually on the film. And I remember struggling very hard over the wording of it; we did something to cover ourselves for that. The events that took place occurred; they weren't staged, but they were taken out of sequence, you know, the chronology, or something like that.

G.R.L. How about him looking for a job? Was that straight?

A.B. Yeah.

G.R.L. He didn't have the job with OEO when he went back.

A.B. Well, no, he didn't look for a job. . . .

G.R.L. I thought he and the boy—

A.B. No, he went there, to the factory, and he sat there, but he wasn't looking for a job. The implication was, I suppose, that he was there looking for a job.

G.R.L. Didn't he fill out the application?

A.B. Well, if you notice he didn't fill one out. He sat there, and he's helping the guy next to him fill it out and his son-in-law; that actually did happen, but I guess we did leave the implication that he was going for the job too. Anyway both pictures are rather contrived, don't you think? They're not real documentary. They're kind of constructions. They're an attempt to create a form, to kind of mesh literature with life. Hence, some people criticize the picture very much as being cruel and a distortion.

G.R.L. Which one, or both?

A.B. More *Babbitt* than *Grapes*. For example, the guy sitting at his desk typing and working, and we're using stuff from Lewis in which he talks about the sadness and the yearning, and how they feel trapped in their work. Well, maybe this guy loves it. We certainly don't validate that narration.

G.R.L. In one of your articles in *Film Comment*,[2] you mention problems with the network and say that you had to put Clark Kerr[3]

[2] "Network Television and the Personal Documentary," in *Film Comment*, Spring 1970, vol. 6, no. 1.

[3] Then Chancellor, University of California, Berkeley.

into *The Berkeley Rebels*. Were there other instances of that kind of thing?

A.B. Oh yes. Oh, God, yes.

G.R.L. Can you tell me of specific instances?

A.B. We had to remove certain scenes from the film. Well, there was one scene in a fraternity house that we shot. We wanted to do a sequence with the fraternity kids who are not activists. We asked Mike Rossman, one of the actors, "How do you relate to the Joe College kids?" and he said, "Well, it's very sad, those kids. They're in college as part of a program process to become part of the establishment, and all they want is a nice home, and a nice job, and a nice car in Westwood, and they're really silly kids. They're not serious people." And to illustrate that we went to a fraternity house, and the rage at that time was something called Tom Jones parties, and we filmed a Tom Jones party. One of the most staggering . . . The cameraman, Walter Dumbrow, has been in coal mine disasters, Vietnam, jumped out of planes with paratroopers, forest fires, and he was so shocked by this scene, like he had to sit down after it was over. He was trembling. What they did was, they took a room in the fraternity house and emptied it entirely of furniture. Then they spread sailcloth on the floor. Then they dumped enormous mounds of spaghetti and meatballs on the sailcloth and threw in chunks of bread, and they blew a whistle and turned on a jukebox with a loud rock 'n' roll record, and then about eighty guys and their dates ate that spaghetti with their bare hands, rolling in it, soul-kissing through strands of spaghetti, throwing it at each other, dancing. It was an obscenity. Would you believe what the emotional force of that scene was? It was unbelievable, decadent, and the kind of awful sexuality . . . Well, CBS cut that scene.

G.R.L. Did they say why?

A.B. That's a very complicated story. You can read about it in Fred Friendly's book, *Due to Circumstances Beyond Our Control*. I wasn't invited to the meeting. Well, you see, Stanton and Paley[4] screened the film, which was something like unheard of after Fred Friendly[5] approved the film and passed it. Apparently, Stanton got a letter from Clark Kerr—and you know they're buddies, they sit in the Rockefeller Foundation[6] together and so forth—and apparently

[4] Dr. Frank Stanton, President of CBS; William S. Paley, Chairman of the Board, CBS.

[5] Then President of CBS News.

[6] The extent of the pressures for certain kinds of conformity on television are clearly unspoken and certainly not codified, but nevertheless very real, as Barron notes above. Indications of the influences behind these pressures can perhaps be seen in the following quote from page 36 of *Survey of Broadcast Journalism*,

the letter, I was told, from Kerr, said, "You better look at this film before it goes on. It's a bad man out here making this film." It's a very long story. I didn't want an objective balance; I wanted to enter the world of these kids, and let them tell it. So one day Stanton and Paley screened the film, and I was called in and I was told here is what you do, "This scene comes out, this scene comes out, this scene comes out, you've got to put Harry Reasoner on-camera, he's got to say certain things."

Let me give you an example. In the film we have a very wonderful rap session with the kids, where they're talking and where one of them says, "The system is providing its own gravediggers. Like man, they give us the Declaration of Independence to read in college." He said, "Think of it. These old ladies in tennis shoes who're expecting a Red Chinese invasion from the Gulf of Mexico, if they knew their tax money was paying for us to read Tom Paine, it would blow their minds. Because you've got to become a revolutionary if you read that stuff and believe it." And it was this kind of discussion. I had to write a narration for Reasoner which goes like this: "The Bull Session, a typical college thing, like in my day goldfish swallowing, sheds much heat but very little light." And that was the narration for Reasoner that went over that scene. And like every scene there was added a particular tone, a particular point of view, which trivialized the kids. Just change after change was made in the film.

G.R.L. Would there have been any point in saying, "Look, if you're going to do that, I'm not going to do the film"?

A.B. Sure, there would have been a point. You're entitled to question that. I question it myself. I was getting my start in filmmaking, learning how to make films. CBS, before that and subsequent to that, gave me freedom to make some heavy political films. Like, I think *Webster Groves* is a very strong indictment of our society. *The Berkeley Rebels* was bad evidence of censorship, but there were other occasions where I was free to do pretty much what I wanted. Also, the guy who was communicating this to me felt so badly, that had some impact on me. And I also know that Fred Friendly fought very, very hard, resisting this, so I felt, win a few, lose a few. The good guys are trying. I want to stay here, I want to

1968–1969: ". . . in addition to being president of CBS, Stanton had served as chairman of the United States Advisor Commission on Information, was once chairman of the board of the Rand Corporation, funded almost entirely by Air Force money, and served as head of the executive committee of Radio Free Europe."

make more films. It's a good place to work. I'm not going to make my fight over this. Also, there was a lot of good stuff left in the film. It was still, I think, the best thing that came out of a nasty year in Berkeley.

G.R.L. I think there were good things too, and I think the kids chosen were bright, but I think the specific instance you gave of Reasoner's voice-over, that kind of condescension really took the bite out of the film.

A.B. Oh, it emasculated it. It destroyed it. It was awful. My original plan was to have no narrator. My original plan was to have a CBS person say at the very beginning of the film, "You're going to see a film about the Berkeley rebels, you may like it, you may dislike it. You may think it's a lie, a distortion, an exaggeration. We're not passing on its validity, but for you to understand that this is what they believe. This is a presentation of how they see it. So sit back, dig it, enter their minds, and good-bye, you will not hear another voice from CBS." That's how I wanted to do the film.

G.R.L. In *Webster Groves Revisited*, the metal shop teacher speaks out about the bond issue the town is to vote on, and how none of the money was earmarked for the metal shop, which needed equipment, and so on. Was money ever given—?

A.B. Well, the metal shop teacher's contract was not renewed, he got sacked. So films do have effects. Not always negatively. And I can't go back to St. Louis. CBS crews now if they try to sign into those hotels, they're like . . . wow!

G.R.L. Would you rather make documentaries than features?

A.B. Nope. I want to make features. That's what I'm heading toward. My work has gone through like a cycle. I began my work in documentary with very heavily staged and contrived and directed things, and then I sort of hit my cinéma-vérité period with three films, *Johnny Cash!*, *Birth and Death* and *Factory*. And now I'm into, I really want to get back into features.

G.R.L. You don't feel that documentary is satisfactory?

A.B. Oh no, no. I don't mean to denigrate documentary. I think documentary can reach a power and a truthfulness and a forcefulness that fiction films can never achieve. But there are things fiction films can do that documentary can't do, and it's just like Picasso had his Blue Period, his Abstract Period. I want to move on, I want to do something else in film now. I want a different challenge and a different experience.

G.R.L. Like features?

A.B. It's just that I want to experience that form, and I want to get back to it.

G.R.L. What do you mean get back to it?

A.B. I've been in the cinéma-vérité period for a while now, but before that I did things that were more relevant to features. For example, in *Babbitt*, like the scene of them sitting in the sweat house, which we constructed to achieve special technical things, and the slow-motion scene with the fairy girl. What I'm saying is, I want now to reaffirm and to refine and to push forward those parts of my creative personality that deal more with fiction feature film-making than with documentary, after a period of fairly rigorous cinéma-vérité documentary film-making. I'm very interested in scripting things now, in writing, in creating characters on paper.

G.R.L. Are there any features close to production?

A.B. Well, I've written two feature films. One for Universal Pictures called *Eric*. It's sort of thinly based on a love affair between Bob Dylan and Joan Baez; it's a film about a rock 'n' roll star. Then I wrote a film with a collaborator, Steve Ross, for Warner Brothers, called *Running*, which was about a young man who leaves Vietnam to come home for his mother's funeral, gets involved with a commune and then deserts from the Army.

G.R.L. Are both of these being made?

A.B. I don't think *Eric* is being made, I don't think it will be made. I think *Running* will go into production. I think Warners wants to produce it. They're not going to let me direct it, however. So, I've done those two scripts. Now I'm adapting Oliver La Farge's novel *Laughing Boy* for the screen, and have been promised that I will direct it as well. By David Ellis, who's the producer. He bought the rights for *Laughing Boy* from MGM for fifty thousand and has assigned me to write the script and direct the picture. That's another possibility. I have others. To get my first feature, I've got to have many things in the works. I've written a long treatment of a film about a Forty-ninth Street prostitute for Cinemation Industries.

G.R.L. Will that be fiction?

A.B. Yes, it is fiction; but in all of these cases, fiction, yes, but with a very strong documentary feeling, flavor, location, based on interviews with people—you know, that kind of thing.

G.R.L. Do you think that you'll be able to make the kind of features you want to make?

A.B. Largely, it comes down to a psychological thing. I mean, do you want to get very personal?

G.R.L. Sure.

A.B. All right. I'm moving in my own personal life toward greater areas of freedom, personal freedom. Before I had the courage to be a documentary film-maker, I was an academic sociologist. Before I had the courage to be a fiction film-maker, director, I'm a documentary film-maker. For me, movement toward the thing I revere and love most, which is *Wild Strawberries, Shane, 8 1/2, La Strada, Zabriskie Point*—for that kind of expression, there has to be a corollary process of individual growth, a closeness to the subsconscious emotional forces inside me, a confidence and ability to direct people. (I'm not saying that this odyssey has to apply to anybody else, obviously it doesn't.) An emotional freedom, in other words, so that my career movement and my desire now to work in fiction films, that desire which I think was always present either consciously or subconsciously, now becomes not merely desire but a practical possibility as I begin to change as a person. Do you understand? That's a very personal expression of where it's at.

G.R.L. The confidence to be able to try to do it and the push to do it?

A.B. Yes. To be more in touch with my feelings, to be able to understand, to be able to enter other people's lives, characters, with a kind of mature understanding of emotional . . . In other words, a certain personal human growth has occurred which now makes it possible. I'm not intimating that people who make documentaries are less emotionally rich or courageous or creative or forceful than people who make fiction films. I'm just saying that the way my individual destiny fell out is that it's the case with me. I think. I'm ready now to begin to try something else; to me, something more challenging and more difficult. I have a theory and a feeling that fiction films must be infinitely more difficult to do than documentary, much more difficult, in certain ways.

G.R.L. What are some of the documentary films, either yours or other people's, that you think reveal something in an important way?

A.B. Oh, many. I think *Death* does, from *Birth and Death*. I think *Salesman* does. I think *Titicut Follies* does incredibly so. I think in its own way *The Anderson Platoon*. What I think they do is provide something that fiction films cannot provide, which is actuality, which is a sense that this is really happening. This woman is really having this baby. She is not an actress. She could die, right before your eyes. Or perhaps a cretin could be born, or perhaps her husband will kiss her and they'll be happy; but whatever is going to happen, it will really happen. Fiction films just can't do that.

G.R.L. They try to create that belief.

A.B. They try to create that belief, but they can't do it, because it is fiction. That's one thing. Another thing is that I don't think that fiction films can affect people's lives in the direct way that documentary films can.

G.R.L. In films that you've worked on, has making a film affected people's lives? Can you give me an example?

A.B. Well, in *The Berkeley Rebels*, with Sally, the film produced a crisis in her life with her parents. The immediate crisis was that she was disinvited from being a flower girl at the wedding of one of her cousins. Her father offered to resign his job at a law firm.

G.R.L. Because of the film?

A.B. Because of the film, yeah. And so, on one level, a thing happened in her life: she was not invited to a wedding that she had been invited to. She did not participate in it. On another level, though, I think the film caused her to confront her parents in a way which might well have been beneficial for her; I don't know, but at least it precipitated an event which caused her to confront with her parents the perimeters of her freedom and her life. That really happened. *Birth and Death* unquestionably helped establish Bruce North as an artist. Norman Cousins, who is on the board of Public Broadcasting Laboratory, as soon as he saw the film, called up Bruce North and bought several paintings. Things happen to people in the films. And the other thing about documentary is it very often causes things to happen in society in a very direct fashion. For example: the film *Hunger in America* that Marty Carr made had an immediate and definite impact on the Department of Agriculture's policies toward food stamps. These things happen time and time again in documentary films. Laws are changed, people are promoted or demoted and so forth. People are fired, inquests are held. Jay McMullen's film *Biography of a Bookie Joint* resulted in the suspension of some policemen in the Boston Police Force for corruption.

G.R.L. Let me go to something else. It seems quite clear to me that documentaries on TV are not objective. But what bothers me is not so much that they're slanted, but that they pretend to objectivity.

A.B. I agree with all of that. They're not objective. And I think we pay a terrible cost for that pretense because it degrades the coin of the realm, it degrades the credibility, and it also means that some films are not done because you can't be objective about those subjects. It means that films that are done are very often vitiated by an attempt to be objective. So lots of bad consequences follow.

G.R.L. In that *Film Comment* article, you talk about documentaries on TV being in the tradition of factual reporting.

A.B. Of reportage, right.

G.R.L. But you're interested in human revelation?

A.B. Right. You see, I feel that you don't have a film unless there's a real commitment, and a real point of view, and that it should be out in the open.

G.R.L. Do you think some of your films make your point of view clear? *Webster Groves*, for example?

A.B. Oh yes. *Webster Groves* was a very point-of-view film. It's not a bit objective in one sense. It's not balanced. It isn't an attempt to show both sides of an issue. It's a definite, passionate expression of a definite and strong point of view. I want every one of my films to be like that, I really do. I'm not interested in being a reporter, I don't want to inform, to educate, to be balanced. I want to do what the novelist, what the poet, what the dramatist does, which is to move people emotionally, and to enable them to enter into the life of the human beings which you will find on film, to enable the audience to become more a part of the human family by that identification. I want to inform the heart, not the mind, and I want all of my films to have a point of view and to express it passionately.

G.R.L. Do you think you'll have the same problems that you had in documentaries in features? Trying to do what you want to do, trying to say what you want to say? At least traditionally it's been very difficult to—

A.B. I think it's very free now and I think the box office is a much nicer and better muse than the network executive. There's a lot more freedom and flexibility in that pragmatic test with the box office than there is in the network thing of FCC, Washington, establishment, objectivity and so forth.

G.R.L. You mentioned several European film-makers. Are there any American film-makers who have made films recently that you like?

A.B. *Faces*, I think, is an extraordinarily important film. It's honest like a cinéma-vérité film, its whole sensibility and style. I find that very exciting. And in a funny kind of way, *End of the Road*, I thought, and that's all. *Zabriskie Point*, but that's not an American film.

G.R.L. When you're listed as producer, do you keep control of the conception, script, editing?

A.B. Yeah. CBS doesn't give director credit because of the union problem; but on all those network documentaries, even though I got producer credit, I was producer-director. I must put in a word for Public Broadcasting, for NET, because there the freedom is just considerable in my experience. Total freedom, thus far. Much more so than the networks. My god, *Factory* could never have been made in network filming.

G.R.L. There was a group at NYU that wanted to make strike films, peace films—that's as clear an intention as I could get from them. Do you think that at a time like this[7] one could make documentary or propaganda films that could help?—if, let's say, one were in sympathy with the demands of radicals? And what kind of films could one make?

A.B. I'd take a reactionary point of view on that. I don't believe the artist should put on the uniform unless he wants to. If he wants to, fine, that's where his sensibility is; but don't try and make Stravinsky John Philip Sousa. You know what I mean? That's my feeling. I would give every encouragement to our students to make radical films, strike films, if that's what they wanted to do. But I think once you start telling artists don't listen to your muse, do this because it's so urgent and so important, I think that's death to art, and I'm opposed to that.

G.R.L. Do you see any way of producing and getting widespread distribution of documentaries other than through traditional means, like TV?

A.B. Oh yes. The whole theatrical thing is opening up quite beautifully now. And I think that it's now becoming possible to make documentary films, to raise money and finance them and distribute them on college campuses, and in special 16mm. theaters and do very nicely on them and not even go network at all.

G.R.L. Do you know anybody who has done this?

A.B. Well, no, not so far. I don't know. Well, *Woodstock* is one. *Johnny Cash!* was made for television, but it has done very well in the theaters. *Salesman*, is that going to work out? Is it going to make some money?

G.R.L. As far as I know, they still haven't made any money on it.

A.B. I think it will be possible. I can't point to any examples, but *Endless Summer* did very well. I think *Mondo Cane* did tremendously well. *Monterey Pop*, too.

G.R.L. But all the ones that you mention that have made money treated very popular kinds of subjects.

A.B. I want to tell you, *Birth and Death* was doing very well. We have made money in 16mm. distribution on *Birth and Death*. Well, that's unfair to say, because PBL[8] paid for it; I mean, if PBL hadn't paid for it to begin with, the film would be very much in the red. But I think eventually it will make it.

[7] V. note 5, p. 283.
[8] Public Broadcasting Laboratory.

G.R.L. Why did you take the job here at Columbia?

A.B. Chairman? Well, I like teaching, and I like working with young people, and I have an academic background, and I like the security. And there's a good possibility of sending my five kids to college for free.

G.R.L. Was there anything in particular that you wanted to do in the way of running a film school that other people aren't doing?

A.B. That's a difficult question. I'm just feeling my way. I'm so new at it I couldn't really give a good answer, other than to say to encourage a lot of production, to teach through production rather than through theory.

FREDERICK WISEMAN

Frederick Wiseman was born January 1, 1930, in Boston, Massachusetts. He received his B.A. from Williams College in 1951, his LL.B. from Yale Law School in 1954. In 1955–56 he served in the U. S. Army. Wiseman was on the student law faculty of the University of Paris, 1956–57, and has also taught at Boston University Law-Medicine Institute, 1958–60, and at Boston University Law School, 1959–61. He was in private practice in Paris, 1957–58; was a Russell Sage Foundation Fellow, Graduate School of Arts and Sciences, Harvard University, 1961–62; and a Research Associate, Department of Sociology, Brandeis University, 1963 to the present. He co-founded OSTI (Organization for Social and Technical Innovation), a social science consulting firm, in 1966 and worked there until 1970.

Wiseman has also been a visiting lecturer at the Yale Law School, Harvard, the University of Iowa, the University of Pittsburgh, Portland State University, and the Flaherty Film Seminar.

A member of the Massachusetts bar, he lives with his wife and two children in Cambridge, Massachusetts.

FILMOGRAPHY*

1964: *The Cool World*. A feature film produced by Frederick Wiseman. Directed by Shirley Clarke. 104 minutes. Distributed by Zipporah Films, 54 Lewis Wharf, Boston, Massachusetts 02110.

1967: *Titicut Follies*. A Bridgewater Film Production. Produced, directed and edited by Frederick Wiseman. Photographed by John Marshall. 87 minutes. Distributed by Grove Press, New York. First Prize for Best Documentary, Mannheim Film Festival 1967. Critics Prize, Festival dei Popoli 1967. Film Best Illustrating Human Condition, Festival dei Popoli, 1967.

* Filmography is supplied by the film-maker.

1968: *High School.* Produced, directed and edited by Frederick Wiseman. Photographed by Richard Leiterman. 75 minutes. Distributed by Zipporah Films.

1969: *Law and Order.* Produced, directed and edited by Frederick Wiseman. Photographed by William Brayne. Approx. 90 minutes. Distributed by Zipporah Films. Emmy Award for Best News Documentary of 1968–69 television season.

1970: *Hospital.* Produced, directed and edited by Frederick Wiseman. Photographed by William Brayne. Approx. 85 minutes. Distributed by Zipporah Films. Emmy Awards for Best Documentary 1969–70 and Best Director 1970. Catholic Film Workers Award, Mannheim Film Festival 1970. Columbia School of Journalism, DuPont Award, Best Documentary 1970.

1971: *Basic Training.* Produced, directed and edited by Frederick Wiseman. Photographed by William Brayne. Approx. 89 minutes. Distributed by Zipporah Films.

Wiseman is presently writing a script for a feature film.

September 24, 1970, in Fred Wiseman's office in Cambridge, Massachusetts.

G. ROY LEVIN: Were you very interested in film when you were a kid?

FRED WISEMAN: Certainly as a teen-ager I was interested in it, but I didn't do much about it. I began to be more interested when I was living in Paris after I graduated from law school, when I was about twenty-four or twenty-five. I wasn't really a film buff except in the sense that I was going to the movies a lot. Like everybody else, but nothing special.

G.R.L. Your films are clearly socially conscious, concerned with social issues; are these things you've always been concerned with? Have you been particularly politically active?

F.W. Not particularly. My films are socially conscious but are not, at least from my point of view, trying to sell any particular ideology. Rather, it's the idea of using film and film technology to have a look at what's going on in the world, or, as the cliché goes, "in the world around us." It seemed to me that that was a use film could be put to, and despite the fact that there had been a lot of work in that area, it was still wide open. The country was relatively unexplored from the point of view of film, so that my interest in making films is not political in the sense that I'm trying to sell or subscribe to a particular conservative or radical or middle-of-the-road point of view, but rather to find out what my own attitude is toward the material that's the subject of the films.

G.R.L. I never got to see *Hospital*, but certainly from what one sees in *Titicut Follies* and *High School*, it seems clear that what's happening in those institutions is not desirable.

F.W. Even in the case of the *Follies* it's not clear-cut. Certainly many aspects of the *Follies* are critical, but it's not a total critique of the institution, because in my view, many of the guards at Bridgewater come off quite well. The middle-class professionals don't, particularly. It's a very complex scene, in that the state is trying to deal in some way or other with different kinds of people. Some of them have committed no major offense other than being mentally ill—whatever that means—and others have committed the most outrageous crimes and have to be segregated. The issue, then, is how do you treat them? And certainly the film deals with that, in a very critical way, but it is not entirely a criticism.

In *Hospital*, for example, the hospital staff doesn't come out badly at all. By and large, the nurses and the doctors are extremely hard-working, dedicated professionals dealing with situations that are quite beyond their capacity to affect, given the institutional circumstances under which they're working. If somebody comes in with a cut or a wound, they can sew it up, but they can't really do much about the social conditions that produced what they have to deal with. So *Hospital* is not a critique. It's too much of a liberal's thing to say, "If only we had more doctors, if only we had more nurses, the situation would be different." The problems are so much more complicated, and so much more interesting. You see people who have never been to doctors in thirty years, who can't read or write, who live in crappy houses, who don't have jobs, are recent immigrants either from other countries or from rural or urban areas. And you see the staff trying to deal with them as best they can—but they can't correct the conditions that led to these people walking through the hospital door in the first place.

So it's not a critique of just the hospital. The film attempts to get at some of the larger issues that are related to the hospital, but that the hospital can only peripherally affect. I guess what I'm saying is that I start the film with an ideological view, then I try to have that change to the extent that it does change as a consequence of what I have experienced and felt about the institution. I try to remain open.

G.R.L. But in choosing the institutions you presumably had some idea of what they were like.

F.W. Presumably, yes. But not really.

G.R.L. Well, you knew about Bridgewater, the hospital in *Titicut Follies*, for example, because you'd taken your law students there.

F.W. I knew it, but I really didn't know it in the way I knew it after being there for thirty days or so. I think it's an interesting, even crucial point, because it's extremely important for the film-maker to try at least to remain open to the material, otherwise you're making propaganda. It may be propaganda anyway, but at least it represents your subjective, hopefully thought-through approach to what you've seen and felt and observed, and not the imposition of an ideology on the experience, or the twisting of the experience to fit the ideology.

G.R.L. But certainly in the three films of yours that I've seen, you manipulate the material in the editing—not to mention that one always selects what one actually shoots.

F.W. Of course the editing manipulates, but the distinction I'm making is this: Say you're at a place for four hundred hours and you shoot forty hours and you use ninety minutes. All that is selection, all that is choice. Sure. But really all I'm saying is that I try to make the selection based on my view of the experience as filtered through what I was before the film and what happens while I'm there. This means not only for the period of time that I was at the institution, but also sitting in front of the moviola trying to think through in my own terms, however successfully or unsuccessfully, what the experience meant to me. And that's what the editing reflects. At least I *hope* that's what it reflects rather than something like all hospitals are shitty, or whatever. Within that framework, of course, it's totally subjective.

G.R.L. When I saw *Titicut Follies*—I saw it at Goddard College—people were mostly horrified at what they'd seen—because clearly it's a horrible scene. A strong reaction from *High School* too, the dehumanization, rigidity of the system, etc. That is, do you have no preconceptions?

F.W. Sure, I had preconceptions. For instance, in the *High School* film, I really didn't know that much about high schools—I really hadn't been back in high school since I graduated in 1947. I remember I hated high school and that I was bored out of my mind, and there may have been some unconscious memories of it, but all I knew was that I was trying to make this *High School* film as part of the institutional series. I thought that it would be better to take a good school rather than a bad school, and a white school rather than a black school. However, I really didn't know how the film was going to come out, even in a general sense, before I was there. I went down to Northeast High School, where the film was made, maybe two or three times before the shooting started. Also there's a difference between stating some generality like high schools are boring, or, the experience is banal, and knowing what that really means. You can accept the view that high schools are a banal experience, and you may have that before you start. But in terms of the specific context of the events you're going to observe, and the relationship of those events to each other, you don't know, because you don't know what you're going to find.

There are certainly a lot of themes in *High School* that I hadn't really thought about until I was there for a while, and some of the connections that I think are in the film, I didn't really think about until I was editing it. For instance, what I think is one of the major themes in *High School* is the kind of unisex theme, or at least the repression of sexuality of any sort. I may have had a vague idea about that, but I had no idea of its dimensions until I started trying to put the film together and thinking about, say, the connection between the variety show they put on, the girls' gym class, and the kind of values that were illustrated by the fashion show. These things, at least in my mind, seem to fit together. All I had ahead of time was kind of a general view, but in order to make the film work, you have to have not only the experience, but to think about the relationship of the various sequences to each other. The structure of the film is the film-maker's theory about the event or the events that constitute the film.

G.R.L. During the shooting, you do the sound, and somebody else shoots. You're the one, I take it, who chooses the scenes to shoot?

F.W. Right. And I work out signals with whomever I'm working with so that he knows the way I want to get the shot, and we talk very carefully both before, during and after the shooting about those stylistic things I like.

G.R.L. Do you edit the films?

F.W. Yes.

[. . .]

G.R.L. Do you see yourself as a cinéma-vérité film-maker?

F.W. I have no idea what that means. I think it's a pompous, overly worked, bullshit phrase.

G.R.L. Well, perhaps we can get back to it. The article preceding the interview with you in *Cinema*[1] talks about how one or two people are often the subject in what are called cinéma-vérité films—even if you don't like the phrase—as in, for example, *Salesman*. Now one of the things I think the Maysles would say, and that other people have said, is that after you're around for a while, the characters get used to the camera and they behave fairly naturally. But you don't concentrate on one or two people, you have a situation where a comparatively large number of people have to get used to the camera quickly. Do you find that a problem?

F.W. No, I don't find that a problem at all. I'm amazed that it isn't and I thought it would be, but now I've made several films in this style and it's really fantastic how rarely people look into the camera. I think anybody working in this field develops a very sensitive bullshit meter so that you know when somebody's putting it on, and you don't use the material. But by and large, I think that the experience—at least my experience—is that when people don't want their picture taken—which is very rare, again much to my surprise—they'll just tell you, "Don't take my picture," or they'll giggle or clown or in some way screw up the shot. But most people can't change their behavior sufficiently so they can act differently than they ordinarily do. And I don't think that's just true of the subjects of my films; it's true of most of us. We don't have that large

[1] *Cinema*, vol. 6, no. 1, p. 35.

a repertoire of alternative gestures or words or feelings. It takes a great actor like Laurence Olivier to be the Entertainer in one play and the Merchant of Venice in another. Most of us don't have the possibility of that kind of range, so I don't think, by and large, that people change their behavior in the presence of the equipment or of the film-maker or whatever. If anything, people will act more rather than less characteristically.

You never know, you get these outrageous scenes. I think the thing you get is people doing what they normally do, because if they thought that what they were doing was outrageous, then they wouldn't do it. For instance, the scene in *Law and Order* where the cop strangles the girl who has been arrested for prostitution. Now, if that cop didn't think that what he was doing was okay, why on earth would he do that when it was being recorded?

G.R.L. Did you have to get releases, not just from him, but from the police department?

F.W. No, no.

G.R.L. Did he object in any way to that scene?

F.W. Well, not at the moment. No. And afterward there was no formal objection. But I remember I was told there was some feeling that he wasn't really choking her, that she was trying to escape from him and was jumping up and down on his hand, on his arm. I think this was just embarrassment over the fact that he'd done that, but there was no formal protest. That's an example. Take some of the ordinary things that teachers do in *High School*. Now, if they thought that those things were wrong, one, they probably wouldn't do them in the first place, and two, they certainly wouldn't do them in front of the camera.

G.R.L. Could I ask about that scene with the prostitute? When did you get the release from the detective?

F.W. I didn't get a written release, I don't get written releases. I have not gotten any written releases since the *Follies*, on the advice of my lawyers. The reason is this: The documentaries that I've made so far have all dealt with public institutions supported by taxpayers. Our view is that the films are all protected by the First Amendment, and the films are as much news as what's in the New York *Times* or in *Life* or on television. Even though they might not appear for six or eight months after the event, because it takes that long to put the thing together, it's no less news. The case law is quite supportive of that view.

The famous case in the field is the one involving *The Desperate Hours*. What happened was that *Life* magazine did a story on the family on which *The Desperate Hours* was based. The family had been held captive by some gunmen. The family sued *Life* for invasion of privacy, and the Supreme Court—*Time* v. *Hill*—found that as long as there was no malice on the part of *Life* magazine, it was in the public interest to know what happened, and the magazine story was protected by the First Amendment. They also held that the New York privacy statute did not apply because of the paramount First Amendment interest. So, if it's okay to report on gunmen going into a private home, by analogy then, the film-maker going into a tax-supported public institution ought to be included within that general rule. That in brief is the rationale for not getting releases.

G.R.L. It's a shame that the people who are shown in, let's say, unkind or perhaps even humiliating circumstances are once again the poor. For example, if asked if one wanted to be in certain scenes in *Law and Order* or *Titicut Follies*, and shown that way, I think that a lot of us would say no.

F.W. The ground rules that I always operate under are that I don't get written releases, but I get consents. I go up to someone and say, "We just took your picture and it's going to be for a movie, it's going to be shown on television or maybe in theaters, and it's going to get a wide release to the general public. Do you have any objection?" If they have any objection, I don't use the material. I either ask just before the shooting or immediately after.

[. . .]

Even in the kinds of neighborhoods where *Law and Order* was made, very few of the people living there have the chance to get the full view of police activity. The same is true of people living in an area serviced by a metropolitan hospital. A patient walks into the emergency ward to get his slit neck sewed up, but he doesn't sit in on staff meetings, he's not over at the children's clinic and he's not upstairs in the adult clinic, etc. All the obvious things.

At least one of my interests in film is to be able to use it to present that kind of information to the general public. It seems to me that that's an important part of it. This is the rationale that allows you to get this kind of information to large numbers of people. I don't think it's done at the expense of the poor.

G.R.L. To return to that scene with the prostitute again. From my point of view, I think it was good that that scene was in there because I feel that what the detective did was wrong and that people should know that things like that happen. Other people might feel differently. But why would that girl consent to have that picture in the film? Why would she want her picture in that scene—that's what I can't understand. She didn't object at any point?

F.W. I have her consent. I have no idea why people allow their pictures to be taken at all, but they do.

G.R.L. I'd agree that it's a very difficult question, especially if one sees it in any way in moral terms.

F.W. Obviously, the problem exists, and I resolved it from my own point of view. If I resolved it differently, I wouldn't be able to make the film. On the other hand, I don't review the final film with everybody in it before the film goes out.

The ethical problem is there too, but it's a complicated one, because what you've got in each case is the individual's rights, however they may be defined; and when I say right of privacy, I don't just mean the technical, legal definition or just the moral and ethical considerations involved in privacy—that's one thing. You also have all the issues connected with the public's right to know and the presentation of information in a democratic society. There are all kinds of limitations on those individual rights that already exist. I'm not even talking about the big political issues of our time—just things like limitations on assembly, people agreeing to live by certain kinds of rules having to do with traffic lights or more income taxes, that kind of thing. It's not a new issue. It's a new technology that raises the issue in a new form. It's a very sticky issue. But it's something I have thought about a great deal.

G.R.L. You said you see your films as subjective, is that—

F.W. I think this objective-subjective stuff is a lot of bullshit. I don't see how a film can be anything but subjective.

G.R.L. I absolutely agree. But I don't know that it's clear to all viewers and it wasn't clear to me when I saw your films that they were supposed to be subjective.

F.W. How can any intelligent person think that they're anything but that? The news that's on Huntley and Brinkley is subjective too.

G.R.L. Bravo!

F.W. I mean, you can't put a subtitle on. "For the wary viewer, for the novitiate, all films are subjective." You can't do it. It might be fun to do it as a joke, but for no other reason. When you're signing the film, you are saying it's your film, this is the way you see it.

G.R.L. That seems crystal-clear to me as it does to you, but to a lot of people it's not crystal-clear. For example, I would think that most people who watch Huntley-Brinkley take that as objective reporting—and they pretend that it's objective reporting.

F.W. That's education in another area that somebody else has to deal with. I don't know how to deal with that. It seems to me to be obvious. A book has a viewpoint, that of the person who writes the book. A book of political reporting is no different, is it?

G.R.L. This is, as you know, an old question and an old problem, but it's multiplied to a great degree in film because—

F.W. Because of the immediacy of film, and they think . . .

G.R.L. That it's reality and therefore objective, which is the way people too often take film. In a sense, I also see it as a problem with your films. I think that most people would take them as objective. I don't think that the point of view is made clear.

F.W. I think my films are fair. I think they're fair to the experience that I had in making the film. They are not objective, because someone else might make the film differently. Instead of spending a month in a place you could spend six months, and instead of shooting with one camera and one tape recorder you could shoot with three or a hundred. I don't know how to make an objective film. I think my films are a fair reflection of the experience of making them. My subjective view is that they are fair films.

G.R.L. I may be beating a dead horse, but let me go on for a moment. Let's take *High School.* I would generally agree with the image of public high schools as presented in the film, that they're very bad news. But take the scene with the counselor, an older woman with bottle-thick glasses. Those extreme close-ups of the woman make her look grotesque, which prejudices us against her in a certain way.

F.W. I don't accept your view of the way she looks. I think that we're all victims of the beautiful Hollywood image of people, and I don't think any of us, myself included, are going to look that smashing on film unless we happen to be very handsome, beautiful people. What we're accustomed to looking at on film, by and large, unless it's a Fellini grotesque, is beautiful people. In a documentary film, where there are literally hundreds of people seen, some of them are going to be prettier and some uglier than others, as people are in real life. And stylistically in *High School* I wanted to use a lot of close-ups because I thought it was appropriate. If I wore bifocals I would not photograph any better or worse than the lady you refer to.

G.R.L. Isn't it clear that if you have a medium shot of the woman we would simply look on her as a fairly ordinary-looking woman with thick glasses, but if you come in for a close-up that she takes on almost grotesque proportions?

F.W. I thought that thematically it was absolutely appropriate in that particular scene. One of the aspects of *High School* that

I think is rarely commented on is the enormous passivity of the students and the difficulty that the faculty had in dealing with the parents. In that particular scene you're talking about, think what the mother was saying. She says, "I've always told Arlene that you got to respect an adult no matter what they say to you," etc., etc. The bromides that mother is coming on with are really infinitely worse than what the guidance counselor is spouting. The guidance counselor is just trying to find out what's been going on.

G.R.L. That was my objection in that scene. I don't remember the details, but as I recall, she was sympathetic, she was not being a terrible person, yet you distorted her by using that kind of close-up.

F.W. I guess that's in the eye of the viewer. I didn't view her as any prettier or uglier than almost anyone else in the film. I felt that perhaps Freud might stir a little bit in his grave if he saw what some of his ideas had come to, but certainly none of the close-ups in the film—including that one—were meant to exploit the physical characteristics of the people. I don't think it's fair to do that. It's like using a dwarf to exploit the fact that he's a dwarf, rather than showing an interest in a character you're dealing with.

G.R.L. What about the scene with the gynecologist speaking to an auditorium full of boys about sex, and the close-shot of him wiggling his finger? That seems very subjective, and in a sense distorting. You're making fun of him because you think what he's saying is not good, or foolish.

F.W. But I think that the close-up of him wiggling his finger is fair under the circumstances. It's not twisting what's going on to suit my point of view, it's totally thematic with what's going on. I think that's the distinction. If you twist the material to impose on it something that is not happening . . .

G.R.L. But a lot of the teachers in that school, for example, or parents, might have heard that lecture and thought that it was good.

F.W. Sure. I don't deny that at all. The meaning of the scene, including the wiggle, is dependent on the audience. This is the ambiguity inherent in presenting unstaged encounters on film. The response to the film is very much dependent on the values, attitudes and experience of the audience. When Louise Day Hicks saw *High School* she said it had "the bittersweet quality of life."

[. . .]

G.R.L. Let me go back to that interview in *Cinema* I mentioned before. In reference to *Law and Order* and your experience with the Kansas City Police, you said, "I don't think anything was concealed from me."[2] When I interviewed Franju, I asked him whether he would be interested in having shot anything on the May "revolution,"[3] and he said something like, "What the hell would I want to do that for? The interesting thing is what goes on in the police station. And no one's going to let you film that." I think that's what bothered me and lots of other people about *Law and Order.* I believe you when you say that the film reflects your experience there, and that cops don't spend all their time beating people up. But certainly they do beat people up, and in some real way one of the functions of the police is to control the poor for the rich.

F.W. I think that's kind of a partially valid cliché. For example, it omits the great demands the poor make on the cops for services. For instance, even in Kansas City, people in the black or poor white neighborhoods with high crime rates wanted more police protection and they didn't care what color the police were, but were interested in their assistance. Last year, the New York chapter of the NAACP put out a report saying that they didn't care whether the police in Harlem were white or black, they just wanted more of them. Okay, that's one point. The other is one that I guess has to be taken on my say-so, because there's no other way of dealing with it: when I was in Kansas City—and I was there for six weeks—there was nothing that I wanted to shoot that was off limits.

G.R.L. Do you think those cops ever beat up people badly in the police station?

F.W. Well, I'm sure it has happened. I don't deny that cops beat up people. That's not the point I'm making. I don't deny that it happens, of course it does, but given the volume of police work it happens rarely, which is not to forgive it when it does happen. The cops aren't better actors than anybody else. In one scene a cop bangs a black boy's head against a car hood and in another a member of the Vice Squad strangles a girl accused of prostitution. If either of these officers had thought their behavior was wrong, they certainly would have controlled themselves in front of a camera and a microphone.

G.R.L. Well, I'll just say it one more time in a little different way, then I won't nag any more. The image that I have of police is from all kinds of sources, from reading, from simple hearsay, from newsreel footage, from personal reports, etc., and there's enough to convince me that cops very often behave very badly—

[2] *Cinema,* vol. 6, no. 1, p. 39.
[3] May 1968, the time of the French student "revolution."

at least with the poor. I don't deny that what you filmed is true, not in the least. But if I were making the film—and again it's completely subjective—I think it would bother me, knowing that other things went on, that I was presenting an image of the cop as essentially a nice guy.

F.W. I would certainly never agree that the only view that the film presents is the cop as a nice guy. What I really object to is the view that the cop, as a class of human being, is really any different than anybody else. I don't believe that's true. I may have believed it was true before I spent six weeks with them, but I certainly don't believe it now. The ease with which some people can classify large groups of people as either being groovy or being pigs just escapes me, because I think it's totally ideological and contrary to all my experience in trying to cope with people in whatever shape, size or color. I'm very suspicious of people that can make those kinds of glib classifications, whatever the classification may be, and wherever it may fall politically. Fortunately or unfortunately, there were no demonstrations going on, no political activity other than some campaign candidates coming through Kansas City, and there was no riot. There is a scene in the film where the cops talk about what they did during a riot and the gassing and shooting. There's no question that these events occur, but they didn't while I was there. There was no Democratic Convention in Kansas City and there were no student riots at the university there, so I'm left with what I saw. And I don't believe that this film—at least from my point of view—is meant to be *the* statement about cops. This is a film about Kansas City cops during the time that I was with them.

G.R.L. But people would clearly take it that it has other, wider implications.

F.W. I think it has other implications. Sometimes you can separate it and sometimes you can't, but the fact of the matter is that even now, with all the horrible things the police are doing in some cities, the fact of the matter is that 99 per cent of the police work is more like what's going on in the film. I don't in any way say that other horrible things that the police may be doing don't go on—things like the police raid on the Panther headquarters in Chicago. What I set out to do in *Law and Order* was to make a film about routine police activity. Now, some of these other activities have become more routine since 1968.

G.R.L. You mention in that same interview that PBL blipped obscenities from *Law and Order*. Were there any other instances of censorship where you had to change material for the TV networks?

F.W. No.

G.R.L. Did you ever leave things out that you thought they wouldn't like?

F.W. No. I did what I wanted to do, and I fought. They wanted to cut out even more from *Law and Order*, and I screamed and yelled and they ended up just cutting a little, and when it was broadcast, I made them put in a statement at the end of the film saying that cuts were made over my strenuous objections.

G.R.L. Can I ask how the films were financed?

F.W. Sure. PBL financed *Law and Order*, and the Corporation for Public Broadcasting financed *Hospital* through a grant to NET. For *High School* I got a foundation grant which covered a good part, though not all, of the cost, and the *Follies* was financed partially by a few investors, but mainly on credit, lab credit. Since the *Follies* I've been able to get outside financing to cover most of the cost.

G.R.L. Do you think that your films or that documentaries in general can help change the social order?

F.W. There are all these words in the air like "social change," "innovation," "change agent," "radical restructuring," all that. I don't make any grandiose claims for the films in that regard. My feeling is that if the films do anything, they may contribute information that people might not otherwise have, and may suggest things that some people may otherwise not think about. The premise is the simple one that the more information you have, the more informed decision you can make. The films don't deal with the various possible forms the social change might take or which are desirable. They present no solutions, they don't present alternatives A through B—at least I hope they don't. I hope they simply explore the issues in ways that please me, and if they please me that's ultimately what I care about most. If that's conveyed to other people, well and good, but I really have no particular propagandistic or social change solutions to offer, and I'm wary of them generally.

G.R.L. Are there any film-makers, past or present, feature or documentary, that you particularly admire?

F.W. I like many of Leacock's films, particularly *Mooney vs. Fowle*.[4] I'm as opinionated as anybody else, and I dislike most films that I see—but that's kind of a film-maker's occupational hazard.

[4] Also known as *Football*.

G.R.L. Do you go to films much?

F.W. Yes, when I get a chance, though not as much as I used to, because I don't have much time.

G.R.L. Do you see many documentaries?

F.W. No, I don't, because they're hard to get hold of unless you're on the circuit. I exchange films with other film-makers. But most of the films I see are feature films.

G.R.L. Your films have gotten much wider distribution than most documentaries, but for most documentary film-makers, distribution is a real problem. Unless it's shown on TV, there's little chance that it will be seen by very many people. And except for NET, the networks almost never show any outside-produced documentaries. Given this, do you see distribution as a problem?

F.W. Well, no. Because I've been screwed so badly in distribution, I set up my own distribution company, Zipporah Films. As far as I'm concerned, I want to get the films paid for, and by and large I get them paid for by these outside sources, but I will not, and I never have and I don't think I ever will compromise any of the films in order to get them on television. I won't go to court to stop them from taking the "fucker" out of "motherfucker" because actually I think it's a fantastic joke to leave the "mother" in and the "fucker" out—as was done with *Law and Order*—but I would never compromise any of the films just so that they could be on the networks and reach eighty million people. I make the films primarily to please myself. I'd like them to be seen by as many people as possible, but I will not water them down, dilute them or change them in order to accomplish that.

G.R.L. You said that you got screwed by the distributors. How was that?

F.W. You never get accurate reporting, you never get any money and all that sort of stuff.

G.R.L. Do you know about Raindance and the Videofreex in New York? They're into video tape. They see it as a possible alternative medium, recording on half-inch tape and trying to set up a different distribution circuit. Does that kind of thing interest you at all?

F.W. Yes, it interests me, but I really haven't had time to do more than vaguely keep in touch with it. I'm not even in touch with it to the extent that I had heard of these two companies.

G.R.L. I read that you got a grant from AFI to do a feature film script. Are you about to do a feature?

F.W. I hope to do a feature, and I'm working on the script now.

G.R.L. Does it deal with social issues?

F.W. What doesn't? A Doris Day movie deals with social issues, although this isn't that kind of movie. Yes, it deals with social issues.

G.R.L. Do you want just to make features now?

F.W. No, I still want to do documentaries, but I would like to alternate maybe a little bit. There are a lot of other documentaries that I want to do, but I also want to see to what extent I can adapt some of the documentary techniques to feature films, and just as a personal issue I want to see whether I can make a film with actors. I think I can. There's only one way to find out, and now I'm having the opportunity.

G.R.L. That's good. What about the possibility of combining real events with fictional characters, in the manner of say, *Medium Cool?*

F.W. Oh yes. That's one of the main issues now.

G.R.L. Your script deals with that kind of thing?

F.W. Yes. That's what it's all about.

ED PINCUS

Ed Pincus was born July 6, 1939, in Brooklyn, New York. He attended Brown University, where he received his B.A. in 1960; while at Brown, he spent a semester studying in Geneva, Switzerland. In 1960–61 he went to Pisa, Italy, on a Fulbright scholarship. From 1961 to 1963 he studied philosophy at Harvard Graduate School. From 1963 to 1965 he studied and then taught still photography at Harvard. And from 1969 to the present he has been teaching film at MIT.

Pincus lives with his wife, Jane, and their two children in Cambridge, Massachusetts.

FILMOGRAPHY*

1965: *Mrs. Smith* (unfinished). A film by Ed Pincus. Camera: Ed Pincus, J. D. Smith. Sound: David Neuman.

1967: *Black Natchez* (filmed in 1965). 62 minutes, b&w. A film by Ed Pincus and David Neuman. Editing assistants: Michal Goldman, Paul Balmuth, Andrew Engvall. Production assistants: Dennis Sweeney, J. D. Smith, Mary King. Commentary: James Jackson. Camera: Ed Pincus. Sound: David Neuman.

1968: *One Step Away* (filmed in 1967). 54 minutes, color. A film by Ed Pincus and David Neuman. Editors: Eden Williams, Alan Jacobs. Assistant producer: J. D. Smith. Assistant editor: Jennifer Chinlund. Additional camera: Peter Adair. Field assistants: Merrill Epstein, Michal Goldman, Rick Zamore. Music: The Hallucinations (recorded by The National Express Co.). Flute: Jane Pincus. Assistant: Sami. Camera: Ed Pincus. Sound: David Neuman.

* The filmography was supplied by the film-maker.

1969: *Harry's Trip* (filmed 1967). 16 minutes, color. A film by Ed Pincus and David Neuman. Camera: Ed Pincus. Sound: David Neuman.

Portrait of a McCarthy Supporter (filmed in 1968). 16 minutes, color. A film by Ed Pincus and David Neuman. Assisted by Dianne Kagan, Jeffrey Jacobs, Robin Zamore. Camera: Ed Pincus. Sound: David Neuman.

The Way We See It ("The Film Generation") 57 minutes, b&w. A film by Ed Pincus and David Neuman. Produced by Jac Venza and Perry Miller Adato. Narrator: Andrew Duncan. Associate producer: David Loxton. Editing assistants: Dianne Kagan, Jeffrey Jacobs. Field assistants: Vic Losick, Bob Brooks. A production of National Educational Television. Camera: Ed Pincus. Sound: David Neuman.

1970: *Panola* (filmed in 1965). 21 minutes, b&w. Production: Ed Pincus and David Neuman. Editing: Michal Goldman and Dennis Sweeney. Camera: Ed Pincus. Sound: David Neuman.

August 14, 1970, in Ed Pincus' office and at his home in Cambridge, Massachusetts.

G. Roy Levin: Why did you start making films?

Ed Pincus: I was doing graduate work in philosophy at Harvard, and through a whole series of things I got interested in still photography, and finally took some still photography courses at Harvard. Also at that time I was really getting involved in politics in all kinds of ways. Lots of my friends had gone down South, to Mississippi.

Also in 1963 Al Maysles had come to show *Showman* at Harvard, and the film really wowed me—it really hit me hard. On one hand I had this mystical feeling of reality, like touching the texture of reality. On the other hand I thought it was an awful film. There was something really beautiful about it, but I somehow felt you just couldn't make a film like that. Partially it was the sound, partially it was the kind of visual quality; but I also really had this kind of mystical high. That's very important to realize what that mystical high meant to me, because I was somebody who denied anything except the hardest kind of concrete line of philosophy in some way. I was in what's called the "hardheaded" tradition of philosophy. I was denying anything mystical, and it hadn't only been in philosophy, it was also in my life too—a kind of very dried-up academic life in all kinds of ways.

In any case, there were all these contradictory stories from Mississippi, and I figured, well, here I could do something for the Movement and resolve all these kinds of problems of not understanding what was going on in Mississippi—not only for me but for other people. And the most natural way was to think in terms of this technique that the Maysles brothers had used.

G.R.L. Had you seen any other films like that?

E.P. No, that was the first and only one. Well, maybe. I'd seen *Lonely Boy*, but that had interviews and relies heavily on a kind of narration track.

Anyway, I really thought there was an important social movement going on and that I wanted to be involved in it because I believed in social change of all kinds. What I meant by social change at that time was very different from what I have meant by social change from say, '63 on. It's continually changing, and that's been reflected in all our films. By the way, also at this time I was somehow just getting interested in films in general. There was this short story by Camus called "The Adulterous Woman" which I had made a very loose adaptation of, and I had borrowed a camera from somebody.

G.R.L. To make a film of it?

E.P. Yes.

G.R.L. You had never made a film before?

E.P. No, I was learning as I went along. The still photography was an incredible help, and I really learned still photography very well. I was a teaching fellow at Harvard, teaching still photography.

Anyway, I had asked these friends of mine who were in Mississippi about doing a film down there, and they had written that people were running scared, that it was impossible. Now a friend, David Neuman, was running a sandal shop in Cambridge, and he was interested in my Camus script, so he ended up helping tape sound for the film. Then these guys came up from Mississippi, who had just organized this project with high school students in Amite County, and they felt this kind of union of consciousness, and they said, "Make a film on it." David and I, in order to tape sound on the Camus film, had bought a Nagra together, so I asked him if he wanted to go down to Mississippi, and he said, "Yes." So from then on we were equals in everything: neither of us knew anything. He only had about an hour experience of taping sound with the Nagra, and I had never shot synch before.

These guys told us they were going to raise ten thousand dollars, so David and I went down to Natchez, where we shot ninety thousand feet of film, almost all on credit—very little of the promised money had been raised.

When we went down there we didn't even know how to load a moviola. We really didn't know what the fuck we were doing. On the other hand that gave us a kind of freedom to try the kinds of things I would probably be afraid to try now. Like if somebody came in and said they wanted to do this film on what civil rights meant in this town, on a kind of grand-scale level, I'd say, "Well, you shouldn't try to capture this whole thing, too many things can go wrong, etc." We were in some sense incredibly lucky. We stayed down there and shot for about a month and a half, two months, shooting all this quiet stuff, you know, people relating to each other, and then, all of a sudden there was this bombing. The bombing brought out all the issues we were interested in, and brought them out really clearly, so that the action in the bulk of the film that is now a film was shot in two weeks although we were down there for over three months.

G.R.L. That is, in part you're depending on luck for dramatic structure.

E.P. Yeah, right. I had this notion that when there's conflict, some kind of abnormality that happens, the normal becomes clearer and all the issues get drawn just much more clearly. So like in Natchez there was this bombing. A power vacuum was created in the black community, and the question was, who was to speak to the black people of Natchez. On one hand you had FDP, which is a political organization, Mississippi Freedom Democratic Party. They were the political offshoot of SNCC in Mississippi. You had them purporting to speak for the poor black people, and they, in terms of 1965 (we shot the film in the summer of '65) were the radicals and the revolutionaries—not that people really talked about revolution at that time. On the other hand you had the NAACP, which found its power base among the black bourgeoisie, the ministers, the businessmen. You had this problem of who was going to speak to the black community. In the film that becomes one of the questions itself—this contending for power, and you could just make a much terser film instead of letting things flow.

At this time, in '65, I had this notion of cinéma-vérité as a kind of flow, and what this cinéma-vérité film-maker wanted to do was capture this flow and editing was an unfortunate necessity, but ideally real time and film time would be the same exact thing—a Warhol kind of idea—and somehow that would demand on the part of the audience this real self-attuning to the minutest detail, that they would really become active participants in the viewing. I don't think that any more.

G.R.L. Did you think of yourself as being objective?

E.P. No.

G.R.L. Did you see that as a problem?

E.P. Well yeah, that was a very important problem. I've really changed the way I feel a lot. Back then I thought the nice thing about cinéma-vérité was in the film-maker making a statement. He also is showing his evidence for his statement, so if you look at it that way, the thing about objective or subjective becomes a little wrong—that's not the right way of looking at it. You can have evidence for a position, the evidence can be correct evidence—and the position can still be wrong. Well, here the film-maker was presenting his evidence, making his thesis about the film, about the subject, and the audience, because it shares with the film-maker his evidence, can come to other conclusions. So it was copping out on the part of the film-maker to hide behind the stance of objectivity.

G.R.L. Are you thinking partially of a cop-out in political terms?

E.P. No, no. In any terms. As a matter of fact, in the editing and to some extent in what the film-maker chooses to shoot, there's a whole lot of choice. How you parse the world is very important. The image that TV shows of the world is very important in forming a person's opinion of what that world is like. They can't show everything. They have to choose. So the film-maker had to take a position, and the way he structured his evidence gave his position—whether he meant it to or not; but since the film itself, from which he edited, had a degree of accessibility to all of the kinds of objectivity, other people could see that film and could say, "The film-maker felt such and such about such and such, but I feel otherwise about it because look at what he did there, look at what he did there."

G.R.L. Did you want to make it clear in the film how you felt?

E.P. Yeah. Like in *Black Natchez,* which is into something really very nice. On one hand we had this early SDS political philosophy of let the people decide, don't manipulate people. The role of the organizer was to put people in condition to decide their own future, but he wasn't to coerce them. The worst thing was to manipulate. That was a real crime. Somehow this fits in very nicely with the kind of cinéma-vérité philosophy where the film-maker goes in, doesn't manipulate reality, tries to capture reality as if he weren't there. So for example in the American tradition of cinéma-vérité the interview is considered not cinéma-vérité because what's an interview but a kind of camera-created reality? The interview wouldn't exist without the interviewer or the camera crew. Well, during the editing, where we felt our presence hadn't affected the action, that it would have occurred even had we not been there, we saw ourselves as non-manipulators, capturing the reality in which, for example, somebody like Charles Evers gets judged harshly because he tries to manipulate the crowd, because he doesn't let people make up their own minds for themselves.

G.R.L. Your point of view about that is you like to keep yourself clear of making judgments about what happens?

E.P. Yeah.

G.R.L. In the shooting or the editing, or both?

E.P. Both. There are lots of choices of shots that we could use. This is a really good example, I think: it was very crowded, and some of the shots were taken of Evers—this is in a particular scene—where I would stay two feet away from him, and I could hardly move. Now there's one part where his head is partially out of the frame and he's saying, "We're going to tell you when to march and how to march." Now, as he says "how to march," his head comes down full on the frame. Well, because he's so close and the wide-angle lens distorts his face, he seems like a very powerful figure—and it comes not through ideas but through authority itself that he's convincing people to do something. There's a kind of happenstance of my position. I didn't have a choice—it worked at what we were trying to say. Yet, we had a choice in editing of using that or not using that.

There's another time when he tells people who disagree with him that they should leave and he points his finger. The camera goes down his arm and it fills the frame with his finger. Well, behind his finger is the Catholic church, and then the camera pans down just as a police car goes by. There are these three symbols of authority coming into the frame at the same time. There in the shooting was the consciousness of it, but there was also the choice of using it or not, and we had a discussion about whether to use that even though the ideas were just what we wanted, because it seemed manipulated to have these three elements in the picture though it comes out of a continuous shot. It looked heavy. That was the phrase we used to use, too heavy. That was partially because we were playing two things against each other, I guess. On one hand we recognized the cinema as illusion, but we knew people didn't take it to be illusion, kind of took it to be hard and fast fact. We wanted to prod, to encourage those feelings of this is objective fact. At the same time we wanted to take advantage of the illusionistic aspects.

An example of the kind of illusionistic aspect I'm talking about is that every time you use one camera—and we've only used one camera, on some level we're committed to that—when you make a cut within a sequence you've actually cut out time. Whenever there's a cut that means real time has been cut out. Well, we always used to be very careful that in the sequences all our cuts were matched cuts, meaning they appeared as though time wasn't cut out, they seemed to be a continuous flow of reality. As a matter of fact, we've always looked at the cut in a cinéma-vérité sequence as a way of emphasizing or pushing forward time, to hasten the pacing. That's us manipulating the way things happened to say what we want to say—to make people take it to be continuous. Lots of film-makers who saw the film said, "You shot that with more than one camera, didn't you?" And we hadn't. It was because we were very careful about that level of editing, making all those cuts appear to be continuous, cuts where we change angles, stuff like that.

G.R.L. Did you do most of the shooting?

E.P. Yeah, I did all the shooting and David did all the sound. We do the editing together.

G.R.L. How long did it take to edit?

E.P. Well, ninety thousand feet of film is over forty hours, so it takes a long time, plus when we came back we didn't have enough money to finish the film, and we had lots of debts, which meant that we had to spend a lot of time ourselves trying to raise money, and a lot of that was in nickels and dimes, very small contributions. Plus we couldn't afford to have the sound transferred. We had to rely on people's good graces to let us have access to their equipment. It took a very long time to get all the sound transferred—we could only do it at night, and things like that. In addition, when we first came back we really didn't know how to use a moviola. A friend of ours showed us how to use it. It finally took us thirteen to fourteen months to edit the film. Right now, I think the film would have taken us three months to edit. Also, we used to argue about every single cut. We used to work sixteen hours a day, six to seven days a week, and what it really was was about nine or ten hours of good hard work and six to eight hours of just arguing about the cinematic, political, personal meaning of every cut, every sequence we had in there.

G.R.L. You must have really learned about making films.

E.P. Oh yeah, right. We discussed every kind of possibility, whether chronology should be straight and true or if we could use theatrical film devices like the flashback, what should we do about point of view, what should we do about narration. One of the problems that has plagued us right from the beginning is how do you start a cinéma-vérité film. You, as a film-maker, have a tremendous amount of information when you look at anything: you've gone and met people, you've heard about what you're filming or you've talked to people about it, you've read about it, whatever. Now, how do you communicate all that to the viewer? Especially given that we just hated narration—the third-person objective narrator just seemed like anathema.

G.R.L. I don't remember. Did you use any narration in that?

E.P. No. What we did in *Black Natchez* was to use the main character, Jackson, the black barber, to give the background comments. But lots of the things he says are not totally true, they're always kind of shaded, so they become an element in the film equal to what somebody says in the film. Like a guy stands up and says, "The only people who should be on this committee should be taxpaying voting citizens." Now you don't take that to be necessarily true. Similarly, the narration—we called it a commentary track—took on that same element, an equal element to what the people say in the film. Like the narrator says he wasn't at a meeting, he doesn't know too much about it, but this is what he heard, or he gives us an anecdote which gives us as much about himself as about the film. Plus we did use the equivalent of the third-person narrator in that we had a beginning crawl on the film.

G.R.L. But presumably also the barber's statements were in effect a reflection of what you wanted him to say.

E.P. Well, the nice thing about working with cinéma-vérité is that a lot of the limitations or mistakes turn out to be the most beautiful things. Like in the way that whole visual quality of cinéma-vérité at first is very hard to take; but sometimes it becomes very pleasant, you see things that you've never seen before. Instead of these very carefully composed images you often get these very haphazardly composed images which often reveal more.

G.R.L. What happened with the release of *Black Natchez?*

E.P. Well, the way we got out of debt was two ways. One, partially from fund raising, but we also got a foundation grant and then we sold—

G.R.L. From what foundation?

E.P. All the Rockefellers have about three hundred different foundations, and it was like a very small one that had a very small amount of money from the various Rockefellers. Then we sold the TV rights to NET Journal.

G.R.L. Can I ask how much you got?

E.P. Yeah, we got ten thousand dollars. That was for three years on American TV, which for a black and white film may have been the highest they paid at the time for an independently produced film.

G.R.L. It's about fifty minutes?

E.P. The actual film was sixty-one and a half minutes. That was part of our—I don't know what you want to call it, a kind of adolescence.

G.R.L. You weren't going to make it less than an hour?

E.P. No. We decided, well, it's a sixty-one-and-a-half-minute film, fuck the media. If they don't like that length that's their problem. Ultimately we cut it down to fifty-eight–forty, which is the kind of standard. It wasn't that we were saying fuck the media, it was that we really just didn't care. We were making this film for the movement on some level. As a matter of fact, when we had to cut out the three additional minutes, we liked that much better. In a way, somebody should say to every film-maker, after he finishes a film, "Cut out three minutes," or five minutes.

G.R.L. Or wait six months before you release it.

E.P. Unfortunately you can't do that, given the way the industry is set up right now.

G.R.L. What did the film cost all together?

E.P. It ended up costing in the low twenties.

G.R.L. Have you sold it elsewhere?

E.P. We distributed it for a while. It took an incredible amount of time to distribute just one film. If you were distributing twenty films it would have taken exactly the same length of time. So then we gave it to Leacock-Pennebaker to distribute, and they did very badly with it. So I don't know what we're going to do now, but we're going to take it away from them.

G.R.L. So you haven't really made any money from it?

E.P. No. When we distributed it in Boston, we often distributed it free. Maybe we might have made a little money, but not very much, nothing worth talking about.

G.R.L. Were you able to support yourselves?

E.P. No, no. Not at all. Nobody got paid salary on the film, except toward the end one of the assistant editors got something like thirty dollars a week. Yeah, that was like a real struggle. We also made a decision not to work for other people. That's really a very difficult thing. We have worked for other people, David as a sound man and I as a cameraman, stuff like that. Almost all of the experiences have been like really terrible, and that's not because of the people we worked for, who were always like really very nice, but just the whole idea of working for somebody else we both found obnoxious on some level. It wasn't our kind of perception, we were using these tools we had learned for other people. I remember just feeling kind of shattered as a person in some ways when I would shoot for other people and I would have to do things I didn't want to do. They really weren't bad, just . . . I'd much rather be a plumber than try to do somebody else's shooting. When somebody calls up and says, "Can you do a week of shooting?" I would say no unless it was a project that I was really into or needed money very badly.

G.R.L. Okay. You'd finished *Black Natchez* and you wanted to make films. What happened next?

E.P. PBL was starting—Public Broadcasting Laboratory. They had just gotten what was supposed to be ten million dollars from The Ford Foundation. All these people from CBS who all their lives had felt that they'd been tremendously limited by working for the network—with all that that meant in relationship to advertising—were now going to leave CBS and instead do good educational television programing. Mostly it came from Fred Friendly leaving CBS over the fact that CBS didn't broadcast the Kennan testimony before the Fulbright Committee and put on instead the eleventh rerun of *I Love Lucy*. Essentially McGeorge Bundy, who was running The Ford Foundation, and Friendly worked out this way to make educational television meaningful. The thought was to take people from the networks who really knew where things were at, but who were tremendously limited in what they were able to do in the way of controversy, and you put them in ETV and all of a sudden you'd get a totally new concept of what television was about. What they hadn't realized was that people who worked for the network and had censored their beings for so long were very limited in the possibilities they could think of. They had given up controversy for so long that whenever they were faced with controversy, they were tremendously scared by it. In any case, what happened was that PBL programing was tremendously bland and uninteresting. But when they started off, Av Westin, who is Executive Producer of ABC News, was the guy who was to become director of PBL. About the same time, people at WGBH, a local ETV station in Boston, wanted us to do a series of films for them.

G.R.L. On the basis of *Black Natchez?*

E.P. Right. They had said, "What do you want to do films about?" We decided we wanted to do films about the American family. We wanted to do a film about an Appalachian family, about a black ghetto family, about an Indian family, etc. So we wrote up this whole proposal, and at the same time PBL came around and we were presented to PBL as GBH's bright young film-makers.

G.R.L. You had stopped trying to get your degree in philosophy? You never got it?

E.P. No, I never did get it. I hadn't done any serious philosophy since 1963.

G.R.L. Was David also an academic?

E.P. No, David had gone to Harvard, but he had dropped out just before he graduated and then went into a craft thing, opened up this leather business. Both of us were really products of the fifties in very important ways. Right now I'm thirty-two and David is about thirty, I guess. That's important.

G.R.L. This is one of the reasons I wanted to talk to you—as kind of representative of this age, this time.

E.P. Okay, so PBL. Av Westin came in and he talked to everybody at GBH, and he comes out with, "This is going to be hard-hitting programing, stuff that's never been on TV before, and we're going to put it on. Anything that's controversial, we're going to jump on it. We're going to talk about American cars and we're going to relate how we're going to rate them for safety, and if Ford comes out badly"—remember Ford was funding them—"we're going to say it. We're going to bring on George Wallace and Elijah Muhammad, and have them talk to each other." I don't know if he said that specifically, but all kinds of things like that. Fred Friendly also gave a talk to GBH which was very similar to that. This was early '67.

[. . .]

E.P. PBL. You want to hear about that whole business? Okay. We were the first major project that was funded. Consequently all the anxieties they had about starting out got laid on our project. Ultimately we were really getting the fuzzy end of the lollipop when it came to their willingness to engage in controversy. The first sign was when they said that we'd convinced them verbally, and they would take our word for it that we had an interesting subject. When we started out we just said we wanted to do a film on the hippies, whatever that meant, on the West Coast, and if we found a subject that was mutually acceptable, they would take our word as being very important. Then they would give us the total amount of money, which was to be around eighty thousand dollars. An hour color. But they would first start out giving us ten thousand, and that would give us a chance to shoot some footage; then we could get a confirmation on the phone that it was okay and we would get the rest of the money.

Now, we had decided that if we had the total amount of money and we didn't take our salaries—or very much of our salaries—we could buy essentially all the equipment rather than rent it. Buying new equipment sort of meant autonomy. But we were also in this funny position of only having ten thousand dollars, right? If we start to rent the equipment for a month it becomes prohibitively expensive and we couldn't buy it, so we decided to buy the equipment and take a chance that we were going to get the rest of the money. They assured us, by the way, that if we didn't do this film, we were going to do another film.

Actually, once we were out in California there was a choice between two films. A film on this rural commune or a film on Country Joe and the Fish. We decided it would be kind of a cop-out to do a film on a rock group personality. That had been the tradition of the whole American cinéma-vérité, a film on Bob Dylan, Jane Fonda, Eddie Sachs. . . . It was in this old tradition of filming personalities and celebrities—we thought that was kind of a cheap way of making cinéma-vérité palatable. I feel a little differently about it now. I think cinéma-vérité has done something very important with celebrities. Like I think the Maysles' film on Marlon Brando shows cinéma-vérité revealing a kind of reality we're not supposed to see, which is very nice.

G.R.L. It demystifies.

E.P. Yeah, it demystifies. Or say even in the film *Jane*. I think that's one of the finest celebrity films made. You get to see all these levels of reality—theatrical reality, cinéma-vérité reality, the reality of Jane Fonda's kind of self-created image. It was a Drew film and has a lot of Drew problems—you know, the heavy narration track creating false conflict, will or won't the review . . . ?

Okay. We started to do the film on this rural commune.[1] Since we had a limited amount of money, we made this really awful mistake of assuming that if we felt anything was repeatable, we wouldn't film it now, we would wait until we got all the money. We would only film kind of unique events. Well, in some sense, everything is unique, and we made the mistake of thinking of the commune as stable so that we could film communal activities later. Anyway, once the shit starts hitting the fan in the film, we never could go back to the commune,[2] and consequently we had to make up for a whole very important part of the film in some way. This really influenced ways of cutting everything, and it would have been just much nicer to have this footage that we normally would have had had we started out with all the money.

PBL had undergone some administrative changes, and ultimately I had to go to New York in the middle of the film to show them some of the footage we'd shot. Now the really difficult thing was that the film that we were now sure we wanted to do wasn't contained in this early footage—it takes a certain amount of time to get film back from the lab and synch it up. In any case, we finally convinced them to let us have the rest of the money, but I began to get very nervous about their willingness to show the film. There were little things that were maybe a little mistrustful, so what we did was, we bought all the non-TV rights back from them.

G.R.L. For how much?

E.P. For like thirteen thousand dollars, which meant that they were giving us like sixty-five thousand for the film—they were willing to just buy TV rights for half a year.

G.R.L. When the commune broke up at the very beginning of the film, did you think about not making that film, finding another commune?

E.P. Oh no, because we thought that here was the very conflict we were looking for, the leader of the commune undergoing this whole problem.

G.R.L. A happy accident.

E.P. Yeah, right. That turned out to be good. Actually I should go through a lot of the editing thing. First conflict came

[1] This is *One Step Away*.
[2] The commune broke up a few days after shooting began.

up was a discussion of what to do with all the curse words. It was decided they would be bleeped, and there would be an announcement before about censorship, FCC regulations on the use of curse words and like it was up to people to pressure the FCC to change those rulings. Actually it's a very complicated legal problem—and that's not clearly the problem. In the meantime stations like BGH have used motherfuck on programing and stuff like that. PBL was very nervous, because ultimately the right to decide on what was to be played rested with the local ETV station—it was very limiting. Southern stations and some northern ones are often controlled by school boards. Very limited controversy.

G.R.L. You weren't willing to go along with that?

E.P. No, we thought that was disgusting. One argument wasn't to bleep them but just cut them out. We said if they're not going to play those words we want them bleeped even if it makes the film look funny, because we were pissed off, right?

Then there came this problem. A very important scene in the film that we wanted to use to establish Harry's and Rickie's relationship[3] involved what Joshua, Rickie's child, should call shit, what should he call peepee. We decided that we were going to cut two versions of the film in case there was any kind of problem with TV. They said that if we didn't use the word "shit," words like "crap" were all right. Well, we were very lucky because Rickie starts out in the actual scene by saying how Joshua made some duty on the floor, then Harry says you shouldn't call it duty, you should call it shit. She objects to that, and he says, "Well, why doesn't he call it crap?" Then they go on to a whole argument about crap and duty and all sorts of things. Well, we could cut the sequence so we didn't have to use the word "shit," just use the word "crap," which they said was okay. And it was important, because in this one scene, which is a very funny scene, you get this whole thing about Harry trying to acculturate Rickie into the ways of hippiedom, and you get Rickie ending up by saying, "Well, I thought you said people could do their own thing. I think it's such a cute word," and you get that contradiction in the hippe's need to acculturate yet at the same time they're opposed to the ideology of letting people do their own thing. It was very terse, just the kind of sequence we wanted, and they said it was okay.

Then there was like this other argument. In the middle of this scene Rickie picks up Josh and wipes him. We had a particular liaison with PBL; he was a really nice guy but he was beholden

[3] An unmarried couple, the two main characters in *One Step Away*.

to PBL—they paid his money. I had understood him to say, at the beginning, that it was okay if Rickie went wipe, wipe, whereas in the actual scene she goes wipe, wipe, wipe, wipe, wipe. Right? Then when he saw a cut he said, "No, she can't do any wiping." I said, "Well, you said it was okay if she went wipe, wipe. How about if she just goes wipe?" Like two grown men sat in the car for about an hour arguing about this. Ultimately we left in wipe, wipe, only to find out later that the whole scene had been deleted—but I'll get into that in a minute.

In any case, PBL had had about half a year of programing when we'd finished the film, and it had been very dull programing, tremendously non-controversial, people had really just taken the easy way out, and so instead of being beholden to advertisers, they were beholden to future jobs. There was a general feeling that PBL was going to collapse and these people would have to go back to media to find jobs. Well, people get used to large salaries, and it's very hard for them to think of taking a salary cut, so everybody was planning out his own future—for when PBL collapsed.

So we brought the film in and showed it to a programing board. These were all the executive producers of PBL—four of the five, actually—and they looked at the film and they just loved it. It was really incredible. They stood up and said, "Wow, this film is going to change our whole image. This is really incredible." One guy stands up and says, "I want to say something. That's not only a good television film, that's a good film, like good films in movie theaters—I've never seen anything like this before." So we walked out of there on a real ego trip, really high. They really loved the film.

There was also some discussion of what to do with the curse words. Next thing we hear is that Av Westin looked at the film and kind of liked it but thought it needed some changes. Then we get a call from Joe Russin, our liaison, that Westin deleted the shit-duty scene. We were really angry. Then we get another call—he changed the placing of another scene to another part of the film, and we didn't know what to do. It wasn't clear whether he could do that legally, but we were told that if we objected to it that we would probably get blackballed and all kinds of things like that. We were also told we could withdraw credit. In other words, the film would be shown but our names wouldn't be on it, and we were thinking of doing that. Then Russin calls us up and says, "Look, Westin doesn't think you can just bring these people into America's living room. You need some kind of excuse, some way of framing the film, so what he's done, he's gotten these two sociology professors from the University of California and they're going to say something about hippies before and after the film." The film was kind of down on hippies and these two sociologists were kind of academic pro-hippie.

Then we went to Russin's office. We didn't want to have anything to do with the film at the time, we weren't even talking about our film because we were both physically nauseous about it and really happy that we had bought back the rights, because we could get a clear release on the film, whatever film we wanted. Well, David happened to look at Russin's desk and there was the script of our film, and right in between scenes in the film are these academics talking about hippies. Russin said, "Oh, that was just an idea somebody had," and then he called us up a week later and said, "They've cut in these academics actually into the film. It's not so bad if you're used to looking at a film on TV because they act like commercial breaks." We said, "Bullshit! people will think that's part of the film. How can they tell the difference?" And like these academics were saying these incredibly stupid things, like, "This film is not about typical hippies because Harry and Rickie aren't middle class. They come from working-class backgrounds and hippies are middle class." Then about five sections later they say, "Harry and Rickie aren't typical hippies because they are middle class. All their values are middle class"—which, by the way, was an actual theme of the film: how middle-class culture has inculcated itself very much into hippie life.

That went on until we didn't know what to do. Russin kept telling us how Westin is really nervous about the film, and he thinks that if he shows it a bomb will explode and all kinds of shit will hit the fan. Plus they had a legal adviser look at the film to tell them it was okay. Then they brought in another guy —someone named Aleinikoff; he walks in, looks at the film, has a viscera reaction and says it can't be shown on television. He thinks the film is disgusting. Plus there are fifty-six felonies shown, of which the film-makers are culpable for twenty-eight, or something like that. He listed about sixty-eight objections to the film. Supposedly there's this really tense battle where he would list his objections and somebody would say, "Is that legal or personal?" and most of the time he said it was personal. Anyway, there started to come rumbles from the legal part of Westin's mind. Finally they were going to show it on such and such a date. After all this shit. We had no idea what version they were going to show. Then they decide the Friday before the Sunday that they're not going to show it. They're going to show it next week. Well, they did that for three weeks in a row.

G.R.L. This was going to be shown on what station?

E.P. On ETV, Channel 2 in Boston, by network hookup of ETV stations, but different channels in different cities. So it kept being delayed. Then Westin showed it to three members of the editorial board that PBL had at that time, which is mostly academic liberals—the editor, ex-editor of *Harper's*, stuff like that. Supposedly he got three opinions. One was the film is obscene, the second that it was in bad taste and the third—the only half-complimentary one—that the film was too strong for the home TV set. So Westin, in great part because of conservatism, ultimately decided not to show the film. Wanted to avoid controversy. In the meantime the TV rights lapsed, there was a shake-up in PBL and some guy from the Johnson administration came to run it who didn't know anything about TV programing or media but was a good administrator. He saw part of the film and supposedly said something like, "This is one of the best films I've seen," and somebody said, "You've only seen three films." In any case, he was thinking of showing the film again, but then all the legal problems got raised, and we were kind of very uninterested in the whole thing, so it just lapsed away.

G.R.L. The film was never shown then?

E.P. Oh no. It was never shown on television. We were very sick about the whole thing. First of all, I think with most film-makers, after they finish a film, they feel that they've paid their debt to whomever they owed that debt. They don't want to cope with the whole distribution problem, and we especially didn't want to. We were told that Leacock Pennebaker was interested in distributing films like this and we went over there and they gave us a whole kind of hype job which we believed, and we didn't want to see any other distributors, so we gave them the film. They turned out to be really very bad distributors. That, by the way, has nothing to do with Ricky or Penny.[4] It's the whole kind of bureaucratic superstructure there. They were never willing to put up any money or effort in any way into 16mm. distribution. We in some ways and they even more so were not willing to take the chance of blowing it up to 35 and trying for 35 distribution. At first that's what we wanted to do, but then we became a little wary of that.

[4] Richard Leacock and D. A. Pennebaker.

G.R.L. What finally happened?

E.P. They distributed it for a couple of years and now we've just decided we're going to take it away from them.

G.R.L. Did you get releases from everybody in *One Step Away?*

E.P. Yeah.

G.R.L. Did you pay anybody?

E.P. I don't think so. If we did, we paid a dollar, but I don't think we paid anybody.

G.R.L. Did you pay expenses, for example, like for food?

E.P. Yeah, we bought food at times. Not that much actually. At first they wanted us to become members of the commune. We said you couldn't film your own thing, we needed this distance. That was very important, by the way, that whole concept. One of the reasons we changed, or I changed in a lot of my thoughts in relationship to cinéma-vérité was the kind of filming that we were doing demanded a strange sort of "egolessness" or voyeurism, since we were committed to filming a situation as it happened independently of our presence. That meant we couldn't interject our personalities in any way, and we had to become as small a part of that environment as possible. That does very strange things to your head, and also affects your perceptions of things. Personally it fit in very nicely with a kind of academic non-involvement that I had at that time in my life. I was always kind of escaping from my emotional self.

G.R.L. Do you think the camera, you guys being there influenced events, people, that they acted differently because you were there?

E.P. I get into a lot of arguments with Ricky about this. Like we both teach this course together and we have to give our advice to the students. We both have very different approaches. If he's doing a film about Lenny Bernstein, he'll swim with Bernstein one day, then he'll film a little of Bernstein, and he'll put down the camera, and they'll chitty-chat for a little while, then he'll pick up the camera. That's one approach. Or say in the Maysles' Levine film, *Showman,* this guy relates on the telephone how he just got fired by Joe Levine. The Maysles brothers asked at that point if they could film him relating it to a friend. Well, that whole concept is just what we didn't do.

What we did was, before we started the film, we explained to people the level of intimacy that we wanted, asked them how they felt about this, in fact, gave them typical situations, said that if ultimately they didn't want us to show things, they could tell us afterward but they shouldn't tell us before the scene, that we would try to remain as uninvolved as possible, would set the action as little as possible, and essentially not become tremendously friendly with people, really try to be in the background. The same if we were doing the hypothetical Bernstein film. I think that ultimately leads to our influencing the action less. That's what we were interested in. But it also depends on what you mean by action, because there are all different levels of action, and Ricky is interested in one thing in his films and we're interested in another thing in our films.

G.R.L. At the end of the film Harry goes off to hitchhike to the east coast. Did you set that up?

E.P. No. We never set anything up, really. Sometimes we fudge in scenes and sometimes we create things to make it appear something has happened when it really didn't happen. Always very minor things and always things which we think we can justify in terms of a higher-level truth.

G.R.L. For example?

E.P. I can't think of anything offhand, but like say we've missed an important scene. Sometimes there's another scene whereby cutting it properly it takes the place of the scene we missed. It's like the Maysles have this notion that what truth is is what they got on film. So when they edit, they're kind of committed to just what they have. Well, that's a bullshit notion, because that's not what the truth is. Truth is a much more complicated thing, and why, because something didn't come out on film, either because you weren't there, camera fuck-up or what, why should that determine truth or not truth?

G.R.L. Two things. One, I think the Maysles have changed from that point of view a bit. The other is that if you are in effect manipulating reality to present what you see as a fundamental truth about something, I would prefer that you let the audience know that this is your bias, your point of view, that this isn't pure objective reality—or rather that you're not pretending it is.

E.P. In *One Step Away* we tried to do that, to very clearly say this is an edited film, this is our bias. We kind of said that the footage is the objective reality—a kind of objective reality accessible to everybody, but as a matter of fact we manipulated it a tremendous amount. We used all kinds of obviously manipulative devices, like the film was cut very anecdotally, punch lines with which we wrapped up sequences of events. There are titles in the film that act in a way that Eisenstein understood titles—some kind of montage in relationship to image—and also as a way of saying that we want you to look at the way we've parsed this flow. We also use those titles as a way of overcoming a lot of narration problems, like identifying people, stuff like that, and to give a distancing effect—à la Brecht, as alienation devices—where we felt we wanted people to stay outside of that flow and look at it, rather than being caught up into it. We still criticize the theater for purging people, making them feel moral because they felt the right emotions, then letting them go out the same old slobs as when they walked in.

It would be nice never to fake anything, never to fudge it, but it would be nice also to never have any bad footage, never have any camera fuck-ups. But the question is what do you do when faced with these things? Now, there are two different kinds of problems. In the Levine film, *Showman*, the Maysles did one thing which I felt was really awful. Levine walks out on the balcony, looks outside and then we cut to a picture, shot from the balcony, of a woman walking along in a bikini. We cut back up to Levine walking in going like, "Whew," kind of the film-maker's little dirty joke—but it was all created. I take it that there was no evidence within the film that that really happened as opposed to being kind of an Eisensteinian montage construct.

That's one level of manipulation which I don't think is right, unless it's made explicit—like I think in *One Step Away* we made those things explicit. It was clear, or meant to be clear to people that this was an edited film, unlike *Black Natchez*, which purported to be a kind of reality flow. But what do you do if you're missing an important scene? Do you use another scene which does a lot of the same things, but actually didn't happen within the real chronology? Well, you often have to decide whether the distortion involved outweighs the good to be gained, and that's a choice you make. Sometimes it does, sometimes it doesn't.

There's not one film-maker I have ever heard of who hasn't made chronology changes, used shock to make it appear as though scenes happened in one place when they actually happened in another. It depends on how serious you think those distortions are. What happens if you lack a cutaway, you need a shot of somebody reacting and you just don't have it in that scene and you use something that looks perfectly okay from another scene? That is a distortion.

G.R.L. Okay. After you had done all this hard work on *One Step Away* and had what you thought was a good film—and which I thought was a good film—what happened next?

E.P. PBL decided that they were going to do this program where they asked five film-makers to do a film on the state of the country, and they could do whatever they wanted to do. The film would be like fifteen to twenty-five minutes long. The only conditions were that it was in color, that it had a sound track and that the first shot started off on the steps of the Capitol. Other than that you could do whatever you wanted to do. The initiative for this program ultimately came from a new cultural affairs guy at PBL, David Oppenheim. He was going to be executive producer on the film.

G.R.L. It's really ironic, kind of absolutely crazy, and perhaps indicative of the whole bloody mess that they give you money to make a film, decide it's too radical, don't show it and then hire you again to make another film.

E.P. Well, yeah, but you see . . . within all these institutions there are a lot of conflicts. Sometimes one part is holding sway, and sometimes another part is holding sway. It was also basically that the staff of PBL really liked our work. It was just the kind of high-up people who were afraid, in all kinds of ways, and I also think some of them had genuine reservations in their ideology.

Anyway, one of the five film-makers was Ricky Leacock, then they had the personal film-maker of H. L. Hunt, the oil millionaire from Texas—very right wing; and then they had Jonas Mekas, LeRoi Jones and David and me.[5] We were really put in a very funny position here. Somehow everything we'd been doing we'd always judged in terms of how much autonomy we had, how much freedom we had, and now somebody says, basically, name your budget and do whatever you want. We had heard about all these Hollywood directors, about the studios, the system where they could never do what they wanted, and then when they all had a chance to do what they wanted, they had nothing to do. We were really afraid of that, and wanted to understand what that freedom meant to us and how we were going to react to it. Then all of a sudden, all the unfreedom things started to come in. Like there was a time limit, right? We had to have the film out in two months or three months. That really affects content in all kinds of ways—how much you can think about things, mull them over, make false starts, stuff like that. Also, it wasn't free—it had to be fifteen to twenty-five minutes, and it had to appear on the tube. What kind of internal limitations does that put on us? Later we would hear from somebody who had never had one idea censored at CBS because he had always done the censoring himself.

So then we said, look, we can't just say we're free. We're not free. We're making this film not only for TV but for PBL,

[5] Pincus' (and Neuman's) film for this program was *Portrait of a McCarthy Supporter.*

which is part of educational TV, reaching a limited number of people, and we have to respond to that fact in some way. Also, they were asking us to do a film because we were young and political. And why did they choose us? Why should the media decide for the movement who its representatives should be? And at this time in New York, a group of political film-makers started Newsreel, and we were wondering why PBL didn't want to cope with them. Well, because from all kinds of professional points of view they were "incompetent," given this notion of TV professionalism. Well, we decided right away what we weren't going to do. They obviously expected us to do something about the radical movement, but we . . .

The way the film evolved was very much like a Platonic dialogue, all the early false solutions are incorporated in the final form, so let me go through the various stages. First we decided the film was going to be purely about being a bourgeois, and we were going to do an event. What we were going to do was just have a piece of shit on the screen for fifteen minutes, sitting on the White House steps with a bum sound track, and then we were going to ask for twenty thousand dollars. The film would be the events surrounding that, all the shit we would get. Well, that idea lasted about two minutes.

We went on to the next stage. We had decided that what the society did—kind of a Marcusian idea—was offer the framework of freedom but none of the content of freedom, and as a matter of fact we really weren't free, both because of the limitations we had inside ourselves, and because we couldn't do anything we wanted to do on television. For example, we couldn't show two animals fucking, two human beings fucking. We couldn't say motherfuck, right? A lot of people use that word as part of their everyday vocabulary. What does it mean that the only kinds of people that can appear on television are the people who are censoring that use of the word or never use it? So we decided that we'd make a film about all the things you couldn't do on television. How do you do that? Well, they had said they wanted a rough idea of what the film was about so they would know how to package it in relationship to the other four films. So we make a list of all the things we couldn't do on television and tell them that's what the film is about and they say you can't do that. Then we clearly establish in the dialogue that we thought we had a budget of like twenty thousand to thirty thousand dollars—that was very important to young film-makers like us. We would then begin to hedge on our position and come out with a film which was acceptable to them, kind of laying out that whole censorship thing in an objective fashion.

The important point is that what happened is a natural evolvement of our ideas. We, the film-makers, had ended up as subjects in the film, and that came out very naturally, very unself-consciously. At that time there was this guy doing a film for German TV about young film-makers, and he had asked us if we would be in the film. That idea never panned out, but we got the idea of saying that these were young German film-makers making a film about us, and that would explain why people were filming us, why we went to talk to Av Westin and Oppenheim about our ideas for this film. Then we figured that Westin was just too smart for that. He would never fall for it. So we decided instead that we would get a friend to film us while we called him up on a tapped telephone. We would give him our idea of what we wanted to put in the film, then he would say no, we would change our ideas, and then we would just present that to him as our film.

The first thing was to make a list of the things we wanted to put on, and we began to hedge right there. We started thinking, well, if you really say far-out things to which people who watch TV are going to say, "Of course they shouldn't put that on," then . . . So what we wanted to do was find things that would make the audience flash on the fact that these are things they never saw on TV yet were the kind of things they thought should be on TV. That kind of limitation was very serious in our thoughts. In any case, the idea was that we were going to let people talk in the language of the ghetto, in hippie language, in a natural flow of talk use the words you never hear on television. We were going to talk about how people like Walter Cronkite could purport to be giving objective newscasting whereas as a matter of fact he would say to an audience how he knew that Johnson was lying yet never say that on television. Then we were going to bring up that whole thing with Daley where Cronkite criticized him for a whole complex of reasons[6] and how they finally got together on it. We were going to point out the relationship between TV, government—we had a whole list of stuff like that. A form of muckraking.

So we get Westin on the telephone while we're actually filming it, and he says, "Okay, you can show all that." I was kind of nonplused and didn't know what to say—kind of had my mouth

[6] This is in reference to Mayor Richard J. Daley of Chicago, the brutality of police in dealing with demonstrators at the 1968 National Democratic Convention and Cronkite's outburst on television against Daley and the police.

open. Later on we talked to somebody at PBL who said that if we tried to get that stuff on it never would have gotten on, but on that level they weren't going to exert any censorship at that point, they would exert it later.

Then we decided that what we had to do was—we were still into this voyeuristic thing—or what this country needed were some Yippie happenings staged for film. One was that we were going to ask Hershey—the guy who's head of the draft—for an interview, and being PBL we could get an interview, right? We'd ask him to stand under the lights, and then one of the crew was going to sidle up to him, rub his body against Hershey's and start singing "I'm a Yankee Doodle Dandy." That was going to be the whole event. Then David was working on this really complicated plot where we were going to tear-gas Mayor Daley and not get arrested for it. It seems incredible. And we were going to stage these happenings all over. We figured out our budget for that. It was really expensive and they wouldn't give us that amount of money.

We decided we still had to do a film about liberalism purporting to offer freedom and actually offering no freedom. But we were in a bind given that perception. As a matter of fact, no matter what we did, they were going to frame us in such a way that . . . Like if we did a really way-out film they would say, "Now we are going to hear from the crazy radicals of the left." It's a form of a zoo story. You can look at the most wild thing, but only behind bars. Well, the bars here were the TV set itself, and the way it was going to be framed or programed, packaged was, here are five film-makers with idiosyncratic points of view and people can look at this wild animal—no matter what we did. Given this kind of perception, we decided that we needed a parody of liberalism itself which would indirectly relate to the media by its appearing on TV.

At this time there was a whole phenomenon in the McCarthy campaign,[7] lots of kids thinking that they could work for really deep-seated change within the political system. There was a lot of discussion in radical literature about what to do with the McCarthy kids, how could you radicalize them and show them—McCarthy had already been defeated—in the face of that defeat that instead of continuing to work in the system or not doing any political work, that they should think in terms of radical political work as the only solution. Radical being understood as

[7] Senator Eugene McCarthy's attempt to win the Democratic presidential nomination in 1968.

working outside the system. What we had started to do were these confrontation-interviews where we'd get two people and they would interview one another. We had these really weird combinations worked out. Like we had this drunk artist and an academic Marxist philosopher doing one of them. Most of them were very unsuccessful. Actually the one with David and his girl friend was very successful.

G.R.L. You shot them?

E.P. Yeah, we shot them. They got into very interesting arguments about themselves, but other than that it was a real failure. Then we discussed this idea of doing a film on my father-in-law, who had as a matter of fact supported McCarthy, and who was a hypocritical businessman. All you had to do was put him on the screen and young people would immediately dislike him, whereas it turned out that people—again people over a certain age—look at him and think he's a fine, happy, upstanding citizen, don't see anything wrong with him, and young people think he's funny, ridiculous. So we did a film on him—*Portrait of a McCarthy Supporter*.

G.R.L. Do you think the film at least makes its point, say, to people under thirty?

E.P. No, a lot of complicated things . . . We showed it to the people at PBL and they liked it, and one of them commented, "Boy, the liberals are really going to hate this thing," and we looked at these guys, because who the fuck did they think they were if not liberals? We realized that their perception is that they're above that whole political system, they don't perceive themselves as actually being part of a functioning system, they think of themselves as objectively out of it and looking down on it. They don't feel themselves to be liberal or not, they really think of themselves as objective in some kind of way. Well, what happened was they had people on the show to make introductions, about a one- or two-minute tape. We really objected to that kind of framing, and we figured that would be part of saying how we were young and radical. We decided, again as a way of escaping caging, that what we were going to put on tape was a quote from Paul himself—

G.R.L. From whom?

E.P. Paul, he's my father-in-law, the subject of the film. The quote goes like this: I say, "David, where do you think this country is going?" and he says, "I think it's going to the rainbow's end, more things for more people"—exactly what Paul says in the film. At first they disliked it, then they thought it was funny and decided to air it. Consequently it was very confusing, because we were the first film to start off. Also the film is not a TV film—it looked just awful on TV. We understood, by the way, if we were going to do an interview, the interview being a camera-created reality, the kind of cinéma-vérité meaning of an interview was to include the creators of that reality.

G.R.L. One of the things I really object to in cinéma-vérité films is the pretense of the omniscient, unseen film-maker.

E.P. Right, but there are all different versions of that. [. . .] You have to realize that sometimes the presence of a camera does make a difference, okay? Sometimes it doesn't. Now when it doesn't and you show the camera, the statement being made is that in this society there are various forms of behavior that are not affected by the presence of the camera. When the camera is shown and it does affect the action, then what you're doing is filming how it affects the action.

G.R.L. I'm saying that it doesn't have to be that extreme.

E.P. No, no, of course you're right. But the key point that I'm trying to make is that showing the camera isn't neutral data. It actually has lots of content and it's not like laying your cards on the table—it's a lot deeper than that. We thought that in our case, since we were creating this reality, that we had to be in the film, plus we also wanted to give young people something to identify with, *épater le bourgeois* kind of stuff. I think our introduction was very confusing on television, plus the fact how we appear in the mirror, often in the background slightly out of focus, kind of very small—facial expressions make a big difference when you see them on a movie screen. It all gets lost on TV. Plus the fact I think the film was very unusual for TV, so unusual that a lot of people couldn't take it for what it was, because generally people have been censored before they get access to TV like that. For example, the reviewer of the New York *Times*, Jack Gould, thought that we were presenting Paul as an expert on economics and business and politics, that he was our mouthpiece.

G.R.L. He thought the film was straight?

E.P. Yeah. Obviously it's a test of his straightness. But my father, for example, also thought the film was straight, as did my father-in-law.

G.R.L. Obviously you set up those scenes in the film—you got people together to talk; but did you try to arrange what they said in any way?

E.P. No. In this scene where we're talking, it's all laid out.

When other people are talking to each other, we don't set that up at all. We never do that.

I learned a tremendous amount about myself doing that film, and about the kinds of limitations of freedom, and I decided to make a theatrical film where in some ways I can do whatever I want.

Given the level of people's consciousness right now, it seems that people only take their serious documentary in a kind of fictional form. Part of the reason is that distribution of cinéma-vérité has been all fucked up; it has also been the level at which the audiences are willing to look at film. And given that people want to look at Doris Day rather than how actual people appear in their everyday lives, then the distribution is just going to be difficult no matter what kind of system you have. It's this vicious circle where people don't know how to look at cinéma-vérité films, don't know how to participate in the viewing of a film because they've seen very few of them, because culture has always been presented to them in ways which are very easy to take, and film has always been presented as entertainment rather than involvement. Until people's consciousnesses are transformed cinéma-vérité is just going to suffer without an audience.

A very important part of cinéma-vérité that can be accepted by people right now is via the constructive theatrical fiction form, and I think Godard has had a lot to do with opening up people to those possibilities. I think *Masculin-Féminin* is perhaps the best film of the sixties. Godard in general has opened up film-makers to incredibly more possibilities than they have ever seen before, partially because he has shown how to do fairly inexpensive films. They're still expensive from where we stand; but he has shown how it's possible to say what you want to say for a hundred thousand dollars. Nobody had been really able to do that before in fiction films.

G.R.L. The Italian neo-realists did, right after the war.

E.P. True. The reason I picked *Masculin-Féminin* is because I think it was just a beautiful film. It goes very deeply into how documentary and fiction forms relate to one another and it does it in a very successful way. Something very important, masculinity and femininity; and that ultimately relates to its form—which is kind of the nice thing about the film. I just picked that out because I think it's his best film.

G.R.L. One of the important things for me about Godard is that he's one of the very few film-makers who tells me, in any direct way, about the reality of the contemporary world the way that I perceive it. His films are about the only ones I've ever seen where young people—let's say hippie or beatnik types, or the French equivalent—aren't just embarrassingly stereotyped. I don't think I've ever seen any even in American underground films. In many ways I think he tells me more about reality than straight documentaries do.

E.P. I think a lot of it has to do with his concept of what plot and narrative is. Like right now, somehow, we live in a world where narrative and plots are just bullshit false constructions. In Godard's films they obviously become either bullshit constructions which are explicitly said to be bullshit constructions, like say in *Alphaville*, which is the kind of story which is a joke on itself, or there's no serious plot, like in *Masculin-Féminin*—and where there are plotlike elements, say the guy falling out of a window and dying in *Masculin-Féminin*, which in most films would be a big scene, here it's just related to us by one of the girls he lives with. This is the abandonment of this notion of a coherent reality, which you get in, say, Hitchcock. Hitchcock is probably the best example of ultimately believing that things can be made perfect sense of no matter how crazy actions are. I don't think people really believe that any more, and the reason they find Hitchcock entertainment—and I think he's a great film-maker—is just because he offers them that whole view of the world which nobody seriously believes in any more.

But I'd just like to make one defense of a concept of cinéma-vérité: how it can relate what young people are like. For one thing, if in fifteen or twenty years you want to find out what young people are like, you're going to be much better off going to a good cinéma-vérité film about young people than a fictionalized account of it. That's what I meant when I talked about a kind of irresponsibility of film-makers, and their responsibilities. I think one of their responsibilities is to present an accurate historic picture, and insofar as they don't do that, they're really irresponsible. The problem isn't with cinéma-vérité. It's partially that very few people have done films about young people. I don't know why.

G.R.L. Hollywood does.

E.P. No, no. Right. I'm talking about cinéma-vérité films. Hollywood now has to be used much more generically; like most of what we mean by Hollywood comes out of New York these days, is committed to plot in a very deep sense, and to plot in a sense of entertainment. Insofar as you're going to deal with young people and their movement, the plot is always going to look phony and fake, the way *The Graduate* looked phony, the way *Goodbye, Columbus* looked phony, the way that *Getting Straight* looked phony. They all have a lot of similarities in appearance: the same kind of color photography, very kitsch; they always have a sequence with peace and popular music, and somebody traveling. A film like *Easy Rider* I just really hated, thought it was real crap. Nevertheless, it gets a very big youth audience. How are you to understand it? I understand it as people needing a transformation of consciousness. What makes Godard an important film-maker is that he transformed consciousness in some part, contrary to the people who use all of his tricks; they fall into the kid school of film-makers; but Godard really transformed the way we see reality. *Easy Rider* just falls back on old soap opera forms. Nevertheless, it had a tremendous audience, which wasn't solely because of hype. What are you going to say about a youth culture that is supposedly radical but still bows down before a guy like Peter Fonda?

G.R.L. I think what you say about Godard is true, but it's taking a long time. Some of the films are just getting distributed here, some have never been distributed.

E.P. Right. It takes a long time. I'm not saying these things happen overnight. I'm not saying people should abandon documentary film because of it. The name documentary itself has a bad name. Like I don't want to go see documentaries. One reason why I don't is because what "documentary" means is that nothing unusual is going to happen on the screen. You know, like you go to a Hitchcock film, at any minute anybody is liable to get murdered. There's interest in that. You go to the average documentary and nothing is going to happen. Now that's not true of the good documentaries—in the good documentaries things do happen. Part of the exciting thing of what cinéma-vérité meant was that all of a sudden film-makers got freed from these limiting studio situations, or from the limiting situations where they couldn't use sound, and all of a sudden things could begin to happen on-camera, unexpected, marvelous, giving us insights where we didn't have ones before. Still, take a typical TV documentary where you see somebody giving an interview on television. You know that nobody is going to leap out and stab the guy. But that happens in *Psycho*. That's a whole different feel of sitting here and looking at a movie.

One of the things we've looked for in our earlier films, like say *Black Natchez* and *One Step Away*, was that kind of conflict where people change, a kind of unpredictability and a kind of excitement as well as to understand important social movements. We thought this was the way to do it, but at the same time we were film-makers, we weren't writers. You can understand an important social movement in some very good ways by writing.

G.R.L. It's also because we're so conditioned to a kind of enjoyment and pleasure in the fiction film that we really can't get pleasure out of the other. Like *Salesman*. I think parts of it are boring, but I accept that because I think he's telling me something worthwhile, because being bored is perhaps part of what he's saying. And in almost every Godard film there are boring parts, but I accept that because the boring parts are integral to what he's saying—and which I think is worth listening to. But lots of people aren't willing to accept this.

E.P. Boredom is really a very difficult problem that all film-makers, but especially cinéma-vérité film-makers, have to contend with, especially if you're into that whole flow of reality that you can potentially have in cinéma-vérité—but most people are bored by that flow of reality. Like take an incredibly interesting conversation you have with somebody, or an incredibly interesting person to listen to, and put him on film and often it's a complete dud. In that kind of transference from one kind of medium to another or from life to a medium, something has to be added. If you just take it as it is, it's much duller, and in some ways it's a falsification because it wasn't dull when it started out. When there's been a question of boredom, we've always finked out, I think, in our films. We've basically always been very afraid to bore the audience. Godard, much to his credit, isn't afraid. But you've also got to cope with the problem of what boredom means, and you have to use it creatively rather than just boring people. The only place where we took a chance on boring people was in *Harry's Trip*, and there the failure of will happened in not releasing it.

But let me tell you about two scenes in *One Step Away* that we didn't show because we thought they were boring and yet are really beautiful scenes. If you remember, there's the scene where Harry and his old girl friend are making out on a couch while Rickie's son is sleeping on the couch, and then Rickie walks in. Well, in the midst of that scene there's a radio blaring, there's this radio advertisement, a whole radio skit about how crispy these potato chips are, and we hear like kids talking and eating potato chips and their mother comes in and they hide the potato chips under the pillow, and then they put their heads down, and because potato chips are so crispy, we hear crash, crash, crash.

But it's all done in skit form. Tremendous kind of visual images that you get from it, and it's all going on during this incredibly tense scene, and you get this kind of conflict of media, and all kinds of things like that. But on the other hand, it's also boring. This was an important scene, it said a lot about what we were into and we were just afraid of taking the chance of boring people. The other thing is Harry, Rickie and Rickie's father take a walk along Haight-Ashbury—there's about a minute of it in the film. It was actually this incredibly beautiful tracking shot eleven minutes long. Like when we saw *Weekend*, and there's this eleven-minute tracking shot of the accident and all, well . . . we thought Godard was willing to do things which we were just afraid of doing.

G.R.L. Yeah, but it was fiction and he was able to set it up.

E.P. I understand that. But there are all kinds of little things that happen, little funny things, sad things, but it's also a tremendous visual trip. We also weren't willing to do that on some level because we were afraid. It might have been right in that particular case not to use that, but I think we've always given up that flow of reality unless something really interesting was happening in that flow. Other people haven't. Like I think *Don't Look Back* is an example of a tremendously lot of boring stuff that's in there to give it a feeling of flow.

G.R.L. I agree that that must always be a very difficult decision, and I think most people would tend to want the drama, because if you don't get an audience you don't make any money and you can't make other films. It's a vicious cycle.

E.P. Oh, I agree. That's what I meant when I said that Godard showed people how to make films in which you really do what you wanted to do. If you really want to be perverse and take your own trip, rightly or wrongly, you still could do it. Godard could do that. Truffaut really can't do that. Truffaut is very much into kinds of traditional forms of narrative. He makes his changes within the traditional forms, whereas Godard has been really in revolt against traditional forms.

G.R.L. Before I forget, did *Portrait of a McCarthy Supporter* ever get shown anywhere else besides on television?

E.P. No, because we don't have any rights to it.

G.R.L. That seems to me an essential part of the problem for independent film-makers—distribution. No distribution, no profit, no money to make films. You end up relying on the system to let you make films which are against the system, which is obviously not viable.

E.P. Yeah, like that's the key problem. Like Newsreel tried to work out its own distribution, and I don't think it's very successful.

G.R.L. Okay. Let's go on to *Harry's Trip*.

E.P. Right. Let me talk about *Harry's Trip* and *Panola* at the same time. *Panola* came out of footage that was shot in 1965 when we were doing *Black Natchez*.

G.R.L. Shot down there?

E.P. Yeah, shot in Natchez. We were seeing Panola one or two hours every couple of days and filming. He was a black wino. *Harry's Trip* came out of the footage we shot on *One Step Away*, and both films were edited, were finished well after the prime film was finished. In the case of *Panola*, which was just finished in 1970, we felt very funny given the rise of Black Power. Some white people making a film about a black wino—especially given that Panola goes into things that most black people felt was very deep. So we were very afraid to edit the film, and then some people we knew wanted to edit it, and we finally let them edit it. We maintained some control over the editing, but basically they edited the film the way they wanted it edited.

One of the things that interested us about *Panola* was the nice unity of the content of the film and its form. Panola kind of lived his whole life by performance. When he first came to Natchez, he said the only way to be free in Natchez is to make people think you're crazy. And that's essentially what he did. He could say all kinds of things that other people just couldn't say. He could be cynical, critical of anything he wanted. He had this whole kind of contrapuntal humor where he would say one thing, then undercut it with something else. So all these different levels of reality came out in how he spoke, in what he said, his different moods, whether he was sober, drunk or very drunk, or what. Of course he was relating to the camera and he would put on everything from a real performance for us, to his just being very, very drunk and working out his aggression or his sadness in relationship to us and the camera. Panola as performer also matched the kind of face Panola felt he had to put out to the world as a black man, and those two things just worked very nicely in the film. It's a very moving film, and kind of scarey in all kinds of ways.

Now *Harry's Trip*. After you're been filming for a couple of months, you kind of go crazy. You want to try experiments. So while we were filming *One Step Away* we decided to interview Harry and Rickie, and the interview really wasn't going very well. It was the first time we had really tried an interview. Harry was at the end of a nasty trip, and we got this idea: leave Harry in the room all by himself with the camera and one light and tell him he has to sit in one space; we turn on the camera, leave the room and let the shot go for eleven minutes, then we'd come back and see what we had. Ultimately the film was called *Harry's Trip*, because Harry was on an acid trip, he was talking about going to New York City, and he also gives his trip, his philosophy of life. What it represented was, first of all, a way of making a cheap film—no editing, no A and B rolling.[8] One eleven-minute film—you just come out with the shot. Actually, the way it finally ended up, we had a little introduction from the earlier interview when we were in the room and we put titles on it—then we let the eleven minutes go. We also wanted it to make some kind of comment about cinéma-vérité: Here's a kind of unmanipulated reality; it becomes tremendously demanding on the viewer, he has to begin to notice the slight changes, say, in Harry, which he normally wouldn't notice, or if he was to notice, the film-maker would accentuate it by a camera movement, a cut or something—like a cut into a close-up of a slight facial movement. But here you have it all rely on the viewer. Also, the viewer would have the same kind of access to information that we had, because we weren't in the room. He could see everything we saw. So it was kind of an experimental film, and again it's a difficult film to look at because nothing happens in some sense.

G.R.L. Have either of them been shown?

E.P. *Panola* was just finished, like a couple of weeks ago. *Harry's Trip* was shown once, but the sound got fucked up at some point, so we have to make another print of it. We just never bothered to finish it, never bothered to correct it, because that means more money and more effort, and it's unclear at this point how we would distribute it.

G.R.L. Now you want to make a feature. Is that because documentary doesn't tell it like it is?

E.P. Yeah. . . . It has a lot to do with just distribution. There are a lot of differences between features and television. When we went to San Francisco we chose Harry's commune. One of the reasons was that a lot of people said it was a very good commune, and it represented what people thought was the best happening in San Francisco. Maybe it was not the most common, in that most people living in communes were living in city communes, but it represented

[8] If original 16mm. film is spliced end to end, the splices show in the final prints and effects—dissolves, etc.—are not possible. Therefore, to make effects possible and to hide the splices, a special but common checkerboard method of splicing the original 16mm. film is employed. Though this is an exacting, tedious job and increases the cost of the film, professional 16mm. films are nevertheless cut this way because of the above-stated reasons.

the ethos of hippie philosophy, of where people thought they should be. Now, we knew that Country Joe and the Fish would have a lot more initial hype, and people would come just to see them, or their women—all kinds of very pretty women—and people would relate to them much more easily than to people who weren't pretty or beautiful. One thing that happened is we heard this conversation while Country Joe was doing a recording session, listening to their women talking about mod, hippie fashions, see-through underwear, and all the time it's just like straight women except the fashions are way-out, and we weren't interested in that. We had these democratic notions that how a person looks shouldn't really affect whether we do a film about them, but that what's important is what they're doing. That has a lot to do with how films are distributed. Like every producer knows that having a star or a pretty person automatically gives you a better chance than if you have an unknown or an unpretty person. That was something very difficult to work with in documentary, but that can actually become the topic of a theatrical film or a fiction film if you're going to relate the levels of both documentary film-making and theatrical film-making in the same film—and which, say, Godard tries to do. That's what interests me. It's not as if Godard was the first person to do it.

The best example of the two levels of reality film is *Never Give a Sucker an Even Break*. Did you ever see that? It starts off as a semi-documentary about W. C. Fields, but he's also trying to sell his film script, and he keeps cutting to it, and it's the most fantastic, incredible, theatrical story. And he intercuts these two levels of reality. It's not only about making films, though, it's about W. C. Fields as a man, and in a very important way relies on those two levels: thinking of him as an actor in a film and thinking of him as a man.

In any case, that relationship between the documentary level and the created fictional narrative level is something that is basic, I think, to film-making in the sixties and seventies. That's what the W. C. Fields film is about. Somehow I think he was doing a film that related to the problems of being a male and being a female in society, and the mutual kinds of sexual oppressions that happen between men and women that in some way related to how actors and actresses are treated. Actors have to be good actors. Actresses basically have to be sexual objects. That's not true all the time—you have Helen Hayes types, right?—but that's what a young actress primarily means.

I'm working on two competing scripts right now. One of them involves an actress. We find out about her as a person and what being an actress means as well as relating that to the kind of story that she's going through in the film.

In any case, the thing that feature films represents is just the possibility of breaking out of the distributional hang-ups of 16mm. It's not like inexpensive fiction films have the distribution either. There are a lot more problems about that too, but if you can make a film fairly cheaply, you might be able to avoid the expensive hype jobs that studios, then distributors put themselves through, and you might be able to get enough money in return so you can pay people for having done it and you can pay people who invested in it. Once you do that with one film and show you can successfully do it—and I think you can get the money for one film—then you have access immediately to doing two or three more films.

G.R.L. But you're not, at least for now, going to try to make documentaries through the system, even though it was on the periphery of the system that you worked before.

E.P. Yeah, right. Like *Black Natchez* wasn't done through the system. Also, the whole feature film business is a whole business system kind of thing too, but much less important than TV. TV obviously has a lot to do with molding people's minds, their whole conception of what they think of themselves, what they think of possibilities, what they think life is all about. The relationship between TV and consumerism, all that shit. So that's a much more insidious system to prop up and participate in.

G.R.L. Do you know about the Videofreex and Raindance in New York?

E.P. I know about the Videofreex.

G.R.L. Okay. One of their ideas is that colleges have all this TV equipment which nobody uses, because the people who have control of the equipment want to use it for like theatrical things, as if tape were the same as film—and students aren't interested in that. What the Freex and Raindance want is to get a whole kind of feedback thing going that they think students will be interested in, and from that start a network that would exchange tapes, free, or at worst at cost. They see this as becoming a genuine kind of alternate medium.

E.P. This is exactly Newsreel's idea. It's precisely the same, except instead of using tape, use films. There are a lot of advantages to tape over film. Cost, immediacy . . .

G.R.L. And very easy to use.

E.P. Right. Easy to use. The point is that people define themselves in very serious ways, and just seeing some tapes isn't going to change their whole consciousness of what culture is. When say the Videofreex put on a show, where do they put on a show right now? they put it on in these establishment places, art galleries, theaters.

G.R.L. Part of the idea is not simply for them to make tapes but . . . Let's say you come into a poverty area. You don't make a tape about them, you let them make a tape, or you work on the making of the tape with them.

E.P. No, I understand that. That's all great stuff. The question is how do you break down people's initial prejudices about that whole notion, about the whole mystification of the arts.

G.R.L. Well, if you give the guy a video camera and he can shoot and he gets something—

E.P. Yes, he gets something, but most people consider that home movies or shit or what. It takes a whole radical transformation of consciousness to think in terms of that being a potential culture. If you go and see what the Videofreex do at these art galleries, people don't respond to it. It's very unresponsive stuff too. There are inherent limitations in what TV can do. Somebody once said that TV can sell things, it can't unsell things. The thing is what will the video tape stuff mean? EVR is one form of it, but that's co-optive in a way because not everybody can record EVR.

[. . .]

G.R.L. What do you think about Wiseman?

E.P. I have a lot of feelings about his films. I think it's amazing that there's essentially only one person, Wiseman, and maybe another, John Marshall, who are doing films about institutions in this society. These institutions are constantly in change, and very important for understanding this society is to know what these institutions are like. I think *High School* and *Titicut Follies* are really interesting films. I think that *Hospital* is unfortunately just an anecdotal, sentimental view of a hospital and really doesn't tell us very much—although the scene of the vomiting hippie is high comedy. In the police film,[9] it's like he wasn't around to get any of the present views of police—it's as though someone were to paint a Renaissance painting right now and didn't relate to any of the art movements that happened in between. A lot of people have very serious doubts or questions about police—Wiseman didn't even cope with those.

G.R.L. He claims that that was the way he found it.

E.P. Oh, I'm not saying it wasn't like that. Say Marx and Engels thought of the police as kind of a civil arm of the bourgeoisie to keep down the proletariat. Now, I don't happen to believe that, but they never doubted that police gave ice cream to little

[9] *Law and Order.*

lost kids or helped women to find their handbags. Now, it would probably be true that 98 per cent of the policeman's life is spent directing traffic, but a film that 98 per cent of the time shows a policeman directing traffic is clearly a tremendous distortion of why people consider police important. Besides, there are ways of showing that a policeman spends 98 per cent of his time directing traffic without actually taking up 98 per cent of the film directing traffic.

First of all, it's not at all the way we find it. The film starts off with a series of mug shots—click, click, click. What do you mean you found it like that? That's an obvious film-makerly conceit. That gives us a whole idea of what the role of the policemen is—to catch criminals. Plus, while he was down there, he found President Nixon giving a speech on law and order—do you remember, the next to the last shot of the film? Then we cut to a policeman involved in a domestic problem where the policeman is very conciliatory, trying to explain why the man should not make a legal case out of it—he's really being very patient. In what sense do you find that kind of montage in reality, cutting from a presidential address to a policeman on the street? It's tremendously confirmatory of Nixon. So the whole thing about "that's the way I found it" is a lot of bullshit.

When I was shooting *Black Natchez,* all of a sudden the perception came to me that when I was in trouble I couldn't call the police. In my whole middle-class existence beforehand, it was the police who were the ultimate protectors of my life and property. Well, here in Mississippi, all of a sudden they were my enemies. That's a particular kind of perception that, for example, Fred Wiseman never gives us. And this is a very important kind of perception. Black people don't consider police their protectors, or insofar as they do, they feel very ambiguous about that because there's nobody else to protect them. So the little black lady has only the policeman to go to to help her find her pocketbook. Why doesn't he give us those perceptions? That's part of reality. Maybe he never saw it. Now, also in a situation where you're filming police there are real legal problems with what the police say and with what they do—the police are not going to give you access to everything. So, for example, the police are not going to let you see them beating the shit out of someone. And that happens all the time. It's tremendously well documented.

Titicut Follies was an important film because first of all it was filmed in a very good way. John Marshall filmed it very nicely.[10] It's a very interesting concept of what the cinéma-vérité camera does,

[10] Marshall was also the codirector.

the wide framing within which lots of action occurs rather than the camera searching out as you find more in *Don't Look Back* and Pennebaker's camera. Somehow it was a horror film and it was a documentary horror film, and it was happening in Massachusetts, home of the Puritans, home of the Cradle of Liberty. The film falls in the muckraking tradition. I think there are more profound social analyses than muckraking, but it's important to have a muckraking film like that. It's a shock film, and it's not the kind of film where the shock is just for the shock itself. It tells us about how people can relate and about how people can be. That's very valuable.

G.R.L. What do you think of *High School?*

E.P. *High School* is really interesting. I don't know what Fred had in mind with it, but you get an image of a system of total oppression. Here all of a sudden the anecdotal style works fine because the way it serves is like there are no ways out. So you think, well, when they get to college, that'll be fine, but then you hear all the advice about what they're going to get in college, how limited college is, the very limited job openings; you get all this meaningless authority laid on people's heads and you know that's going to continue right through college and jobs. So the anecdotal style works there as building up the system of total oppression.

Now there was a lot of criticism of the film. For example, let me just give you two. There's a teacher who reads a Simon and Garfunkel poem, and the students are shown as being very bored. It's obvious from the footage taken of her that she's telling more about herself than she's actually relating to those kids. But still it would be very important and interesting to find out how those kids did react after she finished, over and above their looking bored. Also, how would we take their looking bored? Is it the problem of the situation of being in high school, period, and there's no way that anybody can work within that, no way you can be a meaningful teacher? Or, as a matter of fact, is she just a meaningful teacher, meaningful in quotes, meaningful teacher in a completely meaningless sense, that she tries but can't really relate to the kids, can only relate to her own narrow level of experience?

The second criticism has to do with the whole notion of montage, how sequences going together say things. Also the whole use of close-ups, how people who don't look beautiful are put down for that. That's really bad and really serious, and he often uses that as the only argument or the only criticism of a person, that he looks funny or talks funny.

On the other hand, what the film did to me personally was to revive my high school experience in a very strong way. It really shook me up. That's why I say, he's tremendously important. I think that what John Marshall is trying to do is very much like what Fred wants to do—but very different. But other than Marshall and Wiseman, nobody is doing films about institutions, and there are a tremendous number of institutions, tremendously important, and the really interesting thing is that if the films are good, like say *High School* and *Titicut Follies,* I think anybody can use them, be you right-wing conservative or left-wing radical.

G.R.L. Jean Rouch's objection to *Titicut Follies*—if I remember correctly—was that Wiseman presented something horrendous, but presented it in an inhuman way, that he wasn't involved, that there was no way to tell if he was concerned, that no solution or possible solution had been presented, and that if there was no possible solution, that he—Wiseman—was nevertheless appalled. I think that's one of the things that I object to.

E.P. First of all, I think Jean Rouch expects more from film-makers than I do. Look, Wiseman was concerned enough to go and spend a few months at Bridgewater.[11] I don't know about you, but I couldn't spend three months there. David went and took sound one day and told me what it was like. Wiseman showed enough concern to do that—nobody else did. That's the first thing. Secondly, just silently laying it on like that was much stronger than the kind of low-level horror that the average film-maker would express at it. In some way that kind of toughness and relentlessness was just much, much stronger. Thirdly, I'm not interested in Fred Wiseman's solution for it because I don't think Fred Wiseman is capable of giving a solution for it. I don't think that's Fred Wiseman's problem. On the lowest level we have to do things like see it first, and that's an example of muckraking where you haven't even seen it first. The other thing is I think Rouch . . . I've only seen one of Rouch's films, *Chronique d'un été,* and I just thought it was awful. I found his level of involvement pretentious and laughable. I found his walking along the hallway with his assistant discussing a system of art, reality or acting obnoxious. His whole notion of film is a completely camera-created, film-maker-created reality. Reality plays only the very smallest part in the film.

G.R.L. I think that much of what you say about Wiseman is true; he is important. Certainly his films have gotten more attention, have been seen more than other documentaries, and they raise important questions, have brought attention to important subjects, but there's something about them that bothers me—even though I agree he's important and in many ways damn good.

[11] The state mental hospital where *Titicut Follies* was shot.

E.P. Right. There's this kind of disease with cinéma-vérité film-makers. It's very hard to describe, but it has to do with voyeurism, it has to do with neutrality in the footage itself, which means most cinéma-vérité film-makers come from educated, middle-class backgrounds and ultimately have upper-middle-class tastes. Ricky is probably the best example of that. When Ricky makes a film about the police, like *Chiefs*, the very important thing that happens is you get a cut from this barbershop quartet singing "Glory, Glory, Hallelujah" to a speech about riot weapons—or vice versa, I don't remember which way it goes; but in that kind of montage you get a kind of perception which you see if you have an upper-middle-class sensibility. The fact of the police chiefs running around in their Hawaiian shirts, if you have a middle-class sensibility, you see that. That happens because you have to put this relatively neutral footage together and make your statement in the montage between shots or between sequences, and you generally rely on your cultural background, which in the case of upper-middle-class people is upper middle class. This means a kind of detachment, an unwillingness to get involved in action and lowly street things, or yelling or stamping of feet. Rather, you have a very nice, detached, ironical sense of humor, which, say with Ricky, you get in the strongest form. It's very pleasing, it's very nice. With Fred you get that same kind of thing but with no sense of humor. You also get this weird sensibility that says, "Isn't it amazing the things people will say in front of a camera?" and, "Boy, how stupid can people make themselves look?" That's a kind of Candid Camera mentality. You get that in Ricky's films all the time, say in *Happy Mother's Day*, where somebody is just the worst singer in the world, or somebody makes the most exaggerated claims in a speech, like the mayor saying no mayor has ever had a more important duty laid on him.[12] That's very bad, and in some way you have to fight against that because we all kind of love to see people making fools of themselves.

G.R.L. Most film-makers in the past, and I'm speaking mainly of documentary film-makers, looked on themselves as professionals and accepted working within the system in whatever way they could manage. It was part of their life-style. It wasn't that many of them weren't concerned about social issues, because many of them were. In a sense, though, they separated their work, which was a profession, from their personal lives. That's changed to some degree, I think. The Videofreex and Raindance, for example—and I'd say they

[12] The mayor is talking about the town's celebration of the birth of quintuplets by a woman from the area.

were even more extreme in their views than you are—look on their work as part of trying to transform the system. At least in part, they see the work of the group as more important than the individual—in both groups more than one person will shoot, more than one will edit, and they don't sign their names to the work. You also, I think, though not quite to that degree, see your work as a film-maker as an integral part of your life, not as a function that exists outside of your life.

E.P. Right.

G.R.L. And I would suspect this to be true of a number of younger film-makers. So maybe you would tell me something about the way you see film-making in relation to your life. You're married, you have two kids, you're thinking about living communally, and I think you intend to work outside the system—that you're going to find a way to do that.

E.P. First of all, like this Newsreel film in which somebody, talking of the system, says, "You either own the motherfucker or you work for him." Now, I think in some sense that's really true, and there's no way in which you can escape the system. Everything, be it revolution or what have you, turns into a commodity in this society. Like Marx says, in the highest stages of capitalism, virtue, love and everything are in the market place as a commodity. That's kind of what happens now, so the media can hype revolution and not worry about it, and we all look at ourselves as products and objects in the way we look at other people—that's not the only thing, but it's at least part of us. Some people say there's a pig in all of us and we have to learn what that pig is.

The Videofreex, and in general the people who are in underground video tape that I've talked to, have the same kind of mentality as people in underground film. They think that you can bring about a revolution in people's consciousness, that there can be a cultural revolution without there being a political revolution. I don't believe that. I think that a very important part of the political revolution is the cultural revolution, but you cannot transform people's consciousness for the better just on a cultural level. It will also have to effect institutional change, and I don't think you can do that by going off and living a good life and being a kind of imitation of Christ—which used to be one of the ways to salvation in the Middle Ages—and that other people will then follow you. In other words, that people are going to see people groove in a commune and then everybody is going to move into the commune, because what straight people see in a groovy commune is very different. They see a bunch of freaks with long hair doing bad things to their kids because they have the level of consciousness which doesn't let them see other possibilities.

So in some ways, the films I make have to be tied in very strong ways to the consciousness that people presently have. That is, to try to transform that consciousness as opposed to assuming it is already transformed, which is what I think Brakhage assumes in his films, or like a lot of people in video tape assume. People in video tape also seem to assume too much about video tape in some ways—that it can really bring about a radical change in consciousness. On the other hand, they don't seem to think that it has very many intrinsic qualities like, say, McLuhan would take it to have—a small image of undetermined resolution, which is basically kind of a dull image. It doesn't seem clear to me that you can transmit anything you want on it successfully. Obviously you can show pictures of anything you want, but somehow a still photograph or a moving image just impresses my mind much more than any video image.

Yet when we were walking down the street and I was talking about how in all sorts of ways I now think visually where I used to think in novelistic terms before, well, more so with the present generation. A lot of the basic images that they have of what the world is like comes from television. There was this marvelous *Esquire* cover in which they have a kid eating a hot dog and drinking a Coke while looking at his television set. On the television set is Ruby killing Oswald, and he's looking at it in the same way that, let's say, we looked at Hitchcock movies. That's very important. He'll write a book called *I Lost It Watching the Tube.* In my life it's Pauline Kael saying *I Lost It at the Movies,* and Godard says in *Breathless* and lots of other films about how a basic kind of experience of life is looking at movies. It's not just an interpretation of experience; it becomes part of the experience. That's true with kids looking at TV. But you've got to ask what is it that the kids see on TV—what can they see on TV? Which I guess is more the Videofreex question. Also, are there any intrinsic limitations of what can successfully be shown on TV? In a sense, you call sell Excedrin or you can sell menthol cigarettes by repeating something that people hate. But the question is, suppose you wanted to unsell Excedrin, suppose you wanted to unsell commercialism, consumerism. Maybe that's not possible because of something intrinsic to the nature of TV, because of the way it mesmerizes people, the way it makes them non-active in some ways.

G.R.L. Maybe you don't try to unsell commercialism. Maybe you try to sell something else.

E.P. Okay, right. But you see, maybe the whole notion of selling is a contradiction—you can't sell a cultural revolution that's making the revolution an object and making people consumers again.

I've changed. I've had a lot of ups and downs in the past few years, but right now, I have a very cynical attitude toward the possibilities of political revolution. What I want to do is to make films that say what I want to say and in some way relate to political institutions. Not only political institutions, but institutions that determine people's politics and the quality of their lives, be it family, being a male, being a female, the quality of work people do, the way people buy products and people—in a way that will raise people's consciousness, show them possibilities where they might not have thought of possibilities before. For the time being that's liable to mean two months, or it might mean two years. Right now I can't relate directly to any kind of political movement. The reason I can't relate to the underground, be it the Videofreex or what have you, is first of all a brief in the primacy of the cultural revolution, and secondly, because the stuff they do I don't find interesting. Maybe some of Vanderbeek's early films, and I'm more interested in the existence of Warhol than his films. Those are the only things that I got from the film-making underground. The reason I like film is I learned a lot about the world, meaning that all the films I've done have always changed me. Except when I've worked for other people, I've never been the alienated laborer. I've always learned things. Sometimes the things I've learned have only begun to affect me a year or two later, where I've seen the world and understood a lot of things by having to think about footage, both in what to film and by looking at it many times on the moviola. This is different from philosophy, where I deal with very heady, chesslike intellectual games. Here, in film-making, every level of my being is involved.

RAINDANCE (MICHAEL SHAMBERG) AND *VIDEOFREEX* (DAVID CORT)

RAINDANCE, CORP.

(The following material was written by Michael Shamberg.)

"Here is the data/Dada:

"Michael Shamberg, 26, graduated in 1966 from a university in St. Louis (Washington). After that, newspaper work in Chicago; then a now defunct newspaper named *Chicago's American*—owned by the Chicago *Tribune*—then gradually to New York through South America. Here I worked for both *Time* and *Life* magazines, six months at each, and quit because I felt irrelevant, not co-opted. At the former magazine I did a story on video and met Ira Schneider Frank Gillette and Paul Ryan, who turned me on to video tape. Raindance was originally Frank's idea (an alternate culture think-tank à la Rand, R&D, research and development, Rain-Dance—get it?) but he has since split and the organization has gone through many changes from his original perception, though not necessarily his intent.

"[Besides myself,] the existing company is now:

"Ira Schneider, 31, a former film-maker (his famous *Lost in Cuddihy* trilogy [. . .] won some awards and got selected for the Museum of Modern Art) and doctorate student in physiological psychology who got tired of hassling film technology and got into portable video when the machines came out in '68. Besides shooting a lot of tape (Woodstock, Altamont and a portrait of life in Yellow

Springs, Ohio, to name some) he has also designed video environments, the most notable of which, *Wipe Cycle*, he did with Frank for the *TV as a Creative Medium* show held in May of 1969 at the Howard Wise Gallery in New York, where I met him.

"Paul Ryan, 27, studied with McLuhan for a year when the latter was at Fordham. From there he went to an upstate New York town where he turned high school kids on to making their own video programing which was then transmitted over the town CATV system. He now works with us loosely and is writing a book on the grammar of video tape.

"Beryl Korot, 25, and Phyllis Gershuny, 27, are the coeditors and founders of *Radical Software*, which is self-explanatory.

"In addition we have some business advisers and a full-time circulation manager (unpaid) for the paper."

FILMOGRAPHY*

(The tapes below are listed by group rather than with individual credits because, as Michael Shamberg noted in a letter, "As I indicated when we met, one doesn't really conceive of ownership of tape as with film, so what we call our data bank is attributed to everyone who has contributed, but not by specifics." The same principle would apply to the Videofreex.)

RAINDANCE, CORP.

Summer '68: St. Marks tapes† (street rapping)

Jan.–Feb. '69: Antioch tapes (Midwestern American subculture; interviews and experimental video entertainments)

May '69: Composite tapes for Wise Gallery show—*TV as a Creative Medium* (Panasonic)
Document of Wise Gallery Show
Tony Barsha bathtub sequences

July '69: Apollo 10 (11 and 13)

Aug. '69 Woodstock tapes

* From *Radical Software*, summer 1970, and no. 2, 1970, by Ira Schneider, Frank Gillette, Michael Shamberg, Paul Ryan; Raindance, 24 East 22nd Street, N.Y.C.

† All tapes, unless otherwise specified, made with Sony ½″ portable equipment.

Oct. '69: Abbie Hoffman tape at Conspiracy office, NYC

Dec. '69: Altamont tapes

Feb. '70: Urban ecology tapes: City Mix 1, 2 and 3

March '70: Earth People's park meeting—Electric Circus
Locusts attack Chicago

March '70: California trip (The Rays, and Supermarket, plus Here's to your Goiter Goat Man, Tender is the Tape, Alternate TV sub-edit pre-prototype No. 1, More, and Alternate sub-pilot)

April '70: Earth Day in New York (Uptight about Bushes, I Was an Eagle—I am Extinct)

May '70: Interview with R. Buckminster Fuller, NYC
Post-Kent State—Washington, D.C., peace demonstration
City Hall labor and student anti-administration demonstration

Plus: News taped off TV during the week of the Kent State killings and Cambodia protest demonstrations; President Nixon's State of the Union message; the party the President threw for the astronauts; Keep: composition for four synchronized screens; Loop Sketch: an abstract tape composed of feedback patterns; Computer: document on the home computer; Weekend at White Tank: two-part tape of meeting of video people; Rose Art Museum show—Vision and Television documentary, Jan. '70; Moon: off-air collage; Mountaindale Festival (Frank Gillette); Year of the Mushroom—Upstate N.Y. Commune at home and on stage with musical show (Frank Gillette and Paul Ryan); Robert Schwartz—street dancer; Nam June Paik at WGBH (Frank Gillette); interviews with Levittown, N.Y., housewives and newlyweds about their television viewing tastes; Lower East Side Park Fair; Warren Brody—interviews and verite video of Ecological design commune in New Hampshire; N.Y. State CATV operators convention; Glens Falls, N.Y. profile of a town about to install CATV; Clinton Program's Tapes of and by Junior High School Students in Clinton Program; Tapes by Jud Yalkut; Nicholas Johnson at Raindance loft

VIDEOFREEX, INC.

According to listing in the first issue of *Raindance*, summer 1970, the members of the Videofreex are: David Cort, S. M. Blumberg, Curtis Ratcliff, Parry Teasdale, Davidson Gigliotti, Chuck Kennedy, Bart Friedman, Alan Sholem and Tunie Wall.

Dave Cort was born in 1935. (Since the time of the interview Cort has been spending a lot of time working on video and other projects with communes in Vermont and has not answered letters or phone calls to provide biographical information. Some information about him will be found in the text of the interview and will have to suffice for the present—and which is perhaps fitting to his life-style.)

FILMOGRAPHY*

INDUSTRIAL AND EDUCATIONAL

The Food Line—"Supermarkets for Progress"; The Group; Group Games—March '69
Easter in Spain—April '69
Smokey Bear Commercial—Sept. '69
California Experimental High School; Jessie Ritter at San Francisco State—Nov. '69
Cloisters—Dec. '69

GENRE TAPES

Crawfish and Sally Bell—July '69
Chadis—May '69
Rivington Street Dope Speech—Aug. '69
Tarwater—Dec. '69
The Great White Way—Jan. '70
Eclipse and Elijah; Trippy Meeting, House Hunting I and II—April '70

* From *Radical Software*, summer 1970; Videofreex, 98 Prince Street, N.Y.C.

MUSIC

Buzzy Linhart—last half of '69
Incredible String Band—Nov. '69
Major Wiley; Morgan, Mason and Downs; Hubie—Dec. '69
Charlie Mariano—Jan. '70
The Smubbs—April '70
Sarod Player—May '70

WOODSTOCK

First Aid No. 1
First Aid No. 2
Shithouse
Aqualast

EROTICA

Erotica I; Enchanting Erotica II Kusama; Gallery I, II, III
Far-out Ergenous—Frolies and Excitement 3—Nov. '69
Mango Productions I, II—Jan. '70

POLITICAL

Black Panthers I, II, III; Abbie and Jerry; Abbie Hoffman in Chicago; Mrs. Seale—Oct. '69
Women's Liberation; CCNY-SDS rally (Jerry Rubin) March '69
Junkyard—April '69
Abbie at New Haven; Soho Artists' Festival: Washington I and II; David Peel; NYU/Columbia demonstrations; Construction Workers' Loyalty Day Parade—May '69

INTERVIEWS

Claude and Denise—gallery owners—Oct. '69
Dr. Hippocrates I, II, III; Tony Pig—KSAN (body painting) Nov. '69
Ricky Leacock; Bill Psyche (Brandeis)—Jan. '70
Hell's Angels party—Feb. '70
Odyssey House; Hell's Angels at home—May '70

ARTISTS

Aldo Tambellini—Jan. and April '70
Charlotte Moorman; Nam June Paik—Jan. '70
Salvador Dali—March '70

ECOLOGY

Earth People's Park Meeting I, II, III—March '70

THEATER

70 Grand Taffel—Oct. '70
Prince Street Taffel I, II—Jan. '70

EVENTS

Circus Arts in Central Park—Sept. '69
Martin's Magic Pillow—Nov. '69

St. Marks (New Year's Eve)—'70
Rose Art Museum Show (Vision and Television)—Jan. '70
New School Mixed Media—Feb. '70
Musica Electronica Viva—March '70
Finch College Laser Show—April '70

ELECTRONIC VIDEO EXPERIMENTATION

MC—TV—July '69
Feedback; Chrome I—Sept. '69
Extra Special Effects I, II—April '70

July 15, 1970, in the interviewer's loft in New York City.

(Also present at the interview were Curtis Ratcliff, a Videofreek, and Phyllis Gershuny, coeditor of *Radical Software.*)

[. . .]

DAVID CORT: Let me tell you about the Videofreex. At Woodstock, this freaky kid comes up to me and says, "Man, I can get you anything you want, anything you want. I know a guy at CBS, he'll get you anything you want. What do you want?" Well, it turned out he did know somebody at CBS, the assistant to the president, Frank Stanton. And one Saturday he brought him up to the loft; I really didn't even believe it then and—

G. ROY LEVIN: What was the guy's name?

D.C. Don West. At any rate, I handed him a camera—I was really interested. He was this very straight-looking cat and he kept smiling at me in this weird kind of way and just for like a lark, I said, "Well, we're going out shooting. Want to come with us?" I just flipped him out, and then as he went he said, "Sure, I'll make the appointment." He kept talking about some television program he wanted us to do. I didn't believe him. I thought he was just kidding. I thought he was just a secretary or something like that, which he was, but secretaries at CBS can do strange things. At any rate, he said he'd be back. So he came down one day and he shot with us, just followed us around really. Then the next day he came back and handed me a check and said, "Start doing it for me."

G.R.L. Meaning CBS?

D.C. No, meaning a thing called SQM, which is really CBS, yeah. He said, "Just do whatever you want, but will you put something together for me?" I said, "Okay," which was a mistake in a way, but we really needed the bread too.

G.R.L. Was it a lot of bread?

D.C. Well, it was a little bit, but he said he would keep giving us more and more. In the beginning, it was about three hundred dollars.

CURTIS RATCLIFF: See, this guy thought he was ordained by God to do a presentation for a pilot for CBS, and he was going to make a million dollars and he was going to tell the world what was happening in the United States in 1970. It was called Now Project, and he had started his own production company called SQM Productions, which was funded by CBS, although under a different title.

So he went out and he hired the people with the long hair, the beards, the freaks, and he thought, here are these people who are going to be able to tell me what we want, and at that point we had all sorts of things to do, we were going to do them anyway, and we sort of said, "Well, why don't you come along with us? We're going to go out to the park."

D.C. We weren't going to do anything different. We just wanted to do our thing.

C.R. So for three and a half months we did exactly what we wanted to do and we got CBS to pay for it. It was really a good rip-off, but he got what he wanted in a way.

G.R.L. He got tapes?

C.R. We did forty hours of tapes for him.

D.C. Yeah, they really did a whole number. At the end they were giving us everything we wanted, everything. If we had asked for dancing girls—everything. Cars—there were four cars. Dope.

G.R.L. He paid for dope?

D.C. No, but there was so much money, everything was part of the expense account. There never was that much money. Everything was rented. But like I knew that as soon as anyone besides that maniac saw what we were doing, they'd say, "These freaks are going to stop getting money." And we were getting a little fucked up because he kept wanting more and more and more.

G.R.L. Were any of the tapes ever shown?

D.C. Oh yes, we did a presentation for them and then he . . . We had an agreement with him that he would have to involve us in any editing that ever occurred, and of course, he finked out on it. We had a big argument. He didn't like what we were doing and he wanted to do his own thing. We have some tapes of Fred Hampton[1] before he died, before he was shot—that was what they really liked. They had gotten this country house for us—

G.R.L. You were off in this country estate?

D.C. Yes. They rented this country estate in East Durham.

C.R. David, let me. We did about forty hours of tapes for them. Now, this person had lots of film crews, he had other people doing video tapes, but as far as actually turning out on December 17 for the presentation for Mike Dann[2] . . . that was last year. We had to put together a presentation for Mike Dann, and so everything went up to this big climax. Three weeks before December 17 we had gathered together about forty hours of tapes and we had to edit them down for the presentation. So we said we can't possibly do it in

[1] A Black Panther shot and killed by police in Chicago in 1969.
[2] Then programing chief at CBS.

New York, get us a house in the country. So he went out and he rented this elaborate house.

D.C. No, no.

C.R. Yes. You don't remember what a number we did on them. So we all went out and for two and a half weeks Parry, David and I edited these tapes down to fifty-three minutes, and we had six segments—it was all different things. So we had those six segments totaling fifty-three minutes and some live music. We had all these people come to the studio and it was a live presentation. We had color monitors in a circle. We showed a segment of tape, then we switched the cameras to a live presentation of the music—the music was actually there being performed; then we switched back to the tape. It was a closed-circuit system in the studio.

D.C. It was a presentation for Mike Dann, who was sitting next door. They kept a great many of the tapes. We stole back the political ones, the Fred Hampton and—

C.R. But this Don West person had seen the tapes the night before, on the night of December 16, and he'd said, "I'm shocked, I can't use any of it, blah, blah, blah. I want to use some Fred Hampton Panther tapes," and we said, "No, we've looked at the tapes, we don't think it's proper. We don't think you ought to use them." So between the night of the sixteenth and the night of the seventeenth, twenty-four hours, he flew in a private plane up to the country house, ripped off all those tapes, that forty hours of tapes, brought it back to the CBS studio, and he edited about a thirty-minute segment using our video tapes and some CBS footage of Fred Hampton's woman wailing over the coffin. Pure sensationalism, we thought. He said, "I'm going to show this tomorrow night." Then, the night of the presentation . . . it was five minutes to seven o'clock —that was when it was supposed to begin—he comes in with this little tape and his tape recorder, and he said, "I'm going to show this Panther tape." We said, "You're not going to show this Panther tape." He said, "Yes, I am," and Parry and David and I looked at him, and said, "We're going to pull out all the plugs in the whole studio if you want to show this tape." He didn't know a thing about how you connect video machines together, so there actually wasn't anything he could do about it. He just stormed out and said, "I will never work with you again."

G.R.L. Then you did the presentation for Mike Dann that you described, and that was the end of your connection with CBS?

C.R. Yeah. But we did the whole thing. It was a real bomb. Everybody was shocked and nobody was speaking to anybody for two weeks at CBS, no one wanted to claim anything that had anything to do with this awful pilot. It was very weird. Everybody was wondering what happened to that funny pilot they had spent ninety thousand dollars on.

G.R.L. You got ninety thousand dollars?

C.R. No, no. All the cash we ever got actually went right back into the equipment.

G.R.L. So you didn't really make any money personally?

C.R. No, we never saw any.

D.C. We haven't made any money personally, ever.

G.R.L. What do you all live on?

D.C. Well, we live. Just barely.

C.R. We used to get twenty-five dollars a week, but now we don't even get that.

D.C. Videofreex became very big over this project. Actually, a lot of people were working with the CBS project.

C.R. Yeah, we got all our friends in on the CBS project—share the bread.

[. . .]

Then, after the whole CBS thing, everybody went away for Christmas, then came back about the first week in January and we said, "Well, anybody who wants to come back and be a Videofreek, come." So at that point, there were six of us.

D.C. And we built this studio, built walls, and plugs, and soldered and stuff like that. Because we were so exhausted from all the stuff we'd done for CBS, we really found . . . I found it difficult personally to do any work until just about two months ago. Some other Videofreex could at the time, but I couldn't. I was exhausted by it. It was also not very good for the head. But it brought us along very quickly technologically. I think that in terms of a video underground community, probably we have more equipment than anybody.

G.R.L. Did you "inherit" equipment?

D.C. Yes, we "inherited" equipment and stuff like that. Also Chuck Kennedy really came with us, and I don't think maybe he would have come with us as quickly if it hadn't been for the CBS project. Like everybody really freaked out over it, and then we just kept banding together. You saw who the enemy was very clearly, you saw who you were, and it sort of defined us to a very great extent. We just clung together because of that.

I think the thing about Videofreex that is like important is that there's a kind of group consciousness as well as individual consciousness; no question about it—it's very strong in all of us, and not just in the head. It's like it's technological. We have a system which brings six or seven of us almost electronically together. We've got four cameras connected into an electronic mixer—a video mixer—which mixes the cameras through special effects, devices like fading, superimpositions, split screens, and also there's a sound man, and all this is connected into one organ sort of thing, and we're all intercom-connected. That's a very exciting experience for us, especially when we're involved with the music thing. We always see ourselves paralleling like a band too. That's the group part, which I think is important.

Also, though we seem to be caught into the hardware, I think most of us individually are into the software[3] part of it. I guess we're involved in experimenting with hardware to see if we can get new kinds of software. I think that we see ourselves really as revolutionaries. Very much so. I think we really want to change things with what we're doing. The information is much more than just that. The information does change people, we think. It does more than a lot of things.

Another thing is that we have a lot of interests that are varied. Some people are into designing structures as well. Some people are into politics, some are into sociology, psychology, teaching—like a lot of different things—and we just sort of focused in on video tape because like it's able to take all of us in, sift this information. It's sort of a total commitment to all of those things to be put into the video tape.

G.R.L. I have some questions about that, but let me come back to them later. Now, let me ask Mike Shamberg about Raindance. Perhaps you could tell me something about yourself, something about how Raindance started—what it's all about. Why don't you move a little closer to the mike?

MICHAEL SHAMBERG: Okay. Here's the scene. I'll approach our history from my vantage point, and I'll try to do it quickly. About a year ago at this time I was working for *Time* magazine as a reporter and I did a story on a show up at the Howard Wise Gallery called *TV as a Creative Medium.* Frank Gillette[4] and Ira Schneider, who are now part of Raindance, had a piece in there, and I knew Frank vaguely because I went to school with his old lady. Okay. So Frank got the idea of how to apply for a thing which would be like a hip think-tank, to be to the subculture what Rand Corporation is

[3] *Software* is the information that comes from the information system—the machinery, mechanical or electronic: i.e., the *hardware;* or, software is the information that we get and hardware is the mechanical, electronic means by which the information is disseminated. The terms can also be used more generally, as, e.g., "Software of industry is pollution," or "Software is the illusion of the effectiveness of technology." (Quotes from *Software,* a Great Balls of Fire Film.)

[4] Gillette is no longer with Raindance—December 1970.

to that culture. And his idea was Raindance. R&D for research and development—Rand, Rain-Dance. Like I made up the explanation, he made up the name. Also Raindance is ecologically sound anticipatory design. Okay. So we put together Raindance, and over the summer we picked up some people and Frank had been into video tape. Basically there are five of us.

There's a cat by the name of Paul Ryan, and Paul was in a Catholic monastery for four years and got out of that trip and got a degree in English and then was very heavy into media, studied with McLuhan when McLuhan was at Fordham, and got into video tape. McLuhan hadn't said anything about video tape, but if McLuhan was right, what he was right about was going to work with video tape. That was in '68, and at that point the Sony portables first came out, and Paul conned them out of a couple, took one for himself to fool around with and gave the other one to Frank—and that's when it all got together. And Frank, with another cat, did a series of interviews on St. Marks Place. We still have the tapes. Out-of-sight tapes. Like St. Marks Place in '68 was a lot different than it is now. So Frank and another guy put together this body of theory about what it all meant, and we got together about a year ago last summer and started doing Raindance. We came together formally last fall. We found a freak who had inherited some money and like he gave us about twenty thousand dollars to play with.

G.R.L. Do you want to say who that is?

M.S. No, I don't. So we got into portable equipment then. I had been working for *Time*, but around when we started Raindance I had switched and was working for *Life*. Well, last February I quit that to do this nonsense full time.

I'll give you like the collective rap. Basically it's on what the hardware systems mean. That is, there are certain trends in technology, basically toward decentralization, and as they become smaller, they become cheaper, and any cretin can use them. That's what's going on with video tape. There's a similar phenomenon with computers, but it's not as financially accessible. It's called time-sharing, and it's terminals hooked up by a standard telephone to central computer. Okay. So Frank got the idea—and I credit him for it—that what you had in fact was a way to restructure the entire communications systems in the culture; that is, broadcast fucks us up because it's this huge monolitic thing that's one way, so there's no way to get the into broadcast and they can't let you into broadcast because they have all these expensive machines, see, and they can't afford to let freaks play around because they have this overhead. And how do they substantiate the overhead? They sell advertising.

So, since its inception, broadcast TV has been like the tool of the advertisers.

What happens with the portable equipment is . . . anybody can produce, and you have new modes of distribution. One is cable, the other is video cartridges, which means that broadcast is no longer the only means of video distribution. You can now economically service specialized video markets. So what we're trying to do, in fact, is expedite this process. What we're saying is basically a post-McLuhan rap. McLuhan said, "Listen, the way the culture operates, the way culture communicates, structures . . . there's nothing you can do about it." We're saying there is something you can do about it.

What we're attempting to do is put together a network that replaces the network. I can't speak for David, but none of us has really aspired to get on to broadcast. We don't want an hour a week, or something. That's bullshit, because the whole fucking system is doing us in, man. It's a brutal system. Aesthetically they're into notions that are still the radio and screen, it's the cat with the coat and tie, value judgments, sitting between you and the news—the way they work is scandalous. They go out with five-man crews. They sit above the crowd. If they want to talk to somebody they drag him out of the crowd, and they make sure you don't get in their way while they talk to him. We don't go out of the crowd—we're part of the crowd. The experience of being part of an event has never been considered news on broadcast television. If you've been to a peace demonstration or a rock concert, you know, it's vibes. But that never comes across on broadcast because the only way it could come across is to drag somebody out and, "Hey, tell us about it." They could never get around to showing it. So that whole system is dead. There's no way to get into it.

What we want to replace it with is like the most interactive system possible, which is basically a two-way system. Not only are you a passive consumer, which is what the culture is trying to be, but you can also produce for it. The problem—and David alluded to this before—is that while the technology is available there's no economic structure for what we're trying to do; at the moment it's only *ad hoc*, you know, from job to job, and we're trying to put together a notion of some structure . . . Basically the way we see it, it's a process rather than a product notion—that is, it's a subscription service. You have access to all this studio information, and if you want, you can produce and contribute to that as well. For example, there are about four groups and maybe another dozen individuals who are seriously into video in New York, and there's our publication *Radical Software*,[5] and there are a lot of people around the country . . . If we can put together a structure to get these people in touch and start exchanging tapes—there are some out-of-sight tapes around. So that what we're trying to do is, say, instead of waiting for the hardware to open up, and waiting for a guy who owns a cable station to come to us, or a guy who wants cartridges to come to us, we're doing it. We're just going out producing software, and though we don't have the distribution we would like, if we can hook people on our software, it will find the best channels of distribution, such as cable or cassette.

G.R.L. But again, cable and cassette are big business, and if you continue being part of the counterculture, what chance is there for those tapes to be disseminated through those, in effect, establishment systems?

D.C. But cable isn't as homogenous as broadcast.

M.S. Yeah, I don't think we're adverse to making money. We're adverse to having the economic structure dictate the programing structure, which is what you have on broadcast; but if we can put together an economic structure that brings into play the highest variety of programs, then we've really made it. I mean, I don't mind if we make money and go out and make more programing. That's cool.

D.C. That's all we ever do.

M.S. I'm saying that the structure of this market is going to be vastly different. I can get into somewhat of a high rap on it, but basically it has become a process medium and the people in it now . . . Here's the paradigm. Each new medium is the rearview mirror —that's McLuhan's line. The car was the horseless carriage, the radio was the wireless and so it goes. Like when long-playing records came out, right? They put train sounds on them, they didn't know what to do with them. So all these cats like look at video and they don't see it as an indigenous form. They think it's something else. They think it's something where you can take the Ed Sullivan Show and you see it when you want to, or everybody is going to get do-it-themselves tapes on how to putter around the home. Well, that's bullshit, because we're way beyond that. There are just a lot of indigenous things to video, and basically the most indigenous thing, it seems to me, is that it's not a product medium. It's so involving to watch video that I don't really think there's anything that you will want to play more than four or five times like a record, because it's not background shit. What we're banking on is that what people pay for is access to this process, the timeliness of the information, access to the information and not the product, which means

[5] First issue published summer 1970 by Raindance Corporation.

we don't have to sweat copyright. If I send the tape out, anybody is welcome to copy it.[6] What you're paying for is access to that tape originally.

D.C. It's good, man, because it means that it's not like property. Like property is something when you do it and then you keep getting it. You've got to keep up with video tape. It's a real thing. It's energy. It's not the old stuff. Video tape is really revolutionary.

M.S. It's the first step to a truly information economy.

G.R.L. Certain things you guys want to do aren't exactly clear to me, so let me ask something about Ken Marsh[7]—it might help. One of the things he told me about was setting up a network of outlets, mainly in colleges. That sounds feasible within five years. Already most schools have some video tape equipment; then people in all these schools all over the country would hopefully be making video tapes, sending them into a center for dissemination—[8]

M.S. We've all . . . that's our notion too. The trouble with Kenny's notion is that the colleges are dead, absolutely dead. I mean, we're in the same business they are, the business of structuring and disseminating knowledge—and we're doing a better job. The best people just aren't going to colleges any more. They want an alternate structure, and that's what we're doing—setting up an alternate information structure, which is very important. We don't want to put alternate programing on the existing structure. We want an alternate structure.

D.C. We would like very much to have our own channel on cable. If we had our own channel, that would be a different number. Video cassettes are easy for us to control, because all you have to do is have one office that sends out our video cassettes. Then it has our stamp, it's red, or a red star, or something like that.

We're trying to get through the State Council on the Arts this year a media bus which will try somehow to take this whole sort of flow out of New York City. We want to try to discover where,

[6] Note: From the editorial in *Radical Software*, summer, 1970: "To encourage dissemination of the information in *Radical Software* we have created our own symbol of an x within a circle: ⊗. This is a Xerox mark, the antithesis of copyright, which means DO copy. (The only copyrighted contents in this issue are excerpted from published or soon-to-be-published books and articles which are already copyrighted.)"

[7] Ken Marsh and Elliot Glass now run the People's Video Theatre in New York City; among other aims and plans, one is to facilitate communication between people in the neighborhood of their studio through the use of videotape.

[8] I've recently become aware of a basic problem with this idea: many of the half-inch video tape machines are incompatible with one another. (Half-inch video tape is used in non-broadcast or "amateur" systems and two-inch is used in broadcast television.) (G.R.L., January 1971)

if any, are the places to begin, at least in the state, because that's where they're paying for us to be right now. Where are they? We'll go to universities and find out whether they're really not in universities but in somebody's basement. We want to go out on the road and try to find those places and try to connect them up if we can.

M.S. Yeah, I'll give you some clichés. We've all grown up on TV, being bombarded by TV, so you become literate in television, but there's no way to write in television, so to speak. In other words, it's like learning how to read. Tape is to television what writing is to language; that is, it has all the prerequisites of a total information system—storage, record and playback—so a lot of kids, man, who have been bounced off that thing all their fucking lives, you give them a camera and they know what to do.

G.R.L. How old are you?

M.S. I'm twenty-six.

G.R.L. How old are you?

D.C. I'm thirty-five.

M.S. He's a little older. I'm the first television generation.

G.R.L. David didn't really grow up on TV and neither did I—I'm thirty-nine.

D.C. But I had such a terrible childhood.

[Laughter.]

G.R.L. But cable TV and cassette are going to be controlled by profit-making organizations, and I don't see them using your tapes the way you're going to do them.

M.S. The reason we're getting more exposure is . . . it's the same thing films are going through, and that is the underground filmmakers are not actually making the films, but they're influencing them. You've got things like *The Strawberry Statement, Midnight Cowboy* or whatever. Same paradox is going to take hold in video.

G.R.L. But that's just co-opting.

M.S. Yeah, but my feeling is we're ready to produce. We may be co-opted, but . . . Well, these people are ready to say, "Hey, we'll put you in our catalogue," so we've got to demonstrate that there is a market for our stuff. In other words, the same censorship involved with films because of cost, because of everything, just doesn't apply to what we're doing.

D.C. What about a book? You write a book and you get an audience for a book. The same thing with a video cassette. When those little sets are in everybody's house, then we'll produce video cassettes like you produce books. Eventually the cable will be like magazines or underground newspapers, because each cable carries with it twenty to forty channels, right? and they can get it to be a thousand, and eventually it's going to be two-way. One of those channels can be for a very selected market, or parts of each channel, so it can be like a magazine or an underground newspaper market.

M.S. They're common carriers. Now, the fear of co-option is the fear of censorship more than of co-option. I think as long as we're in touch, as long as we're producing, because we are in touch we will find a market.

G.R.L. You're in touch with whom?

M.S. We're in touch with the head of the cultural edge—like we're the media people out there. We're not the only people out there but we are the media people.

D.C. That's the thing about reality. Do you know what I mean? I mean, reality, wow! Energy is like if you could find why or where it's at, and you can keep with it, you can explode in the front of it.

M.S. What's the publication date for your book?

G.R.L. Nine months after I finish it.

M.S. Now I'm going to give you a piece of information that's not public. We've also applied and apparently received a grant from the New York State Council on the Arts—and this is not a matter of public record, it should be treated in confidence.

G.R.L. You don't want it in the transcript?

M.S. It can be in the book if the book is coming out then, but don't tell anybody now. We're supposed to be getting two hundred and sixty-three thousand dollars, which is a lot of fucking money.

G.R.L. To do what?

M.S. The proposal is this: it's called the Center for Decentralized Television, if you can appreciate the irony, and we got it through The Jewish Museum. We personally wrote the proposal with Paul Ryan and Ira Schneider, but we needed them as a front.

G.R.L. Once again, who are Paul Ryan and Ira Schneider?

M.S. Paul Ryan and Ira Schneider are members of Raindance. Ira is an old film-maker—not old; Ira is into film and did some very beautiful films, but didn't get into the trap that most film-makers got in. Ira was hip to the fact that he was into a process and in that process he was trying to affect people. He wasn't all that concerned with the product. He saw that he could do better with tape what he was trying to accomplish with film, which is basically sensitizing people to their environment and giving them some channels of feedback. Paul Ryan is the fellow I mentioned before who studied with McLuhan. Paul used to work for a thing called the Newbury Media Project, and was giving kids portable cameras to tape the community and then they played that over the cable system—so it's already being done. That's like the most radical thing being done in cable. Ford was putting up some money for that.

So we wrote this proposal and it breaks down as follows: Ten per cent of it has to go to The Jewish Museum—basically we're going to be setting up a video environment in The Jewish Museum, to open concomitantly with a show called Software, which is opening in the fall. The video environment will be the place where everybody's tapes will be shown, uptown, for what it's worth; and two, it's going to like change the environment itself. Like we might come to the Freex and say, "Okay, it's your month at The Jewish Museum, design the environment." So that takes 10 per cent off. The rest of it is basically forty-five thousand dollars for equipment, which is the maximum amount of portable systems we can buy. Probably about fifteen portable systems and then a support system for that in terms of an internal space for like editing and duplication facilities.

G.R.L. Is this half-inch?

M.S. It's all half-inch—we're not interested in anything else. Then there's like forty-two thousand dollars for individual stipends. So if a cat from say Bedford-Stuyvesant comes and says, "Hey, we're having trouble with our community. I can use tape, but I need some money to live on," we can give him money to live on. Then the rest goes for an information and data bank. We're going to put together a data bank and make the tapes generated by this project available to everybody in New York State. Also, we have a cat to go around and rap about it, and we're going to use computers to index the tapes. It won't be an actual direct access; it will just be a printed index. It's like a quantum leap, what's going to be able to be done. By then we'll have some results.

Raindance, somewhat in contrast to the Videofreex, was never going to be a production company. We're not going to put money in production. We have a loft, and we're trying to set up a highly responsive environment. In other words, in the traditional notion of the television studio, the studio structure is the experience, right? They're just terrible. Cats looking at you through glass windows, big cats who won't let you touch their cameras. . . . We're trying to set up a highly responsive environment, designing platforming modular units, then soft modules, or some sort of soft units of plastic stuffed with Styrofoam balls or something so that it's sort of like a giant erector set where you can come in and structure the environment and the interaction of the environment, and to that we're adding video. Like we have notions for a talk show where you sit around in the environment you've structured yourself and you pass the camera around like a joint, because they're highly flexible. The paradox here is basically the recording studio where the performers can become the technicians if they like and can have some control over the environment. That's what we want to do. We want to generate a scene where people are comfortable and put that into video. We have notions like, if you ever got it together, you could have a group doing video like the Fireside Theatre in radio, and people just experiencing themselves with video.

G.R.L. What's the Fireside Theatre?

M.S. Fireside Theatre is a group from California; they've got three records out on Columbia. They're into sound, into doing parodies of old radio, but being very conscious of the medium. The most crude example is calling attention to the fact that they're doing sound effects. It's very stoned stuff. And it's indigenous to the sound medium because they're into feeding back on it and working off it. We want to do the same thing with video. That is, take a group that just feels out the video space and can improvise a rap, feed back on it and keep feeding back on it. This is something we've done with some of our own tapes.

We did some tapes in California when we were all stoned on acid or grass, and feeding back on that because we made this tape of this out-of-sight experience, and then we have that in our minds and we allude to that among the group. This is how a tape has gotten us together, so to speak. We have this collective archive of video, this collective archive of experience that we replay. We know it as a tape and we know that experience, and then we bring that into our own experience. We allude to it, we allude to some of the dialogue, and what we've done is, we've pooled all of our tapes. There's absolutely no concept of who shot what—it's all central archive. And we're all into editing each other's tapes and there are no hang-ups. One day it's my turn to edit a tape, and one day it's Frank's turn and one day it's Paul's turn. So the whole concept of what constitutes information really does, I think, lead you into a different life-style. It's a different form of processing your life-style.

G.R.L. Do you guys live communally in any way?

M.S. No, we don't. We're different in that from the Freex. We all have separate directions and we get together to do the tape thing.

G.R.L. Do you live communally, the Videofreex?

D.C. Some. Some of the Videofreex do.

C.R. There are three basic places, uptown, the studio, and then David and I live together.

D.C. And we have some friends come over every so often.

G.R.L. Do you all share whatever money comes in equally?

D.C. No, not entirely. When we have money we share it equally. When we don't have money, then each of us shares what he can get. In other words, the first priority is to make tapes and keep the studio alive, then the money can be shared in terms of bread and survival for each individual; but to keep the equipment running and the tape there so we can do the tape, that's totally communal. After that, I guess those that can survive within that system and get money from it, do. Those that have to go out and get money somewhere else do that.

M.S. Your book is on film?

G.R.L. The book is interviews with documentary film-makers, but this just seems too relevant now to leave out.

M.S. It's impossible to view what we're doing through the context of film. [. . .]

What you find is that the first generation of video tape equipment is sitting in closets everywhere because people weren't hip to doing it. They took it out of broadcasting, and like let's get the kids together and do a mini Ed Sullivan Show, let's have them write scripts and stand there and read them. I mean, they're doing that, man. The kids don't get turned on by that, so the equipment sits in a closet. A lot of video equipment in this country has to be liberated.

G.R.L. You were describing the environment that you're setting up in your studio. It turns you on to working in it, to rap in it, and let's say some of your friends come down and do the same thing. But would those tapes say anything to other people? Like you were talking about being stoned and doing a whole kind of cyclical number on that. Would that mean anything to anyone else?

M.S. Yeah, I think so. We have a notion . . . [. . .] One of the things we want to do is like a processed look at people, a processed look at the superstars. We don't want a rock star standing there singing his shit and that's all. We want to have him shitting, we want to have him blowing his nose, we want to get into people and show they're people. And this is how you do it—in this environment. And if you do that with superstars, you can do it with ordinary people, and you can find that ordinary people can be entertaining. They're not all the time. I rapped with this cat the other day who was just boring, and it's a boring tape.

The video experience, unlike the film experience, doesn't have to be a public medium. You can make a tape for yourself and it's a totally valid experience. There's nothing wrong with that. You can control it yourself, you can experience yourself, you can pick up body movement like you just can't do in any other medium. We've made environmental tapes, tapes of driving, driving through Manhattan, driving in the country, driving through L.A., and showing them on three screens simultaneously. That, with sound, it's out of sight.

G.R.L. I take it that you see the things you're talking about as implicitly political. I don't mean political in that very narrow sense of people running for office.

M.S. In your sense, then, this is political. This culture is insane. It's the most insensitive fucking culture you could imagine. But it's Fuller's line, reform your environment, don't reform man; and that's what we're into. We're into the hippie, we're into making people aware of their environment, aware of how it's fucking them over, mobilizing their energies for changing it.

[. . .]

This culture has got to change or it's going to destroy us. In that sense we are political.

G.R.L. Neither of you sees change in any essential way, say, by electoral reform?

M.S. I use that as a means, but not as an end. I see the political people—and politics is their end, not a means. Look, I'm using two hundred and sixty-three thousand dollars of money legislated by the state legislature, but not directly, if that's what you're asking. To do the high rap that I work on is that basically the context is this: that mankind is evolving through his technology—this is the great epiphany that I had on the moon landing. That fucking thing is part of me—and this is from Fuller. Our mind is doing things that our body can't accommodate, so it's coming out in the form of the technology, so we are in fact evolving through the technology. And we've got to come to some relationship with the technology. The relationship isn't to embrace it wholeheartedly nor to reject it, but to understand it, to understand that ecologically —and this is Frank Gillette's rap—that technology is ecology; finding that overspecialization of technology leads you to death. Like what's an overspecialized thing? Like an electric can opener. That's bullshit, man. What can you do with an electric can opener? On the other hand, video is generalized technology and has a high variety of uses, as our computers. I mean, general technology, high variety of uses, that's attempting to come to some relationship with the technology.

Where the technology is leading us to is toward an etherealization.

That is, thirty years ago *the* industries of America were the heavy manufacturing industries, the automobile industries, the steel industries and whatever; the industries coming out of the fifties and into the sixties are the information-processing industries. You've got Xerox, IBM, Polaroid, which means in effect that the business of America is now to a large degree information processing, where fifty years ago the cat who was president of a corporation sat in a window and made sure that nobody stole the gidgets and didn't get caught in the machine. Now they're all sitting in buildings in Manhattan shuffling papers around, and the blue-collar industry is moving information around. Management tools today are basically various degrees of computer programs. So what the culture as a whole is involved in is a high level of information processing, and this is in fact evolution. The very mundane business of man is no longer one-to-one farming, it is no longer collective farming, it is no longer industry—it's information processing. That's what we're all caught up in, and the business of the culture is in fact living in this process environment.

D.C. If we could get rid of money and put in place of it information, we'd really be in good shape, because that seems to me a much more real way of exchange.

M.S. Paul Ryan's rap on this is basically that what money creates is a homogeneous structure. In other words, the function of money is to create a very low variety of forms, high homogeneity. Information, on the other hand . . . One definition of information is "the difference that makes a difference," and in fact it is—it's a feedback thing that changes something. The culture generates all this information, it's always evolving, it's always changing. So what information leads you to is a high variety of experience and possibility.

G.R.L. Is the idea that if more people are more and more aware of themselves and their environment, of the culture, the society and the structure of the establishment, and see what it does to them, that they will then, in one way or another, revolt against that and look for alternate forms? Is that the hope?

M.S. Yeah, and it's happening now.

D.C. It seems to me that the thing about money is that the people that get it, in the end they get old and cruddy about it and they don't have any contact, they go and escape with it; but if you're dealing with information and you want to be rich, you have to always be involved. It's real.

G.R.L. What about the poor bastard who isn't too swift?

M.S. But it's open access to this information, you don't hoard it. That is a good question. I'm not sure what—

D.C. I think we're talking about a society that has got plenty anyway, so nobody is going to starve. The cat that can't keep up with the information is going to live, in effect. . . . I'm not sure where that is. Then he's going to live in that area, that is, his environment, he's going to be closed in, but that's as far as he can see, so he doesn't conceive of anything beyond that and he's all right. There, you see? The people doing the information number, they want to go here, they want to have access, they want to have freedom because they can see it, they can conceive of it, and where you can conceive of something, you can go. So it seems to me now that you've got a basis of exchange that's real, and when there is differentiation, it's real, it's based upon consciousness and your mind.

M.S. It's a notion of product versus process, and what we're trying to do is hit people with the process of awareness so that change becomes the standard. We don't resist change. We don't fear it. We go with it. We evolve that way. I'll give you a specific example. You take a cat best exemplified by Agnew; these people see the institutions of the country as being immutable, right? They see the changes the country has gone through as being the contents of the institutions, but not changing the institutions themselves, so they don't see the institutions as being reconfigured. In other words, they studied the civics of what the government was a hundred years ago, and they just see a lot more crazy people putting pressure on that structure, but of course it's an entirely different structure. In other words, we're all looking in the rearview mirror, and some people more than others.

One thing I'm interested in working on is conceptualizing what the culture really looks like. If you go to school these days . . . There was a great Feiffer cartoon in the *Voice* about this, the construction worker whose kids were being taught about racism, about imperialism, and that's not what he learned in school. "Hey, my kids are learning about a different America." You have this product mentality, this concept of immutable institutions that changes the contents. But we're into whole new structures, the medium is the message, and that's what we're trying to hit people with.

G.R.L. The way you both talk about process it has a content, because the process itself is saying that things can change, that there are other ways to live, other viable structures, and that seems good to me—it's a process with content. But is there a danger that we'll get to the point where it's just process?

M.S. That's not a danger, that's an ideal where change is in fact the only concept. I'll give you another example. The example of social experimentation whereby the government will allocate three million dollars per federal program, say Head Start. They did a program in Chicago with the ghettos, and the program is a failure. Why is it a failure? Because they can't repeat it the next year precisely the way it was last year. That's product mentality. It's not a failure. It means that next year you take the three million and you don't make the same mistakes, you make new mistakes, and so it goes. The process is the ideal. You're living in process.

D.C. It's like understanding that you will always make a mistake as soon as you do anything. You're going to make a mistake if you look back, unless you keep going. That's what all these institutions are, they're mistakes. As soon as you institutionalize them, they're mistakes.

M.S. And they're into funding new mistakes.

D.C. They should always fund new mistakes.

M.S. I have another feeling. Because we grew up on the electronic media—McLuhan is right—we see things differently, and they don't see it the same way we do. That's a real conflict. There is, in fact, a whole new consciousness.

G.R.L. Have any of you ever tried talking to construction workers, that silent majority?

D.C. We have a tape on the construction workers.

G.R.L. But I mean not only talk to them, but like here's the video tape . . .

M.S. Not in the context of video. I've rapped with them, you can get into it. This is the reason why Agnew is a cruel man. Agnew is like . . . kill the messenger because he brings you the wrong message. Agnew just wants to change the messages, but those people that Agnew is speaking to are genuinely being fucked over by the medium. Agnew is not telling them why. There's nothing on television that looks like a construction worker. There's nothing that gives them any sense of confirmation as a social group. The only sense they've got is taking it to the streets, man, and then reading about it in the newspapers and seeing it on TV. It's the same thing with the Blacks, the same thing with the kids. There's no feedback. And the lower white middle class is getting shit on as much as anybody else. When I talk about an alternate information system I don't mean one that just has freaks on it, I mean one which is responsive to those people too.

D.C. One of the things I'm really going to be experimenting with on this media bus is to get out to a lot of different people. One of the problems we have is like most of our stuff is very much limited to our environment. It's hard in New York City to go anyplace else.

G.R.L. Then presumably you feel that your structures are in process too, and shouldn't necessarily be set up as institutions, that they should be fluid.

M.S. Yeah, that's the idea of the process environment in the television studio. Sure. We want to go through changes.

D.C. Look, as soon as we built our big studio, remember, I thought it was a mistake because it was too heavy, there were walls in it.

[. . .]

M.S. Well, we did a tape, Paul Ryan and myself; we were out in L. A. and we had some time to kill, and we went into a supermarket and they had a surveillance system, right? They had a sign, "Smile, you're on *Candid Camera.* We have these things here so you won't steal and your prices will be lower." They had these cameras all along the store, and monitors. So we started taking pictures of these TV cameras and the manager comes over and says, "Hey, you can't take pictures in here. You got to have a permit." We said, "You don't have a permit to take our picture, how come we need one to . . ." And there was an incredible rap. We have it all on tape. We have the manager putting his hand over the lens. I said, "Hey, you're just doing your job." He said, "Yeah, that's right, I'm just doing my job. Why don't you go into the Safeway down the street? They just had a grand opening. They'd love to have you take pictures." Then we got this guy to come outside. We said, "Can we take your picture out here?" and it was all right. It was a devastating portrait of this guy—a cat who's been a store manager for six years. That's the kind of thing you can do with video. Paul Ryan terms it cybernetic guerrilla tactics.

What the Yippies and Hoffman are doing is only taking it halfway. They're only using their own system for their own ends. We can take our system—if it's an information environment, if we can get enough people watching our tapes—and we can bankrupt broadcast television. I mean, you can't watch broadcast with a straight face. None of us can. And if we can get enough people to do that . . .

[. . .]

G.R.L. Something that Mike said before: that there's no concept of who shot or who edited what, is that—

M.S. It's like a rock group, man. We've done tapes to the analogy of jam sessions. They're not finished products, they're just get-togethers—and there's a lot of feedback there. The tapes are out of sight.

D.C. Everybody, anybody can cut; I can cut anybody's footage in the studio. And I think what's happening between Raindance and ourselves is that very probably we'll be able to use each other's stuff very soon.

G.R.L. Do you see film as continuing to have a function?

M.S. I think each public medium frees the preceding medium to be more creative, right? Public television has freed film. Film used to be the medium of morality in the country; public television is now the medium of morality. Film has become a free medium. We may in fact free broadcast television, or vice versa. I don't know, where do I see film?

PHYLLIS GERSHUNY: It's very possible that chemical processes will drop out completely and all film will go into electronics.

D.C. Especially when the color comes out. Color possibilities in television are much greater technically . . . than in a chemical process. I think film will be a historical thing essentially. Like there are going to be libraries of film because there was nobody on tape before, and that's going to be very important and it's going to remain important. I think if a head gets into film, he'll approach it that way, like storing documents—in that sense.

M.S. It has to do with the experience. Are people going to want to go to big, dark rooms and sit in rows or are they going to want to get into intimate rooms where they can interact with each other and control the way the information comes at them?

G.R.L. What about the idea of documentary? The classic definition by Grierson is "the creative treatment of actuality," right?

M.S. Give me a good example of a documented *Battle of Algiers*,[9] which is really a documentary. You know what? Those bastards are going to get into video tapes.

D.C. Yeah, yeah. Because they're almost there. The way they shoot, the amount of footage they shoot—

M.S. What's taken them all these years to get to where we started from.

G.R.L. What about documentary? Flaherty is like where it started here.

M.S. I've never seen any of that shit.

G.R.L. What about the Maysles' *Salesman*, or the films of Leacock, Wiseman, Jean Rouch or Chris Marker?

M.S. *Salesman* was a bad film. They victimized those people in *Salesman*. I remember particularly the one family out of Opa Locka, Florida, whom they sold the Bible to. And I want to know how they got their fucking cameras in there, man. We never hide that with video.

[9] Directed by Gillo Pontecorvo; a reconstruction of certain events of the Algerian War; shown for the first time in U.S. in 1967.

P.G. It wasn't hidden, it wasn't hidden. It was absolutely right out there.

M.S. But there was never anybody talking to the cameras, there was never one of the Maysles brothers rapping.

D.C. We just did some shooting of an exploitation film being shot. They were doing an exploitation film and we were doing them doing an exploitation film. It was really fun. We were studying how they were doing it as well as trying to interview some of the people as to why they did it, because we're now involved in the whole business of Women's Liberation, which makes us more conscious of it, and it's really like the camera is very separate from the action in a way. It doesn't seem to be involved. Even like they took this big Eclair off the tripod and the guy went around, but he was always on top of them, where if we were going to do an orgy, we'd like to take off our clothes and get right in there; but they weren't really having an orgy, they were all actors.

M.S. We'll call it a fuck-in.

G.R.L. Why didn't either of you video-tape the fuck-in up at Goddard at the media conference?[10]

D.C. We wanted a fuck-in and we took our cameras along, but the women said we shouldn't do that because we were men. Only women can call fuck-ins now.

[Laughter.]

M.S. Now, another thing to remember is you've got a notion coming out of the nineteenth century that there's a direct one-to-one correlation between what the camera sees and what the eye sees, dig it? Because to make a film you look through that thing, right? Because that's how you know what's going on in the film. In video you've got a cable that's flexible, right? In other words, the camera can be there, the monitor can be there, the camera is no longer an extension of the eye in video.

D.C. It's an extension of your body.

M.S. Right. It's an extension of your body, man. And we've got an idea: do you know what fiber optics are? Fiber optics are fibers of optical quality that can keep light coherent—you can in fact bend light. We have fiber optic lenses. They're probably very costly, but we have notions for a lens, say a five-foot-fiver, dig it? and you can attach it to your body, and you can dance with this lens. It's internally decentralized. The parallel goes all the way down. It decentralizes the relationship between the recording and the

[10] The First Gathering: The Alternative Media Project, June 17–21, 1970, at Goddard College, Plainfield, Vermont.

storage of the image. It's no longer an extension of the eye. You don't have to look through the camera to see what you're getting.

D.C. Right, although it's hard to do because it's really insecure.

M.S. Remember the sequence on tape where I just put a camera down on the sidewalk upside down? It was on Earth Day, and you see somebody's feet.

D.C. Oh, the thing that really bugs me about film and commercial television is the mystique, the priesthood. Like only one guy knows about this, nobody else can touch it. The director walks around and he never touches anything, but he has it in his head, he knows how to do it, and everybody knows his own thing and nobody knows anything else. . . .

Video is a different thing, it's like a revolutionary thing. Film is essentially a middle-class—not a middle-class, a bourgeois, property-oriented heavy medium. It's a product. It's heavy. Video is really a revolutionary energy, process-oriented. It's not—

M.S. I've never made films.

G.R.L. There are two things I'd like to ask while I have the chance. One is, suppose there's somebody who sees or knows about something, and he says, "I have these special feelings about this thing, I want to tell you about this thing and these feelings." Now that's very different from what you two are talking about. Don't answer yet. The other point is that almost anybody can learn to use a video camera in about five minutes—it's a hell of a lot less complicated to operate than a movie camera; and it's silent, no problems with synch-sound—like you don't have to know a thing to use it, and that's great in many ways. So everyone goes around and does all these tapes, and before you know it you've got this bloody mountain of tapes, right? Now, what are you going to do with them? No one would ever have the time to look at even half of them. With film, which is much more complicated to shoot and more expensive, you get comparatively small hills of films, and then you cut out, throw out a lot more of the original material.

D.C. We recycle. We can use tape over again. Eventually we throw it out when it's no good.

G.R.L. But in the meantime are you talking about taking all these tapes and just having a voluminous—

M.S. No, no. You take out what's good and you recycle the rest, you reuse it—you actually physically reuse it. We're not into archives in the traditional sense. It's a much more ecological medium. It's processing, processing of information. Let me make a point I meant to give you before. I'm trying to do basically three or four raps because I'm here as Raindance. Paul has a notion of indigenous data, that is, film and broadcasting have ripped out the information and don't enfold it back into the environment. He calls it a form of perceptual imperialism. They're exploiting you. We're into the notion of indigenous information, and the most indigenous thing is giving the cat the problem, giving the cat the camera to find his own problem.

[. . .]

G.R.L. What about that other question? Some guy who sees a particular situation and wants to tell something about it. If somebody with video tape wanted to do that . . . in a filmic way, would that be a perversion of the use of tape to you guys?

M.S. Oh, I'd never call anything a perversion of tape.

[Laughter.]

D.C. He's just beginning probably. Like if he was doing it for that reason and he used a video camera like I find people out there doing now, eventually he couldn't do it any more because the camera is telling him something else. Something else is happening. Like if you start out with an idea and something else begins to happen, if you're a truthful, honest person you'll begin to see that.

M.S. Yeah, we don't have the tape mentality. We've never tried to shoot the same thing precisely the same way. You go out and you do it with a video camera and right away you play it back. I don't know if you know about it, but the new cameras have a mode whereby you can play back on the scene through the eyepiece of the camera. Dig it. So you feedback on it, you don't go back with six identical rushes and then go out and do it again. There's a loop.

G.R.L. Can you edit?

D.C. Yeah, you can edit better. Video tape editing is going to be much better, much faster. They're using video tape editing now much more efficiently than they are film editing because you can lay it all out, man.

G.R.L. You edit by mixing?

M.S. There are a number of modes of editing. You can take three, four different images and feed them in all at once. You can do fades. . . .

G.R.L. That is the way you edit now? You don't cut?

M.S. No, no, no. You don't cut. It's like sound tapes. You go from a master reel to a pickup reel, then you edit.

D.C. You can assemble—

M.S. Or do sequential editing.

G.R.L. Do any of you do any actual cutting of the tape?

D.C. No, it's all electronic.

M.S. Ken Marsh does because it's sometimes faster and cheaper, but it's not really the way to do it. The mixing thing is the capability you never have with film. I mean, you have it but it's always in the lab.

D.C. But like that's an obvious thing, and you see right away that eventually that whole editing process is going to be much easier. Like it's real, now, instead of having everything up in the head, it's right there. The networks have computers and they've got all the stuff lined up and you can just— It's like playing a piano, man. You just press this button over here, it remembers, it goes back, it corrects, it throws away this, it recombines, it switches around. It does everything for you.

M.S. If you want some hype of the visual aesthetic—and this isn't my line at all—it's basically that the filmic image is a flat image, it's light through. The video image tends to be light emanating from, consequently it's a much more tactile image. A cat named Brice Howard out in San Francisco says that it is because it lives electronically, because it lives as electrons or whatever, it lives in a time sense, really. In other words, the video image only exists in time, not in space, as the film image does. So it becomes a process type of image.

D.C. You can't see it on a tape. If you stop a tape and look at it, it isn't there. It's only there when it's moving around.

M.S. It only exists as a time process.

D.C. When you play old tapes, something happens to them. They degenerate. That's part of their element, almost. But I feel there should be a way to transmit information from mother to child.

M.S. Somebody's working on it. . . .There are ideas for twenty-five-cent video booths. All you get is the process, there's nothing to take home. This cat Paul Ryan who was in the monastery, he comes up with the idea for a confessional booth. And who do you confess to? You confess to yourself. Because he's hip, man. He's hip to the fact that the way the information is structured in this culture there's always somebody telling you what to know. It's the teacher, it's the parent, it's the guy with the coat and tie, it's Walter Cronkite, it's the authority figure. And what does that mean? That means you're passive unless somebody tells you what to know.

Peter Drucker, in a book called *The Age of Discontinuity*, says we've gone from an experience basis to a knowledge basis because experience doesn't mean shit any more. Dig it. It's knowledge, it's information, so if a cat's been doing a job for fifty years, because he's old, that has no more authority with us. We in fact know more than our parents do. I mean, when I was ten years old, I was flying in airplane, flying jet planes. Because of the affluence, too, I was going to Europe as a consequence of growing up. I've had TV, I've had radio. It's not special to me and it is special to them. We're in fact more in touch with that. It doesn't mean you throw everybody out who's over thirty or over forty. But it does mean that in the transition from an experience to a knowledge base we really do have that standing. McLuhan has a line that the next president of IBM is going be nineteen years old. Well, that's typical bullshit, actually.

Again, look at the way we get our information, the authority figure giving you the information. It's the consumer mentality. You sit there, you're passive and you receive. If we keep doing that, we're dead as a species, man, because the cats that are shoveling the shit down—and it is really shit—are going to kill us.

This, by the way, is why Nixon is in trouble. You've got a lot of people who say he's the President, he knows best, let's trust him, or he's got more information than we do. These people very desperately want to be convinced that's true, so they march on Wall Street. We've got too much information to accept him as being omnipotent. What really brought me of age was when I flashed that fucking Lyndon Johnson was a madman and that he was no more competent than I was. Now I know this with Nixon too. I can't trust that son of a bitch when I'm getting too much information. I can't accept his version if he won't acknowledge mine. So it's that whole mentality, man, of we'll do something to you. That's why Ira Schneider, this guy I work with, got out of film—he saw he wasn't getting people into the process. That's why a lot of old filmmakers are . . . they smell. I don't mean like literally. And I don't mean to downgrade all of them because there are some very sensitive people, but that's why film as a medium, as an experience, is going to be overtaken by video.

G.R.L. What about this book, which is perhaps an example of what you're talking about?

M.S. Oh, your book. What's going to happen to print?

G.R.L. Well, does this serve any purpose? The rap that becomes the print that becomes the book?

M.S. Yeah. We do a thing called media ecology. Each medium has its own niche, that is, you don't destroy it; and print, not to be confused with books—although books are the easiest way to get it out—is a high compaction of certain types of information, which is very convenient. It's the worst fucking medium in the world to convey experience, and that's McLuhan's strong point. He saw that there was incredible serverance between what was being conveyed in a book and how you felt it. And I have trouble getting into books these days because I approach it as experience, and I don't want that experience. But I could get into printed information very easily. I read six newspapers a day, I read a lot of magazines, so don't confuse book with print. And I think print is going to be around.

G.R.L. I think a lot of things you say are going to happen—that they are happening; but I do think that film, in one way or another, is going to remain, as a slower medium, if you like, in a sense. The rhythm is slower, more pains, time and exactness in the work, maybe what used to be thought of as fine art.

M.S. Yeah, I love movies, by the way. I really enjoy them, but it's not going to have that grip on the culture.

SELECTED BIBLIOGRAPHY

Books

Armes, Roy. *French Cinema Since 1946*, Vol. II. London: A. Zwemmer Ltd., and Cranbury, N.J.: A. S. Barnes & Co., 1970.

Baddeley, W. Hugh. *The Technique of Documentary Film Production.* New York: Focal Press, Inc., Communication Arts Books, Hastings House, 1966.

Barrett, Marvin, ed. *Survey of Broadcast Journalism, 1968–1969.* New York: Grosset & Dunlap, Inc., 1969.

Bluem, A. William. *Documentary in American Television.* New York: Focal Press, Inc., Communication Arts Books, Hastings House, 1968.

Durgnat, Raymond. *Franju.* Berkeley and Los Angeles: University of California Press, 1968.

Grierson, John. *Grierson on Documentary*, ed. by Forsyth Hardy. London: William Collins Sons & Co., Ltd., 1946, and New York: Harcourt, Brace & Co., Inc., 1947.

Knight, Arthur. *The Liveliest Art.* New York: Mentor Books, The New American Library, 1959.

Manvell, Roger. *New Cinema in Europe.* New York: Dutton Vista Pictureback, London: Studio Vista Ltd., and E. P. Dutton & Co., 1966.

Maysles, Albert and David, and Charlotte Zwerin. *Salesman.* New York: Signet Books, The New American Library, 1969.

Porcile, François. *Défense du Court Métrage Français,* 7e Art. Paris: Les Éditions du Cerf, 1965.

Reisz, Karel, and Gavin, Millar. *The Technique of Film Editing.* New York: Focal Press, Inc., Communication Arts Books, Hastings House, 1968.

Rotha, Paul, in collaboration with Sinclair Road and Richard Griffith. *Documentary Film.* Glasgow: The University Press, and New York: Focal Press, Inc., Communication Arts Books, Hastings House, 1968.

Rotha, Paul, and Richard Griffith. *The Film Till Now.* London: Spring Books, 1967.

Sussex, Elizabeth. *Lindsay Anderson.* London: Studio Vista, Ltd., 1969.

Magazines, Pamphlets, Catalogues

Distribution Catalogue, British Film Institute, 81 Dean Street, London, W 1, England, spring 1962.

Cinema, vol. 6, no. 1, Beverly Hills, California.

Film Comment, vol. 3, no. 2, spring 1965; vol. 6, no. 1, spring 1970; Brookline, Massachusetts.

The Museum of Modern Art, Department of Film Circulating Programs, 11 West 53rd Street, New York.

Les meilleurs documentaires de l'histoire du cinéma, Musée de Cinéma, Palais des Beaux-Arts, Bruxelles 1, Belgium.

Radical Software, summer 1970, and no. 2, 1970, New York.

INDEX

M